MW01617908

Gerrit Dou 1613–1675

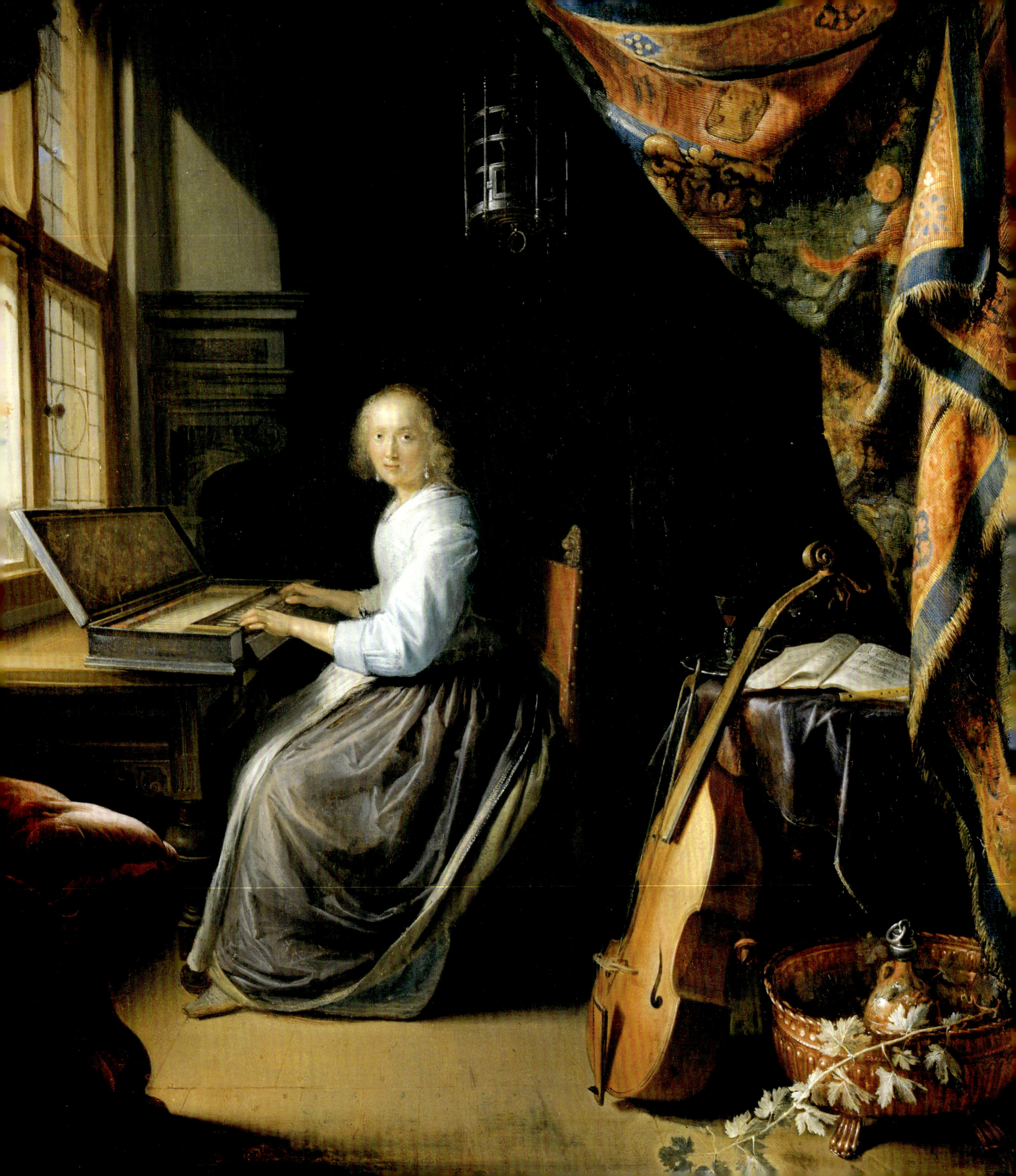

Gerrit Dou 1613–1675

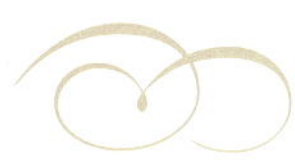

Master Painter in the Age of Rembrandt

Ronni Baer
with contributions by Arthur K. Wheelock, Jr., and Annetje Boersma

Edited by Arthur K. Wheelock, Jr.

NATIONAL GALLERY OF ART • WASHINGTON

YALE UNIVERSITY PRESS • NEW HAVEN AND LONDON

Shell Oil Company Foundation, on behalf of the employees of Shell Oil Company, is proud to make possible this presentation to the American people

The exhibition in London is made possible by The Arthur and Holly Magill Foundation

The exhibition in The Hague is sponsored by ABN AMRO Bank

The exhibition is organized by the National Gallery of Art, Washington, and Dulwich Picture Gallery, London, in association with the Royal Cabinet of Paintings Mauritshuis, The Hague

The exhibition in Washington is supported by an indemnity from the Federal Council on the Arts and the Humanities.

The exhibition in London is supported by an indemnity from the British Government.

National Gallery of Art, Washington
16 April–6 August 2000

Dulwich Picture Gallery, London
6 September–19 November 2000

Royal Cabinet of Paintings Mauritshuis, The Hague
9 December 2000–25 February 2001

The clothbound English edition is distributed by Yale University Press, New Haven and London.

Produced by the Editors Office, National Gallery of Art
Production Manager, Chris Vogel
Editor, Charles Dibble, with Quint Gregory and Stephanie Sonntag
Designer, Wendy Schleicher Smith
Typeset in Van Dijck by Duke + Company, Devon, Pennsylvania
Separations by SeleOffset, Turin, Italy
Printed on Aberdeen Silk by Eurografica, SpA, Vicenza, Italy

Note to the Reader

Dimensions are given in centimeters, followed by inches in parentheses; height precedes width.

In the provenance section of the entries, parentheses indicate a dealer, auction house, or agent. A semicolon between two names indicates a direct transfer of the painting from one owner to another, whereas a period indicates that no direct transfer is documented.

The exhibition history of each picture is given as far as it is known.

Library of Congress Cataloging-in-Publication Data

Baer, Ronni, 1954–
Gerrit Dou (1613–1675): master painter in the age of Rembrandt/ Ronni Baer with contributions by Arthur K. Wheelock, Jr. and Annetje Boersma; edited by Arthur K. Wheelock, Jr.

p. cm.

Catalog of an exhibition held at the National Gallery of Art, Washington, D.C., Apr. 16–Aug. 6, 2000, the Dulwich Picture Gallery, London, Sept. 6–Nov. 19, 2000, and the Royal Cabinet of Paintings Mauritshuis, The Hague, Dec. 9, 2000–Feb. 25, 2001.
Includes bibliographical references.

ISBN 0-300-08369-6 — ISBN 0-89468-248-2 (soft)

1. Dou, Gerard, 1613–1675 — Exhibitions. I. Dou, Gerard, 1613–1675. II. Wheelock, Arthur K. III. Boersma, Annetje, 1950– IV. National Gallery of Art (U.S.) V. Dulwich Picture Gallery. VI. Mauritshuis (Hague, Netherlands). VII. Title.

ND653.D7 A4 2000
759.9492—dc21 00-020298

COVER
An Interior with Young Violinist (detail), 1637, oil on panel, National Gallery of Scotland, Edinburgh (cat. 8)

BACK COVER
Man with a Pipe, c. 1645, oil on panel, The National Gallery, London (cat. 15)

FRONTISPIECE
Woman at the Clavichord (detail), c. 1665, oil on panel, Trustees of Dulwich Picture Gallery, London (cat. 30)

Contents

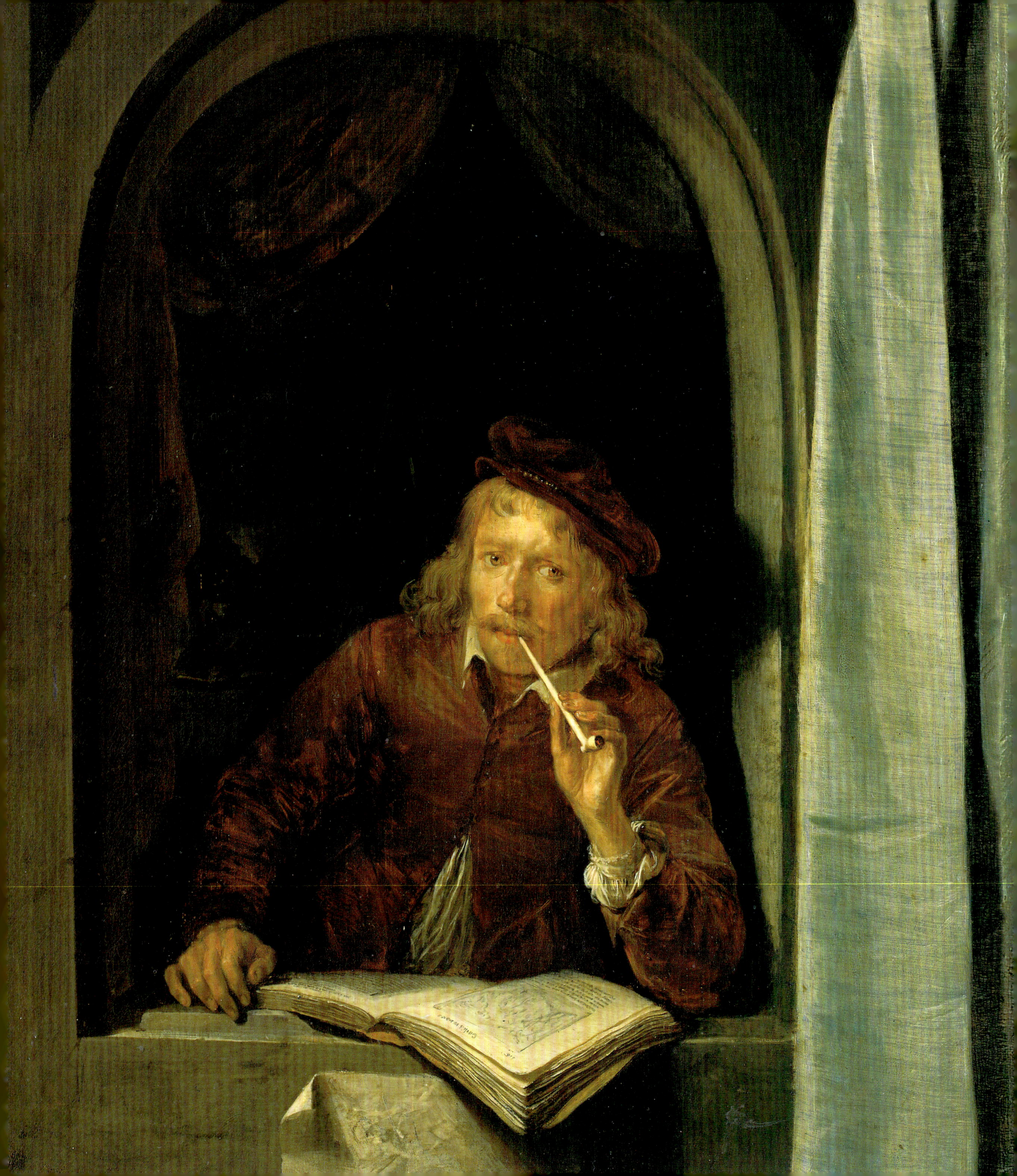

DETAIL
Painter with Pipe and Book, c. 1645 oil on panel, Rijksmuseum, Amsterdam (cat. 16)

Gerrit Dou was one of the most highly esteemed Dutch painters of the seventeenth century, prized for his meticulous technique and illusionistic effects. Dou entered Rembrandt van Rijn's Leiden studio at the age of thirteen, when the great master himself was still a teenager. Although Dou remained with Rembrandt for only three years, the master's influence is reflected in Dou's compositions, use of chiaroscuro, and subject matter. Dou's fame, however, resulted from his own artistic achievements. By the age of twenty-eight, Dou was being hailed both by Jan Orlers, historian and burgomaster of Leiden, and Philips Angel, painter and art theorist, as someone whose style all young artists should emulate. Dou was considered the founder of the Leiden school of *fijnschilders* (fine painters), and his works were sought by collectors throughout Europe, including Queen Christina in Stockholm and Cosimo III de' Medici in Florence, who paid extremely high prices for his works.

By the nineteenth century, Dou's paintings had fallen from favor. His careful execution was faulted as soulless, his stylistic and thematic innovations ignored. Early twentieth-century exhibitions of Dutch art largely excluded his work. In recent years, however, scholars have thoroughly reassessed Dou's artistic achievement. In this, the first international show devoted to this outstanding Leiden master, the fruits of the latest research are presented.

The exhibition is the result of a close collaboration between the National Gallery of Art, Washington, Dulwich Picture Gallery, London, and the Royal Cabinet of Paintings Mauritshuis, The Hague. The fully illustrated catalogue is the work of three scholars: Ronni Baer, curator at the Museum of Fine Arts, Boston, and guest curator for the exhibition; Annetje Boersma, a conservator working in The Netherlands; and Arthur K. Wheelock, Jr., the National Gallery's curator of northern baroque painting and also scholarly editor for this catalogue. He, along with Ian Dejardin, curator at Dulwich Picture Gallery, and Peter van der Ploeg, chief curator at the Mauritshuis, guided the project at their respective institutions.

Gerrit Dou (1613–1675): Master Painter in the Age of Rembrandt is the third in a series of exhibitions in the recently constructed Dutch Cabinet Galleries at the National Gallery of Art made possible by the generous support of Shell Oil Company Foundation, on behalf of the employees of Shell Oil Company. The Gallery owes particular thanks to Steve Miller, chairman, president, and chief executive officer of Shell Oil Company, for continuing Shell's tradition of support for Dutch art. The exhibition in Washington is also supported by an indemnity from the Federal Council on the Arts and the Humanities.

The London showing of the exhibition was made possible by a most generous grant from The Arthur and Holly Magill Foundation. Dulwich Picture Gallery is particularly grateful to Mr. and Mrs. Arturo R. Melosi, trustees of the Foundation, for their inspiring commitment to this project, which has enabled the Picture Gallery to join in this ambitious collaboration. Dulwich has also benefited from the support of The Friends of Dulwich Picture Gallery, its constant and reliable partner in so many projects. The Dutch ambassador to the United Kingdom, His Excellency Baron W.O. Bentinck van Schoonheten, has kindly agreed to be Patron of Honour for the exhibition in London and has offered gracious support.

The Mauritshuis is very grateful to ABN AMRO Bank, which sponsored the exhibition in The Hague.

Above all else, we are deeply indebted to our lenders, whose generosity, cooperation, and goodwill have made this exhibition a reality.

Earl A. Powell III
Director, National Gallery of Art

Desmond Shawe-Taylor
Director, Dulwich Picture Gallery

Frederik J. Duparc
Director, Royal Cabinet of Paintings Mauritshuis

· *Acknowledgments*

This exhibition is the third in a series of exhibitions generously supported by Shell Oil Company Foundation for the Dutch Cabinet Galleries at the National Gallery of Art. Gerrit Dou's extraordinarily refined paintings are best enjoyed within the private viewing experience provided by these wonderful spaces, which were recently created through the support of Juliet and Lee Folger/The Folger Fund. I am delighted that we have been joined in this project by two institutions that were, in many respects, the inspiration for the intimate character of the Cabinet Galleries: Dulwich Picture Gallery, London, and the Royal Cabinet of Paintings Mauritshuis, The Hague. Their participation in the exhibition and the shared enthusiasm of my colleagues in these institutions, particularly Ian Dejardin at Dulwich, and Frederik J. Duparc, Rik van Koetsveld, and Peter van der Ploeg at the Mauritshuis, have greatly enhanced the scope of the exhibition.

I am greatly indebted to Ronni Baer, guest curator, for proposing this exhibition of the paintings of Gerrit Dou and for her many contributions to its concept and character. She joins me in thanking the many institutions and private collectors who have generously lent to the exhibition, and the numerous colleagues who gave it their wholehearted support: P. J. M. de Baar, Jean-Luc Baroni, Tim Baylis, Henrik Bjerre, George Breeze, Jill Capobianco, Dawson Carr, Timothy Clifford, Jack Cowart, Chris Dercon, Magali van Deth, Jeroen Giltaij, Allis Helleland, Selma Holo, David Jaffé, Wouter Kloek, Olaf Koester, Jan Piet Filedt Kok, Ronald de Leeuw, David Levy, Christopher Lloyd, Julia Lloyd-Williams, Neil MacGregor, Evan Maurer, Robert Noortman, Axel Rüger, Karl Schütz, Wilfried Seipel, George Shackelford, Eric Jan Sluijter, Gerald

Stiebel, Peter Sutton, Virginia Tandy, George Wachter, John Walsh, Roger Ward, and Marc Wilson.

We are also indebted to numerous centers for scholarly research, whose staffs and resources were essential to the success of our project, including the Frick Art Reference Library, New York; the National Gallery of Art Library, Washington; and the Netherlands Institute for Art History, The Hague.

In Washington, many individuals worked tirelessly to ensure the exhibition's success. D. Dodge Thompson and Jennifer Fletcher Cipriano in the department of exhibitions ably handled the organization and administration of the loan requests. In the registrar's office Michelle Fondas coordinated the transportation of the works of art. Mark Leithauser, with Gordon Anson, Bill Bowser, Linda Heinrich, and Barbara Keyes, executed the exhibition's design. Many people in the editors office contributed to the production of this catalogue: Mary Yakush supervised the project; Charles Dibble, with great care and patience, worked with the various authors to prepare and edit the manuscripts; and Wendy Schleicher Smith created an especially elegant design.

At Dulwich thanks are particularly due to Ian Dejardin, the curator; to Lucy Till, exhibitions officer; and to Lucy's successor, Victoria Norton, who has handled all the details of loan administration at Dulwich. We are also grateful to the former head of development at Dulwich, Charles Leggatt, who helped to secure funding for the exhibition—his last exhibition in the post and an appropriate swansong.

At the Mauritshuis, André Jordaan handled the administration of the loan requests. Henk Douna and his staff coordinated the transportation and realized the installation of the exhibition. The marketing and publicity campaign for the Dutch venue was organized by Lieke Vervoorn.

Finally, to the staff of the department of northern baroque painting at the National Gallery, I am grateful. Quint Gregory offered a number of keen observations on Dou and his paintings and helped prepare the bibliography for the catalogue. Stephanie Sonntag, an intern who is completing her dissertation on Dou for the Rheinische Friedrich-Willhelms-Universität, Bonn, not only assisted in the editing process, but also wrote the educational brochure for the exhibition. Ana Maria Zavala, our staff assistant, diligently handled many administrative details.

To all those who have helped bring our project to its successful conclusion, we extend our deepest gratitude.

Arthur K. Wheelock, Jr.

Lenders to the Exhibition

Aurora Art Fund, Inc.

Cheltenham Art Gallery and Museums

Colnaghi, London

The Corcoran Gallery of Art, Washington

Trustees of Dulwich Picture Gallery, London

Her Majesty Queen Elizabeth II

Fisher Gallery, University of Southern California, Los Angeles

The J. Paul Getty Museum, Los Angeles

Mr. and Mrs. Michal Hornstein

Kunsthistorisches Museum, Vienna

Manchester City Art Galleries

The Minneapolis Institute of Arts

Museum Boijmans van Beuningen, Rotterdam

The National Gallery, London

National Gallery of Art, Washington

The National Gallery of Scotland, Edinburgh

The Nelson-Atkins Museum of Art, Kansas City, Missouri

Princely Collections, Vaduz Castle, Liechtenstein

Private collections

Rijksmuseum, Amsterdam

Royal Cabinet of Paintings Mauritshuis, The Hague

Statens Museum for Kunst, Copenhagen

Sudeley Castle Trustees, Winchcombe, Gloucestershire

Wadsworth Atheneum Museum of Art, Hartford, Connecticut

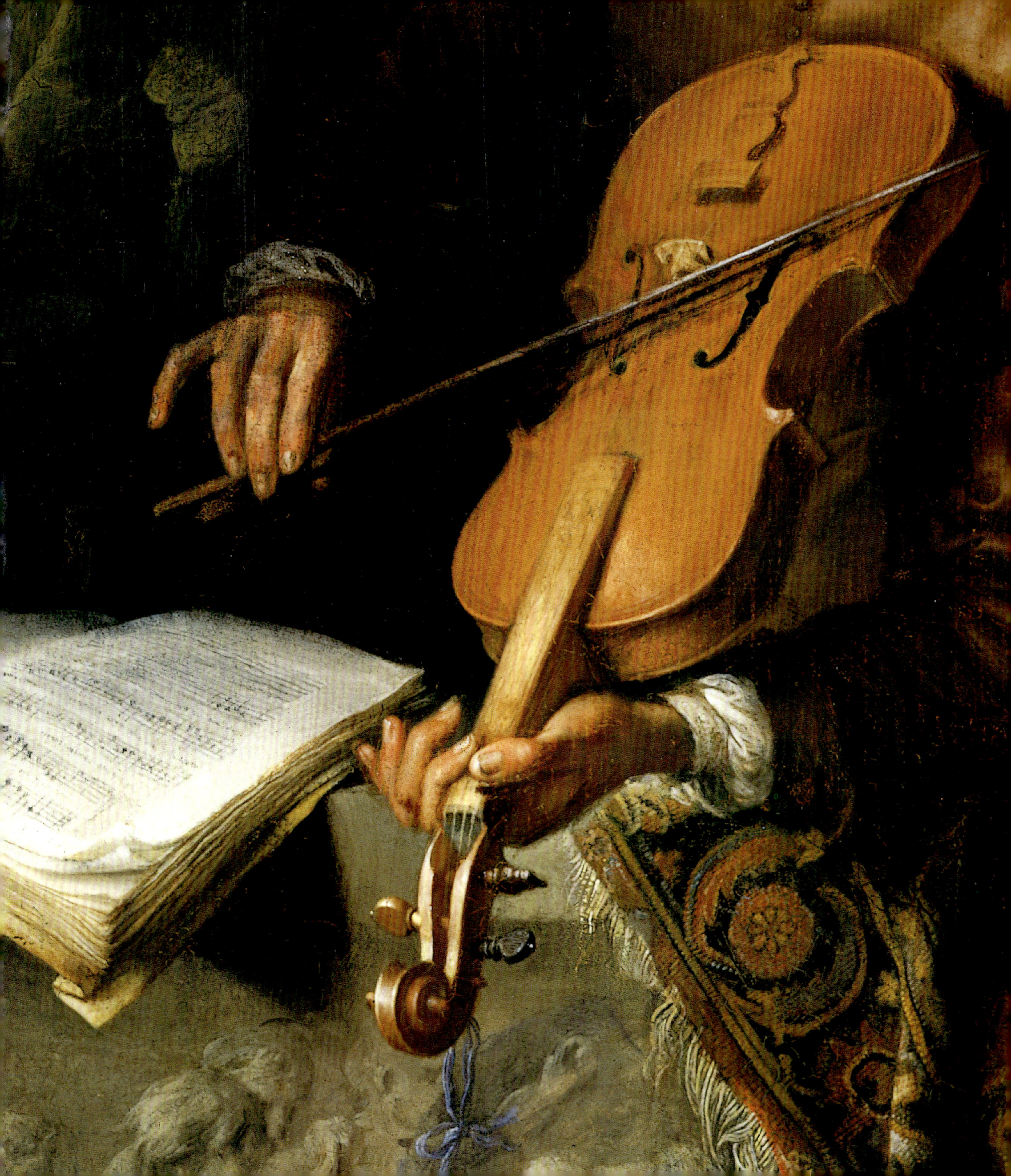

Dou's Reputation

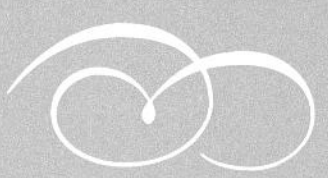

Arthur K. Wheelock, Jr.

DETAIL
Violin Player, 1653, oil on panel, Princely Collections, Vaduz Castle, Liechtenstein (cat. 20)

FIGURE 1
Woman at the Clavichord, c. 1665, oil on panel, Trustees of the Dulwich Picture Gallery, London (cat. 30)

The history of taste is a fascinating subject, particularly when it concerns the ebb and flow of artistic reputations. In Dutch art, stories about the rediscovery of forgotten painters by nineteenth- and twentieth-century art critics continue to astound and fascinate us. That Johannes Vermeer (1632–1675) and Frans Hals (c. 1582/1583–1666), to name only the two most spectacular examples, were virtually unknown beyond a small circle of collectors and art lovers before the 1860s is difficult to fathom. In both instances, a French critic, Théophile Thoré, who published under the pseudonym William Bürger, recognized the remarkable artistic qualities of their paintings and spread the word through his articles and books.

Equally remarkable, although far less often noticed, is the opposite phenomenon: the sudden neglect of masters who at one point occupied center stage in the artistic life of their culture. Any number of Dutch artists can be cited as belonging to this category, but the vagaries of artistic reputation have affected no other master to the extent that they have Gerrit Dou (1613–1675).[1]

Dou, with the possible exception of Rembrandt van Rijn (1606–1669), was the most revered and highly paid seventeenth-century Dutch artist. Viewers marveled at his exquisite technique and masterful images, which elicited such awe and excitement that Johan de Bye, one of his patrons, rented a room across from the

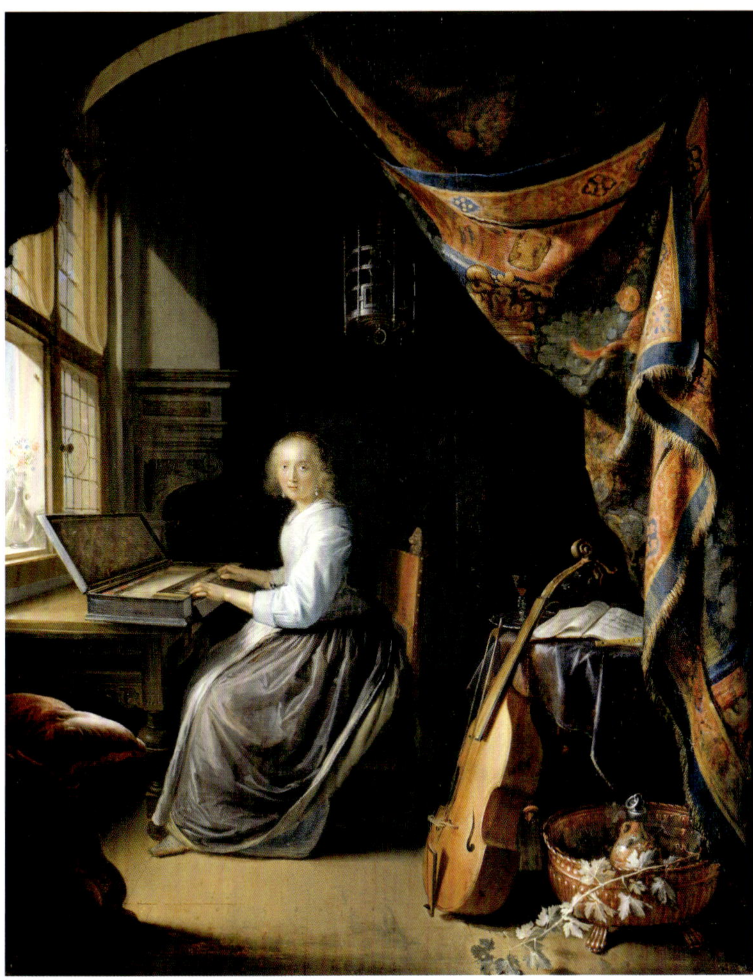

Leiden town hall where paying visitors could come to admire no fewer than twenty-seven of his works, among them, *Woman at the Clavichord* (fig. 1). Dou's paintings, while eagerly acquired by private collectors and courtly patrons during his lifetime, were even more highly valued after his death. Virtually all accounts of his life provide a list of the extraordinary prices paid for his works. A letter written in 1780 by an agent acquiring paintings for the duke of Rutland serves as an example of the prices reached: "I am at last in possession of the Gerard Dou I mentioned to you. The price was 3,000 fl., about 300 £., a very great price considering the size of the picture, but a very small one if you take into account, the great request [sic] in which capital works of the master are held both in Holland and here. . . ."[2]

Dou's fame and the appreciation of his artistic qualities remained unabated until the middle of the nineteenth century. In 1842, Johannes Immerzeel wrote admiringly of Dou in his lexicon of Dutch artists, stating that no other artist, before or after, could match Dou's beautiful manner of execution.[3] He particularly admired how Dou fashioned his "unpayably expensive" masterpieces without giving these highly finished works the look of paintings that required time and difficulty to execute.[4] Dou's paintings, he concluded, bore the "stamp of rare genius." He bound together the lessons learned from Rembrandt about "coloration and effect" with an "unspeakable talent for depicting all animate and inanimate subjects without scrimping on the purity and the freshness of colors or betraying through other means that the wonders of his brush were wrought with difficulty and untiring patience."[5]

Indeed, Dou's untiring patience was a virtue often remarked upon by mid-nineteenth-century critics. One enthusiastic commentary written in 1854 commended Dou's "marvellous" industry. "He would bestow hours in studying new effects, in viewing the contrasts and combinations of light and shade, and in perfecting the most trivial accessories of his subject. He cared not how he laboured or how protracted his labour was, so that he was enabled to attain to that degree of excellence to which he felt his genius was capable of leading him."[6]

However, it was not just Dou's patience that so astounded mid-nineteenth-century art critics but also the compelling narrative of his genre scenes, which he achieved through the truthfulness of human emotions and expressions. The Louvre's *Dropsical Woman* (fig. 2)—the most celebrated of his works at the time—was admired both for its refined painting technique and for the "strong natural expression of each figure: the patient resignation of the lady, the filial affection of the daughter, the anxious attention of the nurse, and the ominous gesture of the doctor, are portrayed with a refinement of feeling that would do honour to the best Italian masters."[7]

Then, just as Vermeer and Hals were being discovered, and their previously misattributed or otherwise unknown paintings eagerly acquired by private individuals and museums, Dou's work began to lose favor. His fall from grace was swift

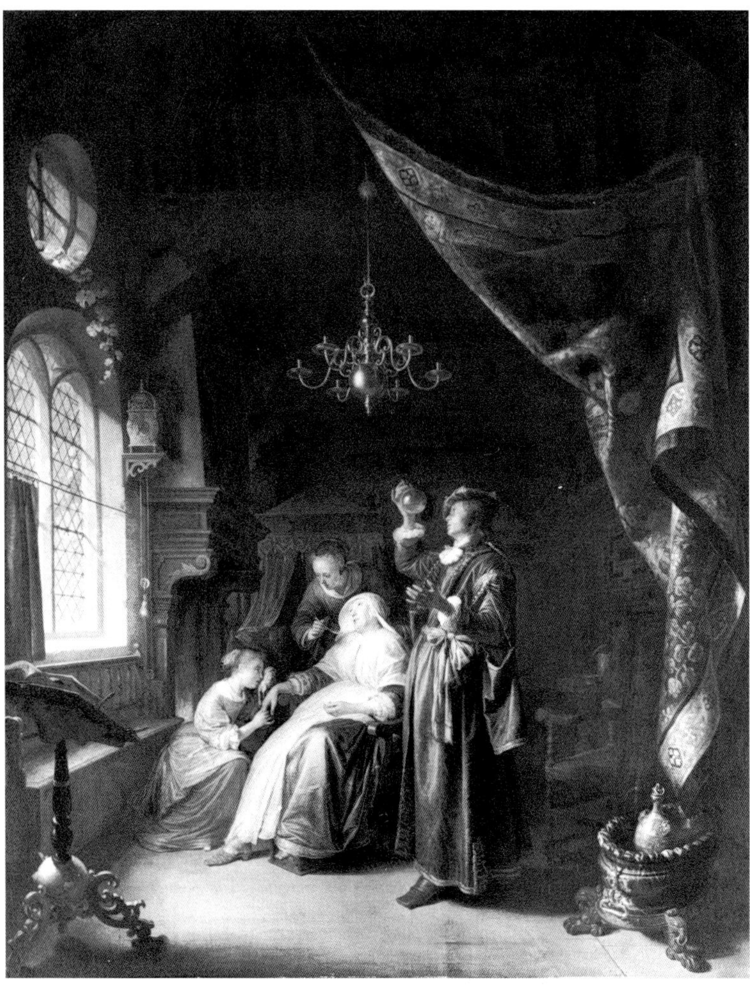

FIGURE 2
The Dropsical Woman, 1663, oil on panel, Musée du Louvre, Paris

and dramatic: the extraordinary craft that had always elicited awe and admiration was condemned as pedantic and dry. The artist who poured his soul into his art, and whose inspiration was felt by generations of Leiden artists, was dismissed as heartless. Just why this reassessment occurred, and what it says about his art, is the question that this short essay will address. The story is fascinating in itself, but it is also important for evaluating the artist and his work as we encounter it anew at the beginning of the twenty-first century.

The story is particularly poignant in America, where serious efforts to collect Dutch art were only in their infancy at the end of the nineteenth century. Thus, there were no long-established princely collections replete with paintings by Dou to obscure the completeness of his fall from favor. During the late nineteenth century, America was in the midst of extraordinary economic growth, spurred by the development of natural resources, the expansion of building industries and railroads, and the rise of banking and financial speculation. Several of the nation's "captains of industry"—among them, Henry Clay Frick, J. Pierpont Morgan, Peter A. B. Widener, and Benjamin Altman—worked closely with art dealers such as Knoedler, Colnaghi, and Duveen to find exceptional paintings and furniture and objets d'art for their homes. The desire to import culture, however, was also civic minded, for these same individuals supported the founding of many of the great symphonies, libraries, and museums—among them, the Metropolitan Museum of Art, the Art Institute of Chicago, the Philadelphia Museum of Art, and the Museum of Fine Arts in Boston—that are at the core of the cultural fabric of America. Indeed, in 1888, one year after the New York banker Henry G. Marquand had acquired *Young Woman with a Water Pitcher*, he donated it to the Metropolitan Museum of Art; it was the first Vermeer to enter an American collection.

The public debut of these collecting activities occurred at the memorable Hudson-Fulton Celebration, an exhibition of 150 Dutch paintings held at the Metropolitan Museum of Art in 1909. Wilhelm Valentiner, who organized the exhibition, wrote in the introduction to the catalogue that the range and quality of the paintings would "astonish" European art circles, particularly the thirty-seven paintings by Rembrandt, twenty paintings by Frans Hals, and, remarkably, six paintings by Vermeer. Little noted or remarked upon at the time was the fact that the exhibition contained no paintings by Dou.[8] Not one of the wealthy collectors Valentiner drew upon for his exhibition—not Widener, Mellon, Frick, Morgan, Altman, nor Marquand—owned a painting by Dou.[9]

This omission is particularly striking when one considers the connections between Dou and the two Dutch artists that Americans most highly esteemed: Rembrandt and Vermeer. Dou, after all, was trained by Rembrandt, and drew a number of his themes, including hermits and self-portraits, from the Rembrandt tradition. On the other hand, his domestic subjects were precisely those that Vermeer favored, among them, women playing musical instruments and scholars in their studies.

Just as the fame of Vermeer and Hals spread through Thoré's enthusiastic descriptions of their work in his writings of the 1860s, so with Thoré can also be found the roots of Dou's slide into obscurity. Thoré's first considered assessments of Dou's paintings appear in his influential *Musées de la Holland* (Paris, 1858–1860), in which he described his reactions to paintings he had encountered in museums and private collections during a tour of the Netherlands. The Dutch paintings this French writer, critic, and collector most admired on his tour reinforced his own aesthetic and political ideals, which were infused with republican virtues of truth, honesty, and freedom of expression. Thoré also felt strongly that human values were broadly shared and that paintings succeeded best when they were emotionally and spiritually, as well as physically, true.[10]

The point of departure for Thoré's evaluations of Dutch art was John Smith's influential eight-volume *Catalogue Raisonné of the Works of the Most Eminent Dutch, Flemish, and French Painters*, published in London between 1829 and 1842. Smith, who was a great admirer of Dou's, began his first volume with an assessment of the artist's work; a lithograph after one of Dou's self-portraits (fig. 3) faces the volume's title page. Smith's description of Dou's extraordinarily meticulous working methods, which by then were accepted as fact by virtually all later commentators on the artist's life, was based on earlier sources.

FIGURE 3
S.M. Smith after Gerrit Dou, lithograph, 1829, National Gallery of Art Library, Washington

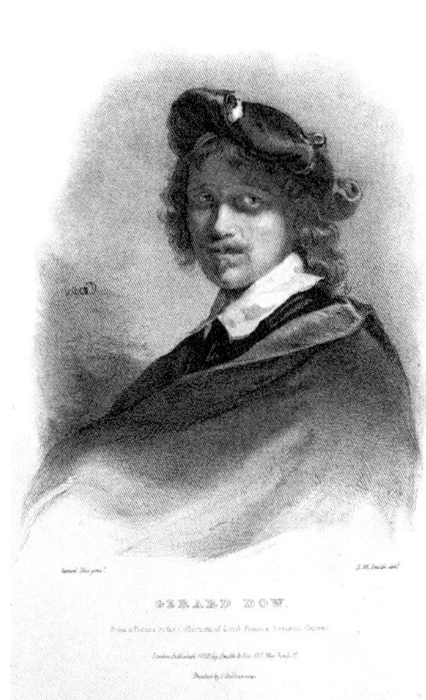

The most important of these was the 1675 treatise of Joachim von Sandrart (1606–1688), a German artist and art theorist who had visited Dou's large studio around 1640. Von Sandrart relished describing Dou's fastidiousness and the way he protected his palette, brushes, and colors from dust by keeping them in a chest near his stool. Before opening the chest, Von Sandrart wrote, the artist would sit silently in his chair and wait for the dust in the room to settle. To illustrate the infinite patience with which Dou worked, Von Sandrart recounted that when he complimented Dou on the care he had taken to paint a broomstick no larger than a fingernail, the artist remarked that he still had three days work to do on it.[11] Smith repeated these anecdotes and concluded by commending Dou as "a perfect master of all the principles of art; which, united with consummate skill and labour, enabled him to produce the most perfect specimens that ever came from the easel of a painter."[12]

Thoré, unlike Smith, grouped together artists who worked in distinctive genres or specialties.[13] He listed the specific categories in the introduction to his first volume: "Rembrandt and Van der Helst and the painters of grand compositions; Gerard Dou and the small, precious masters; Adriaen van Ostade, Jan Steen and the painters of popular and comic customs; Terburgh, Metsu, and the painters of elegant manners. . . ."[14] Although Thoré's logic is understandable, his groupings had the effect of demoting Gerrit Dou from the place of honor Smith had granted him. Thoré not only shifted Dou to the second of his categories but, more importantly, made a pointed distinction between artists who made "grand compositions" and the "small, precious masters." At issue, moreover, was not just the scale of the works Rembrandt and Dou painted but the significance of the images they created.

Rembrandt, in his genius, created majestic paintings that conveyed the vivacity of life and the depth of human experiences. His paintings, Thoré exclaimed, were "mysterious, profound, inapprehensible." When seen for the first time, they create "an indefinable astonishment, for they are never what one would expect."[15] For Thoré, however, Dou's paintings lacked the fantasy and mystery that gave life and vibrancy to Rembrandt's works. Here, he seems to follow the opinion of Roger de Piles, who, in his *Abrégé de la vie des peintres*, published in Paris in 1699, remarked that Dou's extraordinary patience and attention "scarcely accords" with "the ardor that painting demands."[16] One can almost hear Thoré searching to articulate what troubled him about Dou's *Night School* (cat. 28), a painting that Smith had valued highly in his commentary on the artist.[17] Thoré acknowledged that Dou had painted this work with "incomparable industry," but, bothered by the artificial light effects that he described as a "conjurer's trick,"[18] he concluded that "true art has nothing to do with such futile preoccupations": it is more spontaneous and the results are more sincere.[19]

Thoré's most critical remarks about Dou occur in 1859 when he described a painting by Dou in the Galerie d'Arenberg. Thoré wrote that although Dou tried to imitate a certain genre of Rembrandt's compositions, he was the antithesis of his master. "The genius of Rembrandt is [found] in the intimate expressions, the character of movements, and the originality of effects. Gerard Dou has none of these. His manner of painting, as well as his inspiration, is precisely contrary to that of Rembrandt."[20]

Thoré's objection that Dou's paintings lacked the ineffable mystery of Rembrandt's more spontaneous creations was soon echoed by some of the most prestigious scholars of the day. In a remarkable introduction to his 1901 monograph on Dou, the Dutch art historian Willem Martin wrote about reservations he felt about the artist's work: "At a time when nothing leaves men so cool as the art path of the Leiden fine painters, many will wonder why a book is being published about the one who gave life to this path, particularly when the writer begins with the declaration that he, even as Joshua Reynolds, considers Dou's works 'with admiration on the lips, but indifference in the heart.'"[21]

The Rembrandt scholar Wilhelm von Bode, who greatly admired Thoré's writings, acknowledged that Dou painted his intimate and delicately rendered scenes of daily life with utmost care and love. Nevertheless, Von Bode wrote in 1906 that Dou's paintings failed to elicit the same warm responses engendered by Rembrandt's larger works. The reasons were similar to the ones Thoré had intimated: Dou's paintings were too deliberate and neat, included too many details, and were executed in such cool tonalities that they lacked Rembrandt's subjectivity, poetic feeling, and inner life.[23]

Far more critical of Dou than Von Bode, however, was Walter Armstrong, director of the National Gallery of Ireland, who expressly attacked the notion that Dou's renowned patience was a virtue. "As examples of industry, of duty fulfilled, of single-minded conscientiousness, [Dou's paintings] have few superiors. But no one who can enjoy the creative powers of art cares to look at them twice, except as curiosities. Their careful arrangement does not amount to a design; their tints do not amount to colour; their handling is strictly imitative; and they show no gift for aesthetic selection. In short, they are monuments of an irrelevant virtue, and before them we have to say, not 'See what patience can do,' but 'See how patience may be misused.'"[24] Finally, in 1919, the Dutch art historian Just Havelaar summed up Dou's failings: "Dou saw neither more nor better, felt neither finer nor deeper than others: he only had more patience—and it is easy to have patience when the heart beats so insipidly and the spirit is so dull."[25]

That such critical reactions were also felt on the other side of the Atlantic is evident from the passionate critique of Dou's work by John van Dyke, who wrote in 1895 that he found Dou's reputation enormously exaggerated. For Van Dyke, Dou's ability to render objects in microscopic detail was no reason to accord him the popular accolades he had traditionally received. On the contrary, Van Dyke found that Dou's miniature style was consistent with his smallness of vision. He was not an artist who could work on a large scale or with grand concepts. Moreover, his world never penetrated more deeply than the surface of objects. Not only did he fail to examine the psychology of human relations; he never expressed in his paintings his own "faith, hope, sentiment, or feeling."[26] "One is justified," Van Dyke wrote, "in believing that the painter never had either a great mind or a great heart. What he did have was a clever, patient hand."[27] For Van Dyke, the lack of "human emotion, thought, or feeling" in Dou's paintings, and the fact that he objectified reality instead of expressing its subjectivity, effectively removed the painter from the ranks of true artists. He designated Dou as no more than a "skilled craftsman" or "artisan," one whose works should be prized for the "beauty and purity of his workmanship" but not for their profundity.[28]

Dou's reputation as a skilled but superficial artist, incapable of probing the deeper recesses of the human experience, varied little during the first half of the twentieth century. He was practically ignored in the large exhibition of Dutch art held at the Royal Academy in 1929: only one small work, his delicate self-portrait from Cheltenham (cat. 7), was included in this vast show.[29] The monetary value of Dou's paintings, which had always astonished connoisseurs and which, in written commentaries about the artist, had inevitably served as an indication of his artistic worth, declined. One indication of his diminished status in the late 1930s was the decision of the Alte Pinakothek, Munich, to deaccession a number of Dou's masterpieces, four of which are included in this monographic exhibition (cats. 19, 27, 32, and 34).[30] As late as 1956, Wilhelm Valentiner, who was a protégé of Wilhelm von Bode and the adviser to a number of American collectors, including Peter A. B. Widener, wrote that "Dou loses much interest for us after he [leaves Rembrandt's workshop]. His figures, so carefully drawn and colored, lack expression and vitality; smooth technique and minuteness of detail means everything to the artist."[31] Valentiner's opinion of Dou contrasts with his view that "Rembrandt's only object was to bring the soul life of his figures as near to us as possible: he therefore lighted most strongly those parts—above all, the head and the hands—in which the spiritual qualities were most readily expressed."[32]

The slow recovery of Dou's reputation only began in the 1960s when a young Dutch art historian, J. A. Emmens, demonstrated that Dou's mature paintings were, in fact, fascinating and worthy of careful consideration. In two separate articles Emmens demonstrated that these works were not merely prosaic depictions of contemporary life but, instead, incorporated complex philosophical ideas drawn from antiquity.[33] In the first of these articles Emmens discussed a lost triptych by Dou, known today through an eighteenth-century copy by Willem Joseph Laqui (fig. 4).[34] The triptych depicts three different genre scenes: a night school, a mother and child in a large room, and a man sharpening a quill. Emmens argued that the three

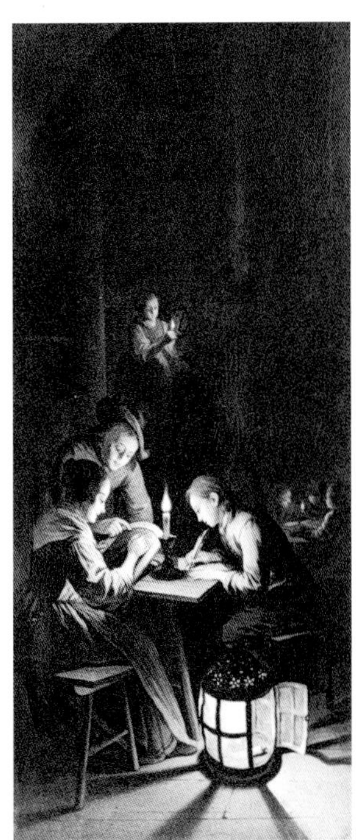
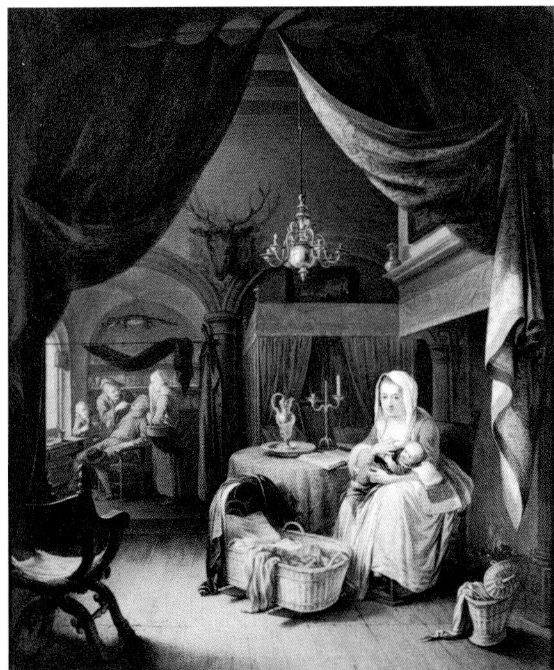
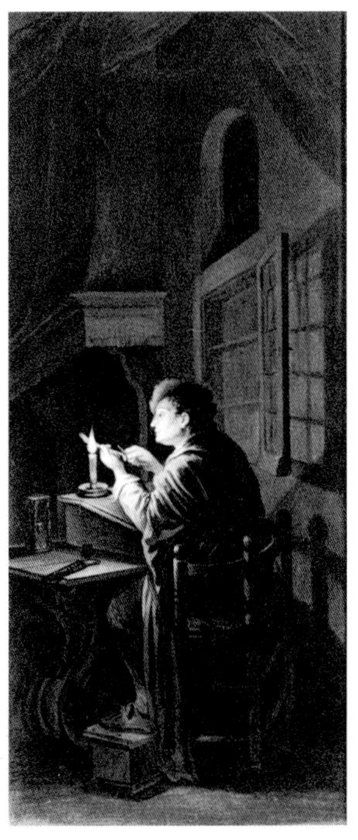

FIGURE 4
Willem Joseph Laqui after Gerrit Dou, *Triptych (Night School; The Lying-In Room; Man Sharpening a Quill)*, oil on canvas (middle), oil on panel (left and right wings), Rijksmuseum, Amsterdam

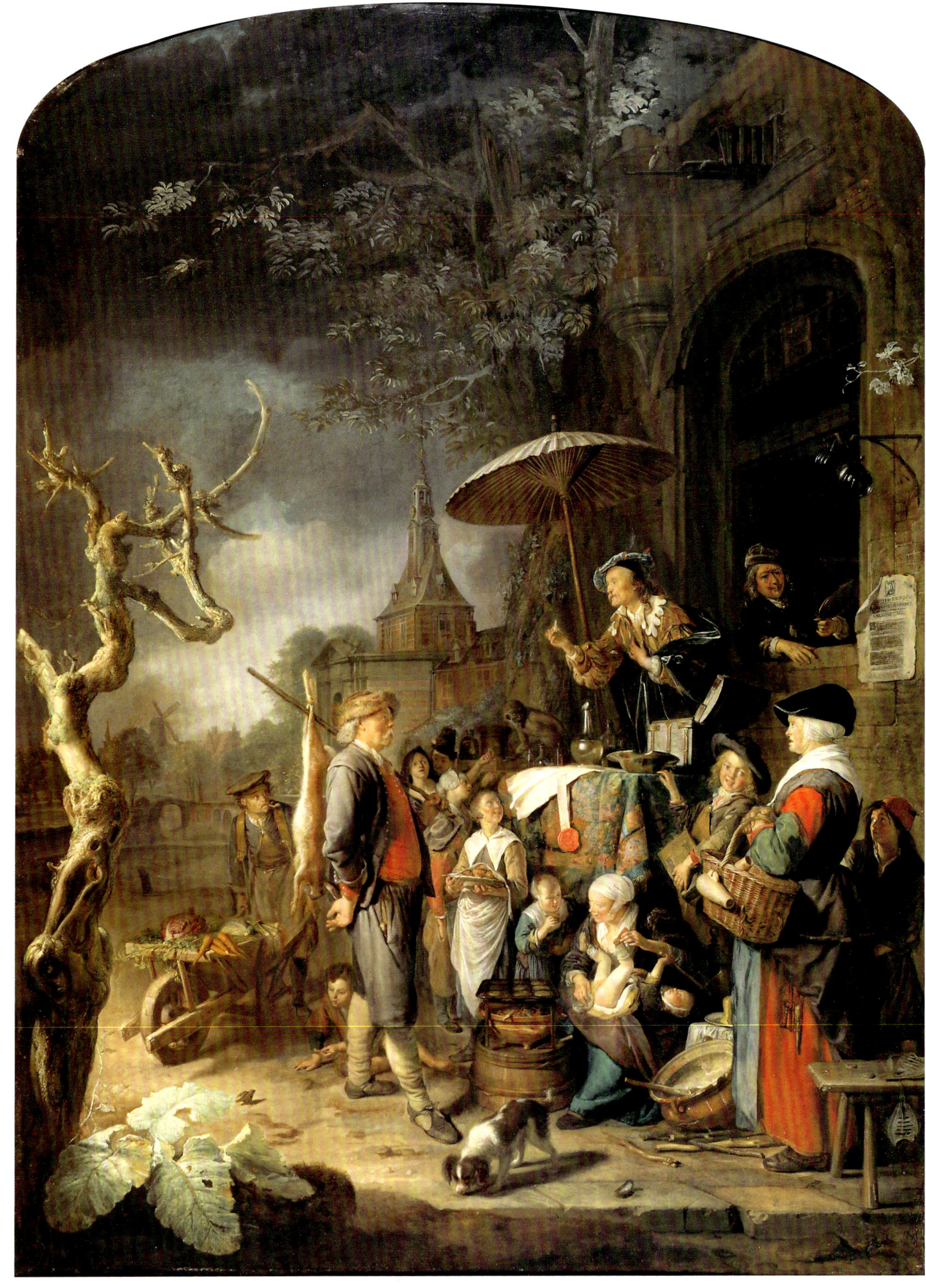

scenes conform to Aristotle's observation that "three things are needed to achieve learning: nature, teaching, and practice; but all will be fruitless unless practice follows nature and teaching."[35] In Dou's triptych, the school represents "teaching," the mother and child represent "nature," and the man sharpening his quill represents "practice."

FIGURE 5
The Quack, 1652, oil on panel, Museum Boijmans van Beuningen, Rotterdam (cat. 19)

Emmens also demonstrated the extensive emblematic traditions that Dou drew upon when conceiving *The Quack*, the artist's largest and most ambitious work (fig. 5).[36] Emmens, who noted that the quack, or charlatan, was a popular subject for seventeenth-century painters because of its moralizing possibilities, argued that Dou here also alluded to long-established philosophical ideas distinguishing between the sensual, the active, and the contemplative life. The quack and the uneducated public he deceives belong to the sensual world; those who actively participate in life, such as the farmer bringing goods to market on the left, and those who contemplate life, such as the artist—Dou himself—peering out of his window at the right, will be able to recognize and avoid deceptions. Moreover, Emmens argued, Dou has also sought here to distinguish between the "good artist," the painter, and the "bad artist," the quack. The "good artist" chooses motifs from nature, which he carefully depicts and thoughtfully combines to convey a moralizing message decipherable by those who contemplate the work of art.

Emmens' reassessment of Dou coincided with an interest that developed during the 1970s and 1980s in the complex character of Dutch realism. Whereas earlier assessments of Dutch art had emphasized its descriptive character, art historians began to recognize that iconographic traditions also affected the types of subjects depicted by Dutch artists. A major impetus for this interest was *Tot Lering en Vermaak*, an exhibition held in 1976 at the Rijksmuseum, Amsterdam, in which Eddy de Jongh demonstrated that many Dutch genre paintings contain visual references to emblematic and moralizing traditions. Dou played a major role in this exhibition, with the Laqui triptych and *The Quack* both featured.[37] While the specifics of Emmens' and De Jongh's interpretations of Dou's paintings have been disputed, their conviction that Dou was a learned artist who imbued his paintings with complex iconographic themes convinced a whole generation of Dutch art historians.[38] Thus, one of the main criticisms of Dou—that he indiscriminately filled his paintings with carefully executed accessories and was uninterested in profound moral issues—was laid to rest.[39]

The particular irony of Dou's reemergence in the 1970s as an artist acceptable within the canon of Dutch genre painting is that interest in his art, in *Tot Lering en Vermaak* and elsewhere, was predominantly iconographic. The artist's meticulous and refined technique, which had always dominated critical assessments of his work, was hardly discussed.[40] Indeed, as has been noted, Emmens' arguments surrounding the triptych were based in their entirety on a copy of Dou's lost original.[41]

The intimate connections between style and content in Dou's paintings, which we now recognize are fundamental to his art, were not explored in the individual entries in *Tot Lering en Vermaak*. Nevertheless, the framework for such discussions was laid out in the introduction to the catalogue. There, De Jongh cited various seventeenth-century texts, including Philips Angel's 1642 *Lof der Schilder-Konst*, to demonstrate that artists were encouraged to imitate life closely and to delight the viewer through the deceptive character of the painting's apparent realism. Indeed, Angel writes: "If [a master] manages to imitate life in such a way that people judge that it approaches real life without being able to detect in it the manner of the master who made it, such a spirit deserves praise and honor and shall be ranked above others."[42] But just as viewers were delighted by such visual deceptions, including trompe-l'oeil paintings, so also were they delighted by veiled references to moralizing ideas within these apparently realistic images. Thus, De Jongh writes, the demands on form and content in the seventeenth century often involve "the combination of two sorts of deceit: the 'pleasant deceit' from the apparent true-to-life imitation, and the deceit that arises through the veiling of the real intent of the representation."[43]

For no other artist is an understanding of the intermingling of these two "deceits" more important than it is for Dou. Yet, it was not until the late 1980s that the inherent bond of Dou's painting style and his subject matter was carefully examined in two important exhibitions about the painters of the Leiden school. In *Leidse Fijnschilders*, held in Leiden in 1988, Eric Jan Sluijter examined the type of accolades Dou received from contemporary sources.[44] For example, the same Philips Angel who advocated that artists strive to imitate reality identified "the never sufficiently praised" Dou as a paradigm for other artists. He commended Dou for his ability to paint in a "pleasing" manner with a "bold yet sweet-flowing brush," and with "a curious looseness that he guides with a sure and certain drawing hand."[45] He warned that artists who failed to follow such guidelines were destined to "smother in that stiff, tidy unnaturalness" that denies validity to the work of art.

Subsequently, when discussing individual paintings in the exhibition, Sluijter emphasized the importance of such considerations for an understanding of the works of art. For example, when considering Dou's *Painter with Pipe and Book* (fig. 6), Sluijter examined the painting's various illusionistic components: the composition, with the figure peering out from the wood-framed stone window; the light effects, with the shadow of the curtain rod cast onto the stone behind it; the careful representation of materials, with the curtain so finely painted that no brushstrokes are visible.[46]

At the same time, Sluijter suggested that Dou's interest in illusionism had broader ramifications for the seventeenth-century viewer. The curtain looked like an actual curtain hanging before a painting, similar to the ones Dutch art-lovers used to protect works of art from dust and light. However, the curtain would also have brought to mind the curtain painted by the Greek painter Parrhasius in his contest with Zeuxis to see who could create the more illusionistic work of art, a topos that continued to epitomize the remarkable ability of artists to create visual deceptions. Finally, Sluijter concluded that Dou's subject, the smoking painter, had *vanitas* implications: smoking, as an

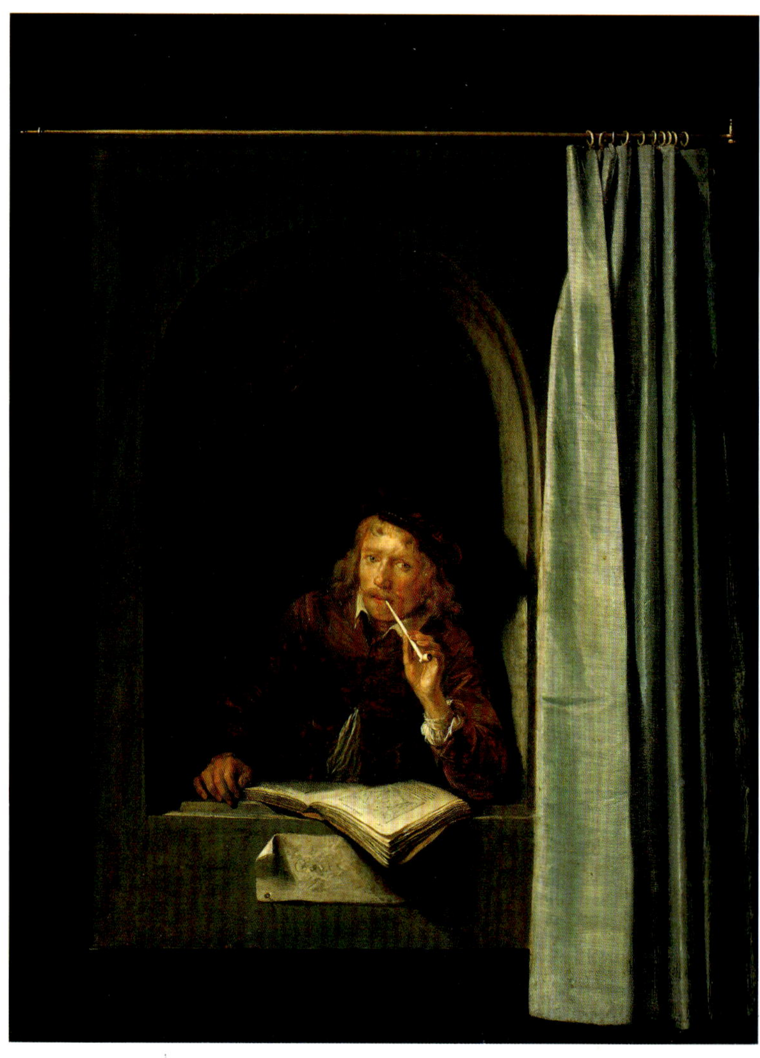

FIGURE 6
Painter with Pipe and Book, c. 1645, oil on panel, Rijksmuseum, Amsterdam (cat. 16)

FIGURE 7
Bust of a Man, c. 1642–1645, oil on panel, The Corcoran Gallery of Art, Washington, William A. Clark Collection (cat. 11)

FIGURE 8
Detail, *Woman at the Clavichord*, c. 1665, oil on panel, Trustees of Dulwich Picture Gallery, London (cat. 30)

ephemeral sensual pleasure, served as a reminder that life itself is transient. In the context of this image, Sluijter continued, the smoker, who looks engagingly out at the viewer, invites us to contemplate the differences between appearance and reality, not only as an artistic phenomenon but also as a reflection upon life's transience.[47]

Peter Hecht, in his 1989 exhibition on the Leiden "fine painters" at the Rijksmuseum, Amsterdam, came to different conclusions than did Sluijter about the character and implications of Dou's illusionism. He interpreted the windows, niches, and large hanging draperies in the foregrounds of Dou's paintings as devices that provide transitions to the pictorial realm within. Much as had Sluijter, Hecht stressed that, as in *Woman at the Clavichord*, Dou enhanced the seductive realism of his technique through compositional means. The young woman's alluring gaze, as well as the poured glass of wine, the open music-book, and adjacent musical instruments induce the viewer to feel drawn to the scene, as though he were the expected guest. However, Hecht argued that such emotional experiences would not have induced the seventeenth-century viewer to contemplate the vanity of the sensual world, as Sluijter maintained.[48] For Hecht, the very seduction of these glorious images was the source of their delight and great appeal.

The vagaries of Dou's artistic reputation are, thus, extreme. Dou's refined techniques and realistic manner of painting were greatly admired and highly valued during his lifetime. However, his extraordinary ability to paint in a detailed fashion and to depict a variety of surface textures—the very qualities that appealed to seventeenth- and eighteenth-century critics—were disdained by late nineteenth- and early twentieth-century art historians imbued with romantic ideals about the power of art to express humanity's spiritual qualities. These scholars found his work cold, calculated, and unfeeling.

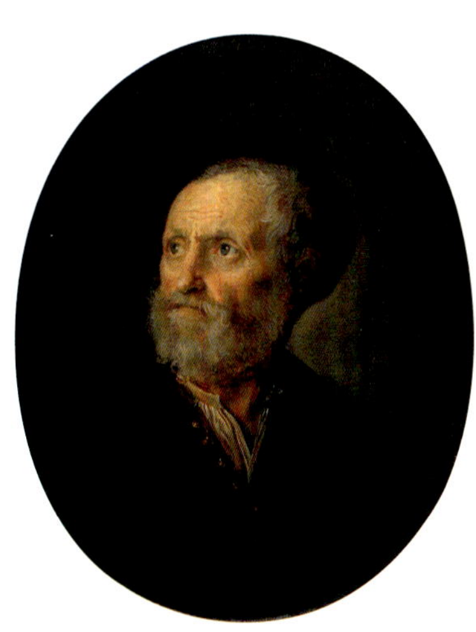

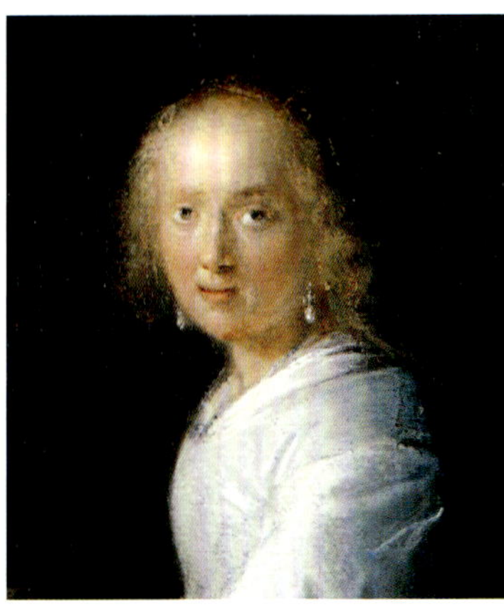

Recent scholars, who have been less judgmental about Dou's work than their predecessors, have sought to explain the unique character of his artistic contribution within its seventeenth-century context. As critics from the 1960s and 1970s sought to uncover the emblematic character of much of Dutch art, they discovered that Dou's paintings were appealing for iconographic reasons. While some scholars from the 1980s embraced this iconographic approach and others rejected it, a common conviction developed that Dou's illusionistic painting style and thematic concerns were intimately connected.

The extremes in these perceptions of Dou's work indicate that the artist, and his place within the broad spectrum of Dutch seventeenth-century painting, will continue to be reassessed by succeeding generations of art lovers.[49] An important part of that story will develop only as more technical examinations of his works are undertaken, for much still has to be learned about the manner in which he created his paintings. For example, as Annetje Boersma notes in her contribution to this catalogue, Dou often worked and reworked his paintings, changing and refining his composition even as he was attempting to replicate reality with delicate brushstrokes and thin glazes. This painterly approach, as well as the probability that many of his paintings evolved over a prolonged period, belies the opinions of his critics that his execution was overly calculated and dry.[50] Indeed, time and again, one sees the remarkable freshness of Dou's brush at work, whether in the evocative head of an old man (fig. 7) or the alluring gaze of a young woman (fig. 8), the "sweet-flowing brush" of an artist who paints with the "curious looseness" so esteemed by Philips Angel.

This exhibition, the first international loan show ever devoted to Gerrit Dou, provides an extraordinary opportunity to reassess the artistic qualities of this fascinating painter. Not since the seventeenth century, when Johan de Bye brought together those twenty-seven Dou paintings in a rented house in Leiden, have so many of his works been seen together. This select overview of his work—from his early years as a Rembrandt pupil to the respected head of the Leiden school of "fine painters" some forty years later—will allow viewers to experience firsthand the artist's remarkable virtuosity in some of the finest portraits, still lifes, and genre scenes that he ever made. It will test his ability to entice and delight with his remarkably illusionistic images, ones such as *Violin Player* (fig. 9), in which a musician leans out of a stone-framed window, his gestures, stance, and expression so realistically portrayed that he seems to lean out of the picture itself.

The exhibition will also engage the viewer in serious consideration of the themes that so preoccupied Dou over the years. His interest in the position and the role of the artist in society, evidenced by depictions of artists in their studios (see cats. 1 and 16) and by self-portraits (see cats. 7, 14, 27, and 29) was one such concern. Another was the *paragone* of the arts—specifically, the debate about the relative merits of painting, poetry, and sculpture. Dou firmly believed in painting's superior ability to produce a naturalistic image, as did his contemporary, Philips Angel.[51] The artist demonstrated in numerous works how the painter could, in a single image, imitate different types of visual phenomena, including soft flesh-tones, the woven textures of carpets, and the smooth surface of carved marble reliefs.

Most importantly, the exhibition will help answer the question that must be asked in light of late nineteenth- and early twentieth-century critics: can Dou's refined technique express an inner, spiritual life as well as surface texture? I have no doubt that the answer to this last question will be yes, and that the intimate grandeur of his paintings will once again seem as compelling and mysterious as it did to his contemporaries some 350 years ago.

FIGURE 9
Violin Player, 1653, oil on panel, Princely Collections, Vaduz Castle, Liechtenstein (cat. 20)

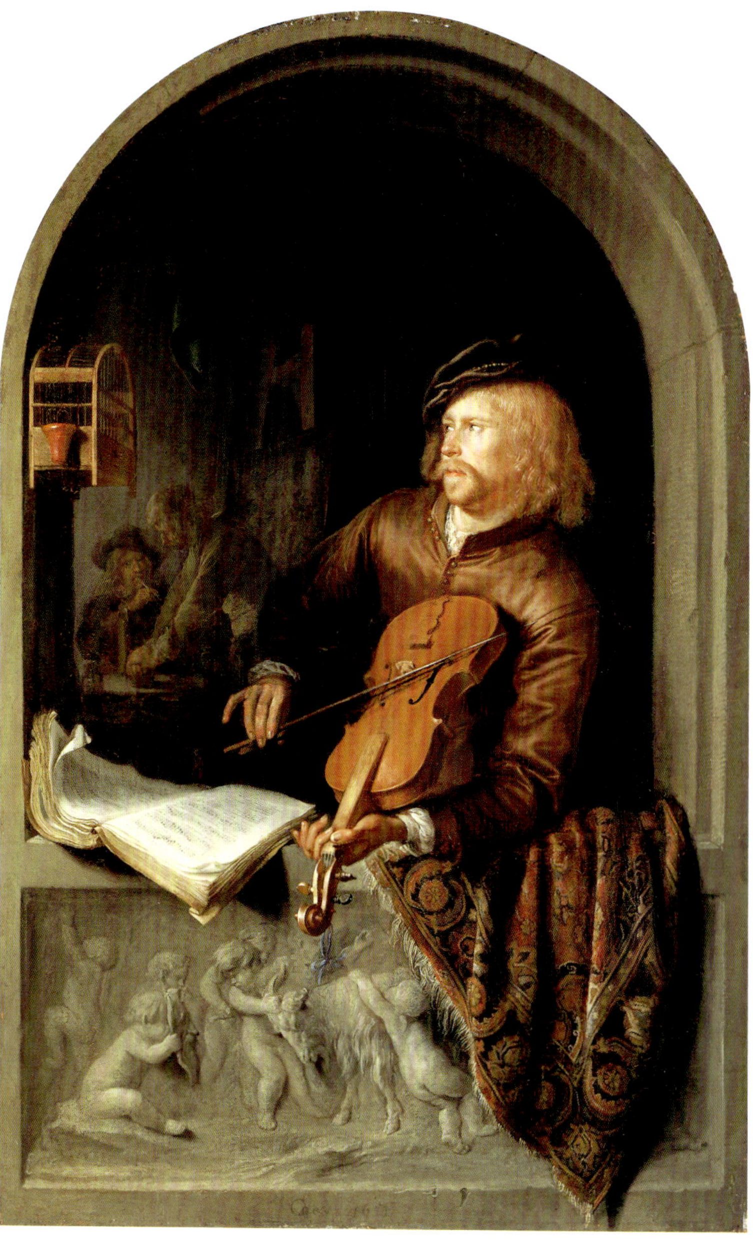

Notes

1 Among the other Dutch artists whose reputations have declined over the years are Pieter Lastman (1583–1633) and Govert Flinck (1615–1660).

2 Quoted in Martin 1901, 157.

3 Immerzeel 1842, 190: "Onder de kunst lichten der 17de eeuw, schittert in de Hollandsche school deze binnenhuisschilder uit, door een schoon uitvoerig, dat niemand vóór of na hem heeft kunnen evenaren."

4 Immerzeel 1842, 190: "van de wijze, op welke hij zijn onbetaalbare meesterstukken bewerkt en doorwerkt heeft, zonder schijn of blik te geven van de tijd en moeite, die er aan besteed is om den hoogst mogelijken graad van uitvoerigheid te bereiken."

5 Immerzeel 1842, 190–191: "het werk van Dou draagt, als kunstwerk, den stempel van een zeldzaam genie, die in hare ontwikkeling in de school van zijner onsterfelijken meester, zich doordrongen heeft van dezelfde beginselen en begrippen ontrent koloriet en effect, die in deze deelen der kunst Rembrandt tot den hoogsten rang van verdienste verheven hebben. Zich vasthoudende aan die beginselen en begrippen, heeft hij daarmede weten te verbinden een onverklaarbaar talent van voleinding van alle bezielde en onbezielde voorwerpen, zonder ooit aan de zuiverheid en het frische der kleuren te kort te doen, of door eenig ander blik de moeite en het onvermoeid geduld te verraden, waardoor zijne penseelwonderen gewrocht zijn."

6 "Gerard Douw," *The Illustrated Magazine of Art* 3, no. 14 (1854): 127.

7 *The Illustrated Magazine of Art* 3, no. 14 (1854): 127.

8 The lone voice noting Dou's absence was Kenyon Cox (Cox 1909–1910), who nonetheless granted that Dou's absence was "not to be regretted." I would like to thank Ronni Baer for this reference.

9 Benjamin Altman, however, did acquire a self-portrait by Dou, which he donated to the Metropolitan Museum of Art, New York, in 1913 (inv. no. 14.40.607).

10 For an excellent assessment of Thoré's views, see Hecht 1998, 166–169. I would also like to thank Frances Suzman Jowell for illuminating discussions about Thoré's attitudes toward the paintings of Gerrit Dou.

11 Von Sandrart 1675–1679, 1:321. This discussion of Von Sandrart's assessment of Dou's work is taken from Wheelock 1978, 62.

12 J. Smith 1829, 3.

13 Smith included seven artists in the first volume of his catalogue raisonné. After beginning with Dou, he catalogued the works of three Leiden artists who worked in Dou's tradition of "fine" painting: Pieter van Slingeland (1640–1691), Frans van Mieris (1635–1681), and Willem van Mieris (1662–1747). The three other artists he included were from Haarlem: Adriaen van Ostade (1610–1685), Isaac van Ostade (1621–1649), and Philips Wouwerman (1619–1668).

14 Thoré (Bürger) 1858, 5: "par exemple, Rembrandt, van der Helst et les peintres de grandes compositions; Gerard Dov et les petits maîtres précieux; Adriaan van Ostede, Jan Steen et les peintres de moeurs populaires et comiques; Terburg, Metsu et les peintres de moeurs élégantes. . . ."

15 Thoré (Bürger) 1858, 22: "l'un est mysterieux, profond, insaissible, et vous fait replier sur vous-même: toute peinture de Rembrandt, même connue d'avance par des déscriptions ou des estampes, cause toujours quand on la voit pour la première fois, un indéfinissable surprise; ce n'est jamais ce à quoi on s'attendait."

16 De Piles 1715, 429: "Car le feu que demande la Peinture ne s'accorde guère avec une patience si extraordinaire, & avec l'attention qu'il faut donner à un si grand detail."

17 J. Smith 1829, 26–27 (no. 79).

18 Thoré (Bürger) 1858, 82: "ces espèces de jongleries en peinture."

19 Thoré (Bürger) 1858, 83, "Gerard Dov, cherchant aussi à créer une spécialité de ce qui fut chez son maître une fantaisie accidentelle, y témoigne sans doute d'une incomparable industrie, c'est le mot, mais l'art véritable n'a point de ces préoccupations futiles. L'art est plus spontané d'impression, plus franc dans ses résultats. J'aime mieux une tête naïvement peinte sous un rayon de soleil, que les plus ingénieuses combinaisons de lumières factices."

20 Thoré (Bürger) 1859, 21. "Le génie de Rembrandt est dans l'intimité des expressions, le caractère des mouvements, l'originalité des effets. De tout cela Gerard Dov n'a plus rien. Et sa pratique, autant que son inspiration, est précisément contraire à celle de Rembrandt." I would like to thank Frances Jowell for drawing my attention to this reference.

21 Martin 1901, "voorbericht": "Dat er in een tijd waarin wel niets de menschen zoo koel laat als de kunstrichting der Leidsche fijn schilders, een boekje verschijnt over dengene, die deze richting in het leven heeft geroepen, zal menigeen verwonderen, vooral wanneer de schrijver begint met de verklaring dat hij, evenals Joshua Reynolds, Dou's werken beschouwt 'with admiration on the lips, but indifference in the heart.'" Martin continued by stating that he would not include many aesthetic descriptions but would write about his subject from a pure historical standpoint ("zuiver historisch standpunt").

22 On Von Bode's admiration for Thoré, see Hecht 1998, 173 note 37.

23 Von Bode 1906, 43: "Die Auffassung des Künstlers ist intim, die Behandlung in der Wiedergabe äusserst delikat, aber Nüchternheit und übertriebene Sorgfalt, eine Überfülle von Details und der kühle Ton der

Färbung lassen uns bei seinen Bildern nicht recht warm werden, sowenig wie bei den meisten, freilich viel grösser angelegten Gemälden seines Meisters, die entstanden, als Dou bei ihm in die Lehre ging."

24 Armstrong 1904, 55.

25 Havelaar 1919, 89: "Dou zag niet méér, niet béter, voelde niet fijner of dieper dan ieder ander: hij had alleen meer geduld—en het is makkelijk geduldig zijn, waar het hart zoo flauwtjes klopt en de geest zoo traag verwerkt."

26 Van Dyke 1895, 73.

27 Van Dyke 1895, 74.

28 Van Dyke 1895, 74.

29 London 1929, 95, cat. 189. The exhibition included 334 seventeenth-century Dutch paintings.

30 See The Hague and San Francisco, 1990–1991, 218–219, for Ben Broos' discussion of the reassessment of Dou at the Alte Pinakothek during the 1930s.

31 Raleigh 1956, 28.

32 Valentiner 1930, 3.

33 Emmens 1963. For an English version of this text, see Emmens 1969.

34 Emmens 1969, 34, notes that the painting, which had been purchased for Catherine of Russia in 1771, was lost in a shipwreck in the Baltic Sea. Aside from the copy of the painting by Laqui, the painting is known from Houbraken's description of the original. See Houbraken 1753, 2, 5–6.

35 Emmens 1969, 34.

36 Emmens 1971, 4.

37 Amsterdam 1976, 86–93, cats. 16, 17. De Jongh based his texts for these paintings on Emmens' articles.

38 For example, Raupp 1984, examined the rhetorical character of Dou's self-portraits. Even those, such as Svetlana Alpers, who strenuously question Emmens' and De Jongh's interpretations of the iconographic underpinnings of genre paintings, do not question the idea that Dou selectively drew from a range of literary and visual traditions in creating a work such as *The Quack*. See Alpers 1983, 116–118.

39 By 1984 Dou seems fully to have been reintegrated into the canon of Dutch genre painters. In that year, five of his genre scenes, among them *Man Writing by an Easel* (cat. 3) and *Astronomer by Candlelight* (cat. 31), were included in Peter Sutton's exhibition, *Masters of Seventeenth-Century Dutch Genre Painting*. See Philadelphia, Berlin, and London 1984, cats. 31–35.

40 The focus of the entries in Philadelphia, Berlin, and London 1984 (cats. 31–35, for example) is on Dou as a learned artist who was interested in incorporating complex emblematic and theoretical ideas into his carefully executed scenes of everyday life.

41 Interestingly, Emmens, who clearly was fascinated by the moralizing implications of Dou's iconography, reiterated in 1972 the harsh criticism of Dou's "oppressive detail" and "petit bourgeois morality" found in the writings of early twentieth-century critics. Emmens' text appears in Emmens 1981, 181.

42 A variant translation of the Dutch text (Angel 1642, 54) appears on Angel 1996, 248.

43 Amsterdam 1976, 20: "Bezien we nu de eisen die in de 17de eeuw aan de vorm, naast de eisen die aan de inhoud werden gesteld, dan kunnen we concluderen dat het dikwijls draait om de combinatie van twee soorten bedrog: het 'aangenaam bedrog', van de schijnbaar natuurgetrouwe nabootsing, en het bedrog dat ontstaat door de versluiering van wat met de voorstelling eigenlijk wordt bedoeld."

44 See, in particular, Sluijter's introductory essay in Leiden 1988, "Schilders van 'cleyne, subtile ende curieuse dingen': Leidse 'finjschilders' in contemporaine bronnen," 15–77.

45 With one exception, this translation of the Dutch text that appears at Angel 1642, 56, is taken from Angel 1996, 248–249. The exception is the translation of Angel's phrase "curieuse loosicheyt" as "meticulous looseness." The correct translation is "curious looseness."

46 Sluijter in Leiden 1988, 98–99, cat. 9.

47 Sluijter's excellent discourse on Angel and Dou (Sluijter 1993) expands upon the ideas expressed in this exhibition catalogue.

48 Here, Hecht specifically takes issue with Sluijter's interpretation of *Lady at Her Toilet* (cat. 32) in Leiden 1988, 115 (no. 16).

49 In 1972 Emmens expressed his belief that, aside from the artist's iconographic interest, appreciation of Dou's work would also increase as a result of developments in contemporary art. For example, he thought that a fascination with "neo-realism" would develop with the passing of abstract expressionism, which he described as the last gasp of "romantic individualism." Emmens also suggested that pop-art, with its expressly "vulgar color effects," as well as renewed interest in surrealism, would enhance the appeal of the so-called photographic realism of Dou's style. For this text, see Emmens 1981, 181.

50 For evidence that Dou worked over a prolonged period on *The Quack* (cat. 19) and the 1663 *Self-Portrait* (cat. 27), see Lammertse 1997.

51 See Angel 1642, 23–26 (English translation in Angel 1996, 238–239).

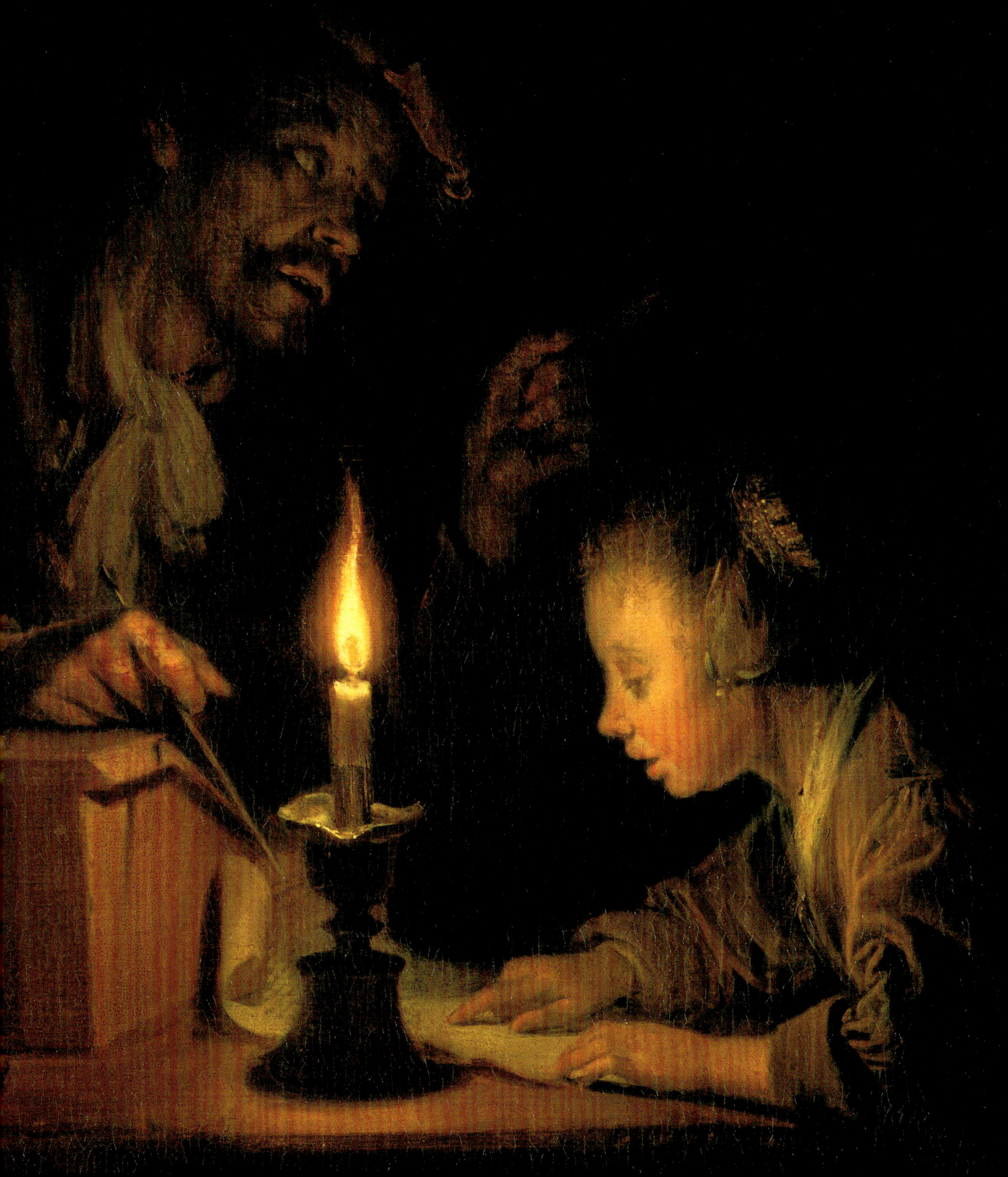

The Life and Art of Gerrit Dou

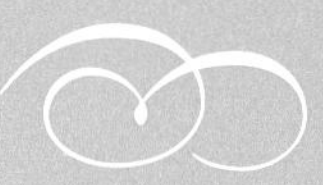

Ronni Baer

Gerrit Dou (fig. 1) was one of the most admired and influential painters working in seventeenth-century Holland. He enriched the pictorial language of art and enlarged the scope of traditional painted subject matter. Known as an artistic innovator and an inspiring teacher, Dou is regarded as the founder of the Leiden school of *fijnschilders* ("fine painters")[1] because he trained so many artists who aspired to replicate his manner of painting. The delicate refinement and seductive finish of his small-scale works elicited the admiration of connoisseurs and painters alike.

Seventeenth-century chroniclers marveled not only at the delicacy of Dou's paintings but also at the true-to-life quality of his depictions and his masterful use of color and light effects. As early as 1641, when the artist was only twenty-eight years old, the painter and theorist Philips Angel (c. 1618–1645 or after) held Dou up as a paradigm for painters and commended his technique to his fellow Leiden artists. Angel noted how Dou combined a meticulous style with "a curious looseness" of brushwork, and warned those less skilled than Dou against the lifeless description of surfaces that would result from painting in too stiff a manner.[2] In the same year, Jan Orlers, historian and burgomaster of Leiden, described Dou's paintings as "small, subtle, and curious things." Orlers, who noted the high value placed on Dou's pictures by connoisseurs of the day, attributed the artist's stand-

DETAIL
The Night School, before 1665, oil on panel, Rijksmuseum, Amsterdam (cat. 28)

FIGURE 1
Godfried Schalcken, *Portrait of Gerrit Dou*, c. 1665, engraving, Rijksprentenkabinet, Amsterdam

FIGURE 2
Willem Isaaksz. Swanenburgh I, *Anatomical Theater of Leiden*, 1610, engraving, The Clements C. Fry Collection, The Harvey Cushing/John Hay Whitney Medical Library, Yale University, New Haven

ing to his incomparable painting technique.[3] In his brief history of Leiden published in 1672, Simon van Leeuwen referred to "the famous Gerrit Douw" [sic] as "the excellent small-scale painter who knew how to depict his living subjects . . . with such perfection that his work seemed so real [that it] could scarcely be distinguished from life."[4]

Dou's name was also associated with certain subjects and pictorial devices that influenced the work of numerous students and followers. The generic hermit surrounded by *vanitas* objects, the doctor examining a vial of urine, and the grocery shop were conventional themes that Dou interpreted in a new light. The manner in which Dou used a window surround as a framing device, a parted curtain or tapestry to reveal a scene within a domestic interior, or the light of a candle or a lantern to heighten the mystery of his images was adopted not only by seventeenth-century Dutch artists but also by German, English, and French painters well into the nineteenth century.

· *Leiden in the Seventeenth Century* The character of Dou's art can best be understood in the context of his native city of Leiden. By the close of the sixteenth century, Leiden was a cultural, intellectual, and commercial crossroads for much of Europe. The University of Leiden—the first Protestant university in The Netherlands—had been founded in 1575 "to fill the need for an intellectual and spiritual center on which the budding nation could draw for its political leadership and religious autonomy."[5] The institution was a powerful presence, and its tenets, primarily those of orthodox Calvinism, permeated the life of the city.[6] The university quickly attained international stature and attracted distinguished scholars from all over Europe, including the classicist Justus Lipsius, the philologist Joseph Scaliger, the historian and rhetorician Guardas Johannes Vossius, the jurist Hugo Grotius, the poet and playwright Daniel Heinsius, and the theologians Francis Gomarus and Jacobus Arminius.

The curriculum of the university covered a range of disciplines: theology, classical and oriental philology, philosophy, Roman law, politics (in effect, practical statesmanship), and the sciences, including mathematics, physics, and medicine.[7] It housed a renowned anatomy amphitheater (fig. 2) that reflected a science grounded in "an absolutely genuine belief in God, deep wonder at the marvels of his Creation and his providential government, and a profound awareness of mystery . . . still bound up with an unquestioning belief in miracles."[8] The amphitheater served as a museum, open to the public, in which "the themes of the Fall, the Fragility of Human Life, and Death were made concrete for the spiritual education and meditation of the visitors."[9] The Hortus Botanicus, which originated as a small herb garden planted in 1594 by Carolus Clusius, was its botanical counterpart.

Those affiliated with the university lived in the city's broad, old main streets. The city's expanding population of laborers occupied the newer parts of town, formed when the city walls were expanded for the first of several times in 1611 to accommodate an influx of Flemish immigrants fleeing anti-Protestant sentiment in the south. These skilled refugees revitalized Leiden's moribund textile industry by introducing a relatively inexpensive, light cloth that came to dominate export markets.[10] As a result, Leiden once again became an important commercial hub.

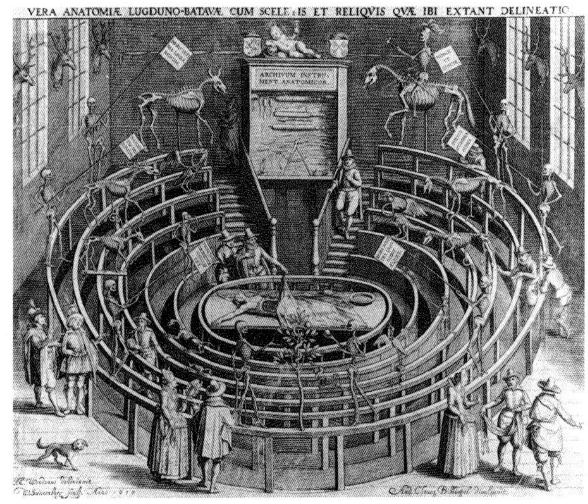

Artistic life in Leiden was not impervious to the climate of social and industrial change. The foundation of the university provided an important impetus for printers and publishers. The Plantin Press, for example, opened a printing office in Leiden in 1583, establishing a scholarly publishing arm for the university and providing it with a means to reach an international audience.[11] This presence, in turn, led to a flowering of the graphic arts. The most important engraver of the time, Jacques de Gheyn II (1565–1629), moved from Amsterdam to Leiden in 1595.

De Gheyn's stay there was short,[12] but his influence can be seen in the work of Zacharias Dolendo and that of his brother Bartholomeus, Dou's first teacher. Little is known about the lives of these artists, but it seems that Zacharias (b. between 1561 and 1573–d. before 1604) made prints exclusively after the work of other artists. Bartholomeus (c. 1560–1626), less skillful than his brother but more inventive, was a goldsmith and cutter of seals and hallmarks as well as a draftsman and printmaker.[13] His engravings—portraits as well as mythological, biblical, and historical subjects—were more often executed after paintings and drawings by others but were sometimes printed from his own designs (fig. 3).[14]

Leiden's most influential artist in the late sixteenth century was Isaac Claesz. van Swanenburgh (1537–1614), who, during almost fifty years of activity, painted portraits and large-scale decorations for the Leiden cloth guild (the *Saaihal*) and the tribunal (*Vierschaar*), among other clients.[15] Between 1586 and 1607, he ran a well-organized studio in which one or more apprentices and perhaps some assistants helped him with various commissions, including designs for church windows.[16] Indeed, Leiden had traditionally been an important center for stained glass, with an impressive roster of native artists who worked in this medium, among them, Aertgen van Leyden (1498–1568) and Lucas van Leyden (1494–1533). Succeeding Van Swanenburgh as Leiden's most successful producer of church windows was the *glasschrijver* (glass painter) Pieter Couwenhorn (c. 1599–1654), Dou's second teacher, who by 1620 had the largest such business in Leiden.[17] Although he was a man of modest artistic talent, Couwenhorn was well connected: glazier for the city of Leiden and the States General, he was also a friend of the famous Leiden humanist Petrus Scriverius and a teacher of Constantijn Huygens' sons. These contacts would stand Dou in good stead.

FIGURE 3
Bartholomeus Dolendo, *Halberdier*, 1590, engraving, Rijksprentenkabinet, Amsterdam

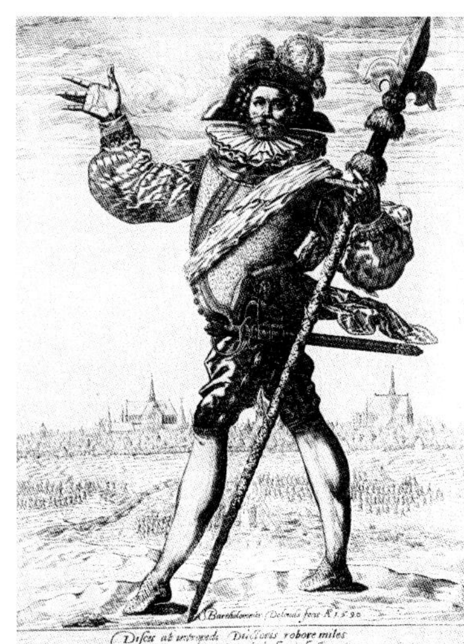

· *Dou's Career* According to Orlers, Dou was born in Leiden on 7 April 1613. His father, Douwe Jansz., owned the second most important workshop for the production of church glass in Leiden after that of Couwenhorn. Active in the community and well-off financially, Douwe Jansz. married the widow Marijtgen Jansdr. in 1609, and apparently soon thereafter took over her first husband's glassmaking business.[18] Dou had a brother, Jan, but his date of birth is uncertain.[19]

Orlers wrote that Dou's father, seeing that his son had "pleasure and desire toward painting,"[20] sent him in 1622 to learn the principles of draftsmanship with Bartholomeus Dolendo, with whom Gerrit stayed for about a year and a half. Subsequently, Dou studied his father's craft for two and a half years with Pieter Couwenhorn.[21] In 1625 and 1627, Dou's name appeared, along with that of his father and brother, in the *glazenmakers'* guild records. It seems, however, that Gerrit did not pursue the family business beyond his early adolescence, for he is no longer listed as a *glazenmaker* in the guild book of 1628.[22] Orlers reported that Douw Jansz. was concerned for his son's safety because of his fearlessness in installing and mending glass, and as a consequence sent the boy to learn the art of painting instead.[23] On 14 February 1628, at the age of fourteen, Dou entered the studio of Rembrandt van Rijn (1606–1669), his elder by just under seven years.

Rembrandt, who had briefly studied in Amsterdam with the renowned history painter Pieter Lastman (c. 1583–1633) in the early to mid-1620s, had

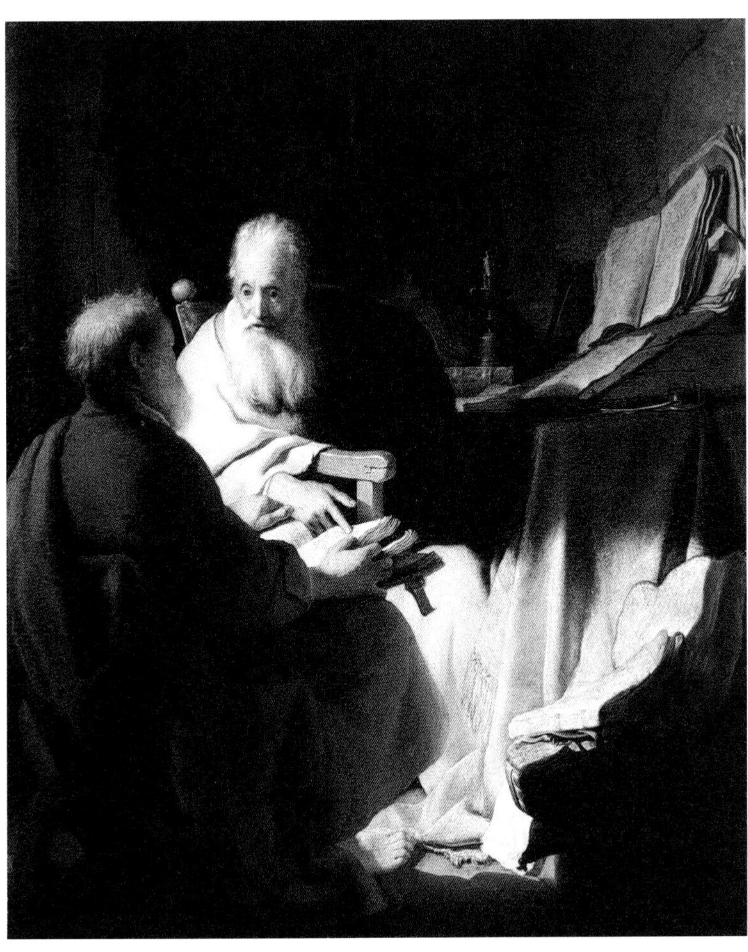

FIGURE 4
Rembrandt van Rijn, *Two Old Men Disputing*, c. 1628, oil on panel, National Gallery of Victoria, Melbourne, Felton bequest, 1934

returned to his native Leiden around 1625 to set up as an independent artist. There, he worked closely with Jan Lievens (1607–1674), a compatriot who had also studied with Lastman. The two young and ambitious artists, who may have shared a studio,[24] were both aspiring history painters. They depicted many of the same subjects in closely related compositions, used the same models, and carried out similar technical experiments.[25]

Around 1627, Lastman's influence on Rembrandt, which was evident in his choice of subjects, compositional arrangements, palette, theatrically posed figures, and rich clothing,[26] was progressively supplanted by that of the Utrecht Caravaggist, Gerrit van Honthorst (1592–1656). Thus, about the time that Dou entered his workshop, Rembrandt's work began to be marked by strong contrasts of light and shadow and the use of artificial illumination.[27] Earlier combinations of yellows, olive greens, light blues, pinks, and violets yielded to tonal harmonies of grays and browns. Rembrandt's works from this period are also marked by the introduction of figures of prophets and hermits and a more subtle description of action that is echoed in Dou's treatment of similar subject matter.[28]

Aside from his growing reputation,[29] Rembrandt might have been chosen as Dou's teacher because the two families resided near one another. The house of Rembrandt's parents in the Weddesteeg, and their properties in the Galgewater (later the site of Dou's own studio) were close to Dou's family home on the Cort Rapenburg. The younger artist may have made Rembrandt's acquaintance through Scriverius, Couwenhorn's friend and possibly Rembrandt's patron.[30]

A young artist's course of instruction and the terms of his apprenticeship had to be agreed upon by the master and the aspiring artist's father. In 1630 and 1631, for example, Rembrandt received 100 guilders annually from the guardians of Isaac de Jouderville (1612/1613–1645/1648) for the boy's apprenticeship.[31] As Ernst van de Wetering has shown, Isaac did not reside with Rembrandt during his apprenticeship, so "the fifty guilders per half-year presumably only covered the tuition fees, and most probably also the cost of materials."[32] Since Dou was also in Rembrandt's workshop during this period, he probably had a similar arrangement with the master.

Dou remained in Rembrandt's studio for three years, during which he became "an excellent master."[33] From Rembrandt, Dou borrowed much of his early subject matter, including portraits, *tronies* (head studies), and hermits. Dou's *Old Man Lighting a Pipe* (cat. 5), for example, is indebted to Rembrandt's *Two Old Men Disputing* (c. 1628, fig. 4), from which Dou appropriated the figure-type, the mise-en-scène, and the dramatic contrasts of light and dark. Rembrandt's abiding fascination with self-portraiture also made a lasting impression on his young pupil.

Dou's training as a *glasschrijver* informed his approach to painting. The technique of cutting glass with a diamond encouraged a steady hand. Dou's technique of applying enamel-like colors in a series of glazes and his choice of bright, saturated blues, greens, and purples may reflect his training as a glass painter as much as the palette of Rembrandt's earliest works. The meticulousness necessary to transfer designs on paper to glass may explain Dou's predilection for small works, while the polish resulting from the firing of painted glass might have provided a model for the characteristic smooth finish of Dou's paintings and governed his use of panel (rather than canvas) as a support better suited to obtaining this finish.

After Rembrandt left Leiden for Amsterdam in 1631,[34] Dou continued to pursue the subject matter and refined style that he had developed in Rembrandt's studio. By 1641, he was being lauded as an exemplary painter in Philips Angel's lecture to Leiden artists, in part because Dou had a patron willing to pay 500 Carolus guilders annually for the right of first refusal of his works.[35] That patron was Pieter Spiering, the second son of François Spiering, the great Delft tapestry manufacturer. He is identified as "ambassador of Her Majesty from Sweden and counselor of finance" in a document dated 19 June 1636, and may have resided in The Hague as a representative of the Swedish crown as early as 1634.[36] Spiering was appointed Lord High Treasurer and moved to Stockholm in 1650 but was back in The Hague the following year, where he died soon thereafter. Spiering collected works by northern artists and acquired a number of Dou's pictures for Queen Christina.[37] Spiering's personal preference influenced his patronage on behalf of the queen, whose own taste ran to the Italianate,[38] so much so that in 1652 the queen returned to Spiering eleven of Dou's paintings.[39]

John Michael Montias has observed that painting style and patronage in seventeenth-century Holland were sometimes closely linked: "'fine painting' was enormously time-consuming and thus expensive to produce, so that the clientele for such works was limited to a small elite. It was simply too risky to produce paintings worth 400 guilders and up 'on spec.' While reliance on a patron reduced an artist's uncertainty, it was also advantageous to the rich consumer who could be sure that he would have the first pick of a fashionable artist's works."[40] This observation would suggest that the subjects of Dou's paintings were of less interest to patrons such as Spiering than the style in which they were painted.[41] Indeed, because his paintings were so much in demand, Dou was one of the few Dutch artists with relative freedom in his choice of subject matter, allowing him to explore an unusually wide repertoire of imagery.

In the latter part of his career, Dou had the good fortune of benefiting from a second patron. Johan de Bye, a pious Remonstrant, had assembled a fine collection of Dou's work by 1665. In that year, De Bye exhibited twenty-seven paintings by Dou at the home of Johannes Hannot on the Breestraat, which he leased from Hannot at the annual rate of forty florins.[42] The contract between De Bye and Hannot, dated 18 September 1665, lists the works in the exhibition, including three self-portraits (indicating that by the time of Dou's artistic maturity, there was a market for his self-portraits, much as there was for his *tronies*) and three nudes, which may have been commissioned by De Bye.[43] *Woman at the Clavichord* ("2. Een claversimbelspeelster met een tapijt, daghlicht") (cat. 30), *The Night School* ("8. Een kaers-avondtschool met veel personen") (cat. 28), and *The Wine Cellar* ("13. Een dubbelt stuck, . . . van binnen een kaerslicht, sijnde een keldertje") (cat. 23) were probably also among the paintings exhibited.

The enthusiastic patronage that Dou enjoyed and the praise he received from contemporary chroniclers made him much in demand as a teacher, and he was reputed to have been a generous one.[44] Gabriel Metsu (1629–1667), Jan van Staveren (1613/1614–1669), Abraham de Pape (before 1621–1666), and Adriaen van Gaesbeeck (1621–1650) were probably all students of Dou in the early 1640s; all four were in any event strongly influenced by him.[45] One of Dou's most esteemed pupils was Frans van Mieris the Elder (1635–1681), who came to work with him in the early 1650s.[46] Arnold Houbraken's report that Van Mieris quickly outshone Dou's other assistants implies that others were studying with Dou at the time.[47]

Dou's high artistic standing was further reflected in his role as a founder of the Leiden painters' guild. Because of its location between Amsterdam and The Hague, Leiden was one of the most important market cities in Holland. Leiden's painters had lobbied for years for protection against outside competition and foreign dealers. In 1648, they finally succeeded in convincing local authorities that a guild was needed to protect their social and economic interests and to govern artistic practices.[48]

The cost of Dou's paintings would have limited their market to the affluent.[49] As Eric Jan Sluijter has argued, the status accorded a painter such as Dou was in part a reflection of the prices paid for his pictures. Angel's championing of Dou as a paradigm for other artists and his argument for the superiority of painting over poetry may be due in part to the financial profit that could be gained by painting.[50] In addition to the stipend Dou received for allowing Spiering his choice of pictures, he charged, according to Joachim von Sandrart, a Flemish pound (six guilders) per hour for his work on a painting. These small panels, Von Sandrart reported, sold for between six hundred and one thousand or more florins apiece. For this latter sum, a prosperous artisan would have been able to buy a house.[51]

Royalty, of course, could afford to buy Dou's paintings, although the court in The Hague, which preferred ambitious paintings in the refined classicizing style, appears to have been indifferent to them.[52] Dou found a market in the courts of other European nations. Queen Christina of Sweden owned at least eleven of his works, and Archduke Leopold Wilhelm owned a painting by Dou, which he might have purchased while he was governor of the Southern Netherlands between 1646 and 1656.[53] Cosimo III de' Medici's journal entry of 23 June 1669 records his visit to Dou's house,[54] where he may have acquired one or two of the paintings by Dou now at the Uffizi.[55] In 1676, the year following Dou's death, Cosimo, who had by then assumed the title of grand duke of Tuscany, eagerly sought to acquire a self-portrait by the artist. Letters exchanged between Apollonio Bassetti, Cosimo's secretary in Florence, and Giovacchino Guasconi, his agent in Amsterdam, between November 1675 and November 1676, testify that an "attempt to move heaven and earth" had been made, first to secure a "miniature" by Dou, and then to obtain a work for Cosimo's renowned gallery of artists' self-portraits in Florence.[56] The acquisition of the *Self-Portrait* of 1658 (fig. 5), still in Florence, was the result of these efforts.

The States of Holland and Westfriesland constituted Dou's most important patron—if not in respect to the number of paintings purchased or continuity of support, then certainly in prestige.[57] In May of 1660, it was decided that the States would present Charles II, on his accession to the English crown, with several gifts as proof of Holland's support for the new ruler. The city of Amsterdam promised a splendid yacht, dubbed the *Mary.* Twenty-four paintings (probably all Italian) and twelve ancient sculptures were bought for 80,000 florins from the Reynst collection on the advice of the sculptor Artus Quellinus (1609–1668) and the dealer Gerrit van Uylenburgh. The States also purchased a painting by Pieter Saenredam (1597–1665) from the burgomaster Andries

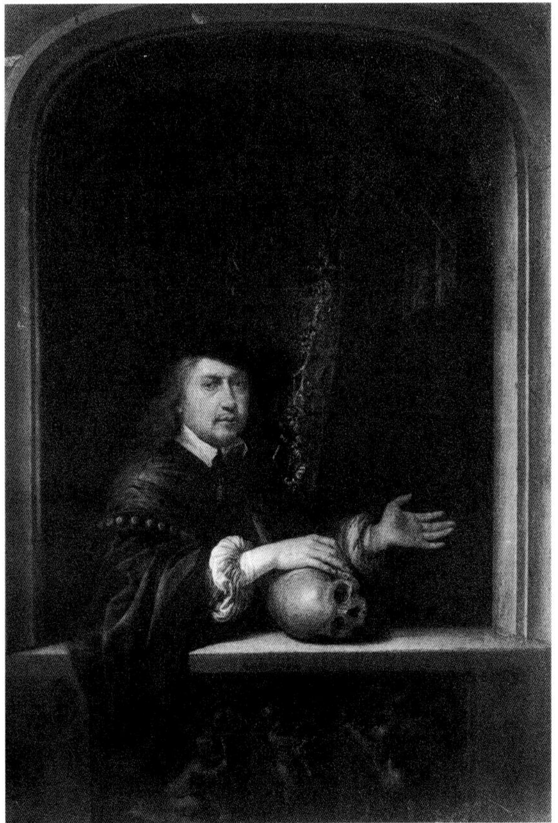

FIGURE 5
Self-Portrait, 1658, oil on panel, Uffizi Gallery, Florence

de Graeff (a transaction for which Dou was appointed one of the appraisers), and three paintings from Dou himself. Letters to Dou, dated 18 and 19 October 1660, from the advisers to the States (the *Gecommitteerde Raden*) instructed him on the logistics of the works' transport. One painting in this group was surely Dou's *Young Mother* of 1658 (cat. 21),[58] while another may have been his *Young Mother* now in Berlin.[59] A third painting was a version of *The Mocking of Ceres* by Adam Elsheimer (1578–1610), a work that Dou may have copied from Elsheimer's original.[60]

The "Dutch gift" was shipped from Rotterdam shortly after 18 October 1660, the day on which the Dutch extraordinary ambassadors to England took their leave from the States General. Two of the ambassadors, Lodowijk van Nassau and Simon van Hoorn, reported from London to Johan de Witt in mid-November 1660 that the presents had been exhibited in the great room at Whitehall, "where the king, with his entire court, all the dignitaries of England and most of the foreign ministers, went to see them and praise them." Charles thanked the ambassadors "and singled out those paintings that seemed most to please him, such as the Titian *Virgin and Child*, the [paintings by] Douw and Elshamer, although he indicated that he held all in high esteem."[61]

The Dutch poet Joost van den Vondel seized the occasion to praise the generosity of the Dutch and to laud the king's connoisseurship,[62] and John Evelyn wrote of the quality of Dou's contribution in his diary in early December.[63] Dou's superior technique, so evident in the paintings sent to England, inspired the poet Dirck Traudenius to compare him to Parrhasius, the artist of antiquity who managed to fool the great Zeuxis.[64] So pleased was the king that he apparently invited Dou to court.[65]

By 1660, the high regard in which Dou's art was held both at home and abroad (as well as his prominent role in assembling the Dutch gift to King Charles) made him famous throughout Europe.[66] In 1661, the Flemish biographer Cornelis de Bie wrote that Dou's paintings are "agreeable works, . . . which scatter all the darkness of our understanding . . . and bear our spirits higher than the stars."[67] In a journal entry of 1662, the Danish scholar Ole Borch, who visited Dou's studio in November of that year, referred to the artist as "the excellent painter of Leiden . . . unequaled in The Netherlands and even in all other countries of the world."[68] The French traveler Balthasar de Monconys described Dou in the summer of 1663 as "incomparable for the delicacy of [his] brush."[69] At this time, perhaps owing in part to his increased fame, Dou took on more pupils. Pieter Cornelisz. van Slingelandt (1640–1691), who was inscribed in the Leiden St. Luke's guild in November 1661,[70] probably studied with Dou shortly before this date. According to Houbraken, Godfried Schalcken (1643–1706), who unlike the others was not from Leiden, was also a student of Dou's at some point between 1662 and 1665.[71] Dou's nephew, Dominicus van Tol (after 1630–1676), must have been in his studio at about this time as well,[72] although family ties were as likely the reason for this choice as the fame of the master.

Several of Dou's students known from contemporary sources came to study with him later in the decade. Matthijs Naiveu (1647–1726), the best documented of Dou's pupils but the least similar to the master in composition or style, paid him 100 florins annually for three years, from the period of 3 May 1666 until 3 May 1669.[73] In a document dated 24 May 1669, Naiveu is described as a "*descipel van Dou*," as are Bartholomeus Maton (c. 1643–1682) and Gerrit Maes, about whom nothing more is known.[74] Carel de Moor (1655–1738) was probably among Dou's last pupils. Houbraken, who knew De Moor personally, mentions that the artist studied with Dou before he was admitted to the Leiden guild in 1683.[75]

Dou executed the first of several wills on 13 August 1657.[76] On 23 November 1669, apparently suffering from an illness,[77] Dou (who never married) executed a second will that left the bulk of his estate to his niece, Antonia van Tol, who was living with him at the time. In addition, Dou made small bequests to another niece, Maria Jansdr., his half-sister, "Trijntje" Vechters, and her son, Dominicus van Tol. A revision dated 24 December

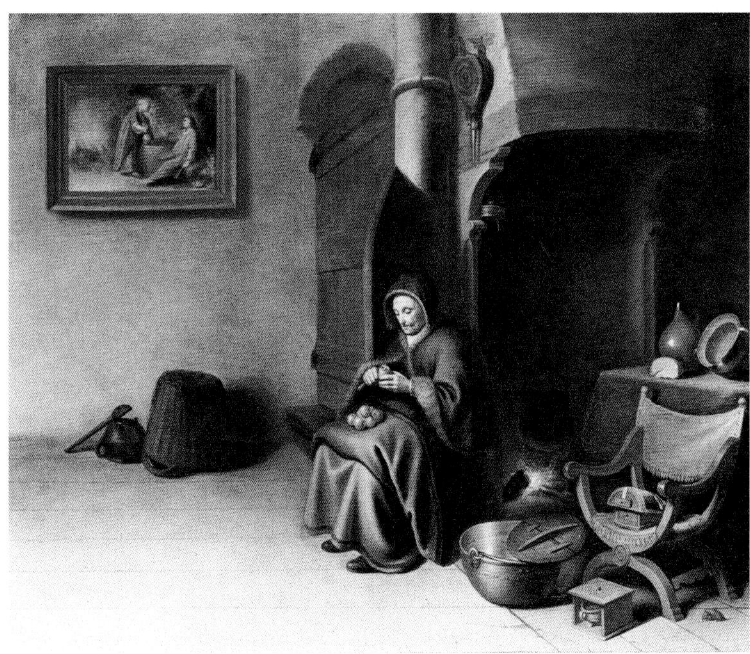

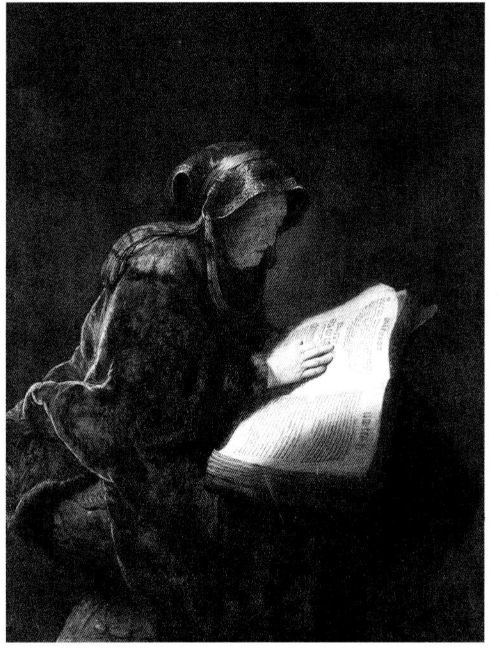

FIGURE 6
Old Woman Peeling Apples, c. 1630, oil on panel, Gemäldegalerie, Staatliche Museen zu Berlin

FIGURE 7
Rembrandt van Rijn, *Old Woman Reading*, 1631, oil on panel, Rijksmuseum, Amsterdam

1674 bequeathed Dou's houses to his half-sister with the proviso that should she be threatened by creditors, they would revert to his other heirs.[78]

Dou died about a month after amending his will, and was buried in the St. Pieterskerk on 9 February 1675.[79] Because he had no children, his death taxes were levied at the rate of five percent of the whole. His house on the Galgewater was taxed at a valuation of 2,000 florins, the three houses on the Cort Rapenburg that he inherited from his father were valued at 1,500 florins, a ruined pleasure garden outside the Morspoort was taxed at 500 florins, and he was further taxed on no fewer than twenty-two debentures (*obligaties*), totaling a value of 27,955 florins. His heirs therefore had to pay slightly more than 1,397 florins in death taxes.[80] We know from other sources that Dou was held in high esteem at the time of his death; the size of his estate reveals that the artist was also a very wealthy man.

· *Subject Matter* The specifics of Dou's training in Rembrandt's studio are not known, although standard practice had a pupil learn to clean palettes, stretch canvases, make brushes, mix colors, and prime supports. He would be set to copy paintings by the master or from the master's collection, with the goal of imitating as closely as possible the master's style, both in execution and conception.[81] Despite the fact that Dou trained with Rembrandt, no history painting can securely be attributed to him, and the only contemporary evidence that he ever painted such a subject is the mention of a *Joseph and Mary* in an inventory of 1669.[82] While under his master's aegis, Dou seems to have concentrated on depicting studious old men (cat. 3) and pious elderly women (fig. 6), a foreshadowing of his later, almost exclusive, interest in genre imagery. These figures echo subjects by Rembrandt that Dou would have seen in Rembrandt's Leiden studio. For example, the figure in Rembrandt's *Old Woman Reading* of 1631 (fig. 7) is probably intended to represent a historical personage—a seer or prophetess.[83] Dou's nearly contemporaneous rendering of the subject (cat. 2), however, might embody a more abstract concept, such as devotion or piety. Although compositionally similar to Rembrandt's work, Dou's painting emphasizes the act of reading, whereas Rembrandt, with his suggestive light effects and less descriptive painting technique, has captured the emotional involvement of the woman in her text.[84]

Rembrandt and the artists associated with his Leiden studio produced *tronies* that closely resemble the images of old women reading.[85] These subjects were painted and sold less for their likenesses to the model than for the type they epitomized or the striking image they presented.[86] While *tronies* might have served originally as studies for individuals in multifigure compositions and were so used by Dou,[87] they were also sold as works of art in their own right.[88]

When Rembrandt left Leiden for Amsterdam in 1631 and Lievens left for England the following year, Dou began to paint portraits and *tronies* in earnest. Perhaps only after his illustrious countrymen moved away did Dou feel ready to tackle subjects that they had executed so well. As their successor, he would have enjoyed opportunities to obtain commissions that might earlier have gone to them.[89] Dou employed the simplest and most traditional of portrait types, which corresponded to the apparent conservative nature of the majority of his sitters. His patrons, often members of the affluent regent class, were little concerned with fashion. Their clothes are, for the most part, sober and unremarkable. Dou's surviving portraits (for example, cats. 12 and 13) are almost all bust- or three-quarter-length views, in which the sitter regards the spectator. The artist made frequent use of the oval format—almost *de rigueur* in the 1630s—both for his portraits and *tronies*.[90] Most often, his upright, rather stiff figures occupy the center of the composition, against a neutral background, while diffuse light enters from the left.

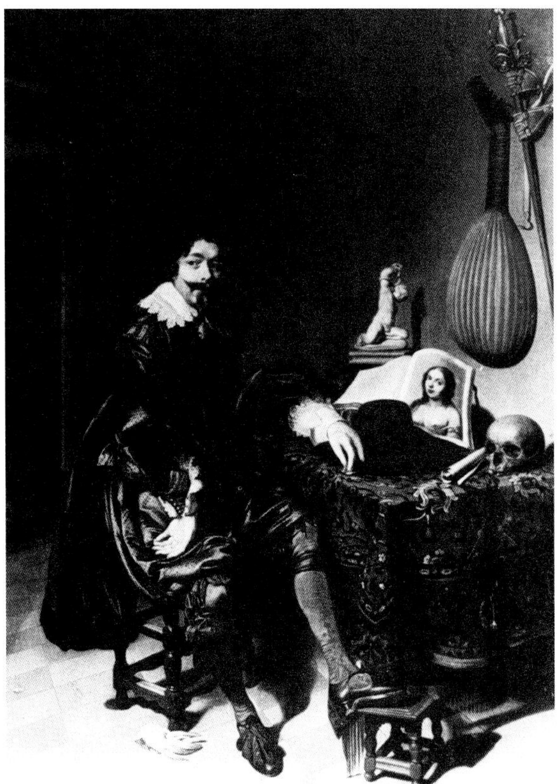

Occasionally Dou includes glimpses of an interior setting in his portraits, perhaps taking inspiration from the work of his compatriot, David Bailly (1584–1657), who painted the background in his own portrait by Thomas de Keyser (1596/1597–1667) (fig. 8).[91] Although Bailly's portraits, like Dou's, are often small in format, they are executed with glazes and thin layers of paint on a green ground, giving them a cool tonality and a uniformly smooth surface (fig. 9). Dou, by contrast, utilizes a range of brushstrokes and finishes in his small portraits.[92] Youths are painted freely, imbuing them with a sense of liveliness; adults, by contrast, are rendered more soberly and with relatively restrained brushwork.[93]

FIGURE 8
Thomas de Keyser, *Portrait of David Bailly*, c. 1627, oil on panel, Private collection

FIGURE 9
David Bailly, *Portrait of Duke Ulrik, Bishop of Schwerin*, 1627, oil on panel, Nationalhistoriske Museum, Frederiksborg, Denmark

FIGURE 10
Self-Portrait, 1647, oil on panel, Staatliche Kunstsammlungen, Gemäldegalerie Alte Meister, Dresden

When Von Sandrart visited Dou's studio in 1639 with the artist Pieter van Laer (1599–1642), he remarked on Dou's diligence and his extraordinarily slow working method. By Von Sandrart's account, it took Dou five days to apply the underpaint for the hand of a sitter. Von Sandrart associated Dou's unhurried approach with the expressions of boredom, vexation, and impatience that he discerned in these portraits.[94] Dou's career as a portraitist spanned only about a decade and a half, perhaps (if Von Sandrart is to be believed) because of his patrons' dissatisfaction with their stilted likenesses. It may be that Dou stopped painting portraits when honor took precedence over profit; profit had already been secured by Spiering's patronage.[95] As Dou was winding down his portrait practice in the mid-1640s, he was concurrently building up his genre-painting repertoire.

Although Dou painted *tronies* and portraits primarily during the 1630s and the first half of the decade following, he produced self-portraits throughout his career. The artist's self-portrait and the closely related theme of the artist in his studio had a venerable ancestry. While their roots lay in fifteenth-century depictions of St. Luke painting the Madonna, by the mid-sixteenth century such paintings had become bound up with questions of professional, social, and artistic identity. They expressed the artist's desire to be recognized as practicing a liberal art rather than a manual craft. Indeed, the proliferation of studio scenes and self-portraits in Holland during the seventeenth century suggests that many Dutch painters were concerned with such issues.[96]

Like Rembrandt, Dou charted his personal and artistic career through his self-portraits. These images of the artist consistently present the comportment he deemed fitting to a man of his social position; they bear no trace of introspection but rather present the public side of the artist. More than half of these paintings are dated, and they fall into two basic types. In the first, Dou presents himself as a gentleman with an artist's attributes (cat. 14). In the second, he surrounds himself with accessories of a painter, to the point that the image becomes a personal manifesto (fig. 10). Dou probably intended these representations, in which he alluded to his learning, ability, and industry, as emblems of the worthiness of the art of painting.[97] The incorporation of objects that evoke the idea of transience (see fig. 5) reinforces one of the primary themes of the work: the painter's immortality, achieved by means of his art.[98]

Dou's masterpiece, *The Quack* (cat. 19), which includes an image of the artist next to a charlatan, stands apart from his other self-portraits. As commentator, Dou here represents his view of the artist's role. By juxtaposing himself with the duplicitous quack, the painter presents his work as a positive deception, a mirror of nature at which the viewer can marvel and from which he can learn.[99] Dou's self-portraits, by showing the artist at work or holding the tools of his trade, invite the spectator to think about the possibilities of imitation, about appearance and reality, vanity and transience.[100]

A correspondence between Dou's approach to painting and Angel's theories on art is readily apparent in Dou's works.[101] His ability to capture the look of things, whether reflections, textures, surfaces, or light—an effect achieved through careful observation—recalls Angel's dictum that "a praiseworthy painter should be able to render . . . differences as pleasingly as possible for the eye (by the art of his brush)."[102] In fact, the substance of Dou's art is almost a point-by-point illustration of Angel's dictum that art should come "as close as possible to life" (*schijn zonder zijn*).[103]

Another theme that Dou explored throughout his career was the solitary religious figure.[104] At least eleven compositions by Dou feature hermits, and most of them are known in more than one version. His first paintings of this figure-type date from as early as 1635; the last in the series were painted in 1670—five years before the artist's

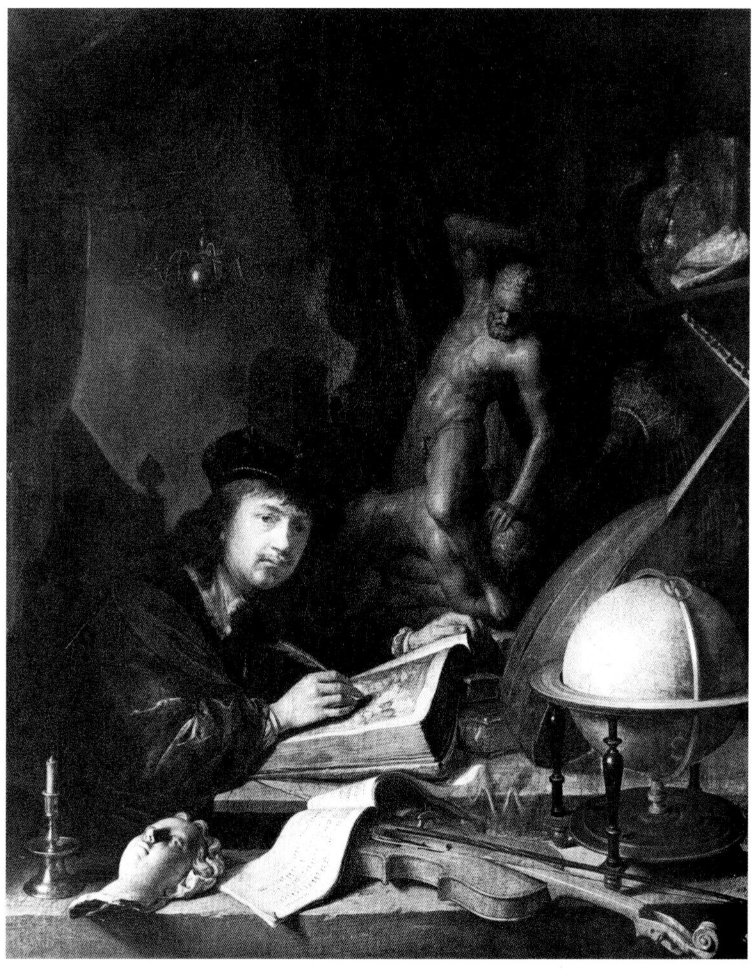

death (cats. 33 and 34). Dou varied the format, showing elderly, bearded figures in full- or half-length, in profile or in three-quarter view. Their postures are variations on a theme: the hermits hold a book, a crucifix, or rosary beads (cat. 33); they clasp their hands in attitudes of devotion; they pray, meditate, or read in a grotto (cat. 34). The settings and attributes give no indication of the figures' identities.[105]

In the same way that Rembrandt "transformed the traditional Catholic iconography of the penitent Jerome into one befitting Protestant views about repentance, individual self-scrutiny, and prayer,"[106] Dou stripped these representations of iconographic references to specific saints or individuals so that his depictions would appeal to a wider audience. While Dou was not the first Dutch artist to depict anonymous hermits engaged in their devotions, he popularized such images. He found an eager market for these paintings, as did many of his followers, some of whom apparently made a specialty of depicting hermits in Dou's manner.[107]

The appeal of the subject of hermits to seventeenth-century viewers may be attributable in part to the ideal of a retreat from civilization to a life of quiet contemplation. The allure of the wilderness and the hermit's life was extolled in The Netherlands and elsewhere by pious authors who endeavored to draw their readers' attention to the spiritual fruits of true solitude.[108] Dou's paintings of hermits allude to spiritual devotion in its most general form. The hermit, withdrawn from society, contemplating God and the vanity of life, is here a symbol of the spiritual life, seen as a necessary counterbalance to the pursuit of worldly goods and pleasure.[109]

By the early seventeenth century, allusions to the impermanence of life were standard in depictions of penitents. Perhaps one reason for Dou's attraction to the hermit subject was the opportunity it afforded him to exhibit his virtuosity in rendering the varied surfaces of *vanitas* objects.[110] Objects such as an extinguished candle, a skull, smoking implements, and the like—symbols of the vanity of earthly existence—also originally adorned the *kas* (case) of at least two of the hermit paintings.[111]

As representations of a spiritual ideal incorporating the concept of *vanitas*, Dou's hermits are closely related to his early depictions of scholars absorbed in study. At first, Dou barely defined the milieu in these works.[112] Gradually, however, he began to fill the space with objects associated both with learning and with *vanitas* (cat. 4). Dou's treatment of the theme of the scholar owed much to the ambience of Leiden, which was profoundly affected by the religious tenor of the university.[113]

Dou eventually concentrated the theme of the scholar in the person of the astronomer (cat. 31). In the seventeenth century, astronomy was viewed in some quarters with suspicion, but Dou's astronomers are presented as men of science engaged in a serious endeavor.[114] The presence of books and candles in these paintings, necessary accoutrements for astronomical study, alludes both to the concept of *studium* and to that of *vanitas*.[115] Dou's choice of the astronomer working into the night as representative of the scholar *par excellence* may have also been influenced by the contemporary association of night work with assiduousness.[116] The subject was, moreover, an attractive one for Dou, since the late hour, necessary for looking at the stars, provided him with an opportunity to explore the visual effects of artificial illumination.

The schoolmaster in such works as *The Night School* (cat. 28) symbolizes the formal aspect of education, a parallel to the pedagogical role of the mother at home. For the most part, depictions of the schoolroom had been the province of "low-life" painters. Unlike many of his colleagues, Dou was concerned exclusively with the positive aspects of education; he never depicted an unruly class.[117] In Dou's works, the schoolmaster's virtue, both by his example and by the effectiveness of his discipline and teaching, was passed on to his pupils. In addition to providing a moral exemplum, the subject also afforded a ready contrast between young and old, a theme that Dou explored throughout his career.

The scholar's study, in addition to the painter's studio, provided a setting for Dou's depictions of male musicians (cats. 8 and 20).[118] These images translate the theatrical paintings of the Utrecht Caravaggisti into contemporary bourgeois terms in which the artist explores ideas about music as a liberal art and the value of life's sensual pleasures.[119] The appeal of the sensual embodied in the theme of music is reflected in the surface of the paintings themselves. Furthermore, the fleeting strains of music traditionally evoked the idea of *vanitas*, a leitmotif in Dou's paintings.

The medical profession is the last exclusively male province in Dou's art. The oeuvre includes representations of the three types of seventeenth-century medical practitioners: the university-trained doctor, the dentist or barber-surgeon, and the itinerant quack (cat. 19). Unlike some of his contemporaries, Dou never painted the *polsvoeler* (the doctor shown taking the pulse of his patient) and only once painted the "doctor's visit."[120] The learned doctor—in Dou's work always a *piskijker* (urinomancer) in consultation (cat. 26)—was, by contrast, a theme he popularized, beginning with the painting of 1653 (fig. 11).[121]

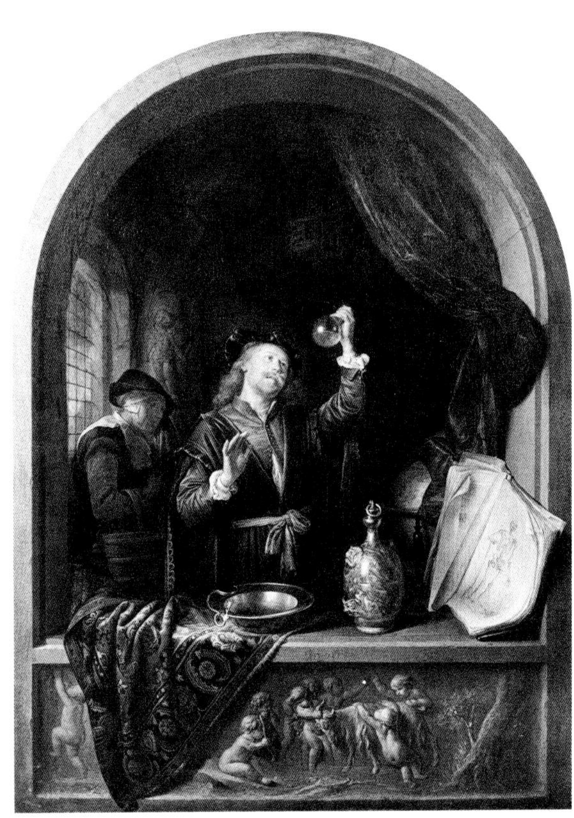

FIGURE 11
The Doctor, 1653, oil on panel, Kunsthistorisches Museum, Vienna

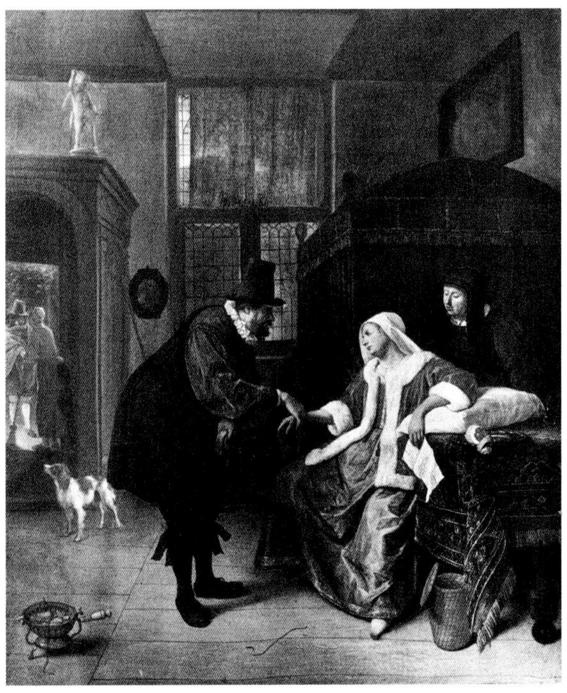

FIGURE 12
Jan Steen, *The Doctor's Visit*, c. 1661–1663, oil on canvas, Alte Pinakothek, Bayerische Staatsgemäldesammlungen, Munich

Dou's dentists and barber-surgeons are shown at work in their shops, their profession often signaled by the stuffed crocodiles above their heads. The mood of public spectacle pervading most contemporary depictions of the theme is absent from Dou's paintings, and there is little recourse to exaggeration to make a point. As befits a practitioner (versus a diagnostician), Dou's dentists are depicted interacting with their patients, and the tone of the paintings is most often serious.[122]

This point is particularly striking when Dou's depictions of doctors are compared to those of his fellow artists. Jan Steen's doctors, shown writing prescriptions or feeling the pulse, are dressed in outmoded clothes and are invariably figures of ridicule (fig. 12),[123] as are Frans van Mieris' medical men.[124] The doctor or surgeon in Dou's paintings, by contrast, is dressed in respectable garb with academic associations, and his comportment, like that of the astronomer, is stately and measured.[125]

Although the precise meaning of many of these medical pictures by Dou is uncertain, several seem to stress the *vanitas* theme.[126] The idea of the helplessness of the doctor confronted by the stronger force of God's will may underlie the earliest seventeenth-century representations of the *piskijker*.[127] In

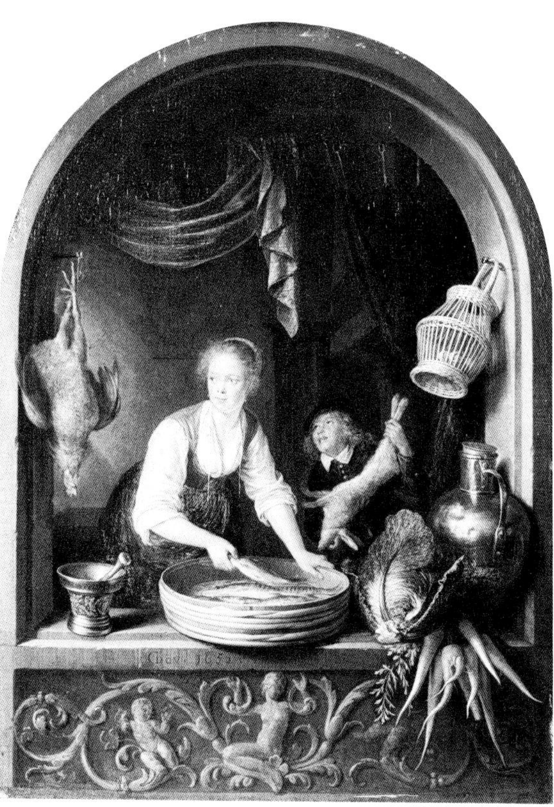

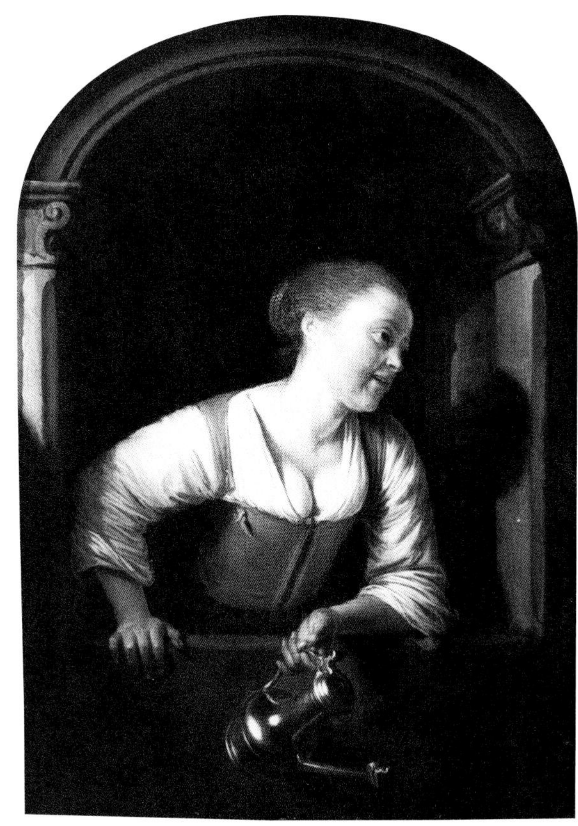

FIGURE 13
Kitchenmaid at a Window, 1652, oil on panel, Staatliche Kunsthalle, Karlsruhe

FIGURE 14
Girl at a Window, mid-1650s, oil on panel, Sterling Francine Clark Art Institute, Williamstown, Massachusetts

FIGURE 15
The Grocery Shop, 1647, oil on panel, Musée du Louvre, Paris

sustaining this general meaning, Dou's images appear conservative, especially in comparison with those of his contemporaries, who depict doctors attending patients suffering from "fashionable" maladies.[128]

Dou's doctor scenes, like those of his scholars and hermits, typically include many still-life details that, in addition to enriching the potential meaning of the paintings, allowed him to display his skill at describing surfaces and deceiving the eye. He was a master at manipulating a set of elements to achieve varied results. By altering the viewpoint, the placement, and the interactions of a few figures, the configuration of an arch, the choice and position of accessories, and the type of illumination, he was able to achieve subtle variations within a circumscribed range of subjects.

Dou was among the first artists in seventeenth-century Holland to depict the everyday activities of the Dutch burgher. The female realm in all its diversity provided Dou with some of his most innovative subjects. His early genre images are often elderly figures in domestic interiors who pursue simple activities, exemplifying moderation and spirituality.[129] In Dou's later work, the old woman reappears, generally placed within an arched window surround and occupied with an ordinary task, such as watering flowers (cat. 25) or winding flax. The old woman seems to have become for Dou a type—the personification of contented old age or a reminder of *vanitas*.

The elderly, however, were not the only women whose virtue Dou extolled during the course of his long career. He depicted mothers, absorbed in their pedagogical duties and overseeing the moral and spiritual education of their young. He also showed mistresses of the house occupied with their chores, represented cooks intent on the preparation of food, and painted servants carrying out their tasks. The domain of the virtuous wife and mother in all its aspects is featured in *The Young Mother* (cat. 21).

Kitchenmaids were one of Dou's favorite female subjects (fig. 13).[130] By the mid-1650s, in works such as *Girl at a Window* (fig. 14), he had transformed his maidservants into generic comely young women. Such pictures of alluring women, which give way to images of elegant ladies in the decade following, have a flirtatious, even erotic, undertone, in con-

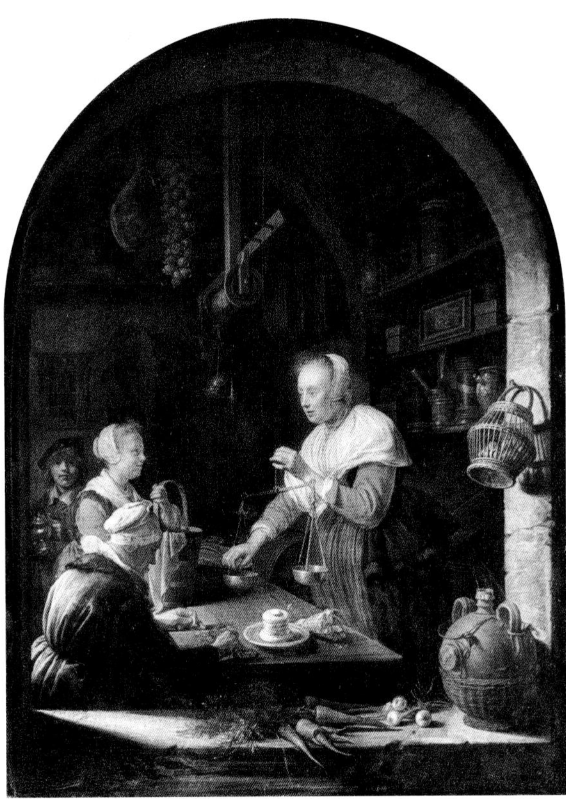

trast to the more standard female images of domestic virtue and industry, piety and duty.

Around mid-century, Dou introduced a new theme into the repertoire of Dutch genre painting. Pictorially, scenes of shopkeepers at work, such as Dou's *Grocery Shop* of 1647 (fig. 15), are descended from depictions of markets by Pieter Aertsen (1507/1508–1575) and Joachim Beuckelaer (c. 1533/1534–c. 1575). Dou's treatment of the subject, however, reflects changes in the structure of everyday commerce. This type of shop, which made accessible a wide variety of wares, had begun to coexist with market stalls, peddlers, and hawkers.[131] The cozy atmosphere that Dou creates in these paintings ties their subjects to the domestic sphere. This correspondence may account in part for the artist's invention of or attraction to the theme, which finds its ultimate expression in the painting in the Queen's collection (cat. 35).

Around 1660, the setting of Dou's scenes shifts from predominantly bourgeois to refined upper-class interiors. In *Woman at the Clavichord* (cat. 30), for example, the costly appointments and spaciousness of the room signal a more affluent milieu. Dou also broadened his subject matter at this time to include scenes of amorous dalliance (cat. 24). The work of Dou's contemporaries, Gerard ter Borch II (1617–1681) and Johannes Vermeer (1632–1675), as well as that of his most successful student, Van Mieris, may have partially influenced this change to "high-life" subject matter.

· *Working Method* Dou's technical facility fascinated his contemporaries throughout his career, but there is little evidence to reconstruct his working method. In 1675, the year of Dou's death, Joachim von Sandrart, who had visited Dou's studio some thirty-five years earlier, wrote in his biography of Dou that the artist had developed a manner of painting never before seen. He mentioned Dou's great diligence and skill at adapting the drawing, color, light, shadow, and polish found in his larger pictures to his very small works, which Von Sandrart characterized as "wonderful, lively, strong, [and] powerful."[132]

Von Sandrart reported that Dou's studio, located in the house on the Galgewater that Dou purchased outright for 2,000 florins on 1 May 1640,[133] was large and high, facing north, on the still waters of the canal.[134] To obtain the purest colors possible, Dou ground them himself (only on glass) and made his own brushes (some of which must have been very small indeed). He protected his palette, brushes, and colors from dust by locking them away. If the weather was not good, Dou would not work; when he sat down to paint, he waited until the dust settled before beginning. Von Sandrart's account confirms that Dou painted in a highly meticulous and painstaking way. Despite the lapse of many years between Von Sandrart's visit to Dou's studio and the publication of his treatise, and his emphasis on Dou's fine manner of painting in order to contrast it to Rembrandt's broadly executed works,[135] there is no evidence to contradict Von Sandrart's characterization of Dou's working method, even if it seems somewhat exaggerated.[136]

Dou apparently made use of a magnifying device of some kind to aid him in his highly detailed work.[137] X-radiographs reveal compositional changes in several of his paintings (*An Interior with a Young Violinist* [cat. 8], *The Quack* [cat. 19], *Lady at Her Toilet* [cat. 32], and *The Hermit* [cat. 34]); by contrast, some works show a careful and consistent method of working. Very few drawings exist, and those that are known are finished works, not preparatory for paintings.[138]

Occasionally Dou painted on a predominantly black ground, which he imaginatively used for areas of shadow (see, for example, the *Self-Portrait*, cat. 27). This unusual technique could, but did not always, make use of bitumen, which was valued for the depth of its color and tone. The presence of bitumen might be responsible for the appearance over time of the wide drying cracks in many of Dou's pictures.[139]

Once Dou had perfected his refined manner of painting, his style evolved only slightly. His early paintings feature a variety of hues—lilac, rose, aqua, and green, with the gradual introduction of gold—and an enveloping chiaroscuro that echo those found in Rembrandt's early Leiden paintings. Full-length figures often occupy the middle ground in Dou's early works; the foreground plane is frequently defined by clusters of still-life objects on either side. The backgrounds of these paintings are often dark.

Around 1650, Dou began to employ a spotlight effect to accentuate his now-larger figures, placed close to the picture plane. Increasingly, his palette is composed of saturated primary colors,[140] and the overall tonality of his pictures seems brighter and more silvery. In the early 1660s, Dou's handling, which combined spirited passages with expert delineation, was supremely assured. In paintings executed after 1665, Dou used color with great freedom. The flesh tones in the Minneapolis *Hermit Praying* (cat. 33), for example, include blue, gray, yellow, and pink. The artist also stretched his technique, expanding his repertoire of brushstrokes, whether to designate a difference in age between the figures or to describe materials and surfaces more accurately.[141] Although not all of Dou's late works are of equal quality, the lively and freely painted passages and glowing chiaroscuro in the hermit paintings of 1670 (cats. 33 and 34) belie Willem Martin's assessment that Dou's late paintings are weak, lacking in freshness and unity.[142]

Dou's subject matter is often situational rather than anecdotal or narrative.[143] Intended to embody ideas, or personify concepts, his works, more often than not, are metaphorical abstractions and do not depict a moment in time, despite the plausible reality of the scene. The posed artificiality of the figures, evoking the *tableau vivant* of the stage, is one of several means Dou employed to signal that his paintings, although based on lifelike vignettes, are deliberate artistic constructs.[144] Dou's metaphorical treatment of his subjects is quite unlike the genre paintings of his contemporaries.[145] His approach is especially marked in those images in which a figure is juxtaposed either with a secondary figure, who is usually smaller, or with a background scene, whose primary purpose is to elucidate, by comment or contrast, the "meaning" of that figure.[146] The painted *kas* cover, which both adorned and protected many of Dou's pictures, served a similar function (cat. 23, fig. 1).

A situational approach underlies the work of Ter Borch as well. But whereas Ter Borch's figures are apparently unaware of the viewer's presence (fig. 16), Dou's figures often engage the viewer directly. Even when his sitters are absorbed or engaged in an activity, the spectator is not excluded in the same way that he is in Ter Borch's work. Through the slight turn of a head or twist of a mouth, Ter Borch could imply something of the figure's interior life. As Sturla Gudlauggson pointed out, the figures' lack of awareness of an audience makes Ter Borch's art appear extremely "true-to-life."[147] The same cannot be said of Dou's art despite the fact that his paintings accurately record the minutiae of life: his figures pose, even when they ignore the viewer.

Dou used a personal set of compositional devices that underscores the nature of his images as painted fictions rather than glimpses of reality. The most ubiquitous of these motifs, which he introduced between 1645 and 1650, is the window surround with its stone ledge. Neither a true window (which is often to be observed in the left-hand wall of the room depicted) nor a true niche (except in rare instances), it nevertheless alludes to these two forms. The device may derive from several sources: Netherlandish still lifes, prints depicting individuals selling wares through a window, the half-length allegorical figure pieces of Van Honthorst, or Rembrandt's portraiture. It announces that the scene depicted, however "true-to-life," is not part of the viewer's world and that the image is more than what first meets the eye. The window ledge erects a barrier between the figure and the viewer, while the window surround monumentalizes the subject and signals its importance. It invites the viewer's scrutiny, cajoles him to look further and contemplate what he sees. This device also stresses the presence of the picture plane, playing with the apparent continuation of space both before and behind the "window."[148] The implied interpenetration of fictive and real space solicits the spectator's participation.[149]

FIGURE 16
Gerard ter Borch, *Parental Admonition*, c. 1654–1655, oil on canvas, Gemäldegalerie, Staatliche Museen zu Berlin

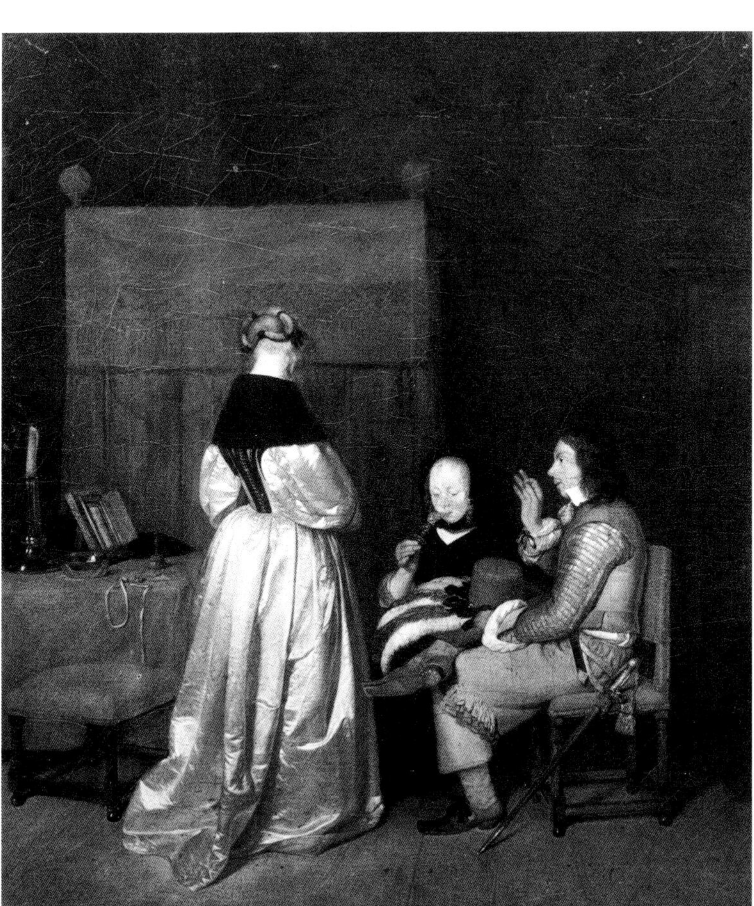

Trompe l'oeil and illusion are important components of Dou's art.[150] Dou's conception of illusion is, to use Marian Hobson's term, for the most part "soft": it suggests an awareness of artifice in the mind of the beholder and points beyond itself. It posits a relationship between art and reality that shifts and overlaps, at once true and false according to the level at which one approaches the work of art.[151] Within the context of trompe l'oeil in Dou's pictures, the curtain—tapestry or silk—plays a special role. Like the window surround, it separates the painted "reality" from the viewer's, in presence and meaning alike. It both excludes the viewer and invites him to pull it aside; it defines the plane closest to him and demonstrates the artist's technical ability. In addition to suggesting the practical function of curtains in the seventeenth century, which were used (much like *kas* covers) to protect paintings from sunlight and dust, their inclusion as elements of the scene also alludes to the exquisiteness of the picture and transforms it into an object of curiosity and fascination.[152]

Bound up with this idea of preciousness is the surface quality of Dou's paintings. It is most often finely wrought and gives an impression of smoothness, but it is also imprinted with the artist's hand, the maker whose brush has visibly described the play of light on forms and the texture of materials. The spectator is thereby invited closer, to scrutinize the beautifully sensuous surface. The small size of most of the paintings makes the act of approaching the pictures practically imperative. The invitation to look and admire is echoed by the implicit proposition, the "come hither" look, of Dou's lovely ladies (cats. 30 and 32).[153] It is strengthened by the objects that protrude from the picture (vegetables, pieces of cloth, a pot of flowers) and three-dimensional bas-reliefs that invade our space. The active engagement of the viewer by all the means at Dou's disposal—the beautiful surface, small dimensions, convincing illusionism, seductive subject—is one of the primary characteristics of his art. This uncanny congruence of medium and message is fundamental to an understanding of the appeal of the artist's paintings. This holds true not only for Dou's pictures of flirtatious women, in which the sensuousness of the painted surface and the seductive nature of the women depicted coincide, but also for the still lifes and self-portraits, where Dou communicates the notion of *ars longa vita brevis* through his careful painting technique and prominent *vanitas* elements.[154]

Dou's conspicuous artistic virtuosity and his gift for delighting the eye are also seen in his artificial light effects. Of course, precedents exist in the Flemish tradition for using candles as the primary light source and compositional focus.[155] Closer to his own time, Dou's light lies somewhere between that of Rembrandt, who created atmosphere in his pictures by sacrificing form and color to light, and that of Van Honthorst, whose light, often hidden and more narrative in purpose, is harsher and more distortive.[156] Like Elsheimer, who worked on a small scale but employed artificial light exclusively in historical subjects, Dou's candlelight is evocative and romantic. Like the curtain, it both conceals and reveals, poeticizes the mundane, and adds interest to the banal.

Dou's use of candlelight situates his subject in a specific time of day; it provides an opportunity for the artist to show his virtuosity. It also carries moral implications, both positive and negative. In the school scenes, candlelight symbolizes the light of understanding; in depictions of hermits, it emphasizes vigilance, piety, and faith. In paintings where the sexes meet, either explicitly or implicitly, the artificial illumination signals easy virtue and loose living.[157] Dou thus employed this pictorial device to function on a practical, artistic, and iconographic level.

Dou's success as an artist was due in large part to his genre paintings, for which he was and remains best known. They look different from the paintings of other great seventeenth-century Dutch artists. Dou does not attain the poetry of Ter Borch, attempt the ribald humor of Steen, or create the tender and quiet world of Vermeer. His art was formed by his artistic training and personal predilections for the small, the precious, and the refined. The crowded university city of Leiden affected his choice of subject matter. Whereas his own seriousness informed his art through the recurring themes of *studium*, *vanitas*, and *ars longa vita brevis*, the tenor of his time is reflected in his attempt to create an art that was "to appear to be without being" (*schijn zonder zijn*). Unlike many of his contemporaries, Dou did not have to work primarily for the open market. The extraordinary patronage he enjoyed came as a result of his own particular style, meticulous yet painterly, illusionistic and refined. His novel subject matter and the sophisticated and thoughtful way he depicted it must also have appealed to connoisseurs of the day.

The many levels on which these pictures can be apprehended and appreciated are enhanced by Dou's ability to engage the spectator's eye and mind, to at once invite him in and exclude him, to create a parallel world that looks real but that operates by means of associations and concepts. The exclusive market for his work that resulted from his innovative technique freed Dou to develop and expand his range of subject matter. Not compelled to specialize, and given the means to pursue his time-consuming method of painting, Dou created and maintained a level of craftsmanship that was the measure against which many of his contemporaries were to be judged.

Notes

This project has had a long gestation. It grew out of my dissertation, which was written under the exacting guidance of Egbert Haverkamp-Begemann at the Institute of Fine Arts of New York University. My first thanks therefore go to my former adviser. In the second place, I am profoundly grateful to Anthony G. Hirschel, Director of the Michael C. Carlos Museum of Emory University, who hired me as curator of European art for that institution knowing that I had this exhibition ahead of me. His understanding and friendship have been instrumental in bringing the show in its current incarnation to fruition.

I owe an enormous debt of gratitude to Arthur K. Wheelock, Jr., who introduced me to the study of Dutch art when I was a first-semester graduate student at the University of Maryland. He allowed me to convince him that Dou would be a fitting exhibition for the newly renovated cabinet rooms at the National Gallery of Art. Finally, I would like to offer my deepest thanks to Steven Elmets, who has seen almost as many of Dou's paintings as I have. He has encouraged my work all along the way and has cheerfully lived with this artist in our midst for seventeen years.

1 In the seventeenth century, *fijnschilder* was used to distinguish a "fine-art painter" from a *kladschilder* (house painter). *Fijnschilderen* as a term for the controlled and elegant technique practiced by Dou and his followers is a modern usage; see De Pauw–De Veen 1969, 17, 372, and Naumann 1981, 1: 12.

2 Von Sandrart, ed. Peltzer 1925, 1: 195–196. Angel's lecture was given in Leiden on 18 October 1641 and printed in a booklet as *Lof der Schilder-Konst* (In praise of painting) the following February. It is one of the few seventeenth-century Dutch tracts on painting. On Angel's description of Dou's style, see Angel 1642, 56. For a full discussion of the writings of Angel and Orlers with respect to Dou, see Sluijter 1993.

3 Orlers 1641, 380. This was the first biographical notice on the artist. According to Cornelis Hofstede de Groot (1907, 337), Orlers may have obtained his information directly from the artist and his relatives.

4 Van Leeuwen 1672, 191.

5 Woltjer 1975, 1. The institution was awarded to the inhabitants of Leiden by William of Orange for their valor in defending the city against the brutal Spanish siege, which had been lifted only the year before.

6 For the University of Leiden, see Grafton 1988. For an account of religious life in Leiden, see Van Deursen 1991a, 233–318. Woltjer 1975, 1–7, and Fix 1991, 30–37, discuss the political implications of Leiden's Calvinist partisanship.

7 Woltjer 1975, 8–13.

8 Woltjer 1975, 10. Pieter Pauw, the founder of the amphitheater, assembled a collection of human and animal skeletons, whose iconographic significance as *memento mori* would not have been lost on a seventeenth-century public. His successor, Ottho van Heurne, added much more, from Egyptian antiquities to prints, evincing the encyclopedic character that marked the collections of his age. See Lunsingh Scheurleer 1975, 222–223.

9 Lunsingh Scheurleer 1975, 268.

10 For the history of Leiden's textile industry, see Blok 1916, 8, 9, 28, 285, 287; Posthumus 1939, 3: 879–1011; Wilson 1968, 31, 32, 58, 234, 238; J. de Vries 1976, 101–103.

11 Van Gulik 1975, 367.

12 De Gheyn is recorded in The Hague as early as 1598, where he was listed in the St. Luke's Guild as painter and engraver. However, he apparently maintained contacts in Leiden: he engraved the portrait of Carolus Clusius in 1600 and designed the title page of Clusius' magnum opus, *Rariorum Plantarum Historia* (1601).

13 For Dolendo, see Bredius 1886; Pelinck 1957; and Ekkart 1974, 189. Only two extant drawings have been securely ascribed to Bartholomeus Dolendo, and although they are incised for transfer, prints after them are not known. See Leiden 1976–1977, 59.

14 Martin 1901, 20.

15 For Isaac Claesz. van Swanenburgh, see Ekkart 1998. Three of Swanenburgh's ten children also became artists, among them his oldest son, Jacob, who was Rembrandt's first teacher, and Willem, an accomplished engraver with close ties to the university, who died at an early age. On art in Leiden at the end of the sixteenth and the beginning of the seventeenth century, see Ekkart 1974.

16 Ekkart 1974, 176. For these commissions, see Bogtman 1944, 61–62.

17 *Register Glazenmakers* (G.A.L. 523, fol. 48) lists five assistants in Couwenhorn's workshop in 1620. His success at this date is remarkable given that Couwenhorn had come to Leiden from Haarlem only the previous year.

The duties and responsibilities of a *glasschrijver* were more varied than those of a mere glassmaker. The glass painter, as head of a workshop, was responsible for receiving commissions and meeting the client's specifications. He could execute the work himself, but most often he would farm out parts of it (usually the design and the manufacture of the glass) to other craftsmen. See Van der Boom 1940, 19; Bogtman 1944, 27; and Amman and Sachs 1568, in which the *Reisser* (designer), *Glasser* (glazier), and *Glassmaler* (glass painter) are three distinct crafts.

18 See Martin 1901, 19, and Montias 1982, 90, on the benefits of this type of arrangement.

19 The 1622 *Register van het Hoofdgeld* (Bon Gasthuisvierendeel, G. A. L., fol. 10) shows that the family—Douwe Jansz., Marijtgen Jansdr., their children Jan and Gerrit, the children from her first marriage, Vechter and Catharina ("Trijntje"), and an unnamed boarder—was living on the east side of the Cort Rapenburg, an extension of the main patrician street of the city.

20 Orlers 1641, 377.

21 It was evidently not unusual for a father to send his son elsewhere to learn the family trade. Montias 1982, 68 note, records a contract in which Willem de Vries, a glass-maker living in France, sent his son to Delft to learn glass-engraving with a well-known master living there.

22 By 1628, only Douwe Jansz. and Jan are listed; *Glazenmakersgildeboek Schilders* 2 (G.A.L. 524, fols. 13, 18).

23 Orlers 1641, 380. The reasons for Douwe Jansz.'s decision to allow his son to learn to paint may have been a combination of several factors. Despite his success and position in Leiden, it is possible that Douwe Jansz., motivated by a practical business concern, could not absorb both of his sons into his business. Perhaps the desire on the boy's part to pursue painting was too strong to deny. Dou's purported recklessness, however, seems at odds with the quiet and patient personality that emerges from the archival evidence, from the reports of contemporaries (in particular, Von Sandrart's description of Dou's working method; see page 39) and from the meticulous type of work Dou produced.

24 Dudok van Heel (1991, 66 note 15) has pointed out that the shared-studio idea is unsupported by any source.

25 Vogelaar 1991, 14, mentions the related versions of *Samson and Delilah*, *Christ on the Cross*, and *The Raising of Lazarus* by the two artists, the fact that the same old man and woman were used as models for their *tronies* (head studies), and that both Rembrandt and Lievens scored the wet paint with the butt end of their brushes to create light effects.

26 Vogelaar 1991, 15. See also Stechow 1969.

27 Rembrandt's *Hannah and Simeon in the Temple* (Kunsthalle, Hamburg), *Parable of the Rich Man* (S.M.P.K., Berlin), and *Christ at Emmaus* (Musée Jacquemart-André, Paris) (Bredius 1969, 450, 337, 452), exhibit the influence of this Utrecht Caravaggist, as do Lievens' depictions of youths blowing on coals or torches (e.g., at the National Museum, Warsaw [Sumowski 1983, 3: no. 1225]).

28 Vogelaar 1991, 16. There is probably a connection between Rembrandt's adoption of the Utrecht style and his aspiration to paint for the court at The Hague, since Honthorst was a favored painter of the stadholder Frederik Hendrik and his wife Amalia van Solms. For the stadholder's taste and collections, see The Hague 1997–1998.

29 Rembrandt had begun to receive commissions for paintings from the stadholder about this time; see Schwartz 1985, 67.

30 On the possibility of Scriverius' patronage of Rembrandt, see Schwartz 1985, 25, 36.

31 Strauss and Van der Meulen 1979, 66, 67, 75, 78.

32 Van de Wetering 1983, 60.

33 Orlers 1641, 380.

34 Dudok van Heel (1991, 54) suggested that Rembrandt traveled from Leiden to his clients in Amsterdam, The Hague, and Rotterdam from December 1631 until July 1633; only after that time did he settle definitively in Amsterdam.

35 Angel 1641, 23.

36 Van Ysselsteyn 1936, 2: 228, doc. 504 and 1: 211, respectively.

37 Von Sandrart records Spiering's appreciation of the northern schools; see Avery 1971, 161, and Van Gelder and Jost 1985, 205–206. His preference for the finely wrought is made clear in a letter from Michel le Blon in Amsterdam to Spiering of November 1635 about a painting by Torrentius (as in Martin 1901, 43): "also UE sin en vermaeck heeft in ongemeene, nette en uytgevoerde dingen. . . ." ("as you desire and delight in uncommon, tidy and detailed things . . ."). On the basis of Le Blon's further description of Dou's work ("de wonderlycke speculatiën dieder bevonden worden daerinne geobserveert en uytgebeelt te sijn") ("the wonderful speculations which are found to be therein observed and portrayed"), Blankert (1983, 18 and 33 note 16) suggests that Spiering may have been as attracted to the ambivalent or puzzling nature of Dou's images as to the refinement of his technique.

38 For Christina's taste in art, see Nordenfalk 1966.

39 Kungliga Biblioteket, Stockholm, S4a, inv. nos. 1–9 and 73–74, marked "rendu."

40 Montias 1987, 462.

41 In 1635, Pierre Lebrun advised the amateur keen to speak about art to consider painting in terms of execution, especially its illusionistic properties, rather than its subject: "Je désire lecteur . . . vous delivrer de ceste peine . . . quand vous voudrez parler de la platte peinture, l'un des nobles artifices du monde, le plus grand trompeur du monde c'est le meilleur peintre de l'univers et le plus excellent ouvrier, car à vray dire l'eminence de le mestier ne consiste qu'en une tromperie innocente et toute pleine d'entousiasme et de divin esprit.

. . . Mais faut tromper l'oeil ou tout n'y vaut rien. . . . Pour scavoir donc parler de ce noble mestier, il faut avoir esté à la boutique disputé avec les maistres, veu le traint de pinceaux, et le jugement asseuré pour esplucher toute chose." Quoted in Merrifield 1967, 2: 767–769. I am grateful to Ernst van de Wetering for drawing my attention to the prevailing interest in Dou's art for style over subject and to this literary source in particular. Blankert (1980, 29), came to a similar conclusion; he wrote that "often the subject seems to have been more important to the painter than to his public." However, given the obvious care Dou took with his compositions, the subject matter could not have been negligible to collectors.

42 Eric Jan Sluijter (1988b, 37) indicated that De Bye probably had some commercial interest in this first "one-man show," as he encouraged interested parties to speak with him, presumably about buying one or more of the exhibited works. As Ivan Gaskell pointed out (1982, 21), given the value of so many paintings by Dou assembled in one place, it is not surprising that Hannot, responsible for the contents of the exhibition room, had to pledge his "person and all his possessions present or future without exception" as security.

43 Leiden Not. Arch. 777, A. Raven. The self-portraits were contract nos. 11, 15, 22 and the nudes were contract nos. 6, 9, and 16. On De Bye, see Blok 1916, 136–138, and 253, and Lunsingh Scheurleer et al. 1988, 3b: 461–465. De Bye's presumed commission of the nudes would explain both the late date of the nudes in Dou's oeuvre (c. 1660–1665) and his choice of a subject apparently unsuited to his painterly abilities. In addition to the nudes, De Bye owned at least ten other paintings by Dou—fully half of the exhibited works—whose subjects could be interpreted as seductive or amorous. It is ironic that a pious man would have had such a collection.

44 Van Leeuwen 1672, 191.

45 The names of these artists appear in the *Schilders-schultboek* of 1644, indicating that they must have been independent masters by that date (G. A. L. 855). For Metsu's dependence on Dou, see Wheelock 1976, 457–458. Van Staveren is mentioned as a pupil of Dou's in the *Lijste van Schilders* of unknown authorship (c. 1776–1785), which reported that Dou touched up many of his works and that Van Staveren's paintings were frequently sold abroad as autograph paintings by Dou (Leiden 1988, 226 note 8). Similarly, Jacob van Spreeuwen (1609/1610–after 1650) is mentioned in the list (on page 20) as a *"Discipel van G. Douw"* in 1643; Van Spreeuwen's works as well were said to resemble Dou's (Leiden 1988, 222 note 6). At his death in 1666, De Pape had fourteen copies after Dou in his possession. It is tempting to extrapolate from this fact that Dou put his students to work copying his own paintings. Copies or variants of at least six of Dou's self-portraits are extant, but it is not known whether these paintings are contemporary or later copies. Van Gaesbeeck apparently moved to Amsterdam, where he resided from 1645 until 1649, shortly after his name was recorded in the Leiden *Schilders-schultboek*. If he had been actually affiliated with Dou, it would likely have been prior to his move, since on his return to Leiden in 1649, he was probably already suffering from the illness that killed him.

46 According to Naumann 1981, 1: 23, Van Mieris resumed his tutelage with Dou sometime before 1658, after a stint with Abraham van den Tempel (1622–1672). Because Van Mieris was inscribed in the Leiden St. Luke's Guild on 14 May 1658, he was likely already an independent master of some standing by that date (Leiden 1988, 127). Eric Jan Sluijter suggested in conversation (7 July 1992) that had Van Mieris returned to work with Dou for a short time around 1655, he would have been about twenty, just the right age for him to become an independent master.

47 Houbraken (1718–1721, 3: 2) records that Dou referred to Van Mieris as "the Prince of his Pupils."

48 On the founding of the Leiden St. Luke's Guild, see Miedema 1973–1975. Sluijter 1988b, 31, draws attention to the fact that the municipality never recognized this group as an official guild. As an example, he mentions that in the *Deken en Hooftmans Boeck*, the Leiden artists are referred to as *opsienders* (overseers) rather than *deken* (deans) and *hoofdlieden* (headmen) as in other guilds. Dou is listed as a member of the St. Luke's Guild from 1648 until 1651, from 1658 until 1668, and from 1673 until 1674. According to P. J. M. de Baar in conversation, few or no contributions were collected between 1652 and 1657.

49 For Dou's patrons and their ownership of his paintings, see Baer 1990, 100–101 and note 254. I would like to extend my thanks to Willemijn Fock for very generously sharing with me her inventory findings on Dou.

50 Sluijter 1988b, 24.

51 Sluijter 1988b, 26.

52 For assessments of the taste at court, see Chong 1987, 104–106, and The Hague 1997–1998.

53 Inventory number 764: "Ein Nachtstückhel in Halbouali von Öhlfarb auff Holcz, warin ein Weibspildt in der linckhen Handt ein Lattern vnndt in der rechten ein prennende Kertzen hatt. In einer schwartzen Ramen von Ebenholtz, hoch 2 Span 6 Finger vnndt 2 Spann 1 Finger braidt. Von G. Dau." Quoted in Berger 1883, cli.

54 Cosimo's journal entry reads: "La mattina . . . andò a vedere un gabinetto di quadri assai buoni messi insieme da un mercante, e di li si portò a casa di Duo, pittor famoso, di dove intrata in carrozza se ne uscì di Leyden pigliando il cammino all volta di Haerlem." See Hoogewerff 1919, 256–257.

55 Chiarini 1989, 105–110. Cosimo's preference for the art of the *fijnschilders* is noted in Goldberg 1983, 194 and Prinz 1971, 40.

56 W.M. de Jongh 1878, 214; Goldberg 1983, 194. Excerpts from this correspondence can be found in Geisenheimer 1911, 56–58. This commission, with the possible exception of the nudes most likely painted for De Bye, is the only instance of a patron seeking a particular subject by Dou—a self-portrait to form part of a collection of self-portraits—rather than an example of his style. Cosimo was initially attracted to Dou, however, because of the technical refinement of his painting.

57 The account of the "Dutch gift" in the following paragraphs is based on Martin 1901, 60–68; Martin 1911, 62–68; Mahon 1949, 303–305, 349–350; and Logan 1979, 75–86. See also Royal Collection 1982, xxxix–xli.

58 There was long confusion about the identity of this picture because of Houbraken's account of it (see note 59 below). With Mahon's publication of the inventory description of paintings in Charles' collection (Mahon 1949, 350), the identification of the painting with the one in The Hague was confirmed: "389: Dow. A Dutch woman at worke her childe in y[e] cradle, her maid by with fowle and severall other things. Dutch Present. 2.5 x 1.10."

59 Houbraken described this painting by Dou in the Dutch gift as follows: "[In het zelve] stont verbeelt een Vroutje met haar Kintje op den schoot, en een meisje dat met het zelve speelt." He was not certain about the painting's provenance, for he had heard from one source that it was bought from Dou by the East India Company for Charles II but from others that the States bought it from Johan de Bye.

60 In the inventory, this painting is described: "334: Elschamor. An Olde Woman holding a candle and a woman drincking, a night piece. Dutch prsent. 0.11 x 0.9." It has been proposed by Logan 1979, 79, that Dou copied this painting from his collection or stock before sending it on to England, based on the observation of Christian Ludwig von Hagedorn (in *Lettre à un amateur de la peinture* [Dresden, 1755], 179): "Gerard Dow ne dédaignoit point de copier le Tableau de Ceres, quand l'original devoit passer en Angleterre, où il fut malheureusement consumé, dit-on, dans un incendie arrivé à White-hall."

61 Leupe 1878, 83.

62 *De Kunstkroon voor den Koninck van Groot Britanje* (Amsterdam, 1660). The poem appears in its entirety in Logan 1979, 76.

63 Evelyn 1818, 315: "Now were presented to his Majesty those 2 rare pieces of drolery, or rather a Dutch Kitchin, painted by Dowe so finely as hardly to be distinguish'd from enamail."

64 Traudenius 1662, 17. Once more, the discussion and appreciation of Dou's art centers on his style rather than on the subject matter.

65 Traudenius 1662, 25. According to Houbraken (1718–1721, 3: 25), who most likely made up the story, Dou refused the king's offer because the restless court life did not agree with his quiet nature and his friends discouraged him from going there.

66 On Dou's standing in Leiden, see Sluijter 1993, chapter 2. Perhaps in recognition of his renown, the burgomasters of Leiden decided to commission a painting by Dou, as well as one by Van Mieris, in the summer of 1669. In February 1670, however, the offer was withdrawn, with no explanation given. See Martin 1901, 81; Naumann 1981, 1: 174. It seems plausible that the commissions were withdrawn because the artists demanded too much money, as Martin supposed.

67 De Bie 1661, 277.

68 Ole Borch manuscript in the Royal Library, Copenhagen, Ny kgl. Samling, No. 373b, 122, as quoted in Madsen 1907, 228.

69 *Journal des Voyages de Monsieur de Monconys . . . Seconde Partie: Voyage d'Angleterre, Païs-Bas, Allemagne et Italie* (Lyon, 1666), 153.

70 The date of his inscription was 22 November 1661 (G.A.L., Lg. A., inv. no. 849, part I). Aside from Frans van Mieris, Van Slingelandt was the only pupil of Dou's mentioned by Van Leeuwen in 1672 (Van Leeuwen 1672, 192).

71 Houbraken 1718–1721, 3: 175: "[Schalcken] begafzig eerst ter onderwiyzinge van S. van Hoogstraaten, naderhant van Gerard Dou, welkers behandeling hy vry wel heeft weten na te bootsen. . . ." The etched *Portrait of Dou* used for Dou's likeness in volume 2 of Houbraken 1718–1721 bears the inscription: "Honoris ergo praeceptorem suum delineavit G. Schalcken" (Hollstein, v. 24, p. 154 [4]). Schalcken studied with Samuel van Hoogstraten in Dordrecht between 1656 and 1662, and he is recorded as back in Dordrecht by 1665.

72 Van Tol was inscribed as a guild member in 1664 (G. A. L., Lg. A., inv. no. 849, part I). He was the son of Catharina Vechtersdr., a daughter from the first marriage of Dou's mother, Marijtgen Jansdr., and Vechter Vechtersz. Although Van Tol's style was not nearly as refined as Dou's, his art was closest to that of the master in every way.

73 Martin 1902, 64.

74 Obreen et al. 1877–1890, 5: 259.

75 Leiden 1988, 182; Houbraken 1718–1721, 3: 343. Houbraken mistakenly gave De Moor's date of birth as 1656.

76 Notary Arent Raven, Notarial Archive Leiden 763. In this will, Dou bequeathed his niece Maria Jansdr. the middle of the three houses he owned on the Cort Rapenburg and two thousand florins. His other heirs were Vechter van Strijtvelt (his mother's grandson from her first marriage) and his half-sister Catharina Vechters.

77 Notary Nicolaes Paets, Notarial Archive Leiden 678. The notary executed the will at Dou's house.

78 Notary Nicolaes Paets, Notarial Archive Leiden 680. For an extract of this testament, see Martin 1901, 168–170, appendix 3.

79 Pieterskerk 6. VIII, Leiden, A° 1665, fol. 233. This church, like the Hooglandse Kerk, the church in which Dou's niece was baptized, was a *hervormde staatskerk* (Reformed church). See De Baar and Moerman 1991, 33.

80 Register vanden XXen Penn . . . Collaterale Successien, Recht. Arch. Leiden 210 (fols. 44v–45v).

81 For Rembrandt's workshop, see Chicago 1969; Amsterdam 1983; Amsterdam 1984; Van de Wetering 1986; Bruyn 1989; Bruyn 1991.

82 *Corpus* 1982–, 2: 848–854, C6, identifies *The Rest on the Flight into Egypt* currently on the art market as the painting described by Ferdinand Bol and Gerrit Uylenburgh in the inventory as "Een Josep en Maria van Gerrit Douw en Flinck." Bruyn et al. believe that Dou painted the figures and objects while Flinck painted the landscape background. The implication is that Rembrandt took the (unfinished?) painting by Dou to Amsterdam where it was worked on (finished?) by Flinck.

Orlers (1641, 380) speaks of Dou's paintings of "persons after life, animals, insects, [and] other things." Neither Angel (1642) nor De Bie (1661) mentions specific paintings by Dou in their texts devoted to the artist. None of the works seen by Traudenius (1662), Borch (1662, as quoted in Madsen 1907), or Von Sandrart (1675) includes a history painting; the latter writes especially of Dou's portraits and still lifes. Sysmus (c. 1669–1678, as quoted in Leiden 1988, 46 note 19) characterizes Dou as "excellent in small portraits." Van Hoogstraten (1678) lists Dou as one of fifteen painters "who have best observed the essence of art and the noblest selection [of subject matter]." Blankert (1980, 32 note 25) suggests that Dou may have been included among these artists because his works often had allegorical meanings rather than because of the particular themes he painted. Houbraken (1718–1721, vol. 2) speaks of the similarity of the "noble" Dou's style to that of the young Rembrandt, but not of the likeness of their subject matter.

After the inventory of 1669, the next mention of a history painting by Dou appears to be that in the catalogue of the collection of the duc d'Orléans (Du Bois de Saint Gelais 1727, 176: "Gerard Dou . . . Le Vieux Tobie, peint sur bois, haut d'un pied six pouces, large d'un pied deux pouces. Une chambre fait le fond du Tableau où l'on voit le vieux Tobie avec Anne sa femme, assis proche l'un de l'autre. Il tient une pipe écoutant sa femme qui lit dans un grand livre. Il y a une table dans le milieu, et à droit un grand rouet à filer."). The description, which underlines the genrelike character of the scene, corresponds roughly to the *Old Couple in an Interior* (Musée du Louvre, Paris [Martin 1913, 138]). While the inspiration for this painting may have been the apocryphal story of Tobit, its theme of a pious couple and their frugal repast resembles that of several other genre scenes by Dou.

83 *Corpus* 1982–, 1: 356, suggests that Rembrandt's old women reading prayer books may have originally been meant to represent the prophetess Anna. Bialostocki 1984, 16, interprets them less specifically, as personifications of piety. This subject was also depicted at about the same time by Lievens in a painting now in the Rijksmuseum (Sumowski 1983: 3, no. 1222).

84 See Alpers 1983, 188, for a different interpretation.

85 Lievens, who had trained with Joris van Schooten (c. 1587–1652/1653), one of the most important portraitists working in Leiden in the first quarter of the seventeenth century, may have been responsible for introducing this type of painting to Rembrandt and his circle. For the definition of *tronie*, see Bauch 1960, 176–180; De Pauw–De Veen 1969, 190–193; Miedema 1981, 215–217; *Corpus* 1982–, 1: 40 note 8; Chapman 1990, 35. For a general discussion of *tronies* in Rembrandt's workshop, see Bruyn 1989, 22–26. For Jouderville's *tronies*, see Van de Wetering 1983 and for those of Van Vliet, see Bruyn 1982, 40–46.

86 Sometimes a *tronie* could be of an identifiable person; see, for instance, the description in a Leiden inventory of 1644: "Een out mans tronie sijnde 't conterfeytsel van den Vader van Mr. Rembrandt." (Hofstede de Groot 1907, no. 101.) However, as Lyckle de Vries (1990, 197), has pointed out, "The likenesses of the models were not commissioned by themselves or by one of their close relatives. Neither the model nor the prospective buyer had an essential influence on the genesis of study heads. . . . A reliable rendering of personal features was not the first objective to produce *tronies*."

87 Dou may have used the *Bust of a Man* (cat. 11) as a study for the *Schoolmaster* in the Fitzwilliam Museum, Cambridge (Martin 1913, 68).

88 Blankert (1982, 26–27), argues that *tronies*, in theory, would have been accorded a higher place in the hierarchy of genres than mere portraits, as they were not slavish imitations of nature, but rather images of nature adorned and commented upon. He also suggests (1982, 57–58) that *tronies* pleased the seventeenth-century burgher because they appealed to his sense of the eccentric and exotic. Blankert's idea that Ferdinand Bol (1616–1680) might have painted *tronies* to attract portrait customers could hold equally true for Dou.

Surviving documents indicate that beginning pupils were often set to work painting copies of *tronies*. These copies were less expensive than works by the master and provided the master with income; see Broos 1983, 40–41, and Amsterdam, 1983, 192.

89 Among the major Dutch cities at mid-century, Leiden had the lowest ratio of artist-painters per thousand inhabitants. It might have been that the absence of a guild to protect their interests had an adverse effect on the number of artists active in the city. Furthermore, Leiden was populated in large part by textile and other workers, leaving a relatively small middle and upper class to patronize artists. See Montias 1990, 62. For a brief discussion of other artists active in Leiden after the departure of Rembrandt and Lievens, see De Baar and Moerman 1991, 36.

90 *Corpus* 1982–, 2: 5 note 7. Dou used a rectangular panel only for the exceptional *Double Portrait* in the Rijksmuseum (Martin 1913, 56), the formal *Portrait of a Woman* in a Dutch private collection (Baer 1990, 34), and the early *Bust of a Negro* in Hannover (Sumowski 1983, 1: 552 [no. 255]).

91 On Bailly, see Bruyn 1951 and Bruyn 1953.

92 The small size of many of Dou's likenesses evokes both prints and portrait miniatures; the latter were often kept in cabinets made for the display of precious objects. Miniatures were especially appreciated at the time in the humanist intellectual circles of Leiden and The Hague. Both the Elder and Younger Jacques de Gheyns, in addition to David Bailly, were known for their meticulously crafted miniature drawings. See Adams 1985, 207–208. The precious nature of Dou's pictures was implied by Houbraken, who referred to "het beruchte konststuk van Gerard Dou" as a "konstjuweel." See Houbraken 1718–1721, 2: 127.

93 An exception to this observation is the loosely painted *Bust of a Man* (cat. 11) in the Corcoran. In this case, the technique may be related to its function as a study.

94 Von Sandrart, ed. Peltzer 1925, 195–196: "Es ist aber die Frau Gemahlin ihm mit grosser Gedult fünf Tag lang, nur eine Hand zu untermahlen. . . . Durch solche Langsamkeit benahme er den Leuten zu sitzen allen Lust, so dass sie ihre sonst liebliche Physiognomie verstellet und aus Uberdruss ganz geändert, wordurch dann seine Contrafäte auch verdriesslich, schwehrmütig und unfreundlich worden. . . ."

95 According to Woodall 1990, 70, "profit" refers to the material standing necessary to a gentleman; "honor" denotes the social position of the gentleman and the intellectual prestige derived from performing a liberal art.

96 Chapman 1990, 6.

97 Emmens 1964–1965, 9–11.

98 The idea of *ars longa vita brevis*, a leitmotif in Dou's self-portraits, is most conspicuous in his *Self-Portrait* in the Uffizi (page 31, fig. 5), in which the artist places his hand on a skull. In the self-portraits in the Louvre (Martin 1913, 21) and the Metropolitan Museum of Art (Martin 1913, frontispiece), the emphasis on the artist's tools, the dignified costly dress, and the steady serious regard combine in a manner similar to that of sixteenth-century engraved prints of artists to create a *memoria*, an image intended to transcend death. See Raupp 1984, 19–23.

99 Sluijter (1990a, 28–33), rightly interprets *The Quack* as an amusing and spirited visual fiction, dependent on pictorial convention, and created by Dou to illustrate the virtuosity of his art.

100 Hunnewell 1983, 99; Leiden 1988, 98.

101 See Sluijter 1993. The similarity in approach between Dou's painting and Angel's prescriptions does not necessarily indicate the influence of one upon the other. Rather, as Sluijter has written (1993, 19), "it simply means that their approximation of painting shows agreement in a number of characteristic aspects."

102 Angel 1642, 55.

103 Sluijter 1988b, 19. In addition to stressing the importance of reproducing materials and skin texture naturalistically, Angel advised that a painting should show a multiplicity of things, and that the light and shadow in the composition should be carefully arranged (that is, not spread out but concentrated). Dou clearly subscribed to these ideas as well.

104 In addition to his numerous paintings of hermits, two paintings by Dou of the Magdalen are extant. They date from relatively late in his career, and reflect as much his interest in the female nude and women's charms as his ideas of saintliness. The sensuous aspects of the theme were apparently what made it so appealing to so many Baroque artists; see Naumann 1981, 1: 90.

105 Martin 1901, 37, maintained that the reason Dou did not designate his hermits as St. Jerome was because he was unable to paint a lion. If by this he meant that Dou could not convincingly portray animals, the accomplished *Goat* in a Dutch private collection (Sumowski 1983, 1: 603 [no. 306]) is sufficient proof to the contrary.

106 Scallen 1999, 86.

107 For the collectors of these hermit paintings, see Baer 1995, 27–28. Paintings of hermits by Jan van Staveren, Pieter Leermans, and Jacob van Spreeuwen, among others, rely heavily on Dou's example. The existence of numerous contemporary paintings after Dou's hermits and the avid contemporary market for such pictures indicate that this type of painting was probably used by Dou for teaching purposes.

108 Knipping 1940, 2: 254–55. For examples of parallel imagery in Dutch literature, see Baer 1995, 28.

109 Baer 1995, 29.

110 The painting of *vanitas* still lifes, though not the exclusive province of Leiden painters, was a specialty in that city. As Elisabeth de Bièvre has demonstrated (1995, 233–234), a preoccupation with death and the passing of time was typical of Leiden (among other reasons, because of the traumatic memories of the Spanish siege and the recurrence of the plague that hit the rapidly growing city hard in 1635). Some of the still lifes Dou painted before mid-century allude more to *studium* and the *vita activa* and *vita contemplativa* (see cats. 17–18)—themes that reflect the ideals of the scholarly life of the university in Leiden—than to the concept of *vanitas*. On Dou's *vanitas* still lifes, see note 111 below.

111 Most of the paintings in Johan de Bye's 1665 show of Dou's works had cases, some of them painted. These cases served a practical, protective purpose and also, on a symbolic level, signaled the preciousness of the painting within. Iconographically, the cover served to comment on or add meaning to the painting within. See Martin 1901, 76–78; Boström 1949, 21–24; Snoep-Reitsma 1973, 285–292. In the contract signed between De Bye, the owner of the twenty-seven paintings by Dou exhibited at the show, and Johannes Hannot, from whom he rented the exhibition space, number 5 reads: "Een groot stuck, een kluysenaer, biddende, geknielt voor een kruysefícx, van buytenen een kaerslicht, lamp en dootshooft." ("A large piece, a praying hermit kneeling before a crucifix; on the outside a candlelight, lamp and skull.") (Leiden, A. Raven, Notarial Archive 777, 18 September 1665.) Further, a fiche in the RKD written by Bredius records that in 1727, Valerius Röver bought for 425 florins from the Delft jeweler Verbrugge, "een cabinetstukje van Gerard Dou, een heremit bij kaarsligt zittende te studeren in een grotte, extra konstig en uitvoerig A° 1661 geschildert met een deurtje daarvoor, waar op een kannetje en toebak en pijpen. . . ." ("a cabinet piece by Gerard Dou, a hermit by candlelight seated and studying in a grotto, extremely artfully and minutely painted in 1661 with a little door before it, on which [are painted] a cannikin and tobacco and pipes. . . .") For smoking implements as symbols of transience, see Bergström 1956, 154–55.

The Wine Cellar (cat. 23) was also originally protected by a *kas* cover, the *Still Life with Candlestick, Pipe, and Pocket Watch* now in Dresden (cat. 23, fig. 1), Dou's only true extant *vanitas* still life.

112 Among Dou's earliest paintings are two works in the Hermitage. One features a turbaned man depicted in three-quarter length studying a book (Martin 1913, 27 right), the other a bust-length figure of a man wearing a skullcap and closely examining a globe (Martin 1913, 22 left). In neither is a setting delineated.

113 Van de Waal (1974, 143), noted that "this age-old theme [of the scholar] had gone through a particular development in Leiden, probably under the influence of the new university."

114 In the sixteenth and early seventeenth centuries, astronomy was disparaged in strict Calvinist circles as dangerous superstition by virtue of its close relationship to astrology (see Amsterdam 1976, 84; Braunschweig 1978, 65; and Brown 1984, 101–102). Negative connotations are also apparent in Brant's *Ship of Fools*, in which the text accompanying the astronomer and a fool reads, "He who puts faith in the planets/May as well buy a [fool's] cap and bells"; and in Kepler's (1571–1630) characterization of astrology as *dolzinnige apekool* (harebrained rubbish) (related to the image of two star-gazing apes provided by Joris Hoefnagel in his *Satire of Astronomy*). By the mid-seventeenth century, such concerns had become largely obsolete.

115 Miedema 1975, 13. This article was instrumental to the reinterpretation of these pictures as images of committed scholarship rather than merely as allegories of transience.

116 Müller Hofstede 1988, 19. Compare Van Veen's emblem "Diuturna Quies Vitiis Alimentum" (*Emblemata Horatiana* [Antwerp, 1607]), which, according to Müller Hofstede, illustrates "the ideal of the 'studia litterarum' of the 'vir sapiens,' who studies even at night following the maxims of 'virtus.'"

117 A direct parallel to Dou's exemplary schools can be found in Bruegel's *Allegory of Temperance* of 1560; Ostade and Steen, on the other hand, tended to represent less positive examples.

118 The most important exception is *The Trumpeter* in the Louvre (Martin 1913, 86 left), in which the background scene suggests a different kind of milieu—a scene of riotous living, with couples drinking and merrymaking.

119 These ideas also inform Dou's *Still Life with Globe, Lute, and Books* (cat. 6).

120 This is the subject of *The Dropsical Woman* in the Louvre (see page 14, fig. 2). As with *The Quack*, when he did treat this theme, it was in a definitive and fully realized picture.

121 Dou's formulation of the theme of the *piskijker* may be dependent on a lost composition by Adriaen Brouwer (Flemish, 1605/1606–1638). However, he transformed the character of the scene completely. As in his representations of dentists, a subject traditionally associated with low-life painters, Dou downplayed references to the lower classes and thereby broadened the repertoire of "bourgeois" genre painting. He used a similar approach in his paintings of pancake bakers, pot scrubbers, and schoolmasters.

122 These depictions can be likened to those of Dou's astronomers in that both run counter to the prevailing tradition of ridiculing the subjects. Perhaps by stressing their solemnity, however, Dou meant to be humorous or gently mocking.

123 See Gudlaugsson 1945.

124 Gabriel Metsu's depictions of related themes focus on the sickness or suffering of the individual; he reduces accessories and subsidiary figures to a minimum. Petterson 1987, 194.

125 Once more, the centrality of the university to intellectual life in Leiden might have contributed to Dou's serious treatment of learning. Not all Leiden artists, however, embraced this dignified approach. Van Vliet, for example, created one of the more memorable images of an inept dentist at work (Bartsch 1797, 1: 53).

126 Feer (1985, 111–112) arrived at this conclusion as well. The ambiguity and complex associations evoked by these images contrast sharply with the more straightforward moralizing behind Dou's school scenes.

127 L. de Vries (1977, 97), in considering this theme as represented by Teniers and Ter Borch, interprets elements in their works as allusions to *vanitas*.

128 For example, *morbus virgineus* (according to Petterson 1987) or *furor uterinus* (according to Dixon 1995). Petterson (1987) has shown that the theme of the doctor's visit in the work of Steen, Metsu, and Van Mieris reflects ideas pervasive not only in contemporary medical treatises but also in the legal system, on the stage, and in the emblem literature of the time. Dou's treatment of medicine is more in keeping with the intellectual current of Leiden as reflected in the *vanitas* associations of the Leiden anatomy amphitheater. According to Dixon (1995, 114), such conservative imagery would have appealed to the "large number of potential patrons among the physicians and students associated with the city's famous medical school."

129 Dou's earliest genre scene (see page 33, fig. 6) depicts an old woman peeling apples in humble surroundings and accompanied by signs of her domestic industry: lacemaking, apple peeling, a clean and shining pot, supper cooking on the hearth. Her piety is directly alluded to in the painting of Christ and the Samaritan Woman on the back wall, evoking the reward of "everlasting life" for those who believe (John 4: 13–14). A later example by Dou is the old woman at prayer before a frugal meal (Sumowski 1983, 1: 570 [no. 273]), who also represents piety and domestic virtue.

130 According to de Bièvre (1995, 234), there must have been many servants in Leiden "where, as in all overcrowded urban precincts, service in a well-built home must have seemed like a ticket to paradise. Besides, with a large and cheap labour force available, even the not-so-rich could afford to employ somebody to do the shopping and cleaning." As Eric Jan Sluijter (1991, 53–55) has shown, the artist combined motifs from sixteenth-century market pictures with the half-length shepherdess type popularized earlier in the seventeenth century by the Utrecht school to create a new kind of genre painting. The purported lascivious nature of serving girls was exploited in seventeenth-century farce and comedic literature; that Dou's voluptuous servant in *Kitchenmaid at a Window* (page 38, fig. 13) literally and figuratively offers her wares to the spectator is obvious from both her gestures and her dress.

131 See J. de Vries 1976, 187–188. Dou's depictions of herring sellers and pancake bakers present a more familiar type of image: the former are related to the hawkers of Metsu and the peddlers of Rembrandt; the latter derive from the pictorial tradition practiced by painters of low-life (for example, Brouwer) and Rembrandt.

132 Von Sandrart, ed. Peltzer 1925, 195.

133 Waarboek PPP, fol. 189, Leiden Rechterlijk Archief 67. The price he paid is within the mean of that paid by artists registered in the Delft Guild of St. Luke at the time; see Montias 1982, 119–122. It seems that by May 1644, he owned more than one house; a document of 25 May (Not. Alervijn Claesz. de Man, Not. Arch. Leiden 549), mentions that "Gerrit Dou, schilder, staat op het punt een wanbetaler uit *een zijner huizen* [emphasis added] te laten zetten." ("Gerrit Dou, painter, is at the point of becoming a defaulter on *one of his houses.*") Investing in houses was a conservative financial measure; see Van Deursen 1991b, 45. At the death of his father in 1656, Dou inherited three houses on the Cort Rapenburg.

134 Von Sandrart, ed. Peltzer 1925, 196.

135 Wheelock 1978, 62.

136 Von Sandrart was probably largely responsible for Dou's reputation as an overly meticulous craftsman. Houbraken (1718–1721, 2: 4) questioned Von Sandrart's description of Dou's working procedure: "Dus ver Sandrart, men sou uit deze beschryving eerder besluiten dat dezelve tot spot dan tot synen roem geboekt was." ("As for Sandrart, one would conclude from this description that he recorded ridicule rather than [Dou's] fame.") While late seventeenth- and eighteenth-century theorists pitted meticulously finished paintings (seen as products of painstaking labor and an artisanal mentality) against more broadly executed works (seen as inspired endeavors), as Wheelock (1978, 63) observed, artists of Dou's time could choose to place themselves in an international framework (as Rembrandt did in relation to Titian) or in a national one (as Dou clearly did). Dou himself may have chosen to distinguish himself from Rembrandt. On the choice between these two poles of painting, see Van de Wetering 1991 and Sluijter 1993.

137 In 1662, Ole Borch wrote: "Quand Dow travaille, il a l'habitude de mettre trois paires de lunettes pour y voir plus clair"; see Madsen 1907, 230. Von Sandrart (Von Sandrart, ed. Peltzer 1925, 195) notes that Dou began wearing glasses during his thirties; Houbraken (1718–1721, 2: 3) transformed these eyeglasses into magnifying glasses, and mentioned that Dou viewed his subjects through a frame strung with horizontal and vertical threads. De Piles (1715, 428) had Dou using a convex mirror. Descamps (1753–1765, 2: 218–219) apparently combined De Piles' and Houbraken's accounts; according to him, Dou inserted a concave lens into a screen. Wheelock (1978, 65) notes that "the preciousness of many of Dou's paintings, in which colors are slightly accentuated and foreground objects are often disproportionately large, are characteristic of images seen through a lens. Dou, moreover, often frames his compositions with curtains or windows as if to avoid distortions occurring in peripheries of images when seen through a lens or reflected in a mirror."

138 Although I have not studied the problem of Dou's drawings closely, I am inclined to accept as autograph only the *Portrait of the Artist's Mother* in the Louvre, signed and dated 1638, and the so-called *Portrait of Anne Spiering* in a private collection, signed and dated 1660 on the verso. For a discussion of drawings attributed to Dou, see Sumowski 1980; for problems in the connoisseurship of Dou's drawings, see Naumann 1978, 5, 19, notes 11–12.

139 Bitumen was found in a cross section taken from Dou's *Young Mother* (cat. 21) and communicated to the author by the conservator there at the time, Luuk Struick van der Loeff. For the use of bitumen, see White 1986, 62. Rembrandt is known to have used bitumen in his paintings as well; see Van de Wetering in the discussion following the presentation of papers published in *Centraal Laboratorium Themadag* 12 (1987): 69. According to Annetje Boersma, responsible for the recent cleaning and conservation of *Lady at Her Toilet* (cat. 32) (see her essay in the present volume), no bitumen was found in the paint layers, despite the wide drying cracks apparent on the surface.

140 It was Dou's use of color and, above all, the virtuosity of his light and shadow effects that were most often praised by early writers on his art (that is, Von Sandrart, Félibien, De Piles); see Sluijter 1988b, 19.

141 For example, the use of a coarse, unblended painting style for an elderly or aged face, to contrast with a more smoothly painted younger face, is found in *The Poulterer's Shop* in the National Gallery, London (Sumowski 1983, 1: 593 [no. 296]), and *The Dentist* in Dresden (Martin 1913, 75 right). In the latter, and in *The Pancake Baker* in Munich (Martin 1913, 172), the costumes are painted more broadly, while the still-life elements are depicted meticulously.

142 Martin 1913, xii. In some late paintings, however, dry and sloppily worked passages and the prominence of red tones do give weight to Martin's assertion.

143 This characteristic is most marked in the paintings whose subjects hover somewhere between the sphere of shop and home; see, for example, the *Woman with Poultry* (Martin 1913, 120), or *Kitchenmaid at a Window* (page 38, fig. 13).

144 This type of painting corresponds to Svetlana Alpers' (1976–1977, 15) description of a realistic representational mode in seventeenth-century art that combines "an attention to imitation or description with a suspension of narrative action."

145 Sutton 1980, 49; Naumann 1981, 96.

146 As Sutton observed in Philadelphia, Berlin, and London 1984, xxvii, this device is related to the idea proposed by Emmens that "the religious elements in paintings by Aertsen and Beuckelaer were not a pretext for the painting of still life and genre, but actually reiterated and explained the moral ideals embodied in the sacred themes; the genre scenes were the concrete demonstration, the actual human and material expression, of biblical and moral truths." The use of background scenes and subsidiary figures in images from the fifteenth and early sixteenth centuries is discussed in Klibansky et al. 1964, 311 ff. See also Dickey 1986 and Stoichita 1997, chapter 1.

147 Gudlauggson 1959–1960, 1: 80.

148 Leiden 1988, 101. De Bièvre (1995, 235–236) argues that since stone window frames were rare in Leiden, their inclusion might symbolize the durability and preciousness of the painting.

149 Jacques Foucart, in Paris 1970–1971, 232, distinguishes between Rembrandt's use of the window or niche and that of his students, Ferdinand Bol (1616–1680) and Jan Victors (1620–1676 or after). Rembrandt uses the device to convey space and monumentality, whereas his students employ it for anecdotal and illusionist purposes. It seems to me that Dou uses the device for all but the anecdotal possibilities.

150 One of the prerequisites of trompe l'oeil is that it be life-size. The small size of many of Dou's paintings militates against the illusionistic impression they create.

151 Hobson 1982, 8–50, as condensed in D. Smith 1987, 425–426. The recognition that illusion is an artifice has no positive value; it is only an awareness of being tricked. This is contrasted in Hobson's view to "hard" illusion, which both "dissimulates" in the sense that it hides itself, and "simulates" in the sense that it creates a replica of reality, which the beholder takes at face value. It is "bipolar," a homogeneous experience, either true or false.

152 Kemp 1989, 20–29.

153 The titillation and tension that results from enjoyment and enticement, on the one hand, and the consciousness of the negative moral implications of the theme, on the other, made such subjects even more attractive to the viewer/buyer. See Sluijter 1988c. This dichotomy is one expression of the tensions in Dutch culture so exhaustively studied by Simon Schama (1979; 1980; 1987).

154 I owe much in this discussion of the seductive surface of Dou's paintings to conversations with Nanette Salomon, the convincing essays on Dou by Eric Jan Sluijter (Sluijter 1988a; Sluijter 1988b; Sluijter 1988c), and the inspiring lecture given by Simon Schama at Hofstra University in May 1988.

155 See Müller Hofstede 1988, 16–28. These works could also include two or three subsidiary light sources as well.

156 These characterizations of the light of Rembrandt and the Utrecht Caravaggisti appear in Van de Wetering 1988, 45.

157 See Müller Hofstede 1988, 18–26.

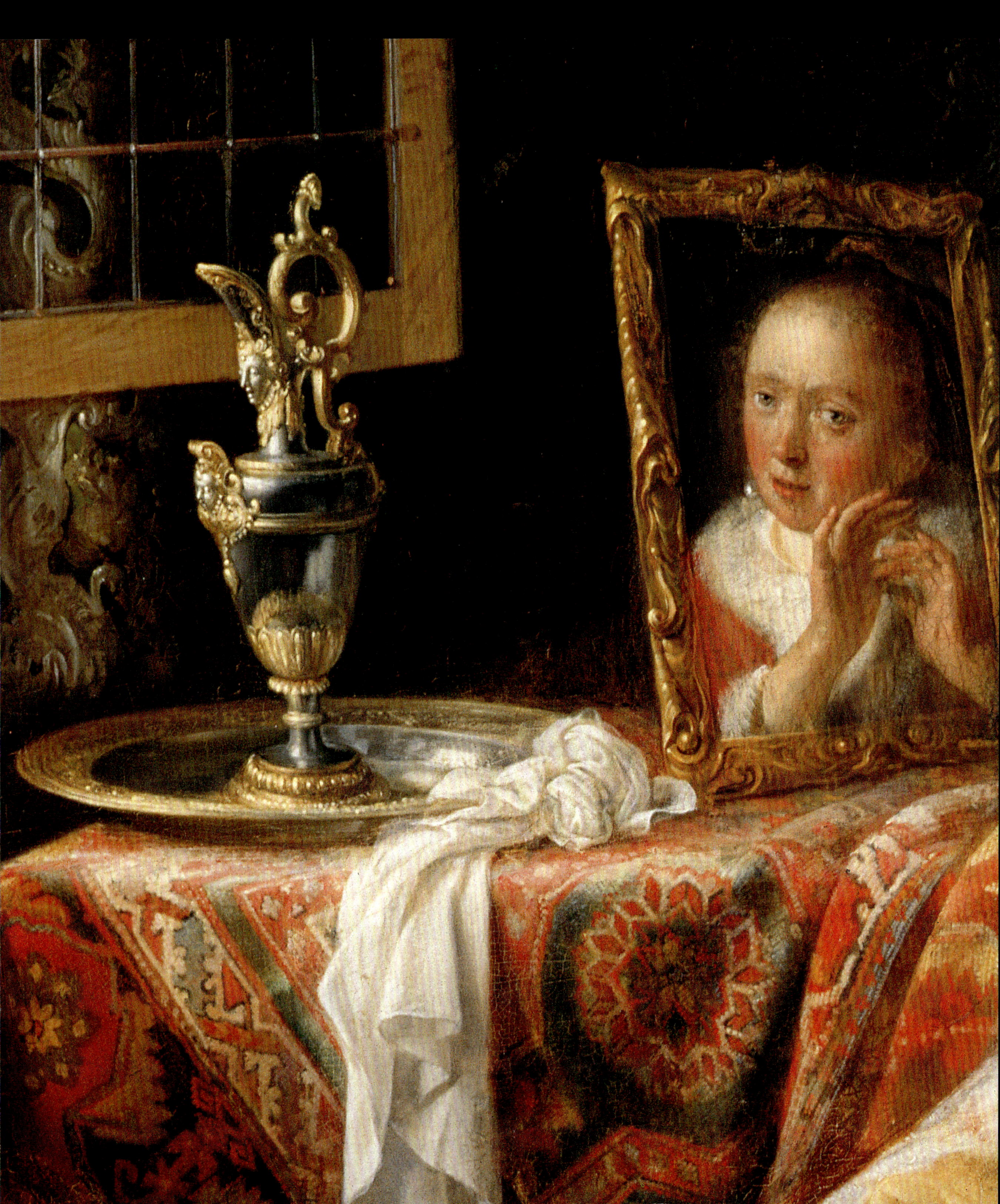

Dou's Painting Technique: An Examination of Two Paintings

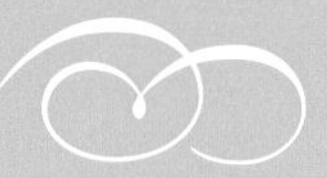

Annetje Boersma

Gerrit Dou's *Young Mother* from the Mauritshuis, The Hague, and *Lady at Her Toilet* from the Museum Boijmans van Beuningen, Rotterdam, are among the most impressive and colorful paintings of interiors in Dou's oeuvre. This technical study of the two paintings examines how Dou created these exceptional compositions, distinguished, among other elements, by their brilliant colors and refined technique.[1] The study is based on research undertaken during the conservation of *The Young Mother* in 1986[2] and of *Lady at Her Toilet* in 1997/1998.[3] The results of this research offer an unprecedented opportunity to compare the techniques Dou used to execute these works.

DETAIL
Lady at Her Toilet, 1667, oil on panel, Museum Boijmans van Beuningen, Rotterdam (cat. 32)

FIGURE 1
The Young Mother, 1658, oil on panel, Royal Cabinet of Paintings Mauritshuis, The Hague (cat. 21)

In the Mauritshuis painting (fig. 1), a mother looks up from her needlework to gaze at the viewer while a young servant kneels by the baby's crib. This figural group and the finely painted kitchen objects in the foreground are illuminated by an open window at the left. The pronounced contrasts in light and dark, which leave the high ceiling and the background staircase in shadow, give the room a mysterious, atmospheric quality. *Lady at Her Toilet* (fig. 2) depicts a well-dressed woman seated on a chair, attended by her maid, in a colorful interior. A curtain has been drawn back on the right to reveal this intimate scene.[4] Bright daylight enters from the left through the open window; it illuminates the figure, creating a strong

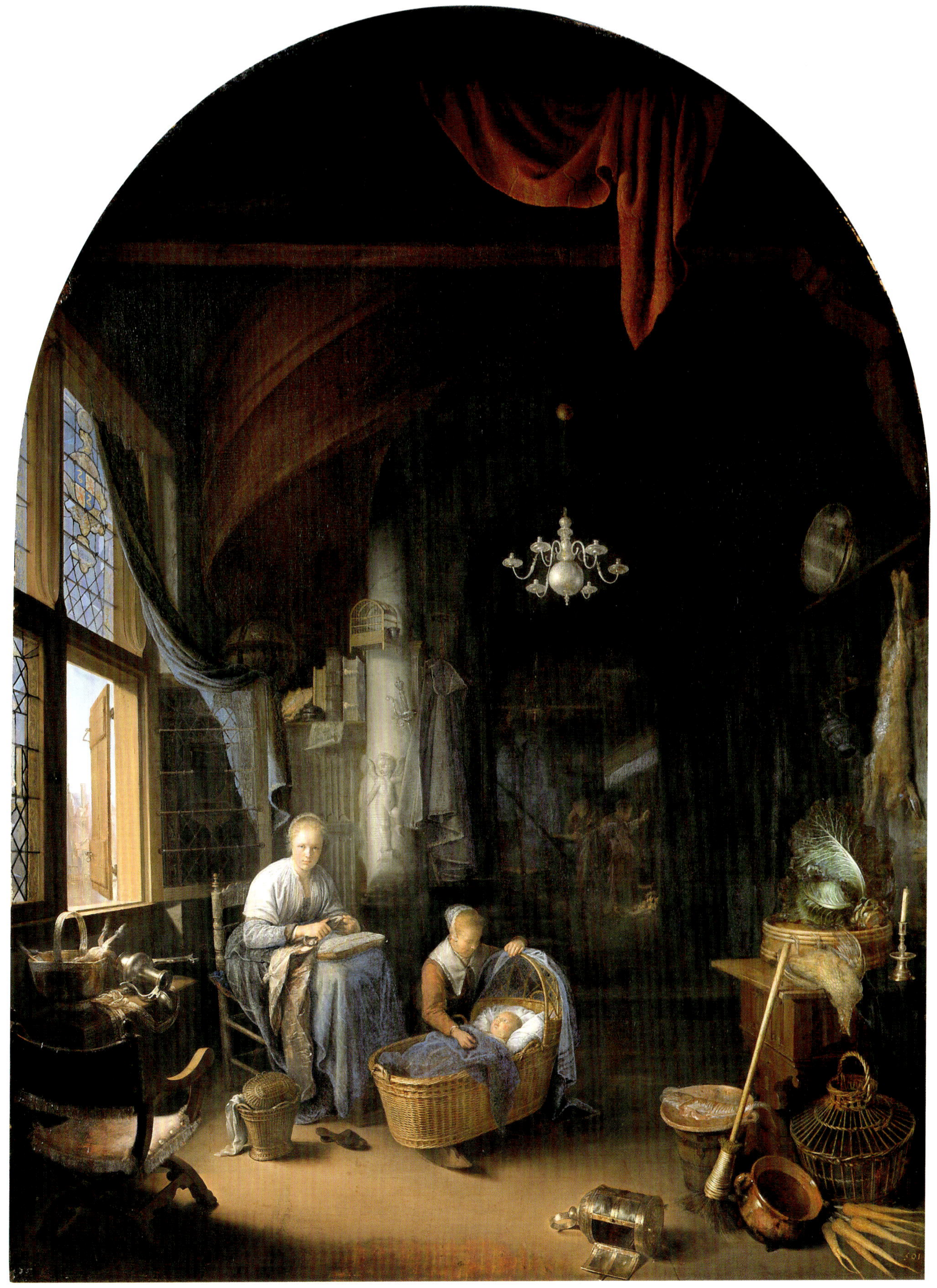

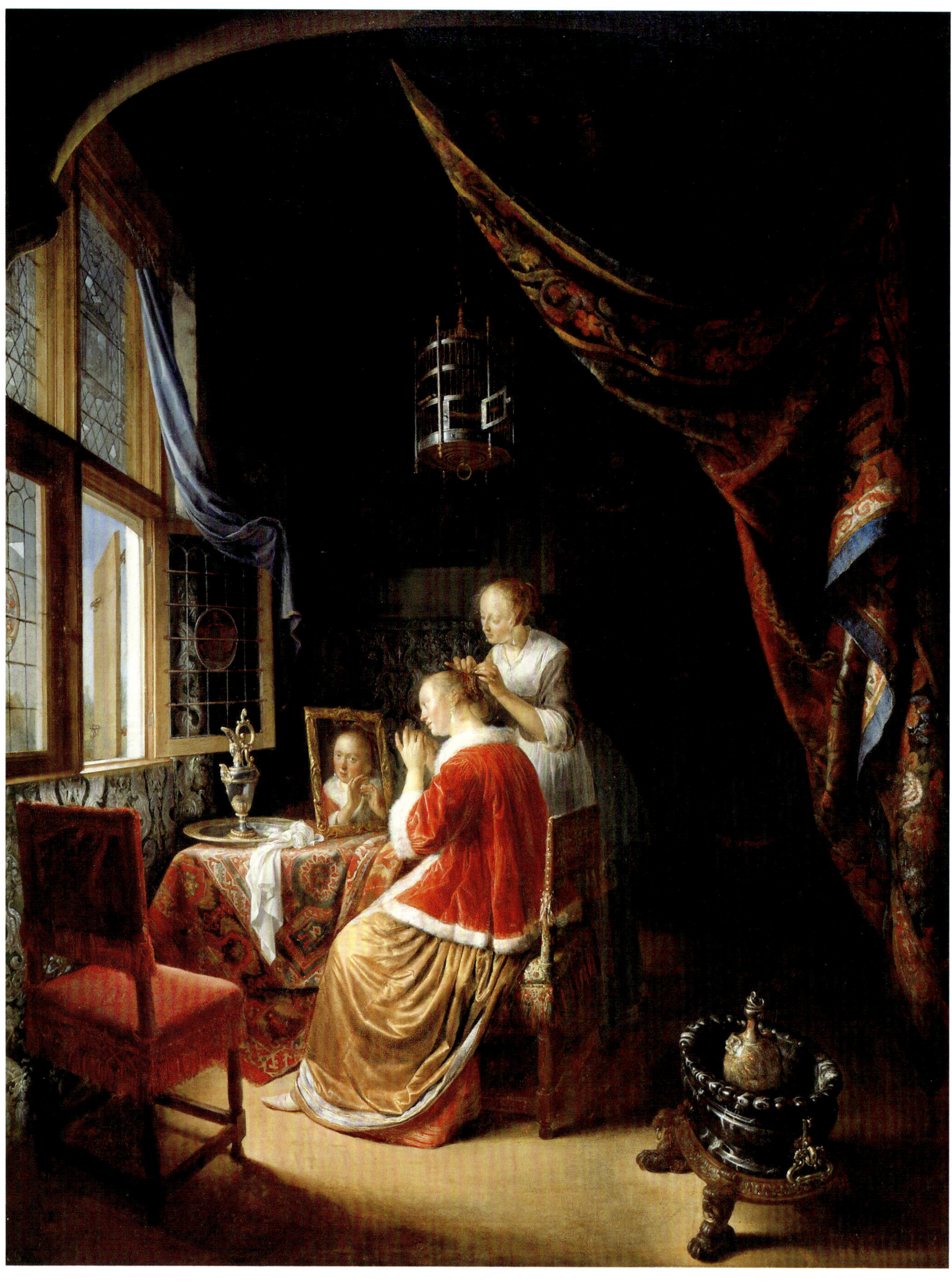

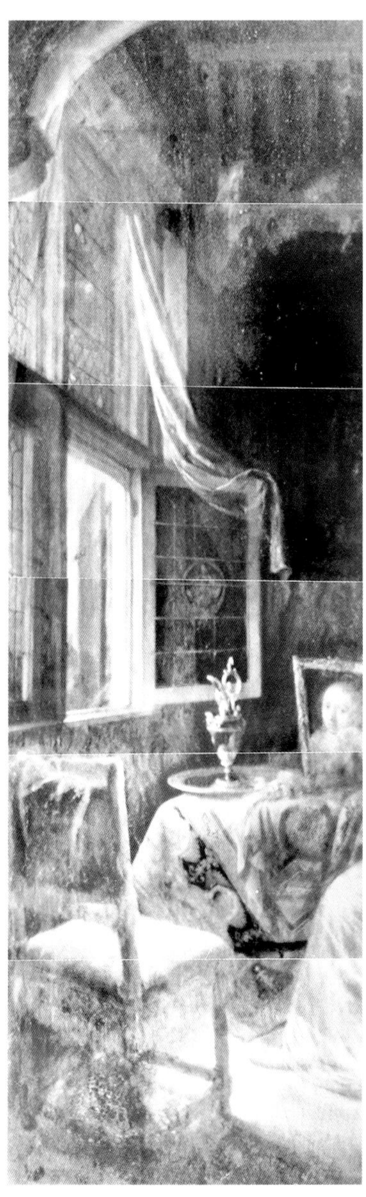

shadow in the foreground and accenting the marble wine-cooler and the metal birdcage.[5] The background of the room is darkly painted, which, in combination with the wide craquelure, makes objects difficult to distinguish: two paintings and a chair placed next to the chimney are barely visible.

Although the two works are dated nearly ten years apart (*The Young Mother* to 1658 and *Lady at Her Toilet* to 1667), they share many compositional similarities, among them, the open window, the blue curtain, and the fall of light. The fenestration in the windows of both paintings is similar (extending even to the broken panes), and in *The Young Mother* a red curtain hangs over a brown balustrade, which can also be seen in the dark background of *Lady at Her Toilet*. The chair in the foreground of *The Young Mother* appears in the background of *Lady at Her Toilet*. In both paintings, the floor is rendered in yellow ochre.

FIGURE 2
Lady at Her Toilet, 1667, oil on panel, Museum Boijmans van Beuningen, Rotterdam (cat. 32)

FIGURE 3
Infrared reflectogram (detail) of *Lady at Her Toilet*

· *Perspective* Dou, like other painters of his time, knew the laws of perspective and experimented with them. In *Lady at Her Toilet*, the spatial illusion is based on a perspective system with a single vanishing point, as is suggested by a pinhole that passes through the paint layer and ground just behind the neck of the seated woman. Visual distortions, particularly noticeable with respect to the empty chair and the wine-cooler in the foreground, become more obvious the farther one stands from the painting. The close placement of the distance points may have been intended to force the viewer to stand near the painting to view the perspective correctly. In *The Young Mother*, a pinhole at the vanishing point at the right is visible in the x-radiograph. Here, the distance point seems to be slightly longer, with the result that the spatial effect remains consistent when viewed from different angles or distances.[6]

· *Pentimenti* The highly finished appearance of the two works suggests that Dou painted them in a systematic and highly deliberate manner. Pentimenti are clearly visible, however, even with the naked eye, and changes in the composition are further revealed through x-radiographs. In *Lady at Her Toilet*, Dou changed the position of the woman's chair twice. The birdcage was initially placed higher and the bowed arch of the room lower. X-radiographs indicate that Dou may have initially painted a piece of fabric over the empty chair in the foreground, which also had a differently shaped back. Other areas are more difficult to interpret, including a round shape in the foreground on the right, which Dou eliminated in the finished version.[7]

Infrared reflectography images of *Lady at Her Toilet* (fig. 3) also provide useful information about Dou's compositional changes. Under infrared examination, changes in the foreground chair become clearly visible. Might Dou have initially painted a coat, perhaps that of a visitor, over the chair? Hatched lines in the pleats of the woman's skirt indicate that Dou executed this area using dark paint; no underdrawing, however, is detectable. A light area, which may have defined a curtain, appears to the left of the window in the infrared image. In the final composition, Dou replaced the curtain with an arch.[8] Infrared reflectography reveals significant pentimenti in *The Young Mother* as well. A significant pentimento, the head of the maid sitting next to the crib was turned in a different direction (fig. 4).[9]

Pentimenti in the signature are clearly visible when *The Young Mother* is viewed with a stereo microscope. The signature is composed of two paint layers, one somewhat black, the other brownish. Dou apparently changed the date from 1653 to 1658, which would indicate that he kept the painting in his studio over several years and reworked it.[10]

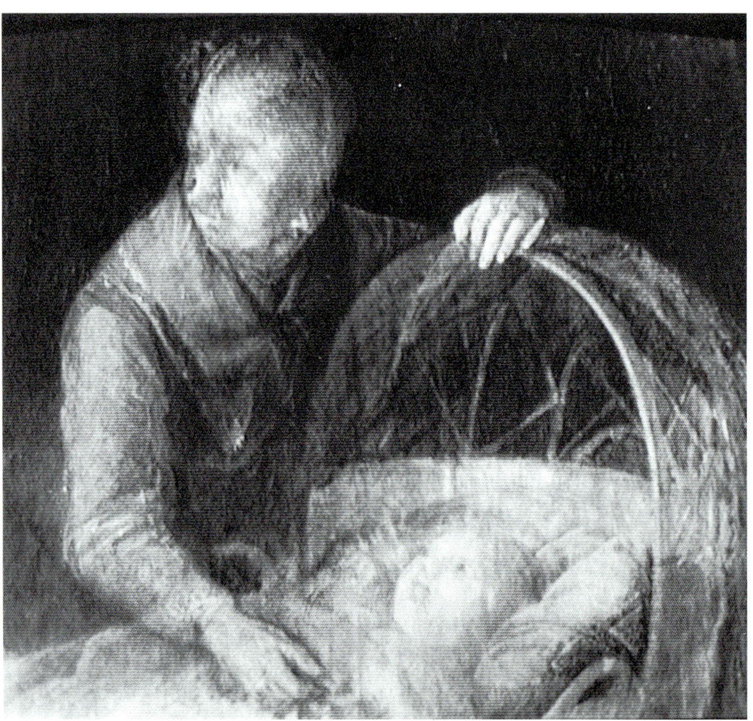

FIGURE 4
Infrared reflectogram (detail) showing alteration of the maid's head in *The Young Mother*

The changes discovered in these two works suggest that although Dou executed his paintings to a high degree of finish, he was uncertain about the compositions at a preliminary stage of the painting process. Infrared reflectography indicates that this first, "dead-coloring stage" (most clearly visible in *Lady at Her Toilet*) was executed with loose brushwork. Cross sections reveal a light-colored gray layer on top of the imprimatura. It is difficult to establish with any certainty at what stage of the painting process Dou made his compositional changes, although we know that Dou often kept his paintings in his studio for years and that he executed paintings over a long period.[11]

Irregularities in the texture of the paint surface of Dou's paintings often provide clues to earlier stages of their composition. In *The Quack* (cat. 19), for example, the portrait of the artist leaning out of the window on the right may be a later addition. Although no underdrawings for this figure were detected by infrared reflectography, loosely applied brushwork is visible, which may represent the dead-coloring stage of this work. Since Dou did not leave reserves for the many figures in this complicated scene, many contours overlap.[12]

· *Supports* Dou uniformly chose wood for his support and preferred single panels to avoid joins that might disrupt the high level of his finish.[13] The support of *Lady at Her Toilet* is a single, rectangular panel of oak, radially cut, and beveled at three sides. The support of *The Young Mother* is also a single oak plank, radially cut, and slightly beveled along the arched top.[14] No dendrochronological information exists regarding the panels that form the supports of *Lady at Her Toilet* or *The Young Mother*, but dendrochronological analyses of other panels used by Dou often indicate a felling that substantially precedes the execution of the paintings themselves (see, for example, cat. 34).

· *Ground* The ground of both paintings is composed of a very thin layer of chalk, so thin that it is mainly present in the hollows of the wood grain. The imprimatura layer above the ground in *Lady at Her Toilet* consists of a thick layer of lead white and chalk with varying amounts of ochre, umber, and black. The color of the imprimatura in *The Young Mother* is less consistent, composed of lead white and chalk, with various additions of red ochre and black.[15]

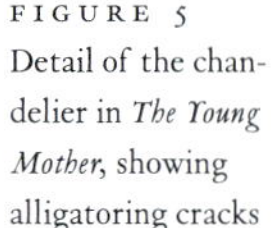

FIGURE 5
Detail of the chandelier in *The Young Mother*, showing alligatoring cracks

FIGURE 6
Wrinkling paint in the yellow foreground of *Lady at Her Toilet*

· *Craquelure* The two paintings contain a variety of craquelure patterns. In *Lady at Her Toilet*, very fine craquelure appears in the curtain at the window and in the painted sky. Areas of the dark background in both paintings are difficult to make out because of the wide craquelure, associated with the use of bitumen. Crow's feet and alligatoring cracks also appear in the red curtain and silver chandelier in *The Young Mother* (fig. 5); the paint has wrinkled in the light yellow foreground of *Lady at Her Toilet* (fig. 6) and above the window in *The Young Mother*.[16]

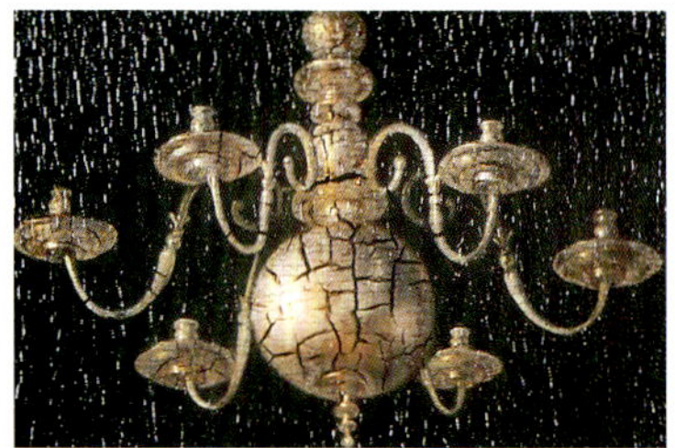

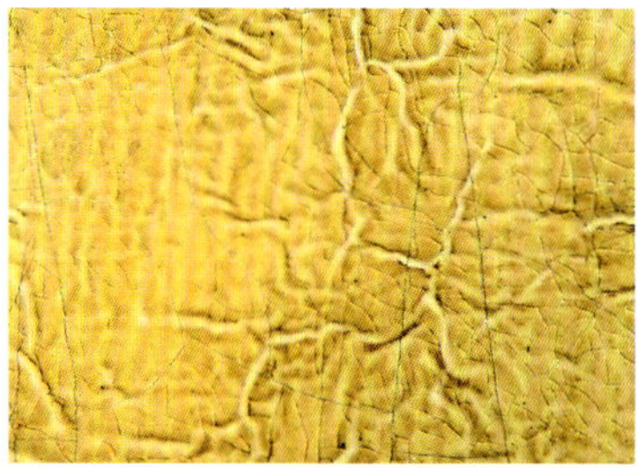

· *Cross Sections* Cross sections were taken from both paintings to investigate several questions about the composition and the application of Dou's paint.[17] What caused the disrupted surfaces in paintings executed by a master renowned for his meticulous technique? What explains the complexity of the paint layers? What caused the discoloration of the blue paint in *The Young Mother*? Are the wide drying cracks evident in many areas of the paintings attributable to Dou's use of dark-brown pigments? Have the red paint layers also changed with time?

The cross sections reveal that Dou used multiple paint layers in executing these works. As many as twelve layers, all of different thickness, have been identified with the aid of ultraviolet light. Most pigments are very finely ground, especially the blue, which in most cases is ultramarine. Brown-colored layers of varying transparency lie between the ground and the upper paint layers in all of the samples.

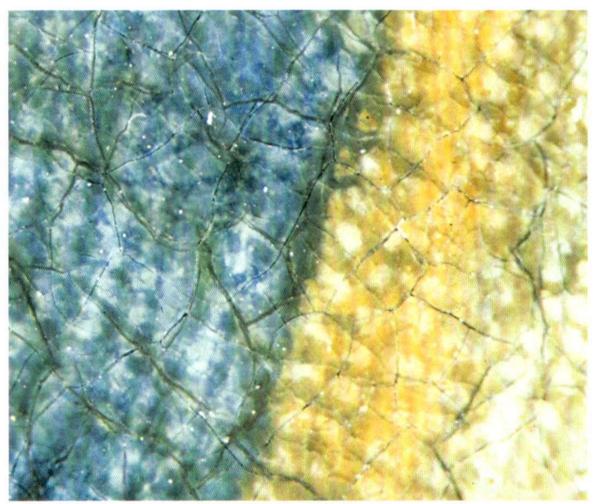

FIGURE 7
Photomicrograph of the blue curtain in *Lady at Her Toilet*

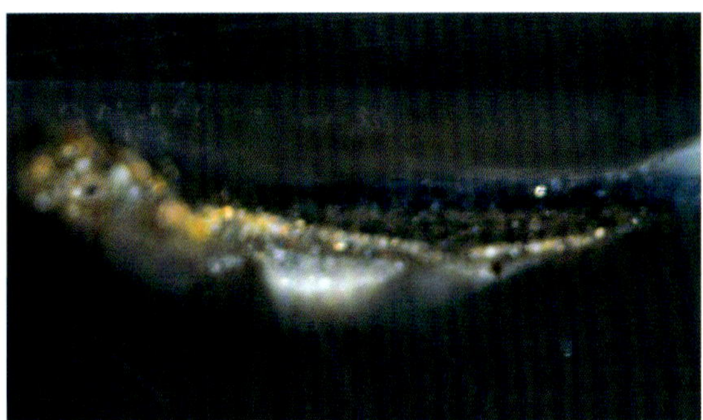

FIGURE 8
Cross section (200 x) taken from the blue curtain in *Lady at Her Toilet*

· *Dou's Use of Color* Warm reds, ochres, and yellows—beautifully preserved—dominate the palette of *Lady at Her Toilet*, and Dou captures the surface effects of the different fabrics—the silk skirt, the velvet jacket with the white fur trimming, and even the little silk slippers—with remarkable skill. Dou creates the illusionistic effect of a heavily woven and patterned curtain with tiny dots of paint in different colors placed next to one another (fig. 7). The bright green used for the leathered wall rarely appears in Dou's palette but is here remarkably well preserved.

The tonality of *The Young Mother* is cooler than that of *Lady at Her Toilet*. It is dominated by blues and grays, accented by the silver chandelier that hangs almost at the center of the composition. The objects in the foreground are painted to a high degree of finish. In particular, the earthenware pot, the copper lantern, and the bird's feathers create the illusion of reality so often noted by Dou's chroniclers.

BLUE The blue pigment that Dou used in these paintings is finely ground ultramarine. In *Lady at Her Toilet*, the blue is beautifully preserved and maintains its bright, deep color. A cross section taken from the curtain hanging over the window shows a thick, blue pigmented layer lying above a number of dark paint layers (fig. 8). Under ultraviolet light, the blue layer fluoresces intensely: bright blue particles are visible in a yellow-white matrix. Analysis of the binding medium reveals the presence of protein, which suggests that Dou used a water-based binder.[18] Artists of the period recognized that ultramarine retained its color better in a water-based medium than in oil.[19] In *The Young Mother*, the blues in the curtain, the mother's skirt, and the cradle blanket have faded to a pale gray.[20] The blue in a cross section taken from the cradle blanket fluoresces when viewed under ultraviolet light—much as it does in the cross section taken from *Lady at Her Toilet*—suggesting that Dou used a water-based binding medium in the earlier painting as well. The blue in the blanket resembles small drops of paint, regularly spaced to imitate a fabric weave (fig. 9); it is uncertain how Dou applied the paint to achieve this effect.[21]

A scumble of opaque, grayish paint covers the dark backgrounds of both paintings.[22] A cross section taken from *Lady at Her Toilet* shows a thin, half-transparent layer of discolored ultramarine lying on top of multiple dark paint layers.[23] Dou may have applied this thin layer of ultramarine to create an impression of atmospheric distance.

YELLOW A cross section taken from the yellow-ochre foreground of *Lady at Her Toilet*, where wrinkling appears (fig. 10), reveals that the uppermost and thickest yellow layer is in fact composed of seven thin layers containing lead-tin yellow and ochre, some of which are more opaque than others. Under the yellow layer is a thick, dark red-brown transparent layer, which contains red ochre, brown ochre or amber, Cassel earth, black, and lead white. Two layers of light gray lie between this dark layer and the ground. These gray layers are perfectly flat, while the upper layers have a meandering distortion that corresponds to the wrinkling seen on the surface. The cross section taken from the area with the blue scumble demonstrates that brown, medium-rich underlayers have also pushed through the upper paint layers (figs. 11a, 11b). A cross section taken from a crack in the lantern in *The Young Mother* shows the same meandering paint layers; here, the dark paint has also pushed through the upper white-colored layer.

This wrinkling and the wide cracks may have been caused by inadequate drying of the paint in the accretion of multiple layers; alternatively, these phenomena may have been the result of Dou's choice of materials, including Cassel earth and bituminous paint,[24] particularly when he applied so many layers of paint one after another. There is no doubt, however, that earlier restorations of the two paintings have adversely affected the paint layers.[25]

Analyses of the binding medium in the yellow paint of *Lady at Her Toilet* reveal the presence of walnut oil and linseed oil. Walnut oil is slow drying and was recommended in treatises of the period for rendering opaque or light-colored areas. It yellows to a lesser degree than do other oils and produces a stiffer-bodied paint useful for highlights.[26] Dou also used linseed oil in the brown-red layers of both paintings, and he may have added lead as a drier.[27]

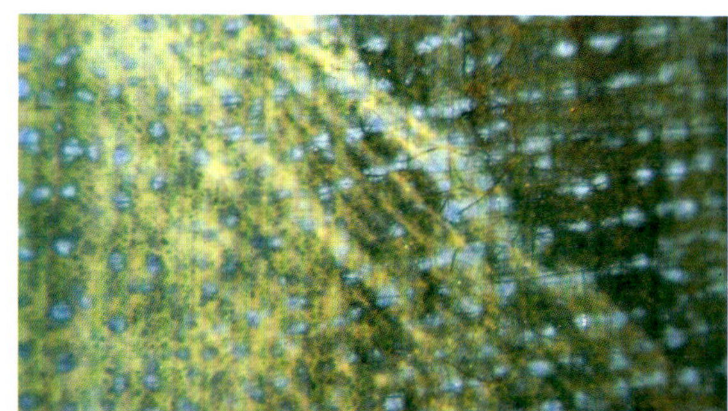

FIGURE 9
Ultraviolet light photograph of cross section (500 x) taken from the crib blanket of *The Young Mother*

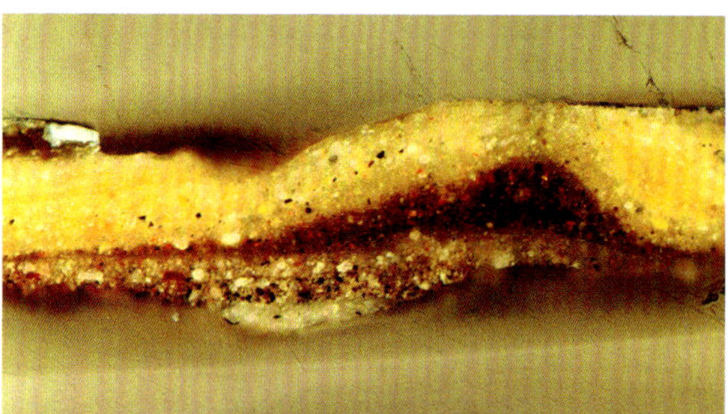

FIGURE 10
Cross section (500 x) taken from the foreground of *Lady at Her Toilet*. Dark underpaints, which may have caused the distortion, are visible; a gray, dead-coloring state lies under the brown layers.

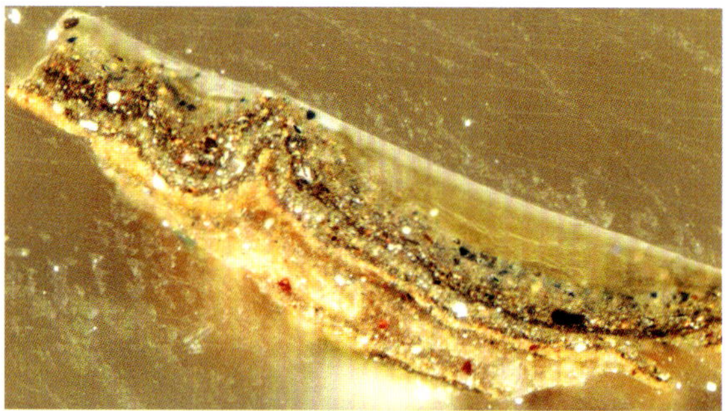

FIGURE 11A
Cross section (200 x) taken from the dark background of *Lady at Her Toilet* showing wide cracks and the blue-gray scrumble on top; meandering dark underpainting is visible. The imprimatura and a gray colored layer, somewhat flatter, can be detected. No ground is apparent.

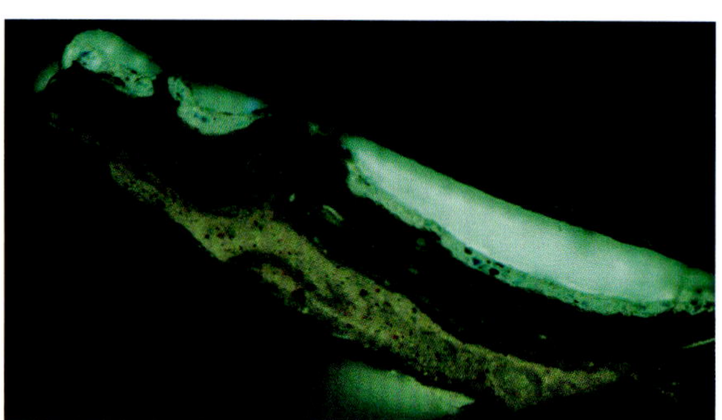

FIGURE 11B
Same cross section (200 x) in ultraviolet light. Blue pigment particles are visible at the surface on the top layer. The light matrix indicates that a water-based medium was used for the blue pigment. The dark underpaints have pushed up the top layer.

BROWN AND RED UNDERLAYERS All the cross sections taken from the two paintings contain brown or red underlayers. Dou's use of Cassel earth in these underlayers may be attributable to its slow drying properties, but his use of these brown-red layers may well have been purely aesthetic. Cassel, or Cologne, earth (also called Van Dyck brown in the 1800s), was widely used during the sixteenth and seventeenth centuries because of its beautiful, deep red-black color.[28] Such dark underlayers intensified the colors of the upper paint layers.

RED AND RED LAKES No cross sections were taken from the red surface-layers of *The Young Mother* and *Lady at Her Toilet*, but it is apparent in cross sections taken from other areas of the two paintings that Dou used a great deal of red pigment, clearly visible in x-radiography, in the underlayers. Although the composition of this pigment has not been established, it may be vermilion or red mercury sulfide. Dou used grays and dark colors for the dead-coloring stage, for painting the first part of the composition, and for creating dark and light contrasts. Red may have served to overpaint areas where he sought to change the composition.[29]

In *Lady at Her Toilet*, both the bright red of the jacket and the red of the chair seat have faded. A bluish gray haze can be seen on the seat of the chair, and a similar grayish paint layer is visible in the pleats of the jacket. Remnants of a dark red glaze were revealed during removal of overpaint in the restoration treatment (fig. 12). These glazes were protected from light by the overpaint and have not faded. The colors of these remnants indicate that the rest of the chair's seat was originally a dark, warm deep red, possibly an organic lake.

An artistic rationale clearly lay behind Dou's choice of binding media and pigments in *The Young Mother* and *Lady at Her Toilet*. Dou chose specific binding media for different colors, most often in accordance with the practices of other seventeenth-century Dutch painters. The application of paint, consisting of multiple paint layers, is characteristic of Dou's painting technique. The buildup of so many layers contributes to the brilliance of Dou's surface, but it has also played a part in creating the extremely wide craquelure and wrinkling that often disrupts his surfaces. We can conclude from analysis of the two paintings that the drying process had a dramatic impact on the eventual appearances of many of Dou's works. No records of remarks by visitors to Dou's studio mention these disturbed surfaces. Indeed, Dou's meticulous manner of painting was consistently noted and praised by his contemporaries. Whether the pronounced wrinkling in Dou's paintings was obscured by heavy layers of varnish or whether it developed only at a later time remains uncertain.

Analysis of *The Young Mother* and *Lady at Her Toilet* also demonstrates that Dou often worked on his paintings over a long period, either to achieve specific aesthetic effects or to satisfy his own compositional demands (or perhaps those imposed upon him by his patrons). Whatever the reasons, Dou made many compositional changes with remarkably loose brushwork in the initial stages of his working process.

However sophisticated our techniques of analysis, we may never be able to fully reconstruct Dou's working method. Many questions remain unanswered, in particular, the extent to which Dou's technique differed from that of his pupils, including Frans van Mieris and other Leiden *fijnschilders*. Additional technical research into Dou's oeuvre and the paintings of his contemporaries may enable us to determine the extent to which Dou's practice is typical of fine painters. Until then, it may be enough simply to marvel at the beauty of Dou's paintings and wonder at the skill of the artist's hand, as Philips Angel, Jan Orlers, and Joachim von Sandrart did nearly three and a half centuries ago.

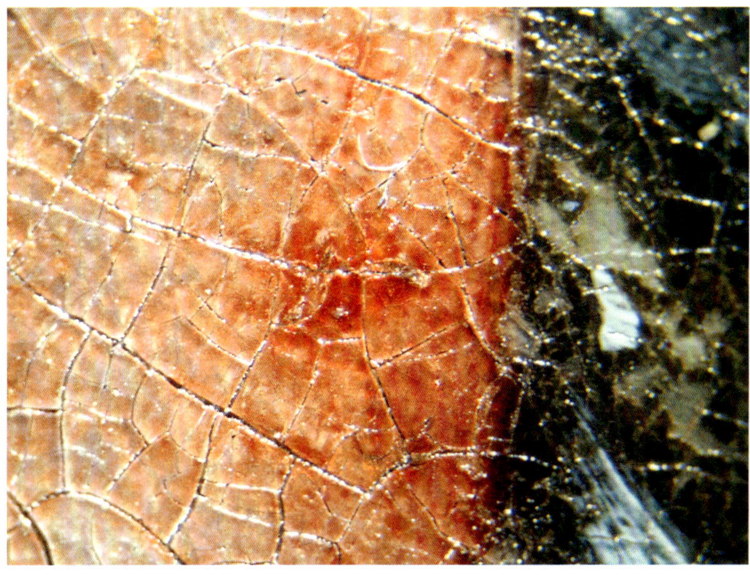

FIGURE 12
Photomicrograph of the seat of the foreground chair in *Lady at Her Toilet*. The deep red glaze, now largely discolored, is still discernible on a small spot.

Notes

I would like to thank Jeroen Giltaij, chief curator of Old Master paintings at the Museum Boijmans van Beuningen, Rotterdam, for suggesting this article and for his comments on it; the conservation department of the Mauritshuis, The Hague, for their help and support; and especially my colleague Elisabeth Reissner, who helped improve my written English and gave good advice on the article's content. I have also benefited from the research on *The Young Mother* carried out by Karin Groen and Luuk Struick van der Loeff, and from research on *Lady at Her Toilet* carried out by the Instituut Collectie Nederland (Netherlands Institute for Cultural Heritage), Amsterdam.

1 For discussion of the two works, see Broos 1987, 111–118; Lammertse 1998, 69–72. Baer 1990 has provided important information for this article.

2 Struick van der Loeff and Groen 1993; Struick van der Loeff 1987.

3 See restoration report, *Lady at Her Toilet*, curatorial files, Museum Boijmans van Beuningen, Rotterdam.

4 On Dou's use of illusionistic curtains and stone arches, see Sluijter 1993, 43–46; Amsterdam 1989, 40–45.

5 As Eric Jan Sluijter (1993, 46–48) emphasizes, Dou carefully considered the arrangement of light and dark in his paintings. This concern accords with the writings of Philips Angel, who writes that, to suggest reality, light must be painted "by properly arranging both the shade and light together. It is the same with a scattered band of soldiers. . . . They can have no hope of victory unless they come together and apply their concerted strength to achieve victory by force. So is it with our divided shadows, which cannot capture the eye of art-lovers while they are scattered. . . ." Angel 1996, 244 [=Angel 1642, 39–40: "wanneer wy de schaduwe, en het licht, ghesamentlijck met goerde orderen by een gheschickt hebben: want dit gaet hier even toe, als het met een *Bende* verspreyde *Soldaten*. . . . toe gaet, dewelcke gheen macht tot overwinninghe en konnen hopen, ten zy dat sy by een rotten ende alle macht ghesstamentlicken toe brengehn, om soo door ghewelt de overwinninge te bekomen. . . ."

6 Houbraken 1753, 1–4. Jeroen Giltaij (Rotterdam 1991) discovered pinholes positioned at vanishing points in several architectural paintings by Gerard Houckgeest (c. 1600–1661) and Pieter Saenredam (1597–1665). See also Wadum 1995, 67–79, for a discussion of pinholes in Vermeer's paintings. For Dou, see Baer 1990, 44. Several theories seek to explain Dou's perspective technique. He may have used the same method as Vermeer, attaching strings to a pin placed at the vanishing point. For a discussion of Dou's probable use of mechanical devices as artistic aids, see Wheelock 1978, 64–65.

7 Lammertse 1997, 111–121.

8 On the arch motif in Dou's oeuvre, see Sluijter 1993, 43–46.

9 A carbon black underdrawing is also visible in the folds of the mother's skirt. See Struick van der Loeff and Groen 1993, 100.

10 Struick van der Loeff and Groen 1993, 100. See also Broos 1987, 117 note 1.

11 Regarding the compositional changes, see Lammertse 1997, 114–116. Dou's 1663 *Self-Portrait* (cat. 27) is signed twice and dated once. X-radiography of the painting shows pentimenti, which, in combination with the two signatures, suggest that Dou returned to it after a period of time.

12 *The Quack* (cat. 19) is also signed twice and dated once—to 1652. The tower depicted in the background was added to the composition later: the tower itself—which marked the limits of the city of Leiden—was not finished until 1667, fifteen years after the signature date.

Further infrared reflectography examinations of Dou's paintings are being carried out by Jørgen Wadum, head of conservation at the Mauritshuis, The Hague.

13 It is uncertain where, or for how long, Dou stored the panels or when he started to work on them. Jørgen Wadum is pursuing research on this subject.

The large plank that Dou used for *The Quack* (cat. 19) is a single piece of Spanish cedar (*Cedrela odorata*), a fine-grained wood, native to Central America and Brazil, that takes a smooth finish; such planks were likely constituents of packing crates: *Cedrela odorata* is also popularly known as sugar- or cigar-box wood. See Lammertse 1997, 111–112.

14 On Dou's use of the arched top, see Sluijter 1993, 43–46.

15 See Struick van der Loeff and Groen 1993, 101.

16 Struick van der Loeff and Groen 1993, 101.

17 The research was carried out at the Instituut Collectie Nederland, Amsterdam, by Karin Groen (microscopy and rapportage), Muriel Geldolf (microscopy), Henk van Keulen (gas chromatography/mass spectometry), Suzan de Groot (Fourier-transform infrared spectroscopy). Also involved were Georgana Languri, Klaas Jan van den Berg, and Jaap Boon (direct temperature-resolved mass spectometry) at the Foundation for Fundamental Research on Matter (FOM), Utrecht (see MOLART Report no. 98.004 [September 1998]); and Kees Mensch (scanning electron microscopy/energy dispersive x-ray analyzer) at the Shell Research and Technology Centre, Maastricht.

18 It is likely that Dou did not use oil as a medium in this area out of concern that oil would darken over time and affect the color of the blue.

19 This color fading is commonly called "ultramarine sickness." However, ultramarine itself usually retains its bright blue color over time. The fading is caused by deterioration in the binding medium, which, in turn, affects the reflective index of the paint surface and, therefore, its appearance. See Groen 1993, 8–10.

20 The change of color in this case is the result of deterioration of the binding medium. Hairline cracks, visible with a microscope, have affected the reflective index of the paint surface. This condition may have been caused by excessive humidity in the air, or may have been the result of an earlier restoration.

21 See Struick van der Loeff and Groen 1993, 101. Similarly textured paint can be seen in Dou's *Kitchenmaid at a Window* (1652) (page 38, fig. 13).

22 "Scumble" designates the softening or blending of an outline or color with a thinly applied uppercoat of opaque color.

23 The presence of blue particles in the topmost layer of the paint, just beneath the varnish layer, may indicate that the paint was regenerated in an earlier restoration treatment; see Schmitt 1990.

24 A sample taken from *Lady at Her Toilet* included traces of phenol, which suggests the presence of a lignite material, most likely Cassel earth. Although bituminous paint was not detected, it should be noted that bituminous material is very difficult to identify in a sample. (See the conclusion of the FOM, MOLART report no. 98.004 [September 1998].) In 1986, Raymond White, of the National Gallery of London, carried out gas chromatography/mass spectometry analyses on *The Young Mother* and found asphaltic/bituminous material in the paint (unpublished report in Mauritshuis curatorial files). (In technical literature, the terms "asphalt" and "bitumen" are interchangeable, although asphalt is more often used.) See White 1986, 58–71.

25 *The Young Mother* has a long restoration history, dating back to 1815.

26 White and Kirby 1994, 64–78. It is likely that painters associated with the School of Rembrandt ground their lead-white pigment in walnut oil and then added linseed oil. Boiled linseed oil was used for impastos and to dry pigments such as lakes, blacks, and possibly Cassel earth.

27 Analysis of *Lady at Her Toilet* using scanning electronic microscopy/energy dispersive x-radiography detected lead in all paint layers.

28 Robert L. Feller and Ruth M. Johnston-Feller, "Vandyke Brown," in Fitzhugh 1997, 157–190. Most seventeenth-century painters gained their knowledge about the quality and drying properties of pigments from treatises. Asphalt was recommended for glazes in the upper layer of paint. Van de Graaf 1958, 58–60, nos. 25, 28, 29, and 30 (fols. 84, 92 v, 94 [r and v], 95 [r and v]). The color was particularly valued for depicting shadows and for glazing. De Mayerne (in Van de Graaf 1958) mentions preparing asphalt-containing paint by adding siccative made from oil with lead (*glit*). The ground asphalt was added to heated oil.

29 Wadum 1994, 11–13.

1.

Artist in His Studio

c. 1630–1632; oil on panel; 59 x 43.5 (23 1/4 x 17 1/8); Colnaghi, London

· *Provenance* (Charles Sedelmeyer, Paris, by 1894). John Wanamaker, Philadelphia and New York; G. F. Plympton, Hackensack, N.J.; (sale, Sotheby's, New York, 17 June 1982 [no. 118]); Frank Martelli, Bel Air, Calif.; (sale, Sotheby's, New York, 19 May 1994 [no. 33]).

· *Bibliography* Martin 1901, no. 114; Hofstede de Groot 1907, no. 311; Martin 1911, no. 235; Martin 1913, 12; Raupp 1984, 276–277; Baer 1990, no. 6; Sumowski 1994, 3525.

· *Exhibitions* Melbourne and Sydney 1997, no. 39.

· The thin, broad application of paint and the purplish brown of the sitter's coat and greenish blue of the tablecloth are characteristic of Dou's early style. Many of the motifs—the propped-up book, the globe, the pen, and the inkstand—appear in other early works by Dou, such as *Man Writing by an Easel* (cat. 3), and *Man Interrupted at His Writing* (cat. 4). In fact, *Artist in His Studio* has much in common with the latter work, especially in its use of chiaroscuro to create an almost palpable atmosphere that envelops the figure and the objects.

The sitter in this painting was identified as Rembrandt by Cornelis Hofstede de Groot and as Dou by Willem Martin; however, his features bear no resemblance to either. The composition owes an unmistakable debt to Rembrandt's *A Young Painter in His Studio* (fig. 1). The monochromatic palette, enlivened by the swath of greenish blue, the unmodulated application of paint, and the strong chiaroscuro are common to both paintings. Dou's artist, like Rembrandt's, holds palette and brushes, and the easel is turned from the viewer's gaze. Rembrandt does not depict a particular individual but, like Dou, offers a generic representation of "The Painter."

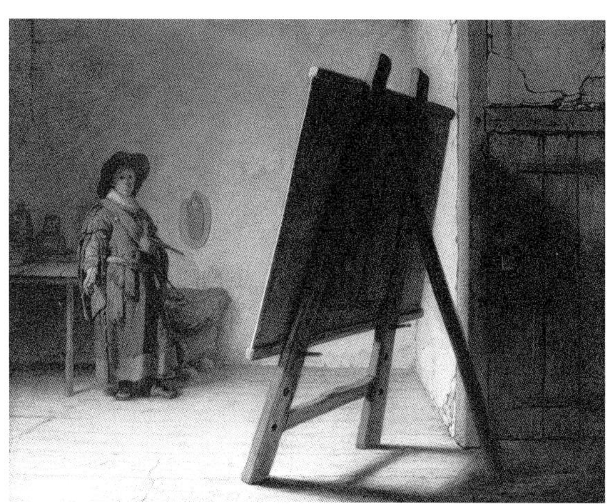

FIGURE 1
Rembrandt van Rijn, *Artist in His Studio*, c. 1627/1628, oil on panel, courtesy Museum of Fine Arts, Boston, Zoe Oliver Collection. Given in memory of Lillie Oliver Poor.

Differences in the artists' compositions, however, are indicative of their contrasting approaches to their art. Rembrandt's painter, his face in shadow, is dwarfed by a looming easel that dominates an otherwise barely furnished space. Dou's focus is clearly the accurate and beautiful rendering of an abundance of surfaces and materials. Care is lavished equally on the painter, who gazes directly at the viewer, and the still-life elements.

In contrast to Rembrandt's painting, Dou's composition is filled with objects, some simply studio props. However, many of the objects depicted—the globe, the plaster cast (a similar one appears in Dou's later self-portraits), the skull, the lute, the books, the sword—were traditionally associated with the idea of *vanitas*, the ephemerality of life. Dou may have included these symbols of transience within his composition to contrast with the artist's achievements, which are lasting (*ars longa vita brevis*). This argument is reinforced by similarities between Dou's *Artist in His Studio* and Thomas de Keyser's *Portrait of David Bailly* (c. 1627, see page 34, fig. 8), a work that has been interpreted as elevating the painter-craftsman to the status of gentleman and humanist and praising art's permanence in the face of transient nature.[1] Indeed, *Artist in His Studio* virtually lifts a number of elements from De Keyser's portrait—the sword hanging on the wall, the lute, the skull, the scroll, and the position of the subject (represented in full length) before the table.[2] Dou's engagement with De Keyser's portrait extended beyond *Artist in His Studio*: the sitter, David Bailly, was a Leiden painter whose influence is evident in Dou's later portraits and still lifes.

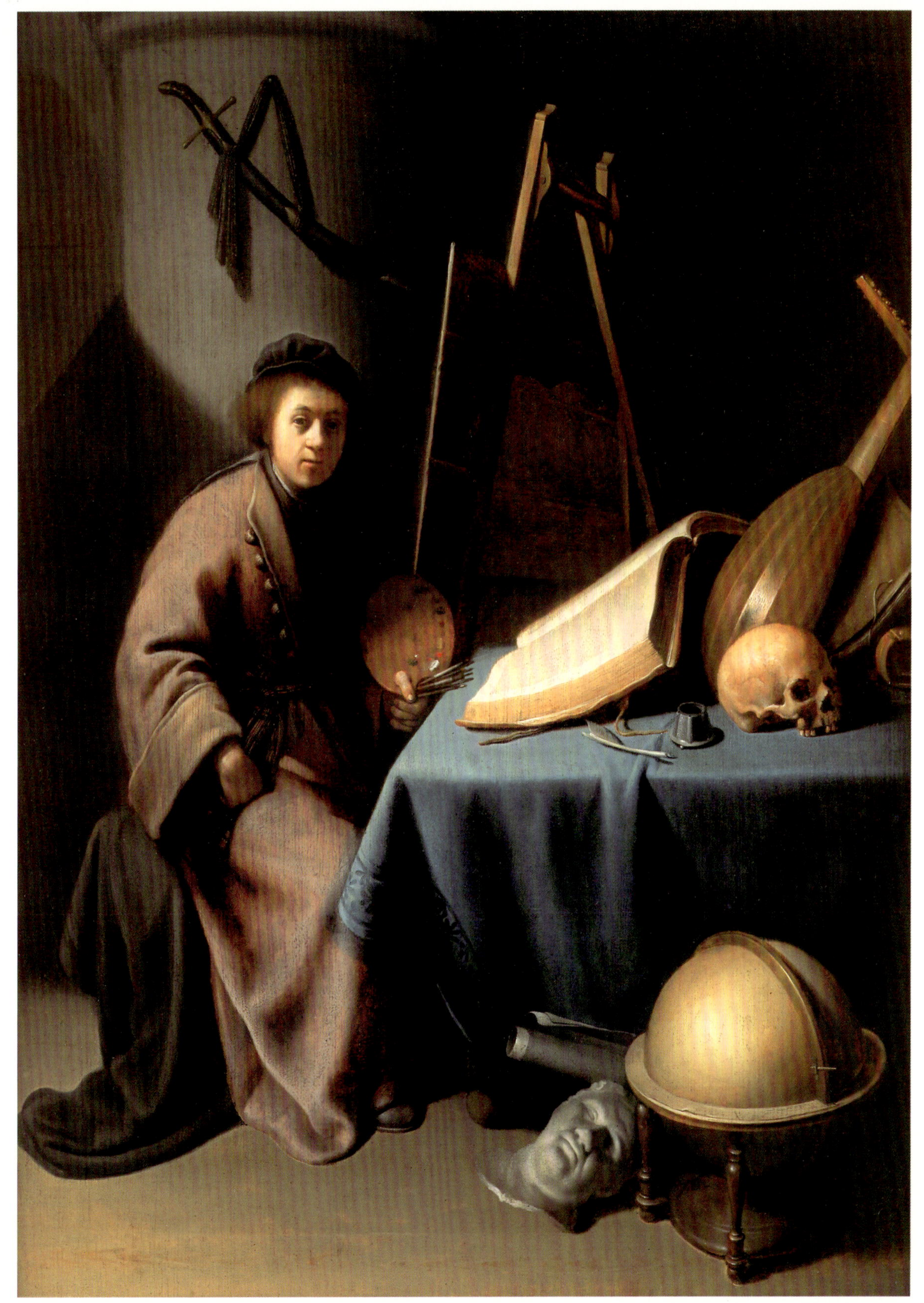

2.

Old Woman Reading

c. 1631–1632; oil on panel; 71 x 55.5 (27 7/8 x 21 7/8); Rijksmuseum, Amsterdam

· *Provenance* C. Hoekwater, The Hague, by 1907; bequest of A. H. Hoekwater, 1912.

· *Bibliography* Moes 1897, no. 9404; Martin 1901, no. 188; Hofstede de Groot 1907, no. 352; Martin 1911, no. 95; Martin 1913, 37; Rotermund 1957, 134; Plietzsch 1960, 38; Rosenberg and Slive 1966, 86; Rijksmuseum 1976 (no. A2627); Alpers 1983, 188; Sumowski 1983, 1: no. 245; Baer 1990, no. 8; Sumowski 1994, 3595.

· This large rectangular picture of an old woman reading is the most imposing of several depictions of the subject painted by Dou early in his career. The painting, which represents Dou's most direct artistic response to Rembrandt's early works, was executed at the time of his master's departure for Amsterdam. In its large size, relatively thick application of paint, and breadth of execution, the work is exceptional in Dou's early oeuvre. Dou has emphasized equally the character of the old woman's clothing, the distinguishing characteristics of her physiognomy, and the type of book from which she reads.

Representations of old women reading from Rembrandt's circle were probably intended as depictions of seers or prophetesses.[1] Dou's image may allude to the prophetess Hannah, whom the Bible described as serving God night and day in the Temple (Luke 2:37). Hans-Martin Rotermund identified the book as a Catholic lectionary, which the woman has open to Luke, chapter 19.[2] The lectionary is illustrated with a representation of Christ talking to Zacchaeus, who has climbed a tree to witness Jesus' entry into Jerusalem.

Though both Rembrandt and Dou used the same model when painting this subject,[3] they express the old woman's piety in different ways. Rembrandt's almost full-length figure, surrounded by an expanse of darkness, is bathed in a mysterious light (fig. 1). For his larger, half-length figure, Dou uses an almost even illumination, which picks out the wrinkles of her hand, the nap of her velour mantle, the print in the book, and the crow's feet around her eyes. Dou may have intended to emphasize the sitter's age by showing her lips slightly parted (as though she were mouthing the words to herself) and by positioning the book up close to her near-sighted eyes.

The difference in approach of the two artists may reveal an underlying difference in meaning of the two works. Dou's painting emphasizes the act of reading, whereas Rembrandt conveys spiritual understanding coming from the written word. This concept was expressed by Svetlana Alpers in another way: for Dou's woman, to see the text is to know it; for Rembrandt's, it is the Word within rather than the surface of the text that is to be valued.[4]

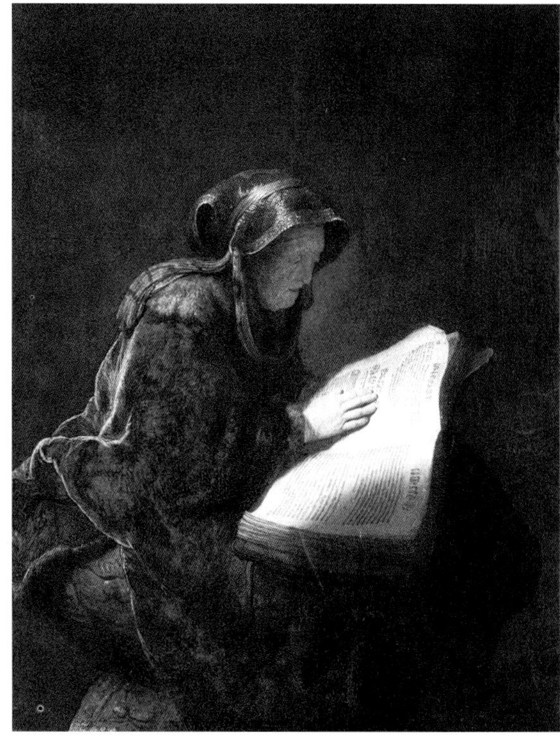

FIGURE 1
Rembrandt van Rijn, *Old Woman Reading*, 1631, oil on panel, Rijksmuseum, Amsterdam

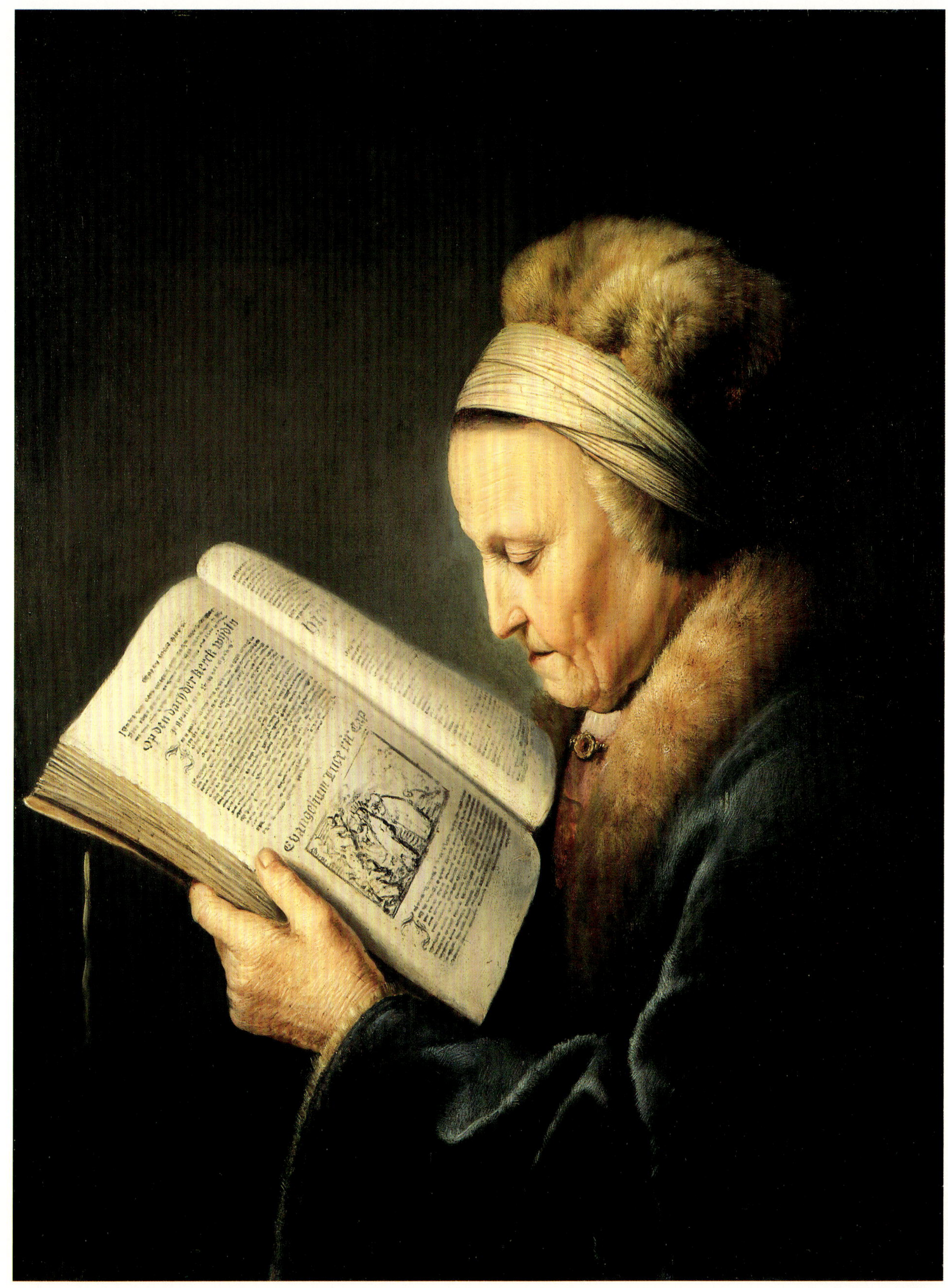

3.
Man Writing by an Easel

c. 1631–1632; oil on panel; 31.5 x 25 (12 3/8 x 9 7/8); private collection[1]

Signed on pages of book in background: GDov

· *Provenance* King William III, London. (G. Bicker van Zwieten sale, The Hague, 12 April 1741 [no. 67] [*f* 400, to Van Heteren]); Adriaen Leonard van Heteren, The Hague, 1752. Rijksmuseum, Amsterdam, 1809; (Rijksmuseum sale, Amsterdam, 4 August 1828 [no. 45] [*f* 510, to Brondgeest]). (Thomas Emmerson, London, by 1829); M. van der Potts. (Charles Brind sale, Christie's, London, 10 May 1849 [no. 65] [£96.12, to Chaplin]). Lord Northbrook, London, 1889 (no. 53). (Thomas Agnew, London, 1976); Michal Hornstein, Montreal; sold by Sotheby's, New York, to present owner, 1999.

· *Bibliography* J. Smith 1829, nos. 13 and 103; Martin 1901, no. 56; Hofstede de Groot 1907, no. 54; Martin 1911, no. 19; Martin 1913, 63; Bauch 1960, 218; Hunnewell 1983, 172–180; Sumowski 1983, 1: no. 267; Baer 1990, no. 9; Sumowski 1994, 3596.

· *Exhibitions* British Institution, London, 1848 (cat. untraced); Burlington Fine Arts Club, London, 1900, no. 27 (cat. untraced); Philadelphia, Berlin, and London 1984, no. 31; Berlin, Amsterdam, and London 1991, no. 56.

· *Man Writing by an Easel*, smaller than *Artist in His Studio* (cat. 1) or *Old Woman Reading* (cat. 2), can best be appreciated with the aid of a magnifying glass.[2] Dou used a tiny brush to describe the wrinkles in the old man's face, the shape of his ear, and the beads on his cap. He suggested the exposed brick of the wall at the left by using tonal variations applied with horizontal strokes. Despite the work's small scale and careful execution, Dou used surprisingly thick paint over much of the surface, a manner of painting that he probably learned in Rembrandt's workshop.[3] Dou may have adopted this controlled technique when he began painting small-scale genre scenes such as this work, *Old Woman Peeling Apples* (c. 1629–1631) (see above, page 33, fig. 6), and *Woman Eating Porridge* (c. 1628–1631) in a German private collection (Sumowski 1994, 3833 [no. 2248]). The unusual color combination of purple, blue, and aqua in large unmodulated areas is also typical of Dou's work in the early 1630s.

An accumulation of accessories defines the space as well as the themes of the painting. Even at this early date, Dou was a virtuoso in describing surfaces and the way they reflect light. In the background, a globe, Bible, and candlestick are visually joined to a violin hanging on the column by a swag of drapery. These studio props, which appear repeatedly in Dou's work, allude in a general sense to man's intellectual and artistic pursuits. Given the advanced age of the sitter in this work, they may also imply the vanity of such endeavors.

This painting resembles Dou's *Man Interrupted at His Writing* (cat. 4), both in the costume that the sitter wears and in the activity he pursues. As in *Artist in His Studio* (cat. 1), Dou here presents an image of the scholarly artist, although his emphasis is now on the "scholar" rather than on the "artist." Other authors have noted that the military objects in the right foreground could allude to the active life of the soldier and contrast with the contemplative, cerebral life of the scholar/artist.[4] This same type of symbolic contrast appears in *Old Man Lighting a Pipe* (cat. 5), and is an important device in the structural organization of Dou's early genre pictures.

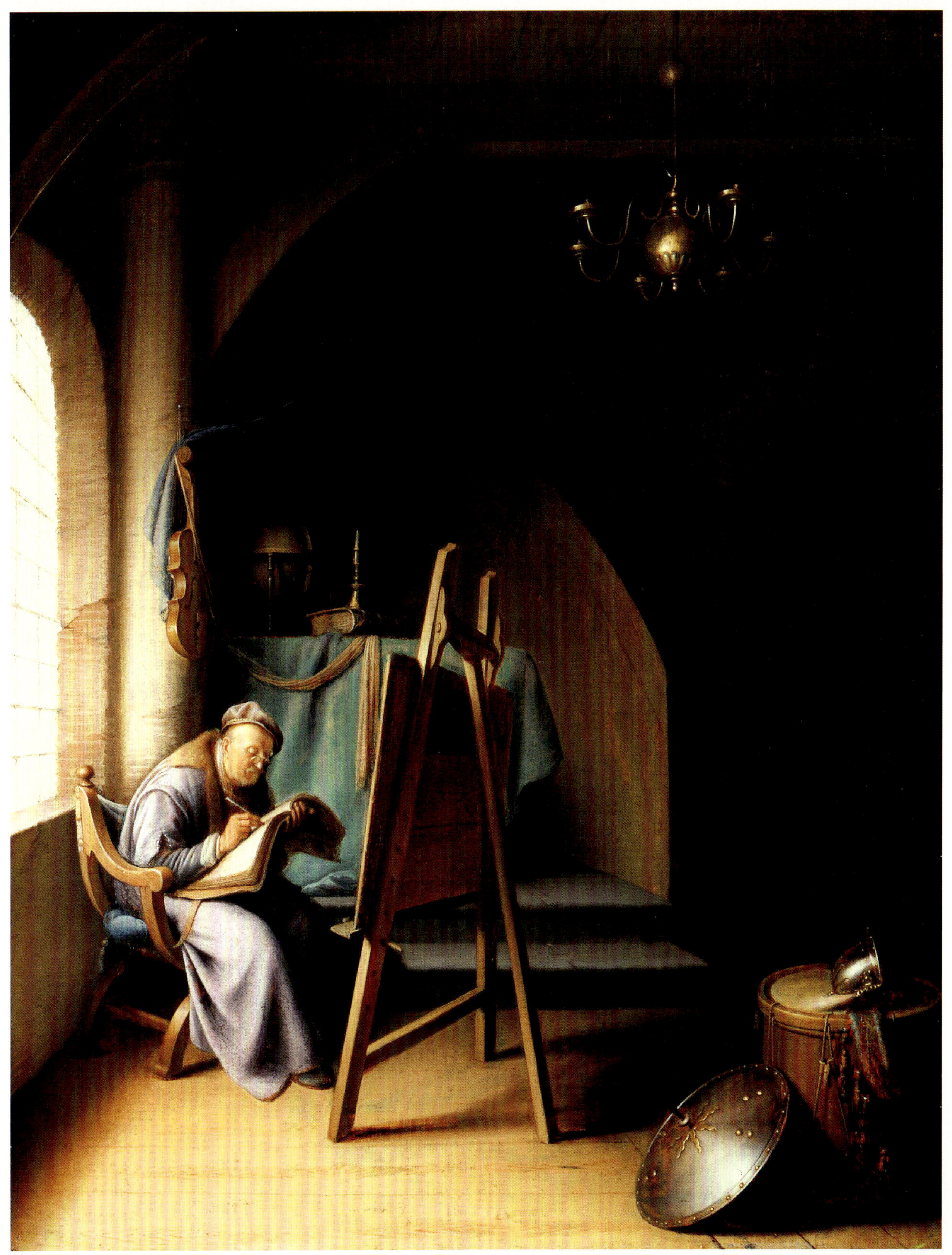

4.

Man Interrupted at His Writing

c. 1635, oil on panel; oval, 24 x 22.5 (9 ½ x 8 ⅞); Sudeley Castle Trustees, Winchcombe, Gloucestershire, Walter Morrison Collection

Signed on paper protruding from the book: GDov

· *Provenance* Probably Queen Christina of Sweden; probably returned to Pieter Spiering by Queen Christina, 1652 (no. 5). (Baron Nagel sale, Christie's, London, 21 March 1795 [£120.15]). (Creed sale, London, 1813 [£131.5, to John Smith] [not in Lugt]); (Smith sale [£262.10]). Edward Gray, London, in 1829. Charles Morrison, London, by 1854; by descent to present owner.

· *Bibliography* J. Smith 1829, no. 87; Waagen 1854–1857, 1: no. 262 (as pendant to Adriaen van Ostade's *Lawyer with a Velvet Cap, Reading*); Martin 1901, no. 57; Hofstede de Groot 1907, no. 55; Martin 1911, no. 20; Martin 1913, 62 (as a print); Baer 1990, no. 14.

· Dou first began depicting figures in arrested movement during the mid-1630s. A date of c. 1635 is further supported by the composition's dependence on Rembrandt's etched portrait of Johannes Uytenbogaert, dated 1635 (fig. 1). In both images, an elderly bearded man, in skullcap and fur-trimmed *tabbaard*,[1] is seated at a table before a large open book. The pictorial tradition of the scholar in his study underlies both works. Rembrandt treated the theme frequently in the first half of the 1630s,[2] and it enjoyed particular popularity in the university town of Leiden.[3] The placement of Dou's signature on a piece of paper protruding from the open book may also reflect Rembrandt's influence.[4]

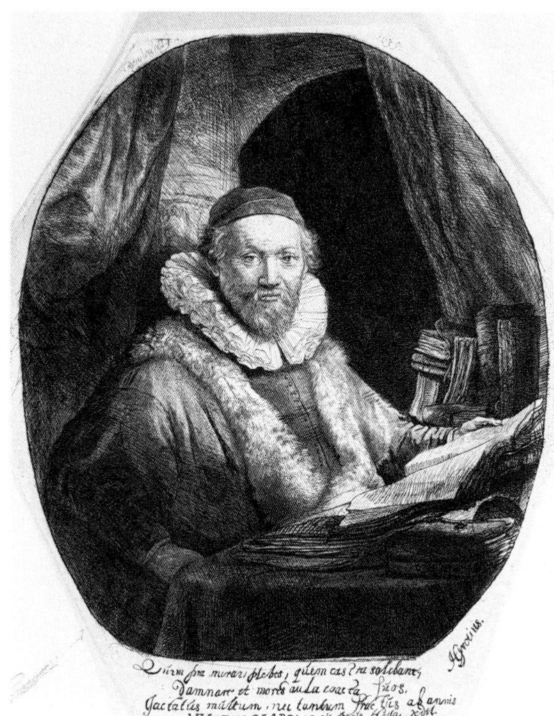

FIGURE 1
Rembrandt van Rijn, *Jan Uytenbogaert*, 1635, etching and burin, National Gallery of Art, Washington, Rosenwald Collection

As is often the case, Dou's image contains many more objects than do Rembrandt's paintings of similar subjects. The skull, hourglass, writing paraphernalia, and globe carry both *vanitas* and *studium* associations,[5] themes appropriate to the man's age and his activity. The birdcage, parasol, and water bottle behind the figure are studio props—opportunities for the artist to display his skill.

Dou achieves a beautiful *contre-jour* effect by placing the shadowed side of the man's face against the highlighted surface of the column. He also subtly focuses the compositional emphasis by varying his painting technique: the old man's wrinkles, for example, are carefully delineated; the form of the ear is suggested by broader strokes. Dou devoted careful and painstaking attention to rendering the still life, whose abundance nearly overwhelms the figure; individual pages of the large book are defined with long, thin, wavy brown lines, while the fabric of the tablecloth is unspecified. This type of selective emphasis in Dou's painting technique is evident in his contemporary portraits as well.

Dou has given the scholar an intensity of expression that bespeaks the figure's seriousness and concentration. His hunched form and the active position of his hands further emphasize his prior engagement in his work. The sudden interruption, implying the viewer's presence, is here the focus of his sharp glance. In this work, Dou established a device he would return to throughout his career: a moment of suspended movement that governs the painting's structure. Dou captured these fleeting impressions as masterfully as he rendered the various surfaces of the still-life objects.

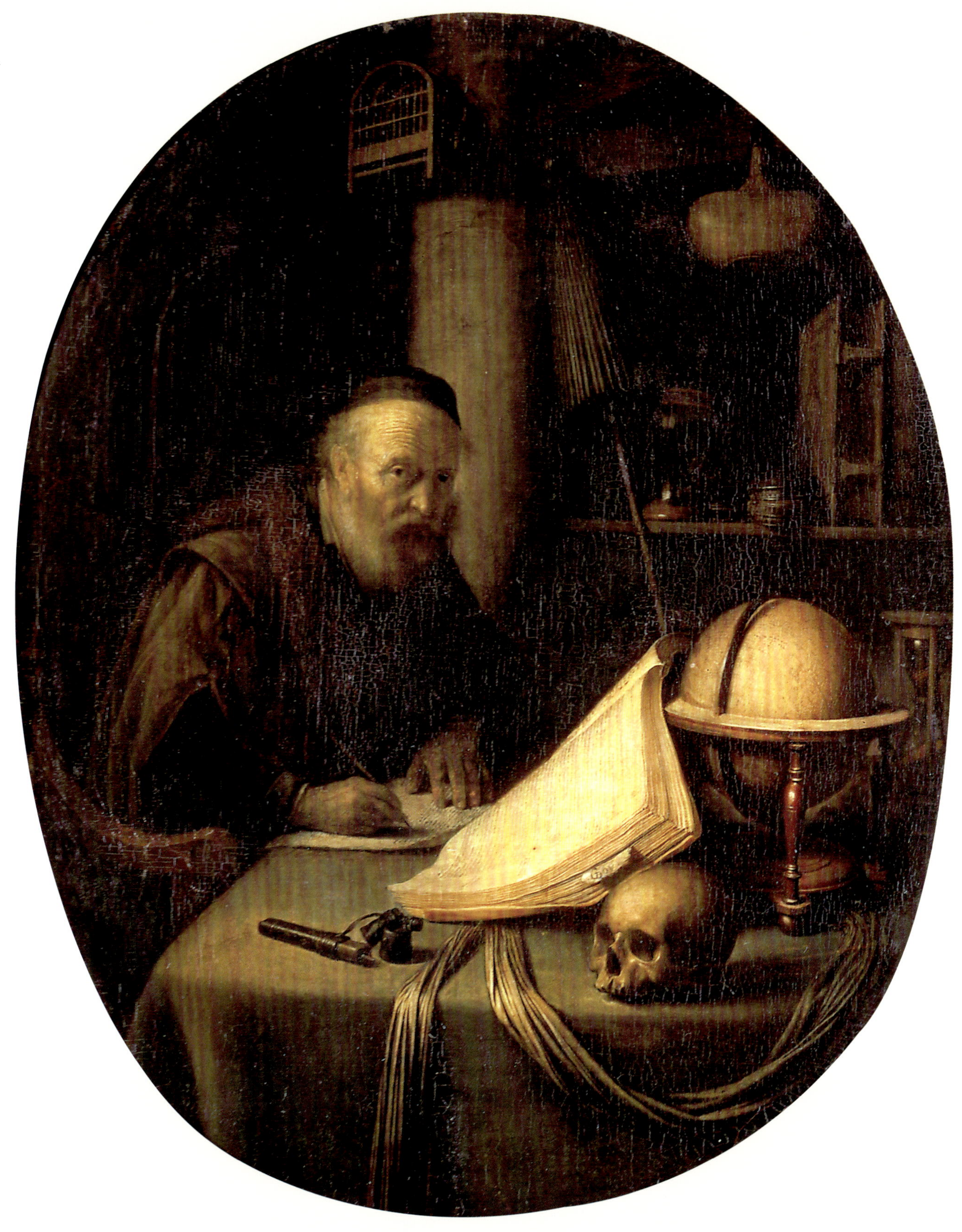

MAN INTERRUPTED AT HIS WRITING

5.

Old Man Lighting a Pipe

c. 1635; oil on panel; 49 x 61.5 (19 3/8 x 24 1/4); private collection, England

· *Provenance* Nostitz, Prague, by 1901. (sale, Christie's, London, 14 December 1990 [no. 111 to Johnny van Haeften, London]).

· *Bibliography* Martin 1901, no. 82 and page 194;[1] Hofstede de Groot 1907, no. 46; Martin 1911, no. 28; Martin 1913, 65, 180 (under S.12), 182; Sumowski 1983, 4: 2549 note 5; Sumowski 1994, no. 2247.

· Dou was in his early twenties when he painted *Old Man Lighting a Pipe.* The work bridges Dou's early genre imagery and the first phase of his artistic maturity, represented by works such as *An Interior with Young Violinist* of 1637 (cat. 8). Horizontal in its format and construction of space—a room divided vertically down the middle—the painting concentrates the elements of visual interest on one side (compare, for example, *Old Woman Peeling Apples* [c. 1629–1631] [above, page 33, fig. 6]). The broad expanses of unmodulated color, as well as the specific hues of purple in the figure's *tabbaard*[2] and blue in the table covering, are characteristic of Dou's early style. Like the contemporaneous *Man Interrupted at His Writing* (cat. 4), the work presents a strong impression of arrested movement; here also, Dou places equal emphasis on the figure and the still-life objects around him. Most of these objects—the pewter drinking vessel (*kan*), the large book with metal corners and clasps, the wicker basket, the globe, violin, pipe, and coal pan—also appear in the more elaborate image of a man seated at a table in *An Interior with Young Violinist.*

The elderly man in a heavy cloak lighting his pipe from a coal pan recalls traditional images of winter.[3] Many of the still-life objects in the image—the books and globe (indicating worldly pursuits), the violin (associated with the transitory strains of music), the smoke of the pipe, and the flask and basket on the floor (alluding to man's journey through life)—are reminders of the fleeting nature of earthly existence, a fitting theme for this depiction of an elderly man.

An air of serenity and studiousness pervades the painting. As in Dou's *Painter with Pipe and Book* (cat. 16), smoking provides the man with an opportunity for contemplation, a theme echoed in many of Dou's other works.[4] Though Dou later explored the dramatic effects of artificial illumination (see *The Wine Cellar,* cat. 23; *The Night School*, cat. 28), here it is the diffuse light from the window that defines the character of the domestic interior.

The sitter, often identified as Rembrandt's father, was among the most frequently depicted models in Leiden during the late 1620s and early 1630s. In addition to works by Rembrandt and Lievens, he also appears in several of Dou's early paintings.[5]

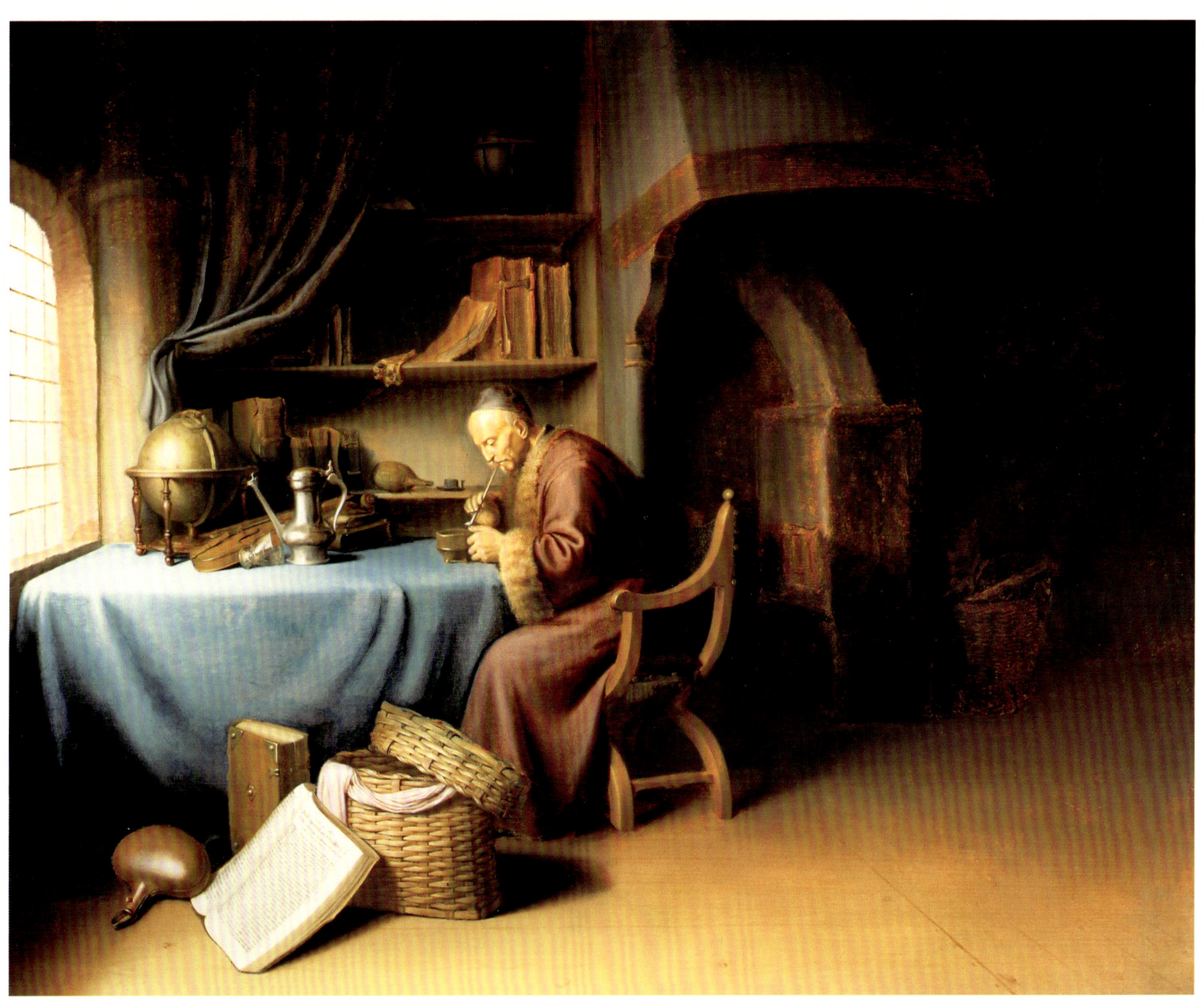

6.

Still Life with Globe, Lute, and Books

c. 1635; oil on panel; 22.5 x 30 (8 7/8 x 11 3/4); Mr. and Mrs. Michal Hornstein

· *Provenance* (Edward Speelman, London); (Galerie Bruno Meissner, Zurich, 1978).

· *Bibliography* Sumowski 1983, 1: no. 307; Baer 1990, no. 19; Sumowski 1994, 3598.

· *Exhibitions* Tokyo 1992, no. 33; Amsterdam and Cleveland 1999, no. 34.

· The conjunction of a lute seen from the back, a ragged portfolio and books, and a globe first appears in Dou's work in the *Artist in His Studio* (cat. 1). Here, the globe (with its text partly legible) and the broken binding on one of the volumes resemble those in the *Flute Player* of c. 1636 in the Proby Collection, Peterborough (Martin 1913, 82, left). The similarities to the Proby painting and the range of brown tones—rust, tan, chocolate, light brown, cream—that links this painting to other Dutch monochromatic works of the 1630s suggest a plausible dating to c. 1635.

The horizontal format is unusual in Dou's work and unique in his still lifes. The picture is meticulously executed, particularly in the rendering of the various surfaces. Alternating thin and thick strokes suggest the raggedness and the weight of the pages of the upright book; thin, calligraphic brushwork describes the volumes' bindings. Dou records the shadows cast by the objects with great care, and the objects themselves are less tightly enclosed within the space than they are in the pendant still lifes from 1647 (cats. 17 and 18). The subtly gradated and modulated background, which Dou used to similar effect in his contemporary head studies, creates an atmospheric perspective for the objects.

Werner Sumowski has interpreted this painting as expressing the incompatibility of faith and avarice, with the globe as a symbol of the visible world, the lute as the ideal of proportion, and the books as representing *vanitas* or salvation.[1] It seems less contrived, however, to view the combination of elements associated with music and study as alluding to the intellectual and artistic life. Dou's focus on the scholarly ideal, never more concentrated than in this work, is central to many of his early paintings.

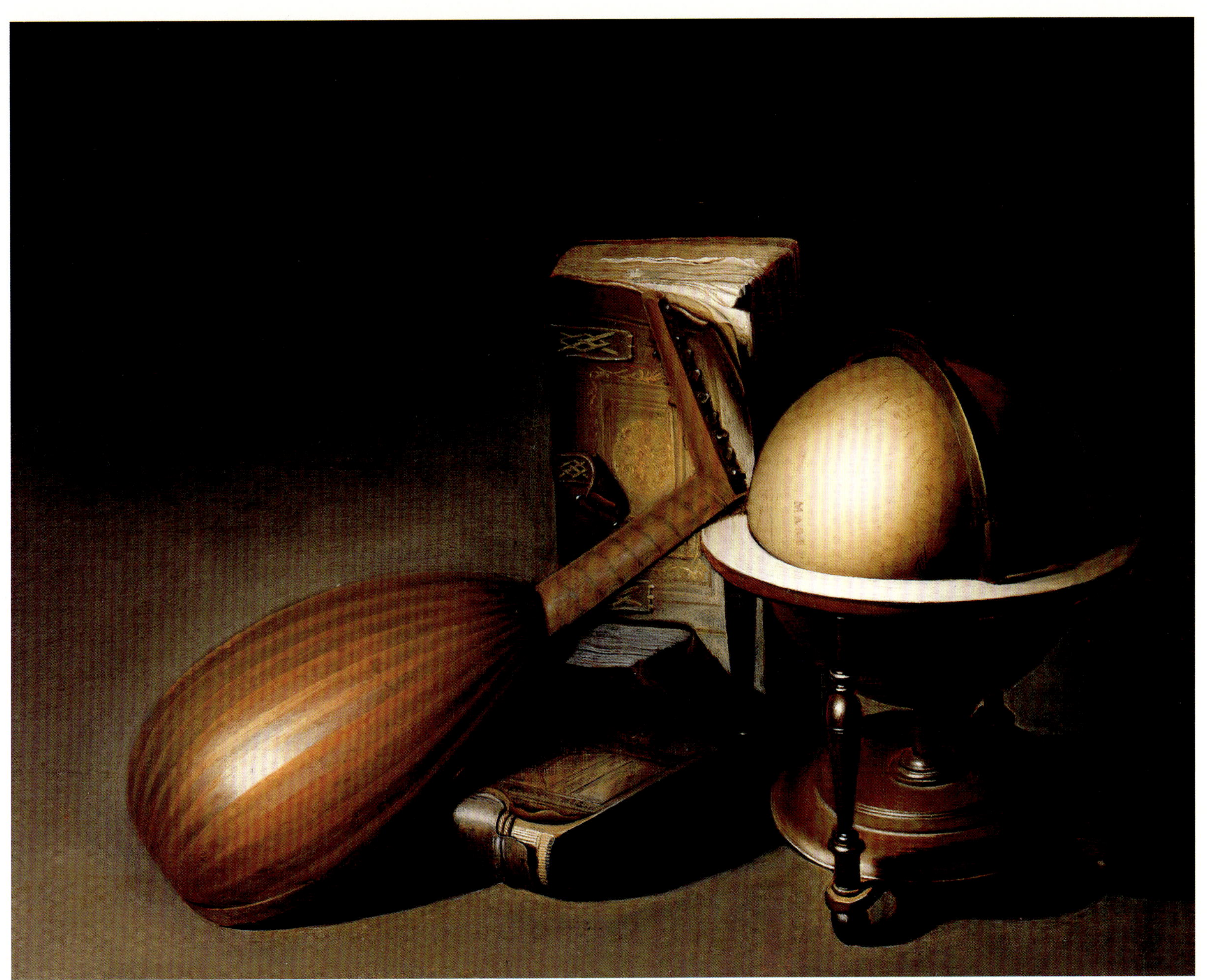

7.
Self-Portrait

c. 1635–1638; oil on panel; arched top, 18.3 x 14 (7 1/8 x 5 1/2); Cheltenham Art Gallery and Museums

Signed on table edge: GDov

· *Provenance* Probably Edward Gray, Harrington Park, Hornsey, 1829. Baron de Ferrières; bequeathed by him to Cheltenham, 1898.

· *Bibliography* Probably J. Smith 1829, no. 100 (although dimensions differ); Moes 1897, no. 2096.19; probably Martin 1901, no. 108 (although painter is described as standing at a window); probably Hofstede de Groot 1907, no. 282; probably Martin 1911, no. 297 (under "ouvrages perdus d'attribution douteuse"); probably Van Hall 1963, 80 (527: 4) and 82 (note to 527: 32); Hunnewell 1983, 24–83; Wright 1988, 18; Baer 1990, no. 20.

· *Exhibitions* London 1929, no. 189; Manchester 1929, no. 51; Birmingham 1934, no. 47; Bristol 1946; Amsterdam 1983, no. 16; Leicester 1988, no. 2; London 1999, 70.

• The Cheltenham *Self-Portrait*, in which the young Dou presents himself as a serious and self-assured artist, is an ambitious and personal statement. The choice of a three-quarter-length format, rather than a bust- or half-length, heightens the importance of the figure. Despite the small size of the panel, the picture gives an impression of monumentality by presenting the sitter close to the picture plane in a frontal, upright pose. The artist looks directly at the viewer, his head inscribed in the double arch of the background. The curtain above the artist's head and the form of the panel itself further heighten the monumental self-presentation.[1] The age of the sitter (between twenty-two and twenty- five years old) dates the picture to around 1635–1638, making it the earliest of Dou's self-portraits.

In choosing to study his own features, Dou is following Rembrandt's example. However, by depicting himself holding the tools of his trade, he departs from his teacher's style of self-portraiture. Furthermore, the youthful Rembrandt most often depicted his own features for their expressive possibilities, whereas Dou's self-portraits are more formal in character.

This image is a simplified variation of Dou's full-length *Artist in His Studio* (cat. 1). Dou has eliminated the abundant accessories that fill the earlier painting and has changed the position of the painter in relation to his easel. Whereas the anonymous painter in *Artist in His Studio* sits directly next to his easel, here the easel has been pushed into the right background. The resulting distance between easel and artist in the *Self-Portrait* shifts the emphasis from the act of painting to the person of the artist. As Richard Hunnewell observed, the artist has chosen to stress the dignity of his profession rather than the practice of his craft.[2]

As in his 1663 *Self-Portrait* (cat. 27), Dou has positioned himself next to a table that supports an object of symbolic importance. The plaster cast on which the painter rests his arm is likely a reference to the training of the artist. Representing the practice of drawing after sculpture, the cast symbolizes the foundation of Dou's art, just as it physically supports his painting arm. This plaster cast, shown from the same point of view and at the same angle, also appears in the *Self-Portrait* of c. 1665 (cat. 29), in which it probably carries similar associations.

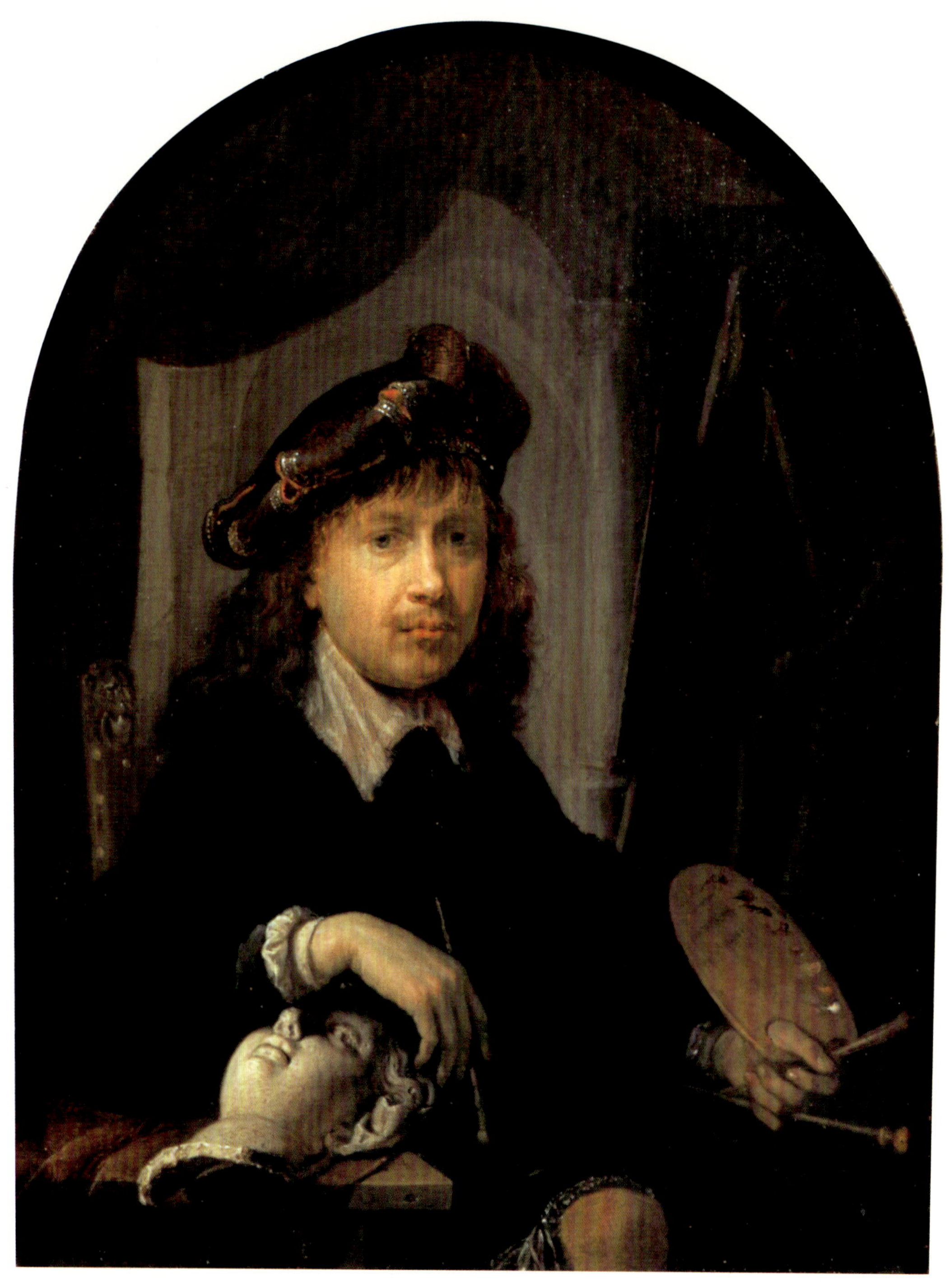

8.

An Interior with Young Violinist

1637; oil on panel; arched top, 31.1 x 23.7 (12 1/4 x 9 3/8); National Gallery of Scotland, Edinburgh

Signed and dated on lowest step: GDov 1637

· *Provenance* Possibly in the collection of Pieter Spiering between 1637 and 1641 (according to Joachim von Sandrart); probably Queen Christina of Sweden; probably returned to Spiering by Queen Christina, 1652. James Brydges, first duke of Chandos (seal on verso);[1] Chandos sale, 6–8 May 1747 (no. 170) (88 gns). (Sale, Christie's, London 29 March 1800 [no. 91] [357 gns]). Possibly Ladbrooke family (inscription on verso). Second marquess of Stafford, by 1808; by descent to John, fifth earl of Ellesmere (later, sixth duke of Sutherland); National Gallery of Scotland, 1984.

· *Bibliography* J. Smith 1842, no. 102; Moes 1897, no. 2096.1; Martin 1901, no. 71; Hofstede de Groot 1907, no. 82; Martin 1911, no. 80; Martin 1913, 85; Stockholm 1966, no. 1296; Van de Waal 1974, 159 note 68; Haak 1984, 269; Baer 1990, no. 26.

· *Exhibitions* Amsterdam 1989, no. 3; Edinburgh 1992, no. 18.

· *An Interior with Young Violinist*, painted by Dou at age twenty-four, is his earliest extant dated work and is, for that reason, an important cornerstone for the dating of his paintings. A prime example of his early mature style, it is one of Dou's most finely executed and thinly painted works. The quality of the picture was recognized as early as 1829, when John Smith wrote that "this little bijou is perhaps, as a whole, the most perfect work that the master ever produced."[2]

Dou's choice of a full-length figure and vertical format recalls those of *Artist in His Studio* (cat. 1) and *Man Writing by an Easel* (cat. 4), but his conception of space is here more fully understood and developed. The arched top of the panel emphasizes the verticality of the painting, which, in turn, gives a monumental aspect to the small work. The beautiful chiaroscuro reveals Dou's continuing debt to Rembrandt and underlines the serenity of the scene. Dou no longer employs the large areas of unmodulated brilliant color that characterized his earliest works but uses more subdued tones to punctuate the closely observed effects of reflected light.

Compositionally, the painting resembles Thomas de Keyser's *Portrait of David Bailly* (page 34, fig. 8) of about ten years earlier. The pose of the two figures is similar, and though the dress of Dou's violinist is not as elegant as Bailly's, his high social status is implied not only by the occupations in which he is engaged but also by his cloak and sword and the spurs on his boots.[3] These accessories belong to the province of the gentleman.

Dou's talent as a painter of still life is shown to great advantage in the profusion of objects that surround the sitter. Most of them are known from the artist's earlier works, in which they generally accompany an elderly figure. Here, the figure of the scholar has been transformed into that of a young man, interrupted during his music-making.

According to Baldassare Castiglione in *Il Libro del Cortegiano* (1528), a gentleman could find "nothing more worthy or commendable to help [the] body relax and the spirit recuperate . . . than music."[4] The sound

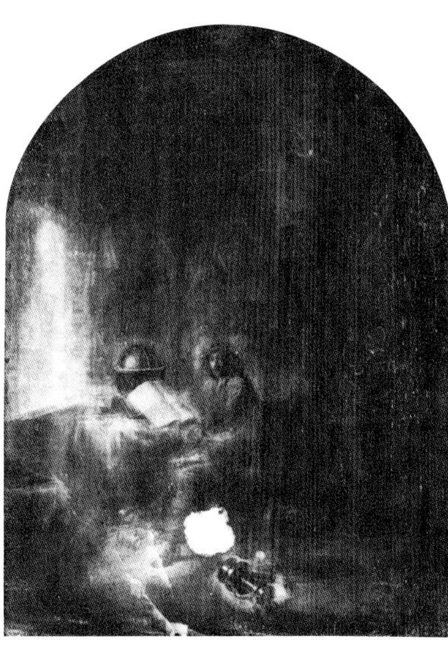

FIGURE 1
X-radiograph of *An Interior with Young Violinist*

of stringed instruments in particular was said to elevate the mind to the contemplation of celestial and intellectual things. For this reason, Sebastian Brant, in *Ship of Fools*, assigns stringed instruments to educated society.[5] As in his *Still Life with Globe, Lute, and Books* (cat. 6), Dou combines elements associated with music and study into an image of the intellectual and artistic ideal, here given a gentleman's gloss.

X-radiography reveals that Dou made several changes in the composition of the painting. The book on the table was once significantly lower, and closer to the man's body (fig. 1).[6] The adjustment of this detail dictated the final position of his body with respect to the table and the viewer. X-radiography also shows that the sitter's features were once substantially different than they now appear. Originally, still-life objects were piled at the sitter's feet, which may account for the somewhat awkward position of the man's right foot, which, in the understate, would have been hidden.

The painting apparently corresponds to "a small painting in which a man plays the violin from a score" that Queen Christina returned to Pieter Spiering in 1652.[7] Joachim von Sandrart may have seen it during his stay in Holland between 1637 and 1641; in his *Teutsche Akademie*, he describes a painting that he had seen at Spiering's depicting "a lutenist sitting at a table, before whom books lie, about a span large."[8] Although *An Interior with Young Violinist* does not correspond precisely to the description, it is closer to it than any other known work by the artist.

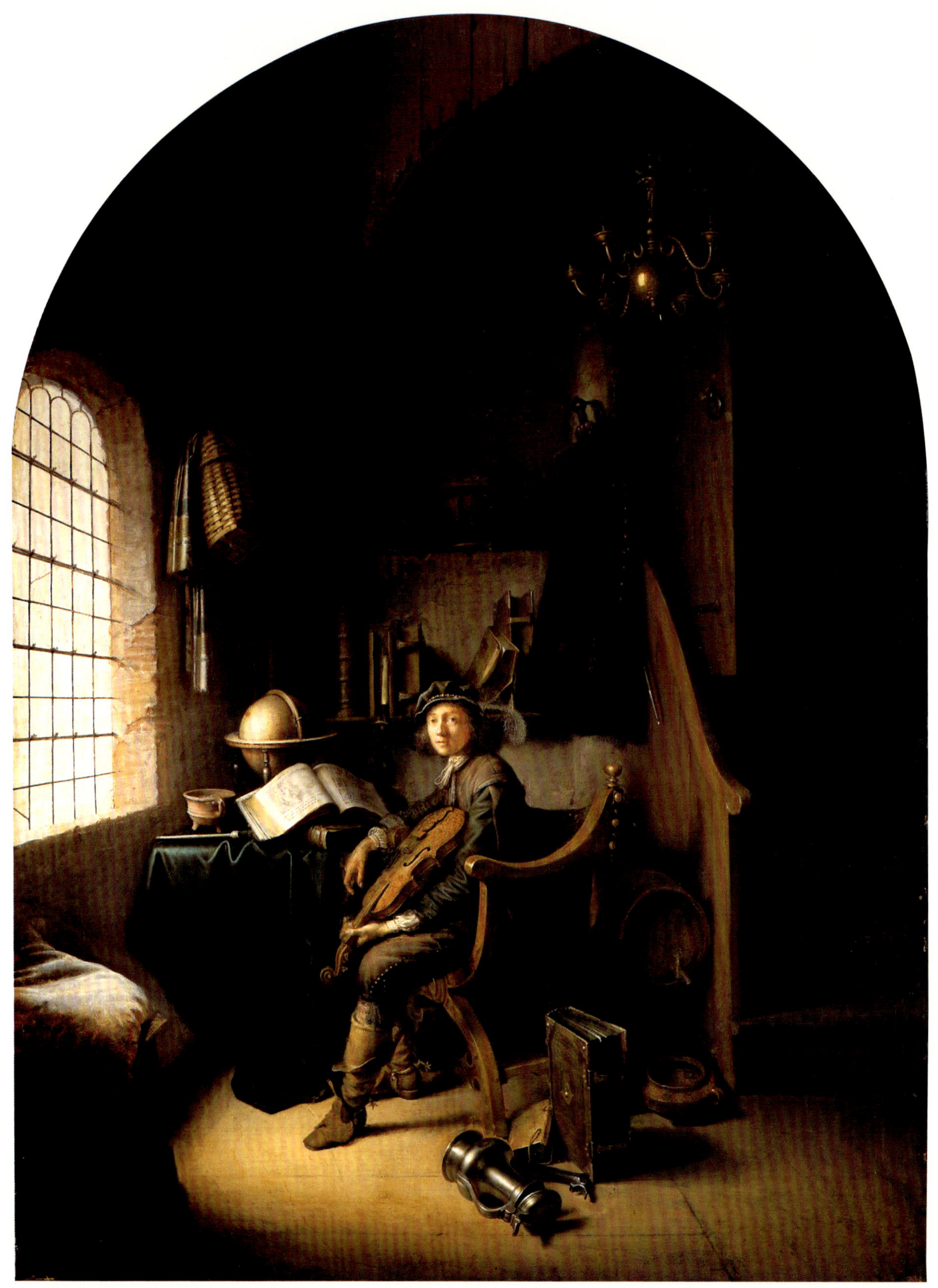

AN INTERIOR WITH YOUNG VIOLINIST

9.

Portrait of a Young Woman

c. 1635–1640; oil on panel; oval, 21.2 x 17.6 (8 3/8 x 6 7/8); Manchester City Art Galleries

Signed at center right: GDov

· *Provenance* Van Loon, 1842. Baron Lionel de Rothschild, 1878. (D. Katz, Dieren). (Edward Speelman, London, 1937); Mr. and Mrs. Edgar Assheton Bennett; by bequest to Manchester, 1979.

· *Bibliography* J. Smith 1842, no. 64; Martin 1901, no. 225; Hofstede de Groot 1907, no. 378; Baer 1990, no. 23.

· *Exhibitions* London 1965, no. 19; Manchester 1965, no. 19.

· The Manchester *Portrait of a Young Woman* reflects a fashion prevalent in Holland during the late 1630s and the 1640s for portraying fashionable women in "arcadian" dress, characterized by "casually strewn veils, scarves, and glittering ornamentation."[1] Contemporaneous descriptions of pastoral dress mention features evident in the apparel of Dou's sitter, in particular, her low décolleté and laced bodice and the shimmering texture and light-green color of her silk dress.[2]

The character of this portrait differs from Dou's usual likenesses; in fact, the arcadian type diverged from the mainstream of Leiden portraiture. Arcadian portraiture had courtly and elevated associations. It appealed to the upper classes, as well as to members of the bourgeoisie who aspired to a higher social status.[3] Details such as the tiny jeweled piece that holds the woman's veil in place and the pearl earrings of high fashion underscore her rank.[4] The delicate hands, one resting lightly over the other, complement the sitter's quiet pose.

Dou did not often use a profile format in his portraits.[5] Here, the sitter faces away from the light source; the right side of her face and the wall behind her are brightly lit, while her features are in gentle shadow. This play of light and shade, which gives plastic modeling to the head, is one of the most sensitive examples of Dou's chiaroscuro effects. The outlining of the woman's profile—an unusual feature in the artist's work—lends the portrait a graphic quality that creates great pictorial interest.

The painting exhibits both smooth and rough passages. Dou has rapidly brushed the background and freely rendered the modulations of tone. The folds of the woman's sleeves are defined with broad, zigzag strokes, and impasto is applied liberally to render the two brooches. By contrast, Dou has carefully observed and recorded the woman's ear and hands. The pearls in her hair and her earring are exquisitely depicted. The overall green-and-gold color harmonies contribute to the serene mood of the portrait.

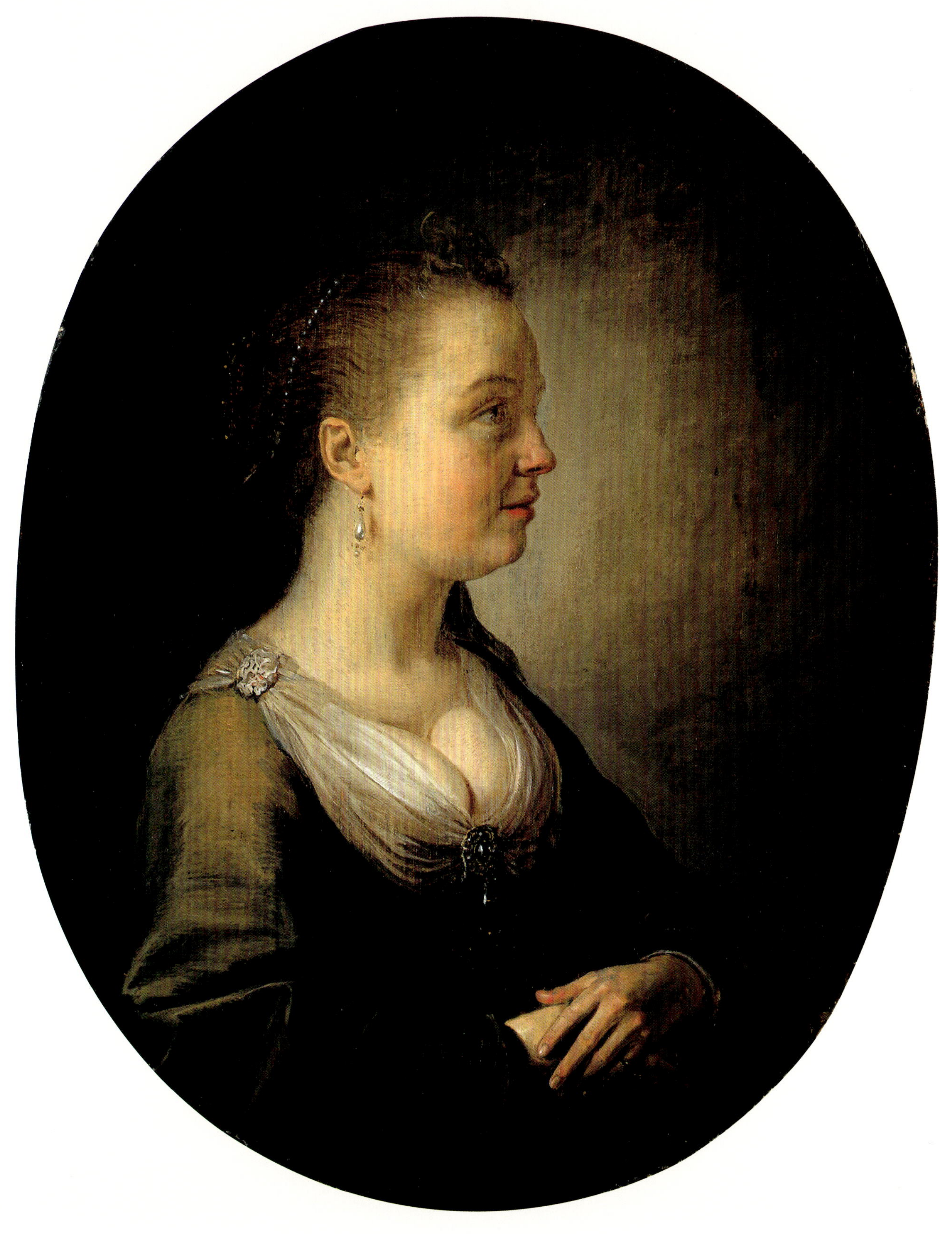

PORTRAIT OF A YOUNG WOMAN

10.

Portrait of a Woman

c. 1635–1640; oil on panel; oval, 13.3 x 11.3 (5 1/4 x 4 3/8); private collection[1]

Signed in dark brown at left center: GDov

· *Provenance* Marcus Kappel, Berlin, 1914; by descent to Henry T. Rathenau, Berlin, and his sister, Ellen Ettlinger, Oxford, England; thence by descent; (Noortman Gallery, Maastricht); to present owner.

· *Exhibitions* On loan to Rijksmuseum, Amsterdam, before 1940 (inv. no. 1173; label on verso).

· This painting is one of a series of small, oval, bust-length portraits and figure studies that Dou painted between 1635 and 1640.[2] The sitter's upright carriage, the calculated placement of her figure in the center of an oval, and the calligraphic treatment of the profile pose resemble Dou's *Profile Bust of a Youth* (c. 1635) in the Fitzwilliam Museum, Cambridge (Sumowski 1983, 1: 556 [no. 259]). However, the supreme assurance in Dou's rendering of the transparent headdress and its lace decoration and the beautiful subtlety of the reflected light under the sitter's chin are hallmarks of a more confident and experienced painter. The handling of the paint, especially in the contrast of the woman's carefully observed and delicately drawn features with the freely rendered sleeves of her fur jacket and the lacing of her ochre bodice, points to a date closer to 1640. The small size of the panel, which creates an impression of preciousness, makes such virtuoso handling even more remarkable.

In many ways, this painting is a complement to the *Portrait of a Young Woman* (cat. 9). In both, the profile format removes the sitter psychologically from the viewer. Here, however, the woman is turned toward the source of light. Her evenly illuminated face shows little of the play of light and shadow apparent in the other. Dou's restricted palette of browns, whites, and grays is here enlivened by the touches of red in the woman's rosy cheeks and full lips. Her costume, with its fur jacket, pearl earring, and lace cap, suggests the sitter's affluence.

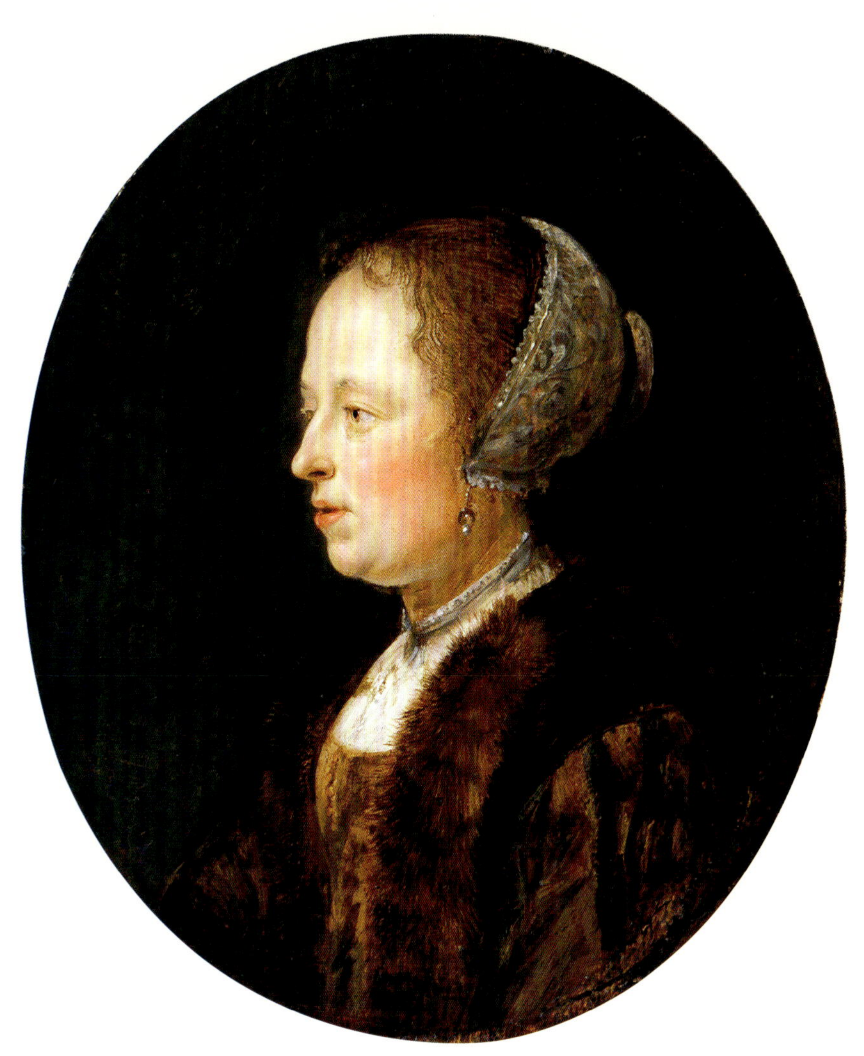

11.

Bust of a Man

c. 1642–1645; oil on panel; oval, 18.4 x 14.9 (7 1/4 x 5 7/8); The Corcoran Gallery of Art, Washington, William A. Clark Collection

Signed over figure's left shoulder: GDov

· *Provenance* Possibly Jacques de Roore sale, The Hague, 4 September 1747 (no. 89) (*f* 141, with pendant). Possibly Johan van der Merck sale, Amsterdam, 25 August 1773, no. 66. Possibly Comtesse Dubarry sale, Paris, 17 February 1777 (no. 79) (FF426). Paignon Dijonval, Paris (died 1792); by descent to his grandson, Charles-Gilbert, Vicomte Morel de Vindé; Paignon-Dijonval and Morel de Vindé sale, Paris, 17 December 1821; (Thomas Emmerson, London, 1821). (Jeremiah Harman, Esq., sale, Christie's, London, 17 May 1844 [no. 33] [73 gns]). (Gottfried von Preyer, Vienna, 1902), William A. Clark, New York; bequeathed by Clark in 1926.

· *Bibliography* Hoet 1752–1770, 2: 206 (no. 89); J. Smith 1829, possibly no. 55 and no. 99 (as *Portrait of the Artist's Father*, companion to *Self-Portrait*); J. Smith 1842, no. 58; Moes 1897, 483 (nos. 3984.2, 3984.3[?]); Martin 1901, no. 135 and possibly no. 135a; Hofstede de Groot 1907, nos. 291 and possibly 292 and 319d; Martin 1911, no. 67; Martin 1913, 29 and 181; Breckenridge 1955, 13; Wheelock 1978; Baer 1990, no. 39.

· This small oval painting is one of Dou's most animated treatments of a figure, due in large part to the sharp turn of the sitter's head in the direction opposite from the turn of his body.[1] The undulating silhouette of the cap, set at a rakish angle, intensifies the effect. The knitted brow and set lips help create the impression of the sitter's intense concentration. The informality of the work, conveyed by the bust-length format and the sitter's pose, is underscored by its spirited execution. The painting is composed almost entirely of small distinct brushstrokes, whose size, shape, and method of application describe the forms. The wrinkles of the subject's forehead, for example, have been rendered by rough strokes and a restrained use of the butt end of the brush (a technique that Dou seldom used). Long, thin, wavy strokes compose the white shirt; short undulating brushwork suggests the curliness of the man's hair and beard. Small dabs of earth color represent the highlights of the buttons.

Dou has carefully drawn the eyes and nose but has largely ignored the anatomy of the ear. A simple line indicates the mouth, mostly hidden by the mustache. Color plays an unusually prominent role in this head study. The sitter's cheeks and forehead are ruddy, and shades of red are also used in the corner of his eyes and around their rims. Gray and brown mingle with the flesh tones in the sitter's face, especially in the area around his eyes and in the deep shadow to the right of his nose. The green backdrop sets off the bulk of the sitter's body. A single dark line suggests the contour of his neck and connects the dark portion of his cap to the brown of his coat.

In 1829 John Smith identified the sitter as Dou's father and paired it with *Man with a Pipe* (cat. 15), which he called a self-portrait.[2] Nearly a century later, Willem Martin supported this identification, based on the resemblance of the subject to a figure in a painting that Dou is holding in his roughly contemporaneous *Self-Portrait* in the Herzog Anton Ulrich-Museum, Braunschweig (Sumowski 1983, 1: 598 [no. 301]). Although the figures in the Braunschweig painting-within-the-painting may well be Dou's father, mother, and brother, the older figure in that picture and the sitter in the Corcoran panel in fact bear very little resemblance to one another.[3] Dou may have used this image as a model for the *Schoolmaster* (1645) in the Fitzwilliam Museum, Cambridge (Martin 1913, 68, right).

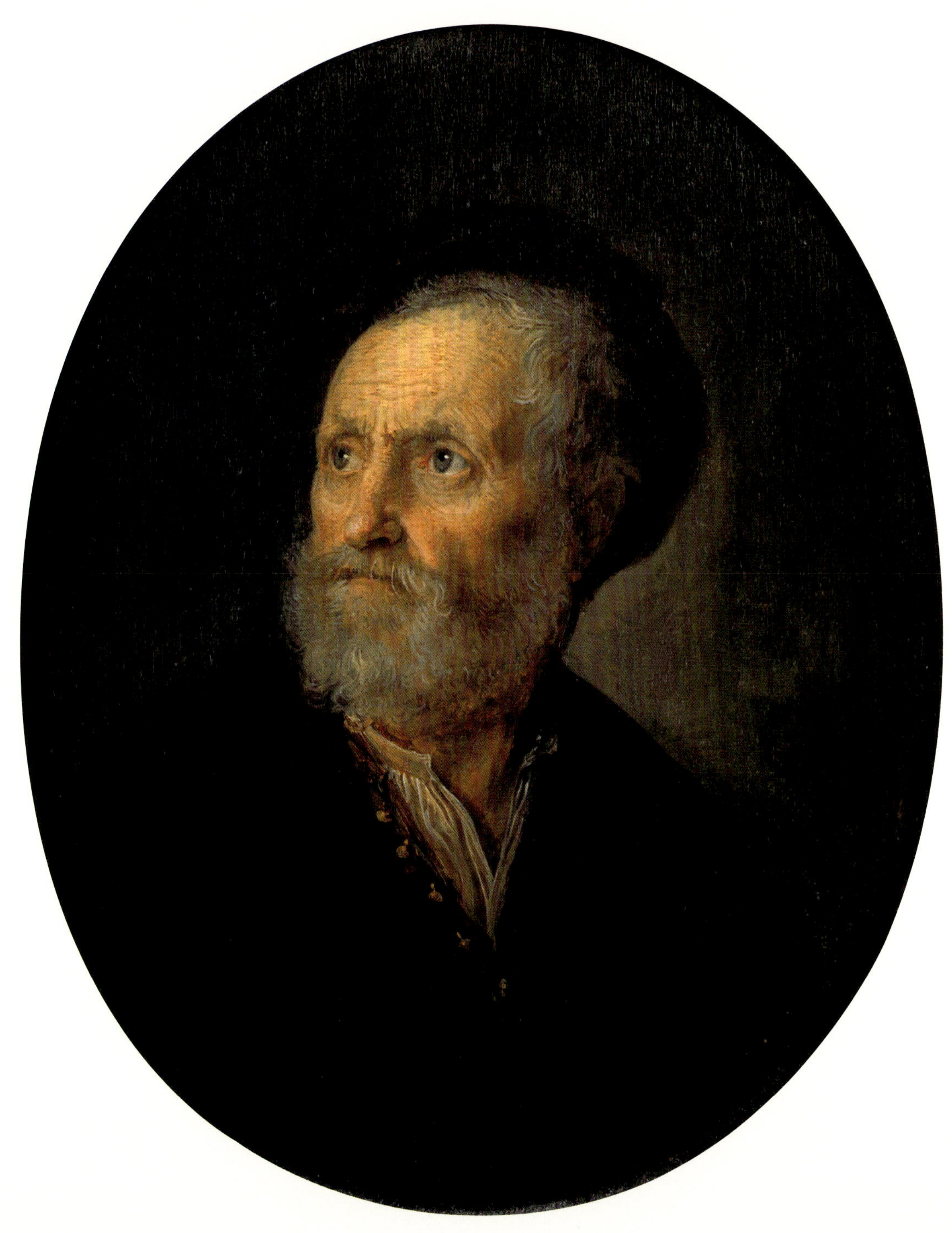

12.

Portrait of a Man

c. 1642–1646; oil on panel; oval, 28 x 23.5 (11 x 9 ¼); Aurora Art Fund (courtesy Rosenberg & Stiebel)

· *Provenance* A.B. Roothaan sale, Amsterdam, 29 March 1826 (nos. 26, 27) (*f* 2120, with pendant, to Roos). Steengracht, The Hague, in 1829; Steengracht sale, Paris, 9 June 1913 (nos. 14, 15) (FF 90,050, with pendant, to Hamburger). Dr. and Mrs. Walter von Pannwitz, Berlin, by 1926. De Hartekamp, Bennebroek; by descent to present owners.

· *Bibliography* J. Smith 1829, no. 132; J. Smith 1842, no. 74; Martin 1901, no. 144; Hofstede de Groot 1907, no. 324; Martin 1911, no. 68; Martin 1913, 32; Friedländer 1926, no. 39; Baer 1990, no. 40a.

13.

Portrait of a Woman

c. 1642–1646; oil on panel; oval, 28 x 23.5 (11 x 9 ¼); Aurora Art Fund (courtesy Rosenberg & Stiebel)

Signed on the arm of the chair: GDov

· *Provenance* As above.

· *Bibliography* J. Smith 1829, no. 132; J. Smith 1842, no. 75; Martin 1901, no. 197; Hofstede de Groot 1907, no. 363; Martin 1911, no. 98; Martin 1913, 49; Friedländer 1926, no. 40; Baer 1990, no. 40b.

· These pendants, depicting a man and a woman turning toward one another while regarding the viewer, are the only paired portraits by Dou that remain in the same collection.[1] The artful arrangement of the man's full sleeve as he rests his elbow on the table and his relaxed posture endow the male figure with more visual interest than his female mate. The man's pose, the costume, and several of the accoutrements (including the tall hat and the column in the background), anticipate Dou's only signed and dated portrait—the 1646 portrait of Johan Wittert van der Aa in the Rijksmuseum, Amsterdam (fig. 1). Here, the man sits stiffly with splayed legs, as he rests his hand on his hat (rather than on the table, as in fig. 1). Spatial effects are less confidently treated than in the Rijksmuseum portrait, which suggests that this painting dates slightly earlier.

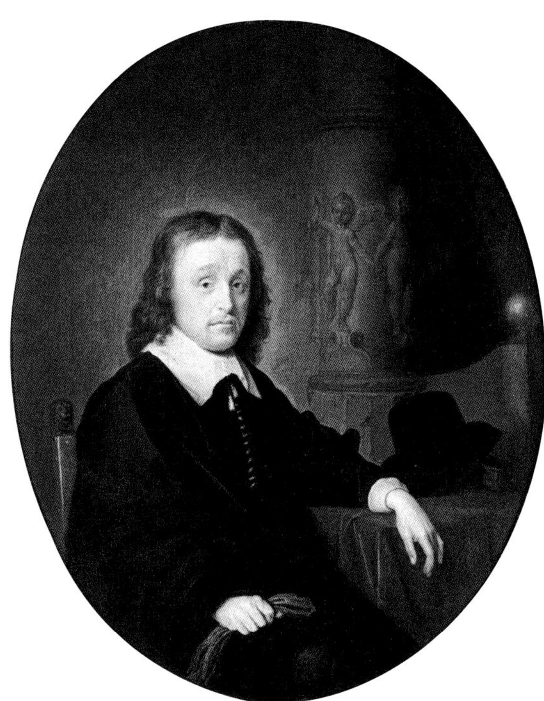

The conservative nature of the woman's dress finds no parallel in Dou's other female portrait subjects.[2] Her head is framed by a succession of arched shapes, culminating in the form of the oval panel itself. The woman's carefully modeled face is thinly painted; horizontal strokes on her forehead, delicate drawing on the bridge of her nose, a sweep of the brush under her eyes are all that betray the artist's hand. Dou used a wet-in-wet technique for the man's hair. In both paintings, a few touches of red and flesh tones enliven the palette of subtle grays, whites, blacks, and browns.

The practice of holding both gloves in one hand, as the woman does, is common in seventeenth-century Dutch portraiture. As David Smith explains, it not only suggests a fashionable convention but may also symbolize polite accessibility—to the viewer, to her husband, or to both.[3] The removal of the man's hat may well convey similar associations.

An early critic identified these pictures as portraits of the painter and his wife,[4] perhaps on the basis of a comment in the 1826 sales catalogue that the paintings came directly from descendants of the artist's family. The notion is an appealing one, but Dou never married.

FIGURE 1
Johan Wittert van der Aa, 1646, oil on panel, Rijksmuseum, Amsterdam

DETAIL
Portrait of a Woman (cat. 13)

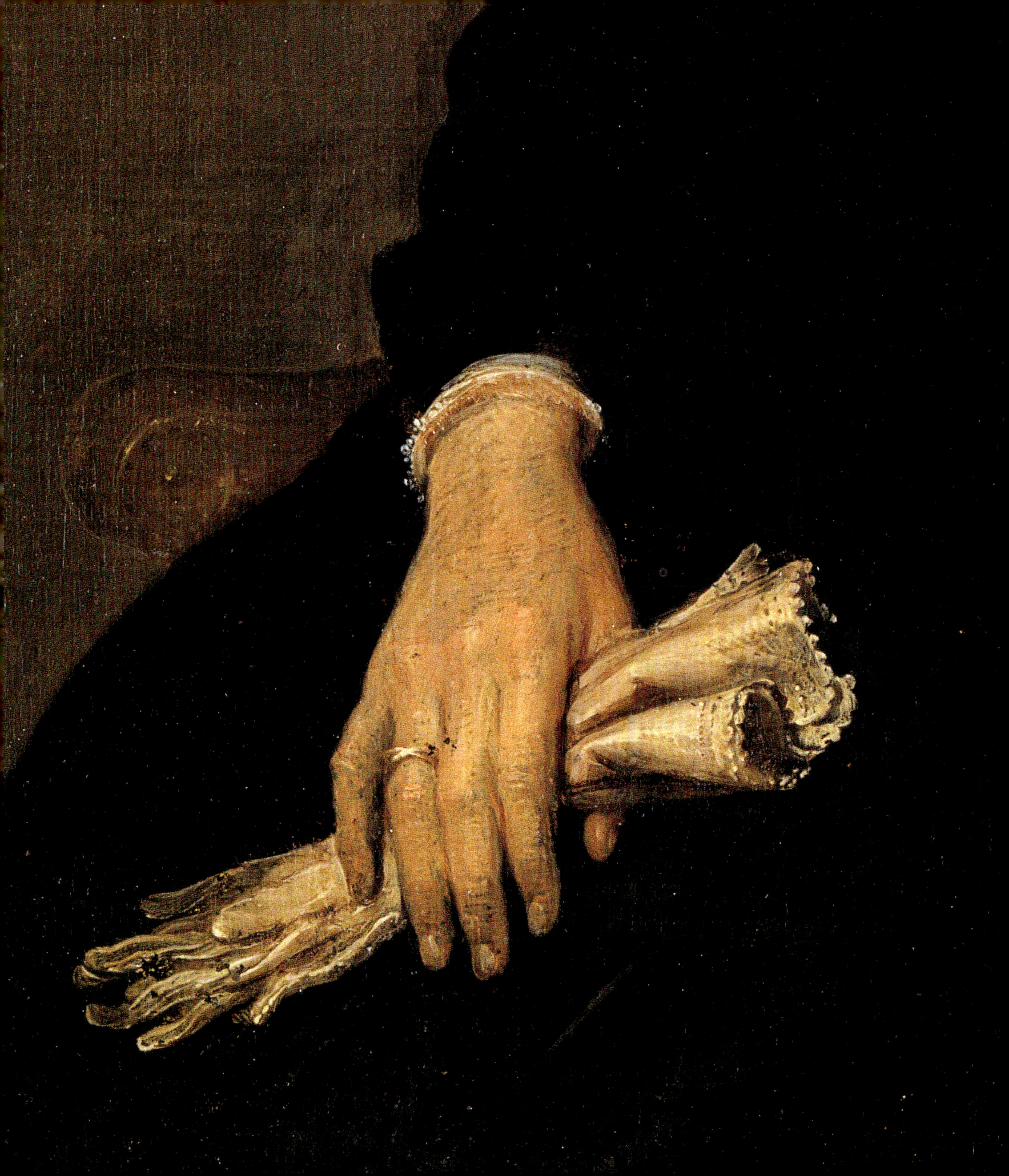

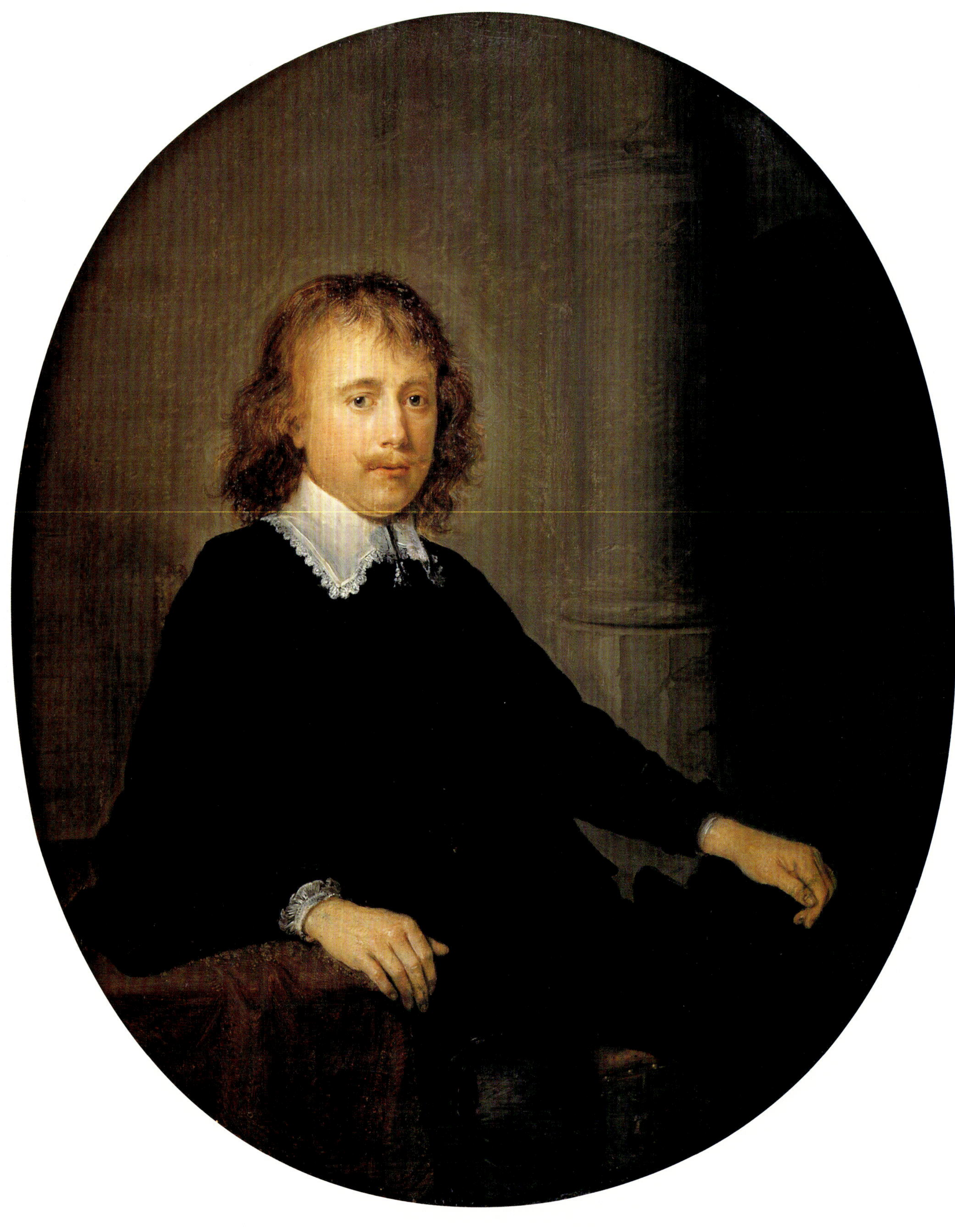

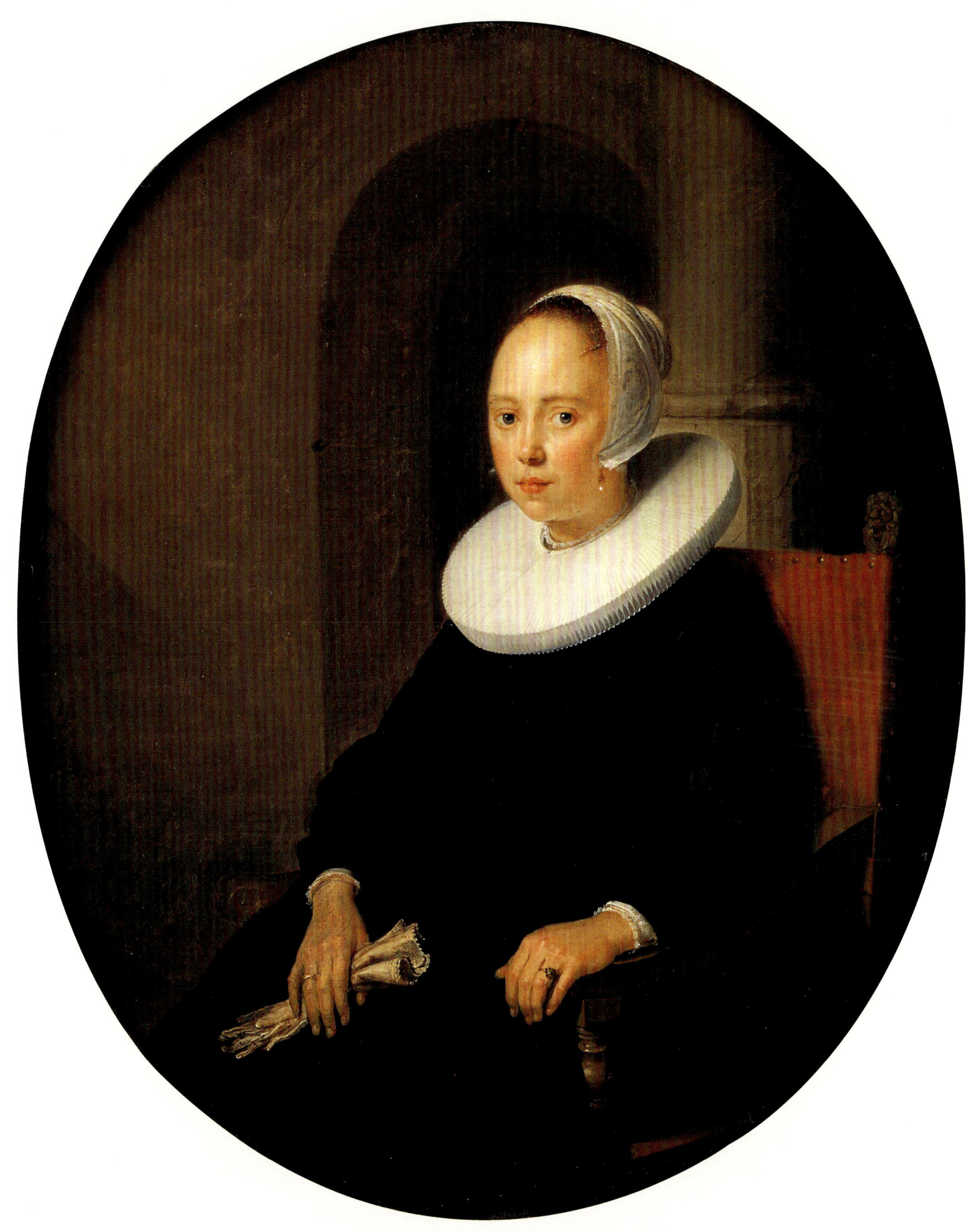

14.

Self-Portrait

c. 1645; oil on panel; arched top, 12.4 x 8.3 (4 7/8 x 3 1/4); private collection, Spain

Signed upper left on the curtain: GDov

· *Provenance* Possibly Count Fraula sale, Brussels, 21 July 1738 (no. 123) (*f* 105). Duque de Cadaval. (Sale, Christie's, London, 8 December 1995 [no. 33A]); (Noortman, Maastricht); to present owner.

· *Bibliography* Hoet 1752–1770, 1: no. 122; Hofstede de Groot 1907, no. 279b.

· *Exhibitions* Melbourne and Sydney 1997, no. 40; London and The Hague 1999, no. 89.

• This *Self-Portrait* is remarkable for its extraordinarily small size. There must have been a market for such tiny self-portraits, and they seem to have been an especially congenial subject to the *fijnschilders*.[1] Dou's image, especially in details such as the curled upward sweep of the hat brim, the long, curly hair, and the placement of the figure in the picture space, calls to mind the image that Rembrandt created of himself in the impression of the second state of his self-portrait etching of 1631 in the British Museum (fig. 1), in which he drew his shoulders, cloak, and collar in black chalk.[2] The present painting illustrates Dou's continued reliance on Rembrandt's example into the mid-1640s.

Dou, in full command of his technique, here suggests complete forms with remarkable economy, employing a few strokes to render the painting-within-the-painting and the still life on the table in the background. The placement of the signature—on a bit of gold and pink at the left that appears to be an embroidered edge of the curtain—is unusual.

Dou's serious demeanor in this painting, softened by the delicate play of light across his face, resembles that in his other self-portraits (compare cats. 7, 27, and 29). It differs, however, from the others in that the easel faces the viewer, revealing a depiction of the Rest on the Flight into Egypt. Although Dou did not paint historical scenes himself, the appearance of the subject here reinforces Dou's dignified demeanor and elegant self-conception by associating him with history painting, the most important category in the hierarchy of artistic subjects.

Joachim von Sandrart, writing about a visit to the artist's studio in 1639, reported that Dou protected his palette, brushes, and colors from dust by locking them up and waiting for the dust to settle before beginning to paint.[3] The parasol placed over the easel alludes in a particularly literal way to Von Sandrart's description of Dou's meticulous working method. The other objects in the background, like the parasol, are among Dou's standard studio props. Dou appears somewhat younger here than he does in the *Self-Portrait* of 1647 in the Gemäldegalerie Alte Meister, Dresden (page 35, fig. 10), suggesting a date of c. 1645 for this self-portrait.[4]

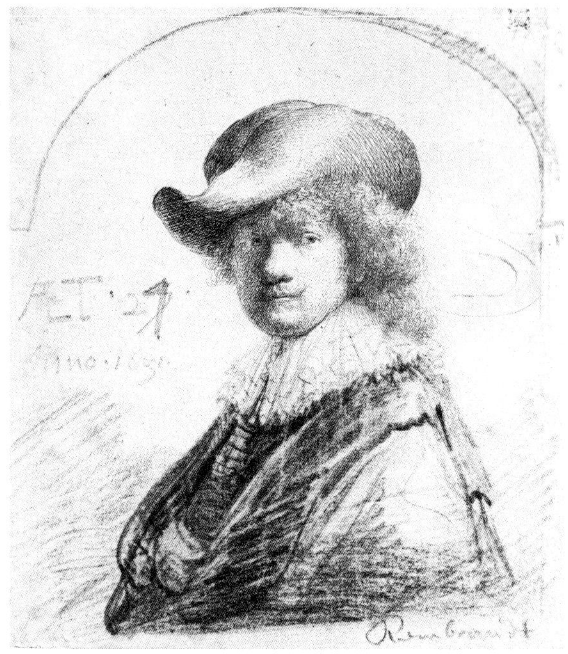

FIGURE 1
Rembrandt van Rijn, *Self-Portrait*, 1631, etching with black chalk, British Museum, London

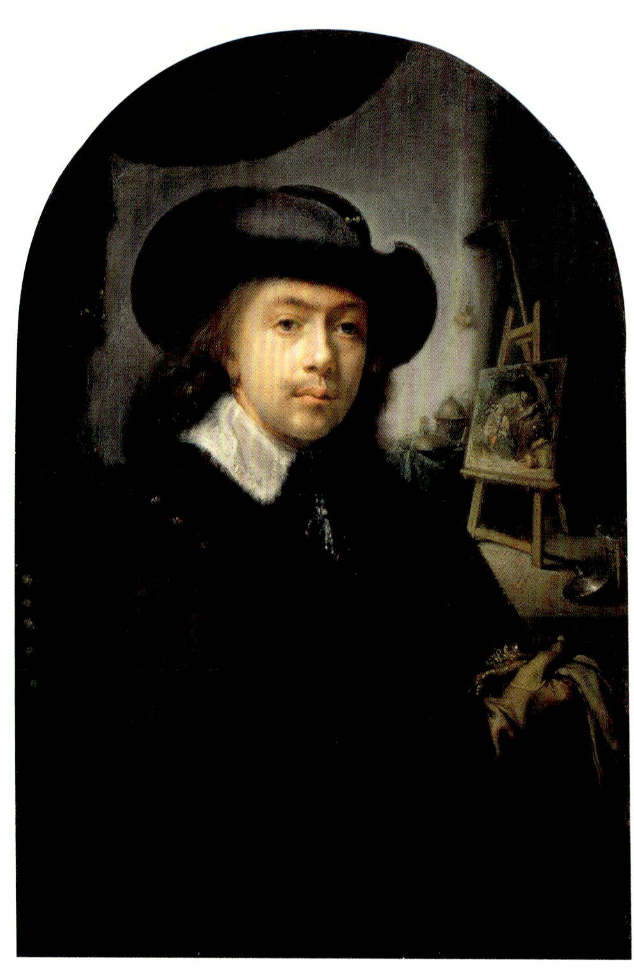

15.

Man with a Pipe

c. 1645; oil on panel; oval, 19 x 14.7 (7 ½ x 5 ¾); The National Gallery, London

Signed at right center: GDov

· *Provenance* Probably in Pieter Locquet sale, Amsterdam, 22 September 1783 (no. 76) (*f*75, to Braam Helsdingen). Possibly in Anna Catharina Putnam sale, Amsterdam, 17 August 1803 (no. 23) (*f*180, to Roos). Or possibly Paignon Dijonval, Paris; possibly by descent to his grandson, Vicomte de Morel Vindé; (Paignon Dijonval and Morel Vindé sale, Paris, 17–18 December 1821 [no. 21] [*f*819, to Hazard]). Jeremiah Harman by 1842; (J. Harman sale, London, 17 May 1844 [no. 34] [125 gns, for the National Gallery]).

· *Bibliography* J. Smith 1829, no. 98; J. Smith 1842, no. 57; Moes 1897, no. 2096.14; Martin 1901, no. 105; Hofstede de Groot 1907, no. 272; Martin 1911, no. 53; Martin 1913, 16; MacLaren 1960, 103–104 (no. 192); Van Hall 1963, no. 527.46; Sumowski 1983, 1: no. 257; Baer 1990, no. 43; MacLaren and Brown, 1991, 1: 106 (no. 192); Sumowski 1994, no. 3596.

· This almost tender image, in which a man smoking a pipe wistfully engages the viewer, seems to capture a specific moment in time. The spontaneity is enhanced by the dazzling range of brushwork. The sitter's features—long wavy hair, mustache, tuft below his lower lip, and humped nose—resemble Dou's own, but they are so generalized that the work cannot really be considered a self-portrait.[1] Rather, it is among Dou's later *tronies* and illustrates the virtuoso and informal manner that Dou perfected in his mature works of this type. It shares a liveliness of execution and similarity of format with the *Bust of a Man* of c. 1642–1645 (cat. 11), and the subject and sitter closely resemble those of the *Painter with Pipe and Book* of c. 1645–1650 (cat. 16).

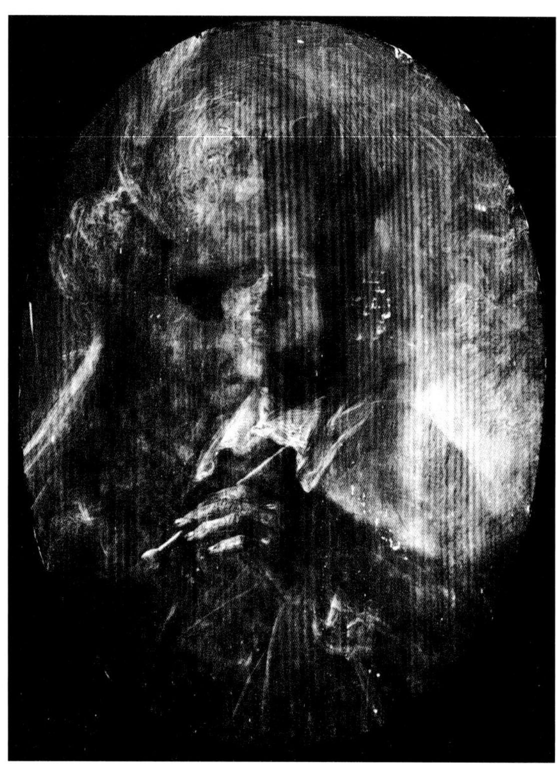

FIGURE 1
X-radiograph of *Man with a Pipe*

As the pictorial emphasis on the pipe suggests, the sitter's likeness is less important than his identification as a smoker. A man with a pipe was a recurring subject in Dou's art (compare cats. 5, 16, and 20). In appearance, this seated smoker in fine dress recalls similar figures in the "Merry Company" paintings by Willem Buytewech (1591/1592–1624).[2] However the tenor of Dou's painting, one of quiet and perhaps melancholic contemplation, is very different from the dandified elegance of Buytewech's images. It is consonant, in fact, with Dou's other depictions of pipe smokers, in which smoking is associated with reverie.

X-radiographs reveal a bust-length portrait of a woman beneath the painting's surface (fig. 1).[3] It is not clear why Dou abandoned or transformed his original image. However, several of Rembrandt's *tronies* and portraits from the late 1620s and early 1630s also appear to have been painted over other pictures.[4]

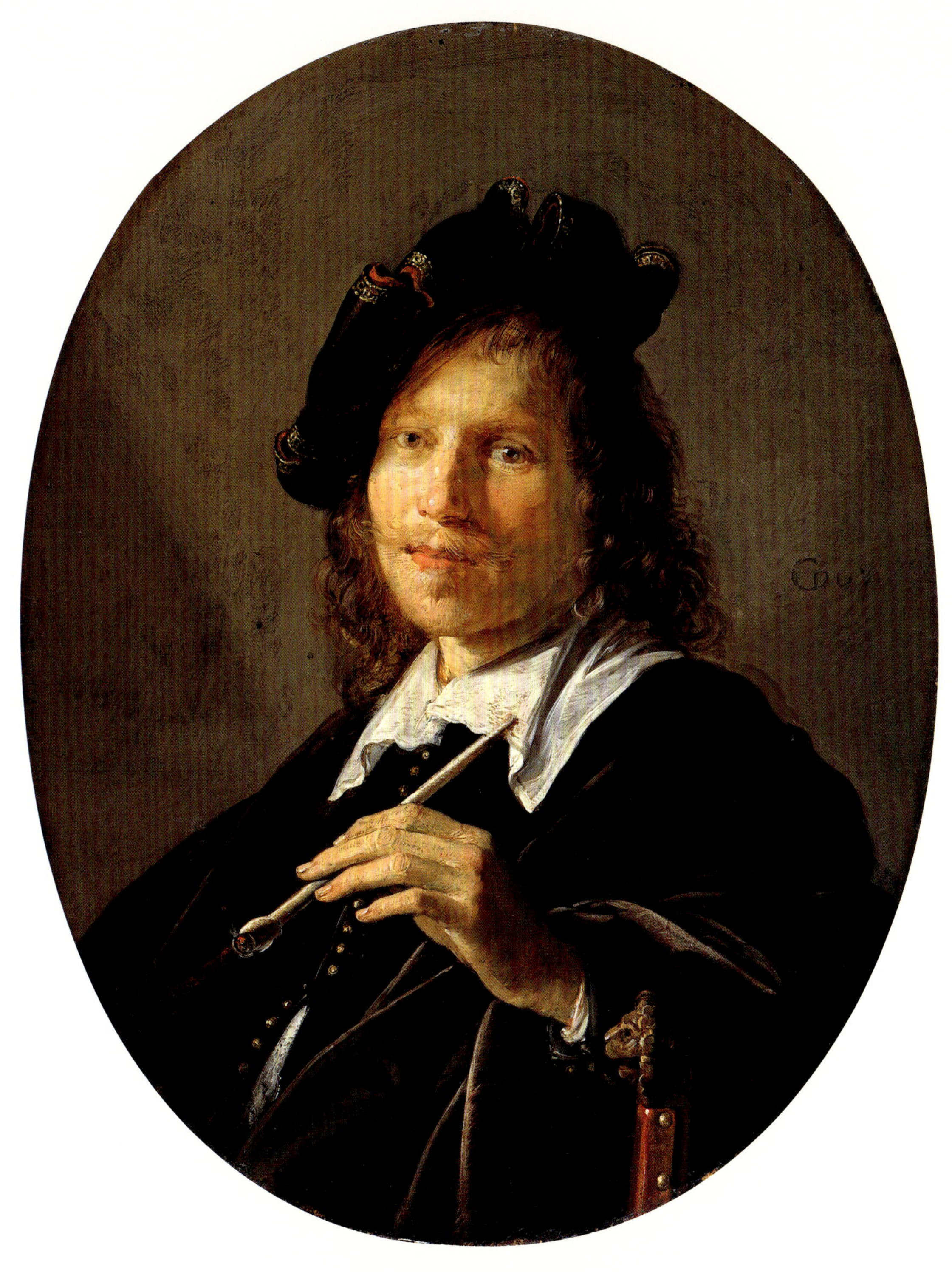

16.

Painter with Pipe and Book

c. 1645; oil on panel; 48 x 37 (18 7/8 x 14 1/2); Rijksmuseum, Amsterdam

Signed on paper tacked to the sill: GDov

· *Provenance* In the estate of Franco van Bleiswijck, Delft, 1734 (valued at *f* 200). Hendrik van Slingelandt, The Hague, 1750; by descent to Diederica Catherina van Slingelandt (valued at *f* 450 in her estate in 1811); Daniël Jbzn. Hooft sale, Amsterdam, 30 October 1860 (no. 1; according to catalogue, by descent from Slingelandt) (*f* 6,400, to Roos for dealer O. de Kat, Dordrecht). Leendert Dupper, Dordrecht; bequest of Leendert Dupper, 1870.

· *Bibliography* J. Smith 1829, no. 9; Moes 1897, no. 2096.12; Martin 1901, no. 104; Hofstede de Groot 1907, no. 267; Martin 1911, no. 51; Martin 1913, 16; Reutersswärd 1956, 107; Van Hall 1963, no. 527.47; Mastai 1975, 186–190; Rijksmuseum 1976, no. A86; Hunnewell 1983, 99–106; Sumowski 1983, 1: no. 271; Raupp 1984, 291 ff; Baer 1990, no. 44; Sluijter 1990b, 295–298; Sluijter 1993, 20, 70–71; Sumowski 1994, 3597.

· *Exhibitions* Brussels 1946, no. 22; Dordrecht 1949–1950, no. 7; Zurich 1953, no. 29; Rome 1954, no. 31 (cat. untraced); Milan 1954, no. 36 (cat. untraced); Paris 1961–1962, no. 1; Leiden 1988, no. 9.

· True trompe l'oeil is rare in Dou's oeuvre. Here, a curtain (used in The Netherlands during the seventeenth century to protect paintings from light and dust) is pulled aside to reveal a painting of a man posed at a window with pipe and book. Dou's refined technique, which makes the finely rendered curtain, rings, and rod almost palpable, is essential to the painting's illusionism. The man, who casts a shadow on the stone window surround, seems real, as does the book projecting out of the niche, yet their "reality" is contradicted by the thin black frame that surrounds the image. The trompe l'oeil tradition of "pasting" a piece of paper to a painting's surface[1] is used in this instance for the placement of the artist's signature, which appears on the curling *cartellino*. Many of Dou's other illusionistic paintings are so small in scale that one would never mistake the painting for what it purports to represent; here the trompe l'oeil succeeds completely because a painting—the subject of this work—can be any size at all.[2]

Pliny (in the *Natural History*, 35:65) recounts the story of the Greek painter, Parrhasius, who, envious of Zeuxis' standing, challenged his rival to a competition. Zeuxis produced a picture of grapes so true to life that birds flew up to eat them. Proud of the verdict of the birds, Zeuxis asked Parrhasius to draw back the curtain on his own painting so that it could be viewed, not realizing that Parrhasius' curtain *was* the painting. Zeuxis yielded up the prize, saying that whereas he had deceived the birds, Parrhasius had deceived Zeuxis. The prominence of the curtain in this painting by Dou is a deft and perhaps intentional allusion to Parrhasius' famous work.[3] Referring to the story, the Dutch poet Dirck Traudenius, a contemporary of Dou's, called the artist the "Hollandschen Parrhasius"[4]—high praise for an artist of the time, since the ability both to render the appearance of reality (*schijn zonder sijn*) and to provide amusement (*aangenaam bedrog*) was prized by theorists and the public alike.[5]

Thematically, this painting closely resembles *Man with a Pipe* (cat. 15). An important pictorial tradition linked artists and smoking in the seventeenth century. While in other contexts, smoking alludes to sensual pleasures or *vanitas*, here the act of smoking is more plausibly associated with contemplation.[6] A suspended moment without distracting movement, smoking is a particularly apt subject for trompe l'oeil. This moment of quiet, an implied component of the painter's creativity, contrasts with the painting's active background scene, in which a standing figure, turned away from an easel, leans over and confers with a seated colleague. Rembrandt used similarly complementary images in prints of the 1640s, supplementing the central figure with a narrative moral exemplum that elucidated the image's meaning.[7] As in the *Violin Player* (cat. 20), Dou may be contrasting the subsidiary background scene with the painting's main subject.

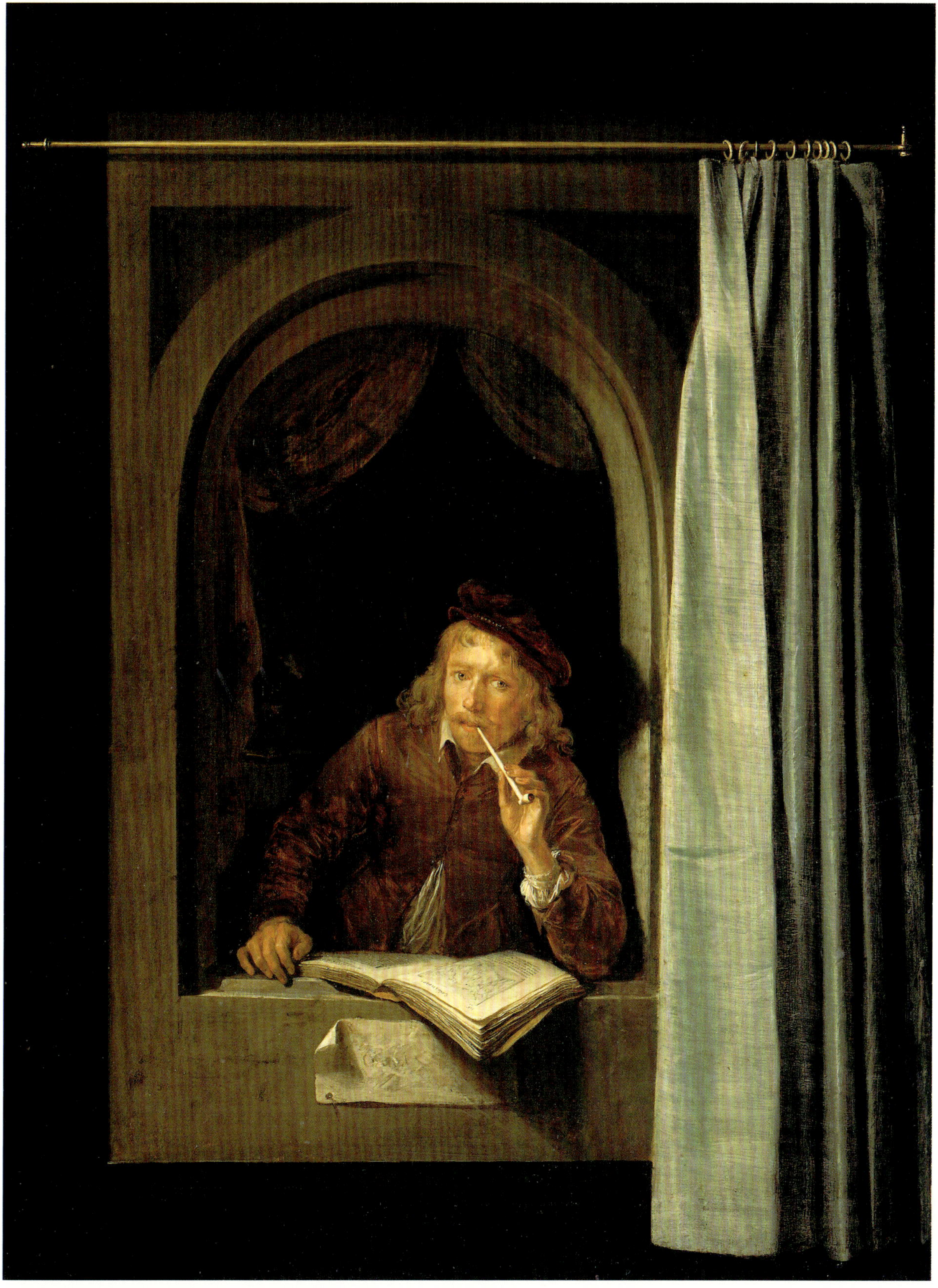

17.

Still Life with Hourglass, Pencase, and Print

DETAIL
Still Life with Hourglass, Pencase, and Print (cat. 17)

1647; oil on panel; original panel 23.1 x 16.4 (9 1/8 x 6 3/8); with added strips 24.7 x 17.9 (9 3/4 x 7); Wadsworth Atheneum Museum of Art, Hartford, Connecticut. The Ella Gallup Sumner and Mary Catlin Sumner Collection Fund

· *Provenance* (Piet de Boer, Amsterdam); purchased in 1937.

· *Bibliography* Boström 1949, 23; Bergström 1956, 182–184; Miedema 1975, 15; *Wadsworth Atheneum Bulletin* n.s. 3 (1937): 3; Mastai 1975, 186; Wadsworth Atheneum 1978, 131 (no. 38, by O. Naumann); Baer 1990, no. 48b.

· *Exhibitions* Hartford 1938; Frankfurt 1993, no. 26; Amsterdam and Cleveland 1999, no. 35a.

18.

Still Life with Book and Purse

1647; oil on panel; 22.9 x 17.8 (9 x 7); The Armand Hammer Collection, Fisher Gallery, University of Southern California, Los Angeles

Signed and dated in black on surface of book pages: GDov 1647

· *Provenance* Charles Stein, Paris; C. Stein sale, 8 June 1899 (FF830). Armand Hammer, 23 May 1947; gift of Armand Hammer, 1964.

· *Bibliography* Martin 1901, no. 368 (as dated 1697); Hofstede de Groot 1907, no. 392b (as dated 1697); Wadsworth Atheneum 1978, 131; Baer 1990, no. 48a.

· *Exhibitions* Amsterdam 1929, no. 41; Raleigh 1956, no. 19; Greenville, S.C., 1957; Omaha 1977; Los Angeles 1987, 14; Amsterdam and Cleveland 1999, no. 35b.

· These pendant still lifes depict closely viewed objects from the same angle and in the same light, which comes obliquely from the left. In each painting, Dou has placed objects in an implied niche but has indicated only one side and the bottom of the wooden structure.[1] The illusionistic character of the two paintings is emphasized by this close vantage point and constricted, nichelike space, from which several of the objects protrude.

The two paintings are studies in light and tone. In the Los Angeles still life, the tan-taupe color of the purse predominates, but it is relieved by the coral color of the book pages and the brown of the mullion and the shelf. The Hartford picture is more monochromatic, its palette limited to tan, brown, black, and white.

The image in the Los Angeles painting is simple and poetic, with Dou masterfully rendering the effect of light glancing off the pliant leather of the purse. In the Hartford pendant he focuses on contrasts of light and materials. The soft leather cover of the book is juxtaposed with the solid wood of the hourglass against which it leans. The chiaroscuro is more pronounced than in the Los Angeles still life, and Dou has carefully applied the highlights, which describe and define the forms. The book is loosely rendered, while the hourglass, pencase, and inkwell are meticulously described.

The hourglass, writing implements, and books in the Hartford still life are attributes of *studium*. Their juxtaposition implies the necessity of making good use of valuable, fleeting time and reinforces the notion of *ars longa vita brevis*.[2] Both paintings point explicitly to "the monetary benefits that can be derived from study."[3] In the Los Angeles painting, a conspicuously full moneybag rests on a thick book, whereas in the Hartford painting, the print of Gula (gluttony) cautions against excess.

One way that the artist of the seventeenth century distinguished himself from the craftsman was through intellectual endeavor and study. Ingvar Bergström traced the themes of the Hartford still life to fifteenth-century Italian *intarsia* representing intellectual pursuits and the liberal arts.[4] But for Dou's biographer, Philips Angel, financial gain was also an important measure of an artist's success; wealth was the surest way for an artist to rise above the social level of a craftsman. Just as Pliny in the *Natural History* (35:75) named several painters in antiquity who were well paid for their work, Angel cited Dou as a contemporary example of the financial profit that could accrue to a learned and successful artist.[5]

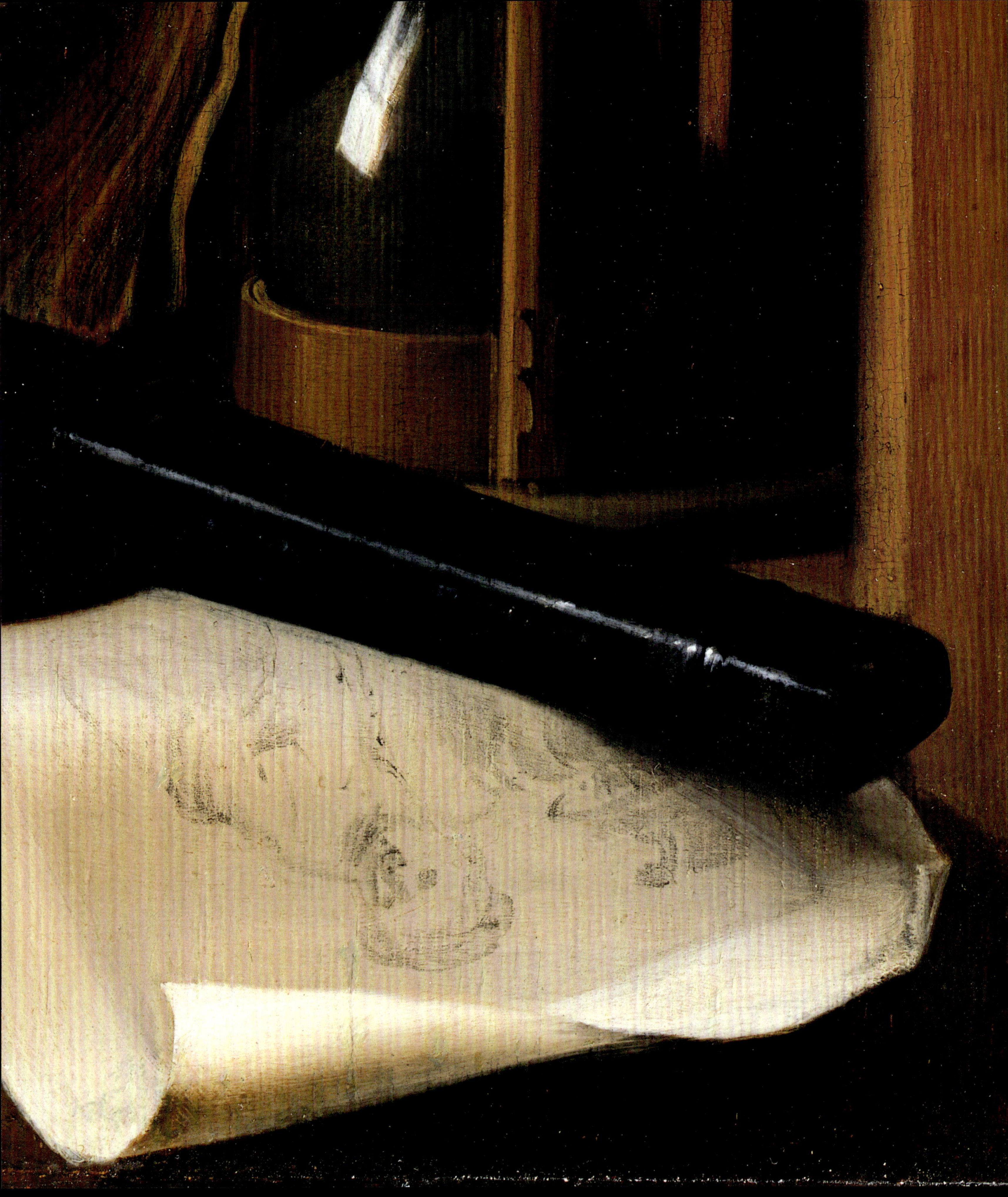

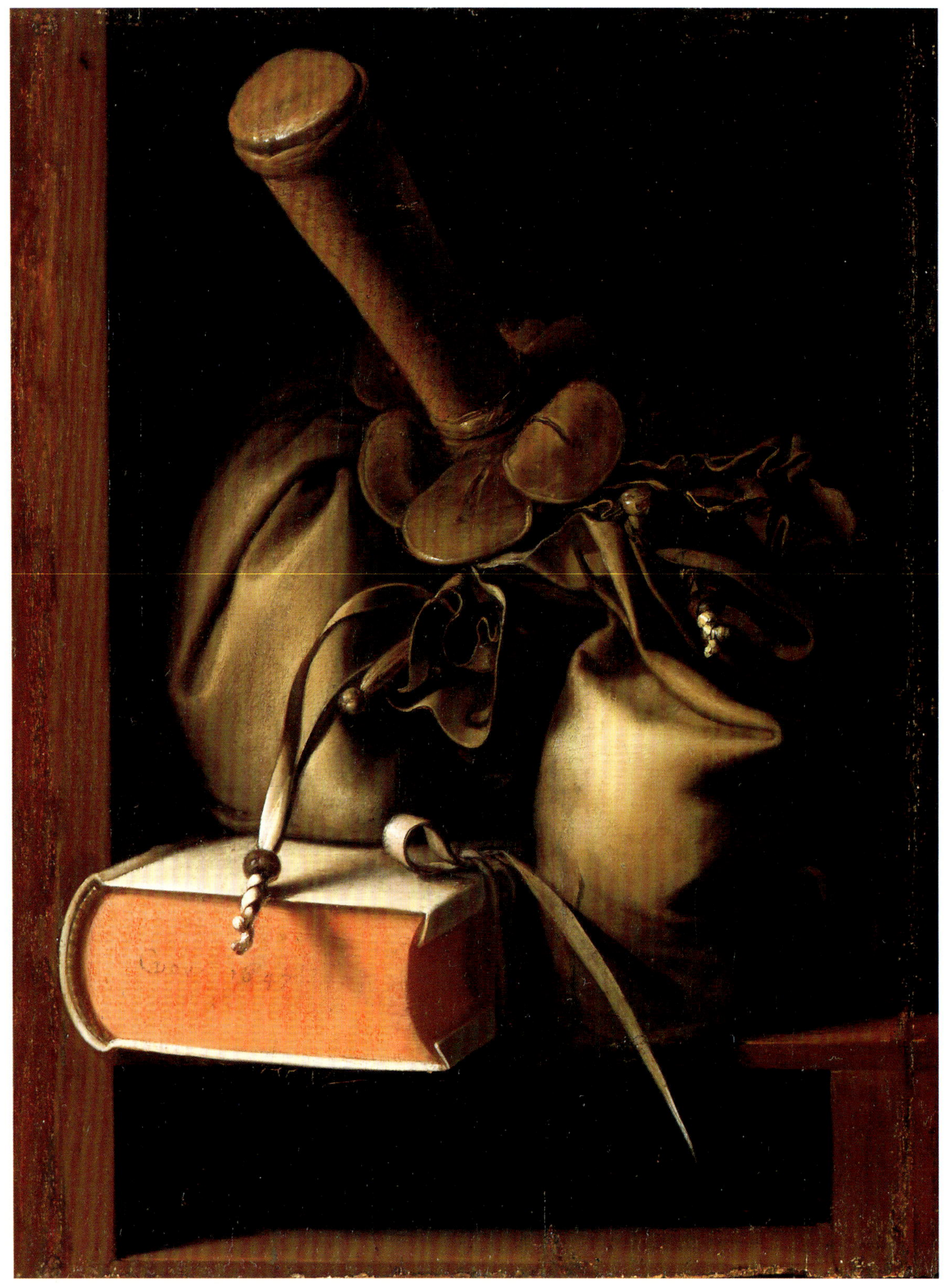

CAT. 18

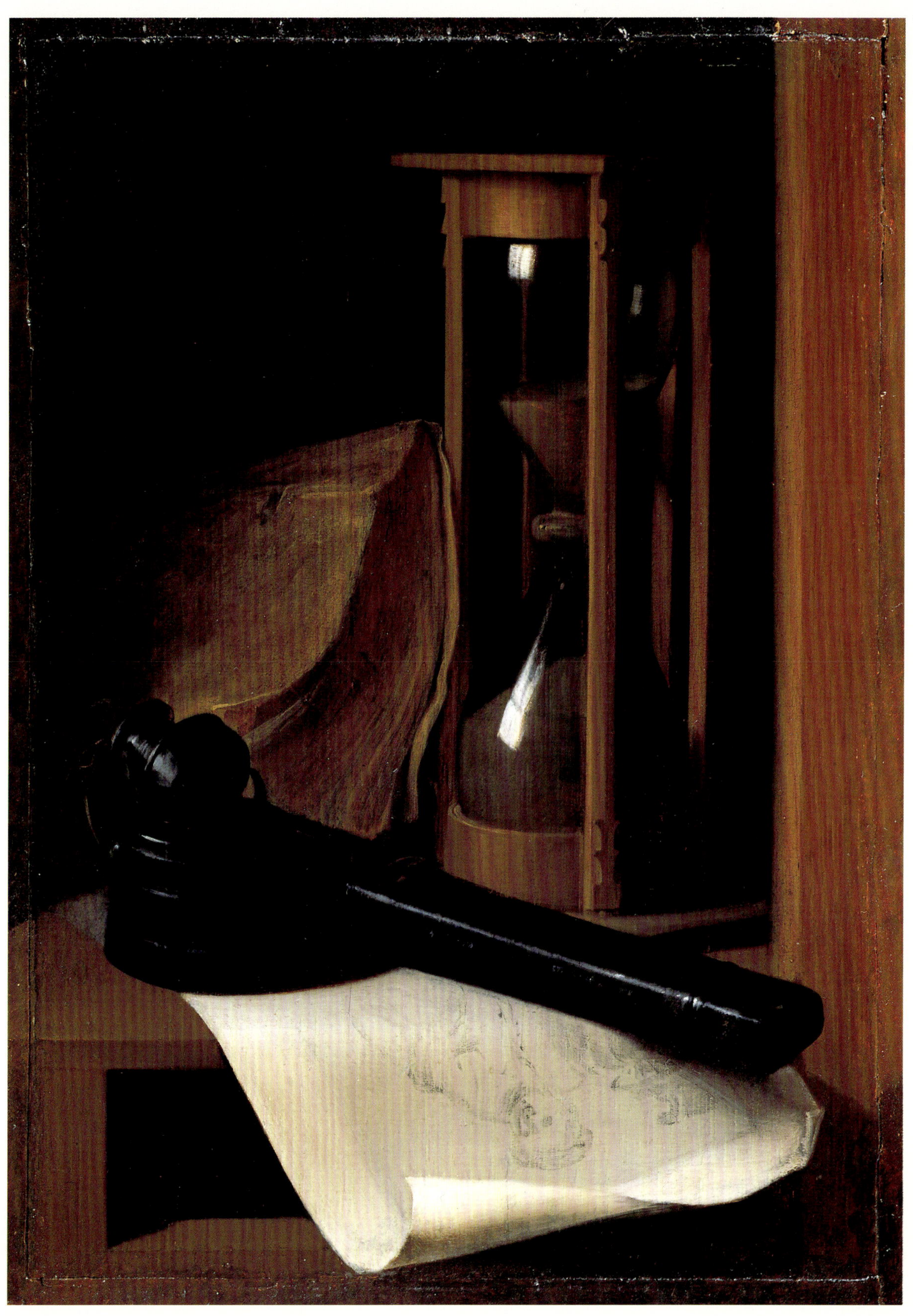

CAT. 17

19.

The Quack

DETAIL
The Quack (cat. 19)

1652; oil on panel; rounded top, 112 x 83 (44 1/8 x 32 3/4); Museum Boijmans van Beuningen, Rotterdam

Signed and dated on stone step: GDov 1652; *signed on mortar and again on parchment*

· *Provenance* Johann Wilhelm, Elector Palatine (d. 1716), Düsseldorf; Elector Carl Philipp (d. 1742), Düsseldorf; Elector Carl Theodor (d. 1799), Düsseldorf; Elector Maximilian IV Joseph, later King Maximilian I, Joseph (d. 1825), Düsseldorf and Munich; transferred to Munich on 7 November 1806, remaining in the Königliche Gemälde-Galerie, later the Alte Pinakothek, until 1938; sold with ministerial approval on 5 September 1938; (Agnew's, London); (Edward Speelman, London); Arthur Goldschmidt; W. van der Vorm, Rotterdam; presented to the Museum Boymans Foundation in 1939; inv. no. St. 4.

· *Bibliography* Van Gool 1751, 2: 538; Reynolds 1781; J. Smith 1829, no. 108; Martin 1901, no. 86; Hofstede de Groot 1907, no. 68; Martin 1911, no. 36; Martin 1913, 81; Gerson 1942, 246–251; Plietzsch 1960, 41 ff; Van Hall 1963, no. 527.32; Gudlaugsson 1965, 135; E. de Jongh 1967, 70–74; Eckardt 1971, 40; Emmens 1971, 4a–b; Gaskell 1982, 18–20; Alpers 1983, 116–118; Hunnewell 1983, 108–119; Sumowski 1983, 1: no. 280; Brown 1984, 43–47; Raupp 1984, 257; Feer 1985, 42–49; Stone-Ferrier 1989, 443; Baer 1990, no. 58; Sluijter 1990a, 28–33; The Hague and San Francisco 1990–1991, 219, 222; Sluijter 1993, 72–73; Dixon 1995, 189–190; Lammertse 1997, 110–120.

· *Exhibitions* Rotterdam 1939–1940, no. 14; Amsterdam 1976, no. 16.

· *The Quack* is in all respects exceptional in Dou's oeuvre. It is his largest panel and is painted on Spanish cedar rather than his usual oak.[1] The composition is populated by a greater number of figures than in any of Dou's other works, and they display an unparalleled diversity of age, type, and engagement.

The quack—a medical charlatan—is hawking his wares to a small crowd on the outskirts of Leiden. He is distinguished from Dou's other representations of doctors by his ruffed collar, slashed sleeves, cape, and wide beret.[2] Among the onlookers listening to his pitch are an elderly woman at the right, whose pocket is being picked; a schoolboy, who places one hand on the quack's table while turning toward the old woman; a pancake baker, wiping a baby's rear[3] while listening to a girl who is speaking eagerly to her; a hunter with a dead hare hanging from his rifle barrel; a trio of youngsters standing between the hunter and the quack's table, all looking up at him; a couple at the back (she listens attentively and offers a coin to the quack while her companion seems more interested in her décolleté); and a pipe-smoking farmer wheeling his produce. The figures clearly occupy a social stratum below that of the painter and his patrons.[4] The absorption of the spectators in the quack's chatter is alternately comic (the leering man in the background taking advantage of his companion's distraction) and disturbing (the pickpocket at the far right and the schoolboy neglecting his duty). The young boy at the left, whose action of luring a bird mimics that of the quack, and the sniffing dog in the foreground show no interest in the quack.

From an arch-shaped window, a painter with Dou's features holding palette and brushes, addresses the viewer. By including himself as a spectator, the artist compels the viewer to identify himself with the crowd around the quack.[5] The step in the foreground, which removes the scene from the viewer's space, and the frozen action of the figures create the impression of a staged *tableau vivant*.

The building in the painting's background—the Blauwpoort—did not assume the form in which it is depicted here until 1667, a full fifteen years after Dou dated the panel. The painting was certainly reworked to include the later form of the Blauwpoort's tower, but there is no stylistic reason to doubt that the genesis of the composition dates to 1652.[6]

The robust, carefully modeled forms, the studied chiaroscuro, and the ambitiousness of the scene exemplify Dou's mature style. The use of bright, local colors is characteristic of his work from the late 1640s and early 1650s.[7] Lightning strokes of white and an assured looseness of technique call attention to the quack's costume, and hence, to the quack himself. The meticulous description of the various textures—in particular the skilled differentiation of the fur of the monkey, the dog, and the hare—are evidence of Dou's virtuoso handling of paint.

Dou took pains to situate the event geographically and temporally. The paper tacked to the brick wall in the foreground is inscribed with the word *kermis*, and the tankard hanging above it, signaling the building as an inn, also conjures up the freedom and license enjoyed at the annual fair. The Blauwpoort marked the city limits of Leiden; a spire of a church and a windmill of the city can be glimpsed in the background. Including such a readily identifiable landmark heightens the impression of contemporaneity in the same way that genre scenes give a "realistic" impression of everyday life. However, as Eddy de Jongh has noted, the deliberate combination of such disparate human activity already calls into question the realism of the image.[8]

It is clear, as has been noted by many writers on the painting, that Dou intended some sort of symbolic comparison to be drawn between the quack and the artist.[9] The various interpretations of the painting differ, for the most part, only in where they place the emphasis.

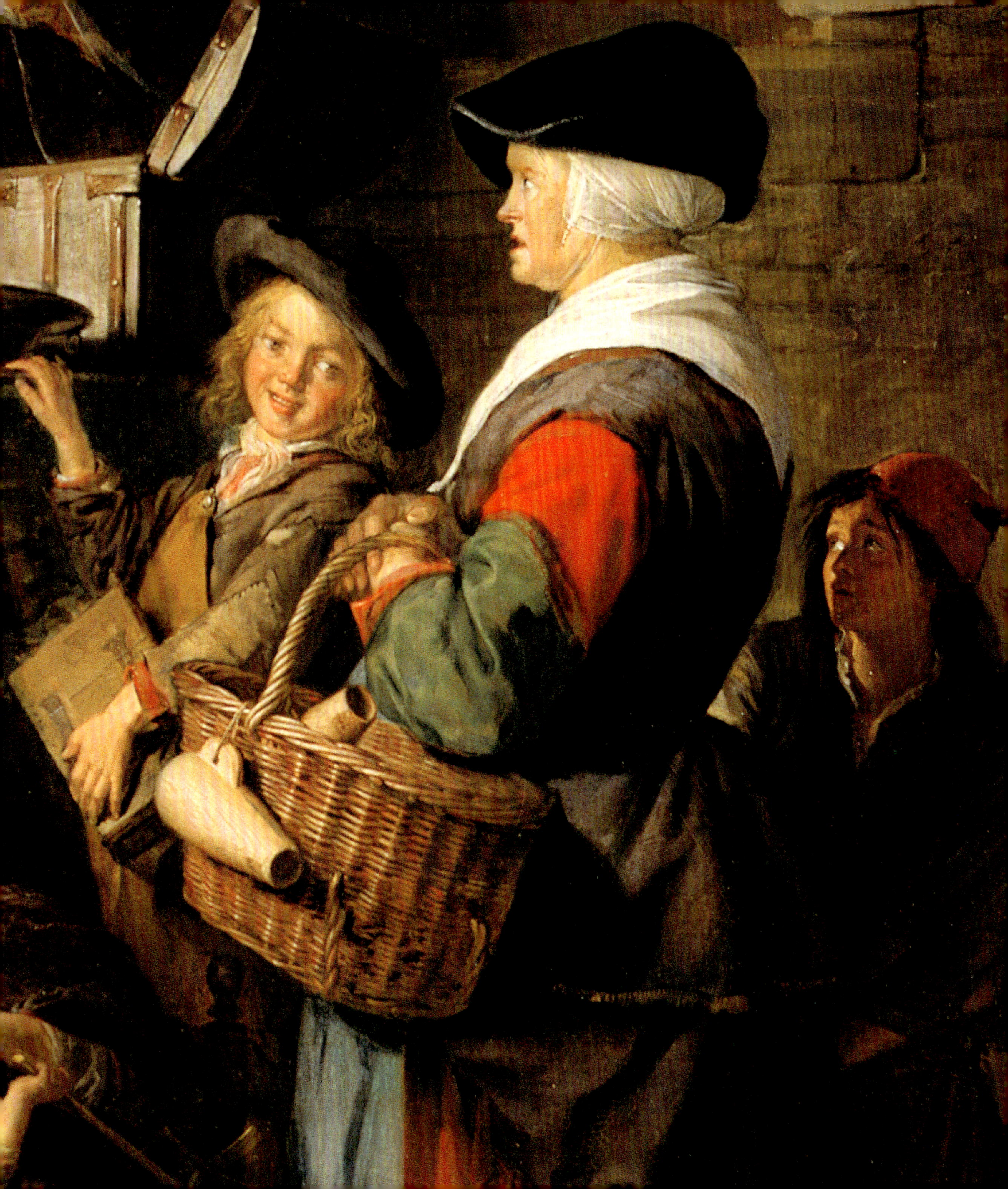

One reading of the painting, which seems overly programmatic, stresses the Aristotelian concept of the superiority of the contemplative life, represented by the painter, over the active life of the farmer and the sensual life of the quack.[10] Another sees it rather as a taxonomic assembly of instances of human behavior, alerting the spectator not only to the duplicity of the quack but also to the deception of the painted surface.[11] A middle ground treats both the artist and the quack as masters of deception. However, choosing between the two has moral implications: to choose the quack's useless wares is to be wrongly deceived, whereas to choose the painter's edifying and beautiful products both benefits and delights the viewer.[12] Dou's contemporary, the artist and theorist Samuel van Hoogstraeten (1627–1678) explained that "a finished painting is like a mirror of nature, so that things which are not there seem to be there, the result of deception in a permissible, entertaining, and praiseworthy way."[13]

In refining this reading, Eric Jan Sluijter has recently contrasted the pernicious deceit of the quack, preying on the simple and gullible public, with the amusing deceit of the artist, who presents the scene to us as real.[14] The painting, Sluijter argues, contains outwardly comic elements: people laughing—a cue to the audience that they too should laugh; the figure of the rascal, juxtaposed with the man of honor; and the monkey, whose antics, it was believed, were a remedy to melancholy. Sluijter ties these comic elements to peasant scenes of the sixteenth and early seventeenth century in which city dwellers mediate between the comic behavior of the country folk and the viewer of the painting. Dou here fills that role.[15] Dou, then, has juxtaposed himself with the quack both to comment on the nature of artistic deception and to mediate between the viewer and the artist's "deception"—the painting in which he displays his mastery by rendering a variety of types, surfaces, and activities.

Because of the unusually complex iconography and the size of the painting, it is possible that *The Quack* was made in response to a specific commission. Many of the ideas reflected in the painting echo those in emblem books, as well as in contemporary prints and comic literature.[16] The program would not have had to have been devised by an unusually learned patron.[17]

In many ways, *The Quack* exhibits those artistic qualities that Philips Angel (and by extension, Dou's patrons) deemed most important: delighting the eye, depicting the range and multiplicity of creation, and presenting a careful arrangement of light and shadow. The ideas that *The Quack* represents—that painting is intended to delight, amuse, deceive, and instruct—were central to Dou's art. Its scale and subject make it an artistic manifesto of sorts, in which Dou displays his virtuosity while commenting explicitly on the role of the artist.

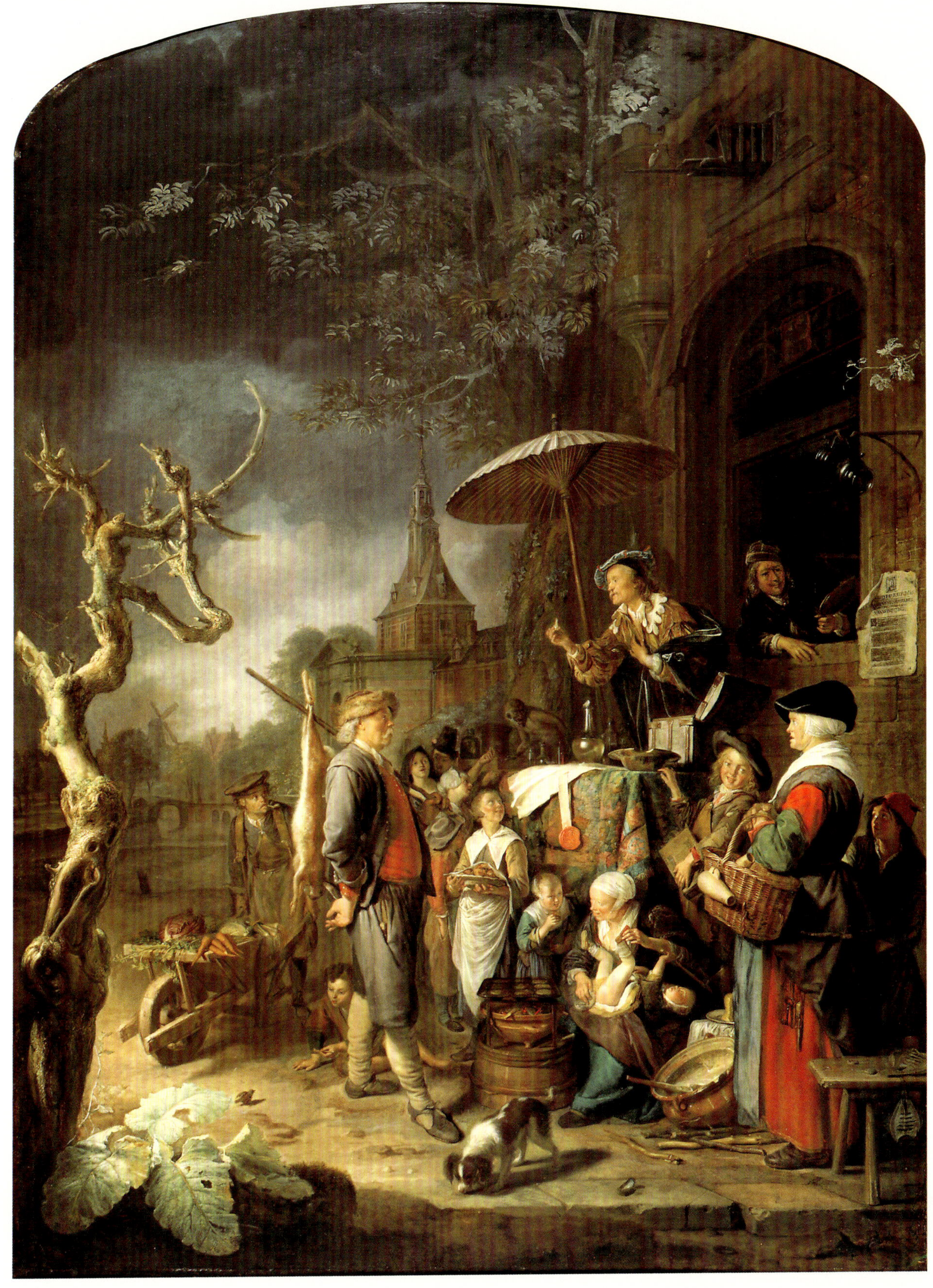

20.

Violin Player

1653; oil on panel; arched top, 31.7 x 20.3 (12 ½ x 8); Princely Collections, Vaduz Castle, Liechtenstein

Signed and dated bottom center: GDov 1653

· *Provenance* Philippe, duc d'Orléans, Paris, by 1727; Louis Philippe Joseph, duc d'Orléans, Paris. Thomas Moore Slade, London, 1792; (probably Thomas Moore Slade sale, Pall Mall, London, 1793 [300 gns to John Davenport]); (John Davenport sale, Christie's, London, 21 February 1801 [no. 90] [304.10 gns, to Meyers]). Richard Walker, Liverpool. (Sale, Christie's, London, 5 March 1803 [no. 6] [304.10 gns, to Birch]). (Possibly sale, Phillips, London, 21–22 March 1815 [no. 173] [346.10 gns]). (Possibly sale, Phillips, London, 2–3 June 1815 [no. 46]: [52 gns]). Charles, duc de Berry, Paris; (duchesse de Berry sale, Paillet, Paris, 5 April 1837 [no. 59] [FF11,228, to Héris] [sold for FF10,700 to Demidoff]). Baron Alphonse de Rothschild, Paris. (Alex Wengraf, London). Joseph Ritman, Amsterdam, 1980; (Noortman Gallery, Maastricht and London); private collection Maastricht; the Prince of Liechtenstein, 1999.

· *Bibliography* Du Bois de Saint Gelais 1727, 179; J. Smith 1829, no. 74; J. Smith 1842, no. 51; Moes 1897, no. 2096.4; Martin 1901, no. 173; Hofstede de Groot 1907, no. 154; Martin 1911, no. 83; Martin 1913, 86;[1] Raupp 1978, 109–110; Raupp 1984, 240; Sumowski 1983, 1: no. 278; Baer 1990, no. 63; Sumowski 1994, 3597.

· *Exhibitions* Amsterdam 1983, no. 17; Leiden 1988, no. 10; Amsterdam 1989, no. 6; *The Amateur's Cabinet: Seventeenth-Century Masterpieces from Dutch Private Collections*, exh. cat., Mauritshuis (The Hague, 1995), no. 8.

· Gerrit van Honthorst (1591–1656) was the first Dutch painter to depict a half-length figure of a violinist leaning out from behind a window ledge (fig. 1). Dou has similarly portrayed his violin player illusionistically leaning out of an arched stone opening, but the exuberance of Van Honthorst's life-size figure has here given way to Dou's smaller, pensive image of a violinist playing his instrument. The painting's illusionism is enhanced by Dou's realistic portrayal of the worn pages of the music book protruding into the viewer's space and by the nubby texture of the carpet hanging over the stone relief. The figure of a youth busily grinding pigment behind the violinist indicates that the scene takes place in an artist's studio. Seated at the table with the youth is a man smoking a pipe, perhaps an artist or a visitor to the studio.

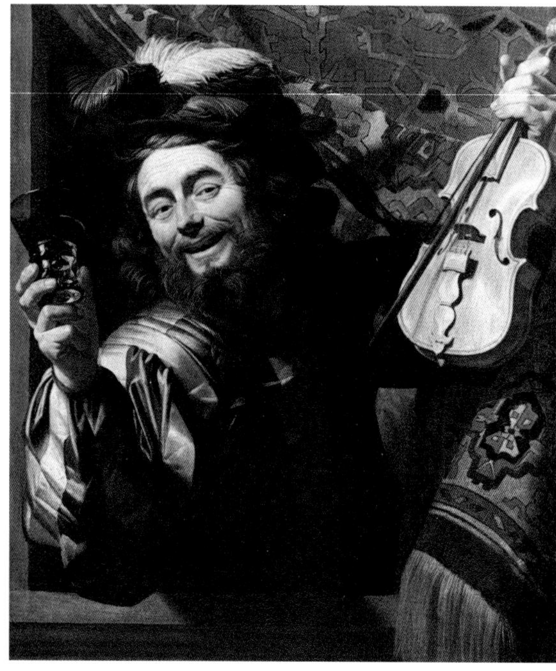

FIGURE 1
Gerrit van Honthorst, *Merry Violinist*, 1623, oil on canvas, Rijksmuseum, Amsterdam

Depictions of artists as musicians appear in several other seventeenth-century Dutch paintings, and it seems likely that the violinist in this painting is an artist.[2] In some contexts, music-making was viewed as a seductive distraction to be avoided, or as a source of sensual pleasure, or as an idle pursuit. The character of this image, however, indicates that Dou intended to suggest music's power to inspire the painter's creative faculties.[3] Indeed, music and painting were often allied as liberal arts that instilled harmony and balance in life.[4] They also provided diversions that were both pleasurable and enlightening. Perhaps it was in this context that Dou intended the bas-relief below the figure to be read. The mask held by the putto, a symbol of *Pictura*, may allude to the pleasurable deception of this illusionistic painting.[5]

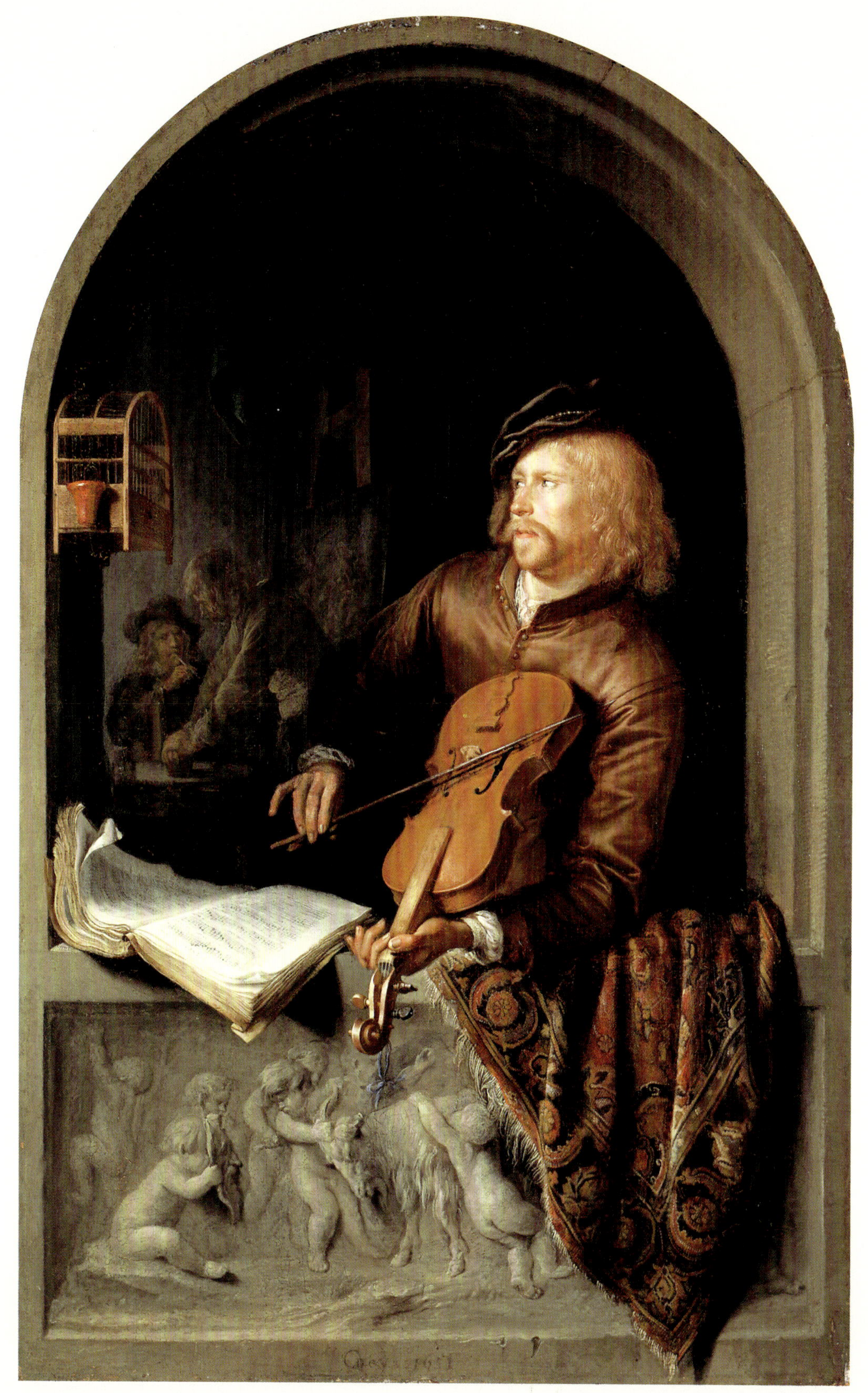

21.

The Young Mother

1658; oil on panel; arched top, 73.5 x 55.5 (28 7/8 x 21 7/8); Royal Cabinet of Paintings Mauritshuis, The Hague

Signed and dated in lower part of coat of arms: GDov 1658

· *Provenance* Purchased directly from the artist by the States General; part of the gift of the States General to King Charles II of England in 1660; King James II, Whitehall, London, 1685–1688; William III, Het Loo, Apeldoorn, after 1688–1702; Johan Willem Friso, Het Loo, 1702–1711; in Het Loo, 1712–1713 (1712 taxation inv. 4; 1713 inv. 897); Maria Louisa van Hessen-Kassel, Princessehof, Leeuwarden, after 1718–1731; William IV, Het Loo, Apeldoorn, after 1734, 1747 (?); 1757–1763 (1757 inv. 86); William V, The Hague, 1763–1795; taken by the French at the conquest of Holland and sent to the Louvre, Paris, 1795–1815; King William I, The Hague, 1815; Mauritshuis, 1821.[1]

· *Bibliography* J. Smith 1829, no. 90; Martin 1901, no. 305; Hofstede de Groot 1907, no. 110; Martin 1911, no. 165; Martin 1913, 90; Sumowksi 1983, no. 284; Mauritshuis 1985, no. 28; Broos 1987, 111–118 (no. 20); Franits 1987, 63 and 119 ff; Baer 1990, no. 76; Franits 1993, 16, 84, 202 note 52; Struick van de Loeff and Groen 1993; Sumowski 1994, 3597; Slive 1995, no. 102.

· *Exhibitions* Brussels 1946, no. 26; Amsterdam 1952, no. 36; Leiden 1956, no. 29; London 1964, no. 7; Amsterdam 1965, no. 3; The Hague 1988–1989, no. 4; Amsterdam 1989, no. 7.

· *The Young Mother* is a bravura demonstration of Dou's technical skill. The skin tones of the mother's face appear almost translucent. The wisps of hair escaping from beneath the mother's cap and the feathers of the dead bird on the table at the right have been meticulously described using a tiny brush. Dou has also carefully observed and captured the varied reflective surfaces of the many objects that furnish this spacious interior. The woman's clothes, particularly the whites of her shirt, are more freely painted.

A convincing chiaroscuro suggests depth and atmosphere in the complex and voluminous interior. The balustrade at the top, over which a curtain has been thrown, is a device used often by other seventeenth-century Dutch artists (to greatest effect by Jan Steen) but rarely by Dou. The broad arch of the painting recalls the proscenium of a theater. This device, which echoes Dou's use of the arch-shaped window (compare cats. 20, 29, and 35), heightens the presentational aspect of the painting.

The figures that form the subject of *The Young Mother* are united by a play of glances: a young girl looks fondly at a baby in its cradle, who gazes at its mother as she sews. The mother, in turn, looks out at the viewer, engaging him in mute dialogue. The home is amply furnished. The provisions that fill the corner of the painting serve a dual function—as indications of the household's abundance and as painterly still-life elements. The bustling activity of the servants in the background signals that the household is running smoothly.

Dou here depicts the world of the Dutch housewife, engaged in her duties as mother and mistress of the home. Sewing was traditionally associated with diligence, domesticity, and by extension, virtue. The activity also carried with it pedagogical associations (in this case, at the very least, she sets a good example for her daughter), an important aspect of the woman's role as mother. The value inherent in the proper education of children may be implied in the comportment of the young girl, solicitously caring for the baby in the cradle. The mother's discarded shoe and the unlit, overturned lantern (for use out-of-doors) may be further reminders that the woman's place is in the home.[2] The man's domain, suggested in the painting by the sword and cloak, globe and books is, by contrast, outside the house. Indeed, the husband is absent, although the cupid, which figures prominently on the column and the birdcage (which often carries erotic associations [see cat. 32]) suggest the union of the two realms in marital love.[3]

The Young Mother may originally have been commissioned to celebrate a wedding.[4] Abraham Bredius and Cornelis Hofstede de Groot identified the coat of arms in the window as that of the Van Adrichems, a regent family from Delft.[5] Magdalena van Adrichem (1639–1684) married Dirck van Beresteyn, *advocaat voor het Hof van Holland*, on 20 November 1652. However, Van Beresteyn died on 23 September 1653, and the commission may as a consequence have been withdrawn. This might explain Dou's alteration of the date, as well as the felicitous presence in his studio of such an important piece at the time that Dou received the commission from the States of Holland and Westfriesland.[6]

The number "501" in white at the lower right edge of the painting corresponds to its inventory number at the time of the reign of James II (1685–1688). Its presence confirms beyond doubt that this painting was part of the Dutch gift to Charles II.[7]

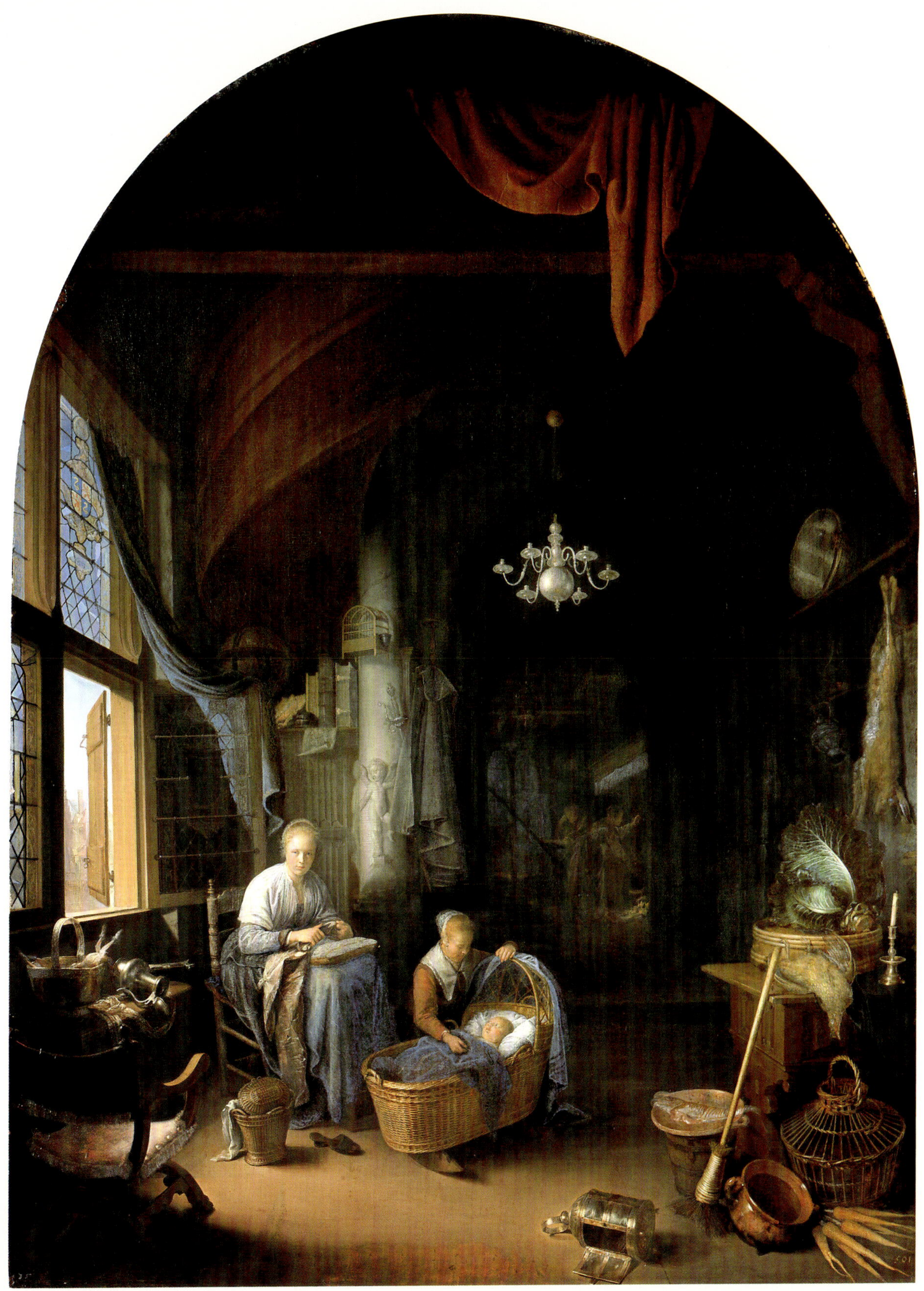

22.

Young Woman in a Black Veil

c. 1660; oil on panel; oval, 14.5 x 11.7 (5 7/8 x 4 5/8); The National Gallery, London

Signed at left: GDov [1]

· *Provenance* Robert de Saint-Victor, Rouen; R. de Saint-Victor sale, Paris, 26 November 1822 (no. 95) (FF501, to Mme Hazard). [According to J. Smith, in Paignon Dijonval, 1821, purchased en bloc by Mr. Emmerson, but not in Paignon Dijonval and Morel Vindé sale, Paris, 17–18 December 1821]. John Farquhar sale, 10 October 1823 (no. 220) (29 gns, to Townley). Henry Fulton sale, London, 20 June 1834 (no. 93) (43 gns, to Charles Brind); (C. Brind sale, Christie's, London, 12 May 1849 [no. 47] [46 gns, to Emery]). Bequest of Wynn Ellis to the National Gallery, 1876.

· *Bibliography* J. Smith 1829, no. 99; J. Smith 1842, no. 53; Martin 1901, no. 215; Hofstede de Groot 1907, no. 364; Martin 1911, no. 104; Martin 1913, 51; Sumowski 1983, 1: no. 303; MacLaren 1960, 106 (no. 968); Baer 1990, no. 78; MacLaren and Brown 1991, 1: 108 (no. 968).

· *Exhibitions* British Institution, London, 1848, no. 27 (cat. untraced).

• The dating of this exquisite portrait of a young woman, who confronts the viewer with an open expression, has been the subject of much disagreement.[2] However, the woman's fur-trimmed, green velvet jacket with gold piping appears exclusively in Dou's works from the 1660s.[3] Such a late date for this intimate portrait would suggest that the sitter was in some way important to the painter, who had for all intents and purposes given up portrait painting some twenty years earlier and who was then at the height of his fame and artistic activity.

X-radiography indicates that the pose of the figure was not arrived at easily. The sitter was originally posed looking to the left; her chin appears narrower and her mouth somewhat puckered. The image revealed by the x-radiograph may in fact date to the late 1630s or early 1640s, which would account for the panel's resemblance to Dou's portraiture of the earlier period.

Despite its small size, *Young Woman in a Black Veil* is very freely painted. Parallel horizontal strokes on and around the sitter's nose, to the right of her mouth, and around her eyes enliven the surface. Although Dou has carefully drawn the woman's delicate features, he merely suggests the sensuous quality of her slightly parted lips by leaving them softly diffused. The color range is equally subtle and beautifully orchestrated. The gray used for shading around the woman's eyes is complemented by brown and gold for the modeling at the side of her face and the pink of her cheeks.

Individual strokes of gold and brown describe the woman's long, curly hair. In contrast to the carefully drawn and traditionally modeled pearls at her neck, the delicate dangling earrings are defined by the highlights in the pearl orbs and the gold filigree work. The lacy trim of the jacket's white collar seems to have been incised with the butt end of a tiny brush, and the brushwork emphasizes the spiky nature of the fur. The black bow and veil in the woman's hair are very thinly and fluidly painted.

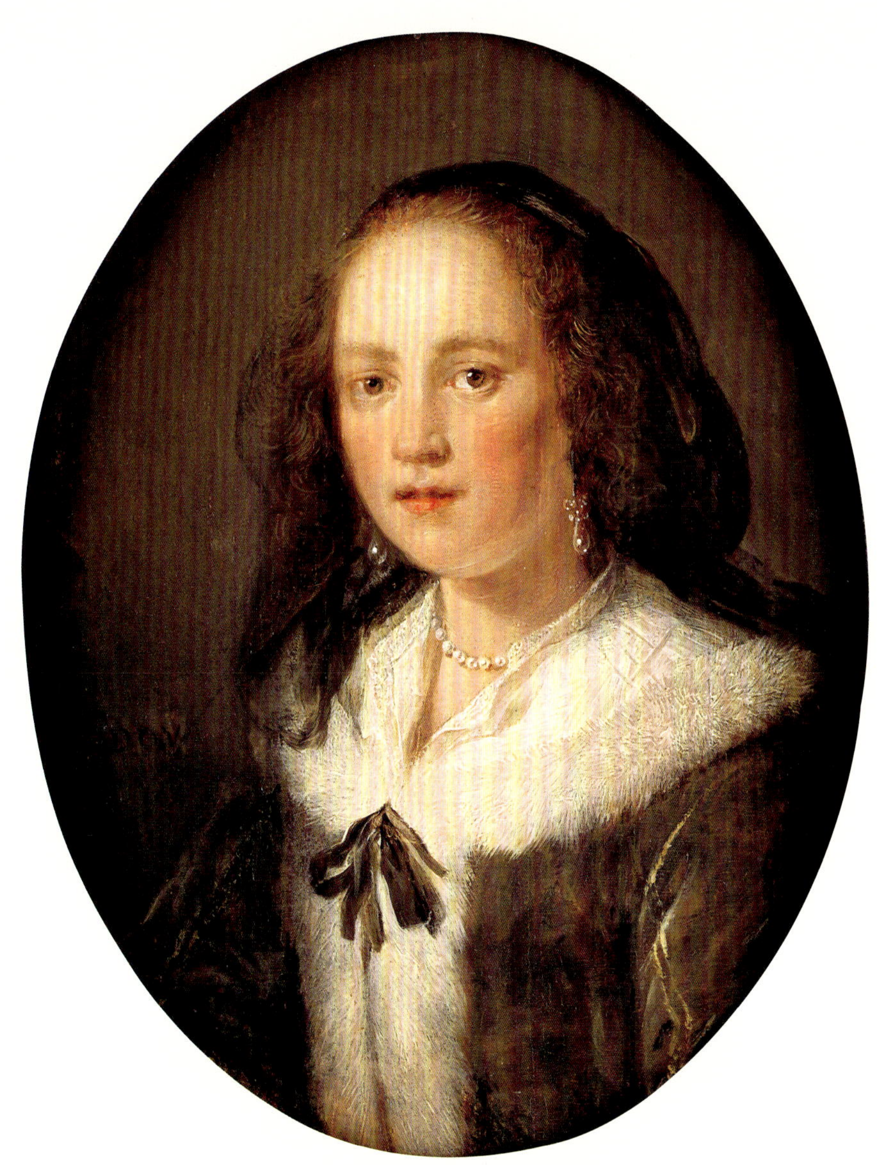

YOUNG WOMAN IN A BLACK VEIL

23.
The Wine Cellar

c. 1660; oil on panel; 30.5 x 25.4 (12 x 10); private collection, Switzerland

· *Provenance* Possibly Johan de Bye, Leiden, 1665 (no. 13). Antony Grill sale, Amsterdam, 14 April 1728 (no. 2) (*f*810). Gerrit Braamkamp sale, Amsterdam, 31 July 1771 (no. 57) (*f*845, to H. Pothoven). Six van Winter, Amsterdam. Van Loon, Amsterdam, 1829; purchased en bloc by Rothschild, 1878. Clarence McKay, Long Island, 1945; (sale, Christie's, London, 29 June 1973 [no. 22] [*f*22,000, to O. Swann]). Graham, on loan to the Ashmolean Museum, 1984; (sale, Christie's, London, 11 April 1986 [no. 37]).

· *Bibliography* J. Smith 1829, no. 42; J. Smith 1842, no. 70; Martin 1901, no. 350; Hofstede de Groot 1907, no. 256; Martin 1911, no. 204; Boström 1949, 23; Bille 1961, 2: 14 (no. 57); Baer 1990, no. 83; Sumowski 1994, no. 2249.

· *Exhibitions* Arti, Amsterdam, winter 1867 (cat. untraced).

· Dou has markedly differentiated between the foreground and background figures in *The Wine Cellar.* The full-length figures of the maidservant and young man are comfortably set into an indeterminate, but rather deep, space. They are painted in a detailed manner, with the muted red of the girl's dress and its green overskirt relieving the predominant brown tones of the painting. The interaction between the figures is unusually lively and engaging.

Dou has paid careful attention to the still-life details in the lower left corner. His free and spirited touch is most evident in the core and the veining of the cabbage and in the wooden hoops encircling the wine cask. By contrast, the figure of an old man hunched over a fire in the essentially monochromatic background, his back turned to the young couple, is sketched in a series of shorthand strokes that merely suggest his spectral form and the hearth before which he sits. Three sources of light dispel the enveloping darkness. Dou has captured the inherent quality of each type of illumination: the sparks and glow from the fire; the diffuse, flickering and freely painted light from the lantern; and the steadily burning and bright flame of the candle.

Dou often included a background scene in his paintings to comment on or elucidate the meaning of the foreground action (compare, for example, cats. 16 and 20). The theme expressed in the foreground of *The Wine Cellar* is young love. The flirtatious interaction of the figures and the surreptitious nature of their meeting, together with the presence of wine—love's nectar—and the mousetrap—the symbol of love's sweet slavery—make the subject clear. The milk jug, the cabbage, and the candle, with their uterine and phallic shapes, reinforce the erotic undertone of the scene. The shrouded and huddled man in the background, symbol of winter and old age, contrasts with the implicit warmth and youth of the foreground. Admonitory in nature, he probably alludes to the transience of all earthly things (and in this context particularly, of youth, beauty, and love). The warning he embodies was echoed and strengthened in a *vanitas* still life painted on the cover of the case originally designed to protect this picture (fig. 1).[1]

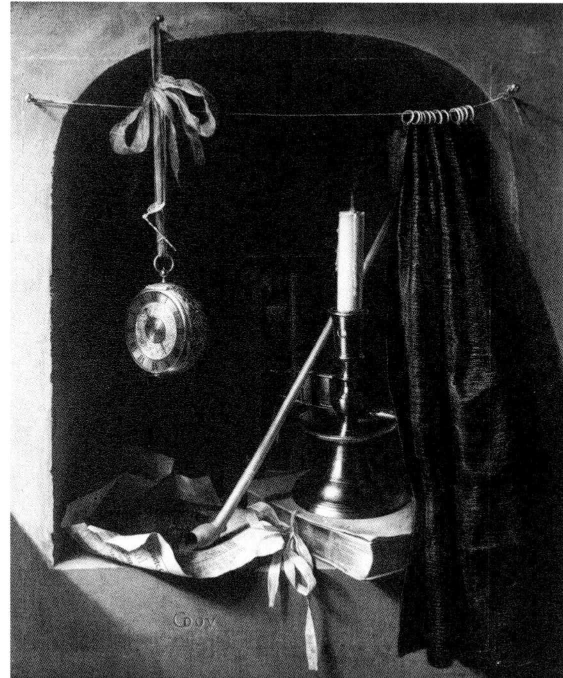

FIGURE 1
Still Life with Candlestick, Pipe, and Pocketwatch, c. 1660, oil on panel, Staatliche Kunstsammlungen, Gemäldegalerie Alte Meister, Dresden

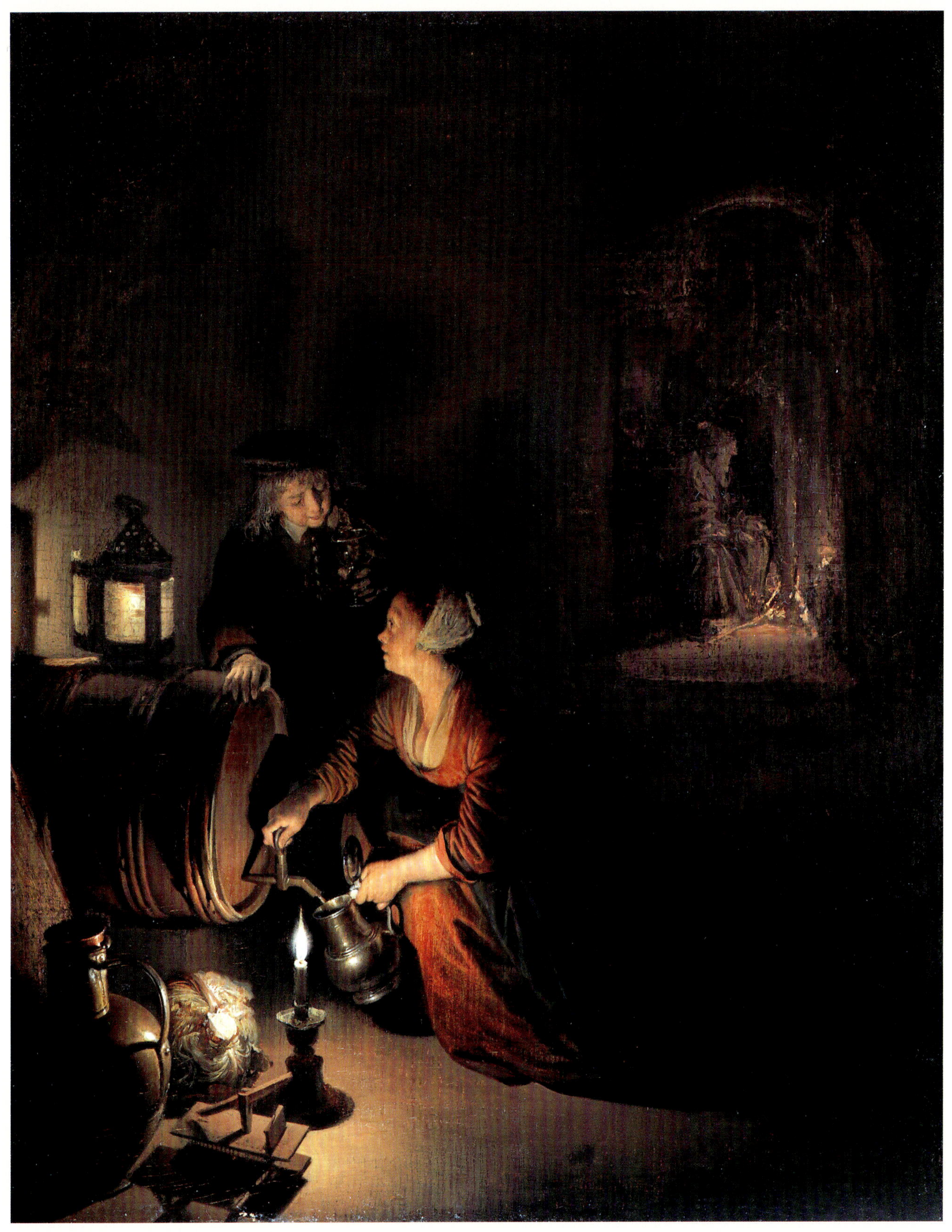

24.

Woman Asleep

c. 1660–1665; oil on panel; arched top, 30 x 21.5 (11 7/8 x 8 1/2); private collection, Switzerland

· *Provenance* (Floris Drabbe, Leiden, 1 April 1734 [no. 5]). Baillie, 1774. Adrian [d. 1781] and John Hope [d. 1784], Amsterdam and London; John Hope, Amsterdam, The Hague, Heemstede; by inheritance to Henry Hope [d. 1811], London; by inheritance to Henry Philip Hope [d. 1839], London (in possession of Thomas Hope [d. 1831], London); by inheritance to Henry Thomas Hope [d. 1862], London; by inheritance to his widow, née Adèle Bichat [d. 1884], London; by inheritance to Henry Francis Hope Pelham-Clinton-Hope, London; (Asher Wertheimer, London, 1898); thence by descent; (Sale, Sotheby's, London, 28 March 1979 [no. 67]); acquired by present owner.

· *Bibliography* Reynolds 1781, 2: 358; J. Smith 1829, no. 134; Waagen 1854–1857, 2: 117; Martin 1901, no. 351; Hofstede de Groot 1907, no. 258; Martin 1911, no. 311; Martin 1913, 177; Baer 1990, no. 93; Sumowski 1994, no. 2250.

· *Exhibitions* London 1881, no. 70 (cat. untraced); London 1891–1897, no. 41 (cat. untraced).

· Like many of Dou's paintings, this scene of two cavaliers at a table with a sleeping woman has the character of a *tableau vivant*, with theatrically dressed and posed characters revealed by a parted curtain.[1] Unlike many of Dou's subjects, however, this representation has an anecdotal rather than emblematic character.[2]

There are three sources of artificial light in the painting.[3] The lantern has been placed so as to spread a decorative pattern of light on the floor. Most strongly illuminated is the woman's décolleté, strikingly framed by the gauzy and rapidly brushed bodice. The candle and the dress cast pink and blue reflections on her skin. The patch of her right sleeve, which catches the light, is broadly brushed in a lighter blue that elicits the texture of velvet. Her smooth, rosy face is set off by tiny wisps of hair that have escaped from under her cap.

The cavalier's face is a lighter pink, and Dou has picked out individual strands of his long hair with a thin brush. The man's costume and boot are composed of daubs of paint, skillfully blended. The freely rendered light reflections on his sleeve are painted in flesh tones on brown. Dou's sketchy technique is most evident in the figure of the seated man. His fingers, formed by single disjointed strokes, have no delimiting outlines, and his cloak is painted rapidly.

The seated man holds a lit piece of rope or wick beneath the woman's nose.[4] This action relates the scene to images of "tickled sleep," in which the dozing protagonist is subject to ridicule by those around her.[5] It calls to mind the Dutch proverbs "He who goes to sleep knows not how he will awaken" and "Wine is a mocker."[6] The action of the man placing the glowing ember under her nose is echoed by the man lighting his pipe, which takes place in the center of the composition. The intoxicating power of tobacco may be intended to parallel the ostensible drunkenness of the woman.[7]

Mocking representations of women in drunken sleep seem to have been a particularly favored subject among Leiden artists.[8] Dou's painting is one of the earliest such depictions. Nanette Salomon sets this work somewhat apart from other representations of the theme because she sees the man's actions as solicitous rather than mocking. However, what Salomon reads as expressions of concern on the faces of the man and the servant could as plausibly be interpreted as wily or knowing smiles; the psychology of the image may be intentionally ambiguous. Perhaps Dou meant to be only gently mocking or slightly admonitory. The sleeping woman's moral laxity is alluded to in her prominently displayed bosom, her limp, unconscious body, and in the pearls that wreathe her neck and adorn her ears.[9] That she is a woman of the night is further implied by the apparent lateness of the hour.

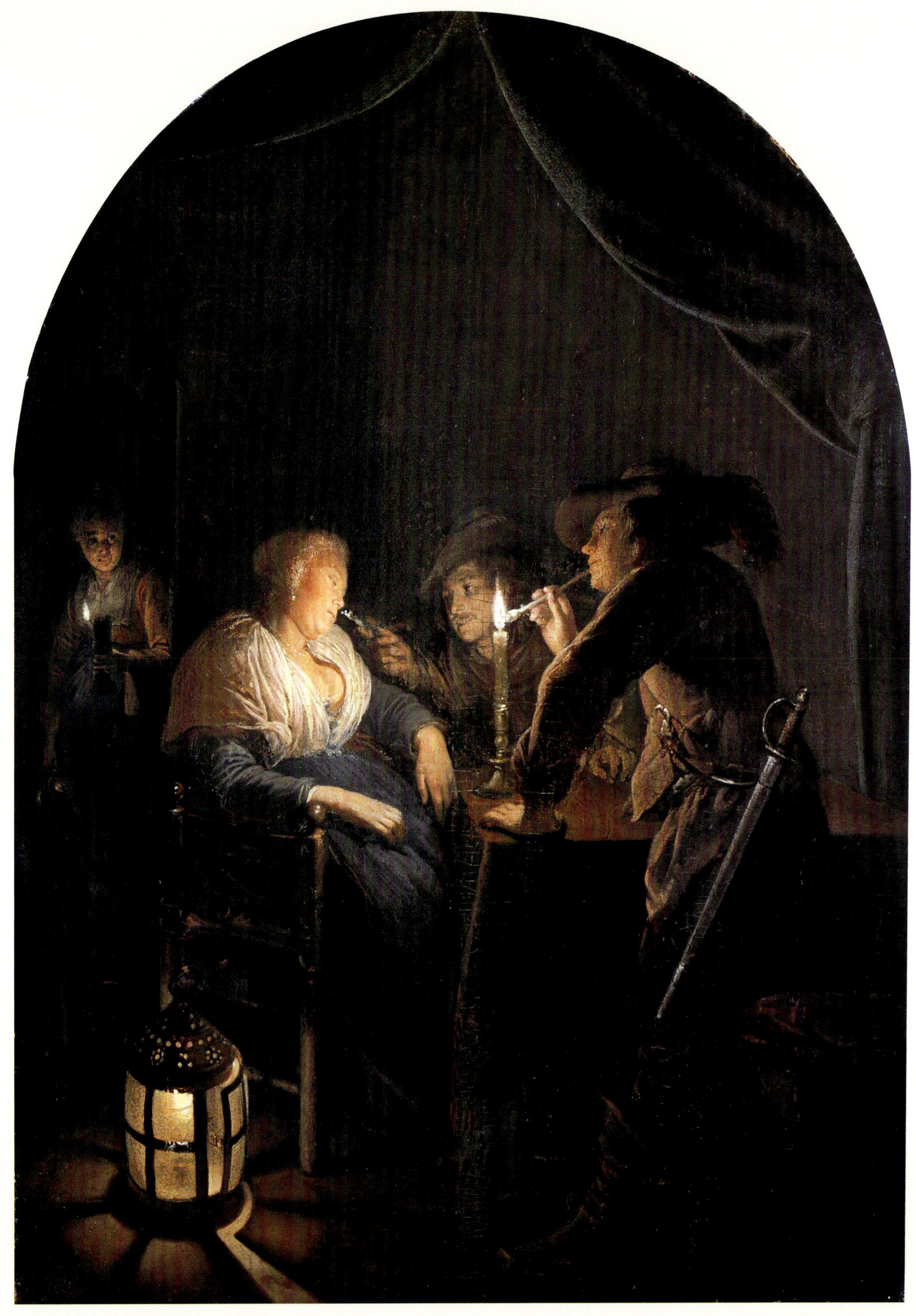

25.

Old Woman with Jug at a Window

c. 1660–1665; oil on panel; 28.3 x 22.8 (11 1/8 x 8 7/8); Kunsthistorisches Museum, Gemäldegalerie, Vienna

Signed on the birdcage: GDov

· *Provenance* H. von Reith, Vienna, acquired in 1811.

· *Bibliography* J. Smith 1842, no. 42; Martin 1901, no. 240; Hofstede de Groot 1907, no. 168; Martin 1911, no. 122; Martin 1913, 106; Kunsthistorisches Museum, Vienna 1972, no. 624; Robinson 1974, 46; Schama 1980, 7; Naumann 1981, 1: no. 39; Sumowski 1983, 1: no. 294; Baer 1990, no. 94.

• Dou uses the familiar compositional arch (compare cats. 20, 29, and 35) as a functional window in this painting; an old woman leans out to water a pot of flowers placed on a bench just under the sill. The theme is rare in seventeenth-century Dutch painting prior to Dou's treatment; the many copies and versions of Dou's composition attest to its subsequent popularity.

Simon Schama sees the woman as a withered hag, her countenance shrivelled by lust and avarice. He interprets the empty birdcage and white flowers as allusions to departed innocence.[1] The action of watering the flowers, however, suggests a more beneficent meaning. The care of plants had a moral dimension in sixteenth- and seventeenth-century emblem literature. An image of two figures watering plants in a French emblem book of 1553 is accompanied by the verses

Comme trop d'eau fait les plantes mourir,
Et les nourrist donnée à la soufissance:
Trop de labeur fait maint engin perir,
Mais (moderé qu'il soit) donne allegeance.

(Just as too much water makes plants die / And the right amount makes them thrive / Too much labor destroys many a thing / but, if moderate, brings relief.)[2] In the same vein, the motto "Poco a poco" (little by little) accompanies an emblem of plants being watered in Gabriel Rollenhagen's *Emblematum* (Zeeland, 1611, no. 95). A similar painting by Dou of a woman watering flowers (c. 1660–1665, in the collection of Her Majesty Queen Elizabeth II [Martin 1913, 106]), includes a pair of scales hanging at the figure's right, perhaps an allusion to the virtues of moderation and temperance, and a fitting symbol of the woman's industriousness.

The figure-type and costume of the old woman, as well as the color scheme, tonality, and lighting of the painting, resemble those of Dou's *Old Woman at a Half-Door* (fig. 1). The panels are virtually the same size, and it may be that they were intended as complements—two visions of contented old age, the one figure chatting with a neighbor, the other tending her plants.

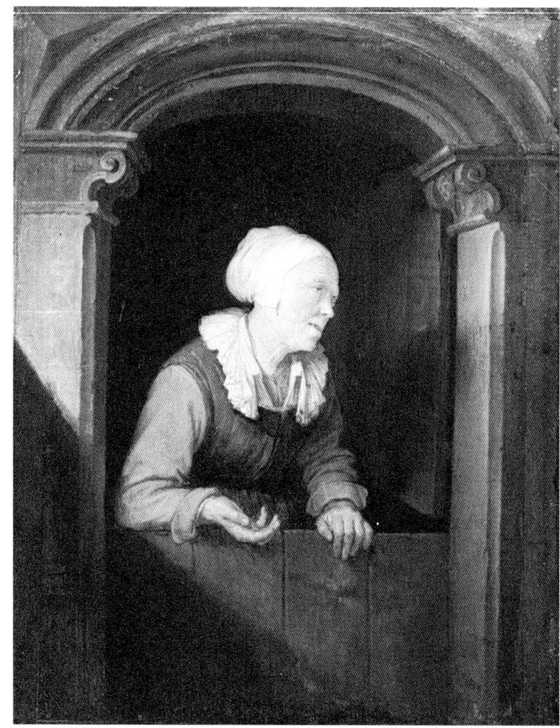

FIGURE 1
Old Woman at a Half-Door, c. 1660–1665, oil on panel, Civico Museo d'Arte Antica, Milan

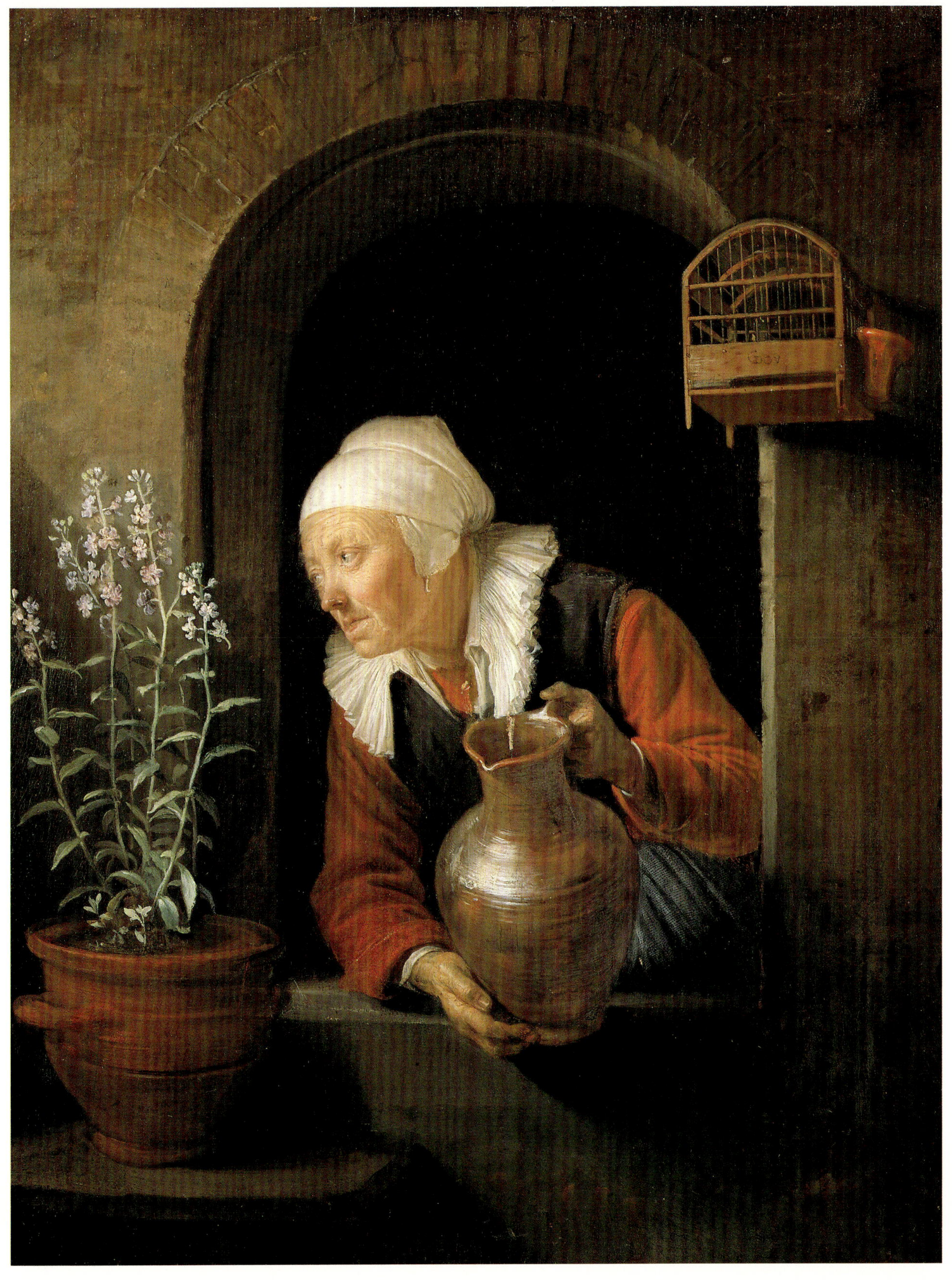

26.

The Doctor

c. 1660–1665; oil on panel; 38 x 30 (15 x 11 3/4); Statens Museum for Kunst, Copenhagen

Signed in the center of the window ledge: GDov

· *Provenance* In the Royal Cabinet of Curiosities, 1700.

· *Bibliography* Martin 1901, no. 95; Hofstede de Groot 1907, no. 139; Martin 1911, no. 44; Madsen 1911, 112 and 114 ff; Martin 1913, 74; Copenhagen 1951, no. 185; Bedaux 1975–1976, 18–19; Feer 1985, 55–57; Sumowski 1983, 1: no. 277; Baer 1990, no. 98.

· Dou's painting depicts a *piskijker*, or urinomancer, examining a vial of urine. He gestures to the woman standing behind him, who clasps her hands tightly and wears a concerned expression. She is likely a servant rather than the patient and has brought the sample (her mistress'?) in the basket on her arm.

The examination of urine was a diagnostic tool; consequently, the doctor pictured here is a consultant physician, as distinct from a practicing surgeon or itinerant doctor.[1] The clothing worn by the physician ties him to the world of the scholar, and in particular to the University of Leiden, which was renowned throughout Europe as a center for the study of medicine. Dissertations presented at the university during the last half of the seventeenth century indicate that women's illnesses were a subject of special interest to Dutch medical scholars,[2] and depictions of pale and listless women in the sickroom were a common subject in the works of Leiden artists at the time (fig. 1). It may be that physicians trained at or associated with the University of Leiden were the patrons for such images.[3]

The coal warmer that sits on the table in front of the woman in *The Doctor* had a practical function: to heat the sample. Contemporary plays make reference to the practice: the doctor in Petrus Baardt's *Deughden-Spoor* (Road of virtues) advises "Here, for a bit is a brazier, and warm the urine through and through."[4] In *Zeven Spelen van die Wercken der Bermhertigheyd* (Seven plays of the works of mercy), dating from 1591, a doctor tells his patient "Let me see [the urine], and heat it well."[5] Urine with a reddish cast, like that in the vial that Dou's doctor is examining, was indicative of the late stages of *morbeus virgineus* (uterine hysteria), "signifying too long a 'concoction' within the body."[6]

The proliferation of objects, the theatrical presentation of the image, and the luxurious accoutrements are characteristic of other paintings by Dou dating from the first half of the 1660s. The objects are painted with the artist's customary finesse. Dou has taken particular care to capture the play of light on the bowl, the keys to the chest, the vial of urine, and the clock, and he has

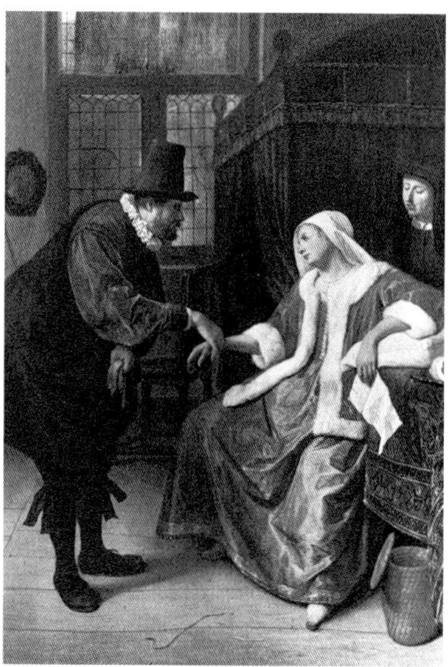

FIGURE 1
Jan Steen, *The Doctor's Visit* (detail), c. 1661–1663, oil on canvas, Alte Pinakothek, Bayerische Staatsgemäldesammlungen, Munich

skillfully distinguished among a variety of materials—terra-cotta, metal, glass, leather, tapestry, linen, and wicker. Dou's gift as a colorist is evident in the terra-cotta flowerpot, in which green, yellow, and brown are combined with red for the ornamentation, and in the tapestry, in which finely modulated greens and blues, along with yellows, reds, and oranges compose the decorative pattern.

On the ledge in front of the doctor are an elaborate tooled leather case, the sash to his *tabbaard*, a barber's bowl, a stoppered vial, and the doctor's diploma, which bears a large red seal of a rampant lion. The snail that appears in the shadow at the bottom of the picture is probably an allusion to transience, an interpretation supported by the presence of the clock (which literally marks the passage of time) and the flowers in the chipped pot, one of the more standard symbols of *vanitas.*[7] These elements probably allude to the ephemerality of life and specifically to the helplessness of the doctor in the face of death.[8] The evocation of *vanitas* was an immediate appeal to the life of the spirit.[9] Jan van Beverwyck, author of the widely read *Schat der gesontheyt* (Treasury of good health), first published in 1642, wrote that the afflicted should take refuge in God, the cure for all illness.[10] Richard Burton, in *The Anatomy of Melancholy* (1621), counseled the sick to surrender themselves to faith in God: "Nay, what shall the Scripture itself? Which is like an apothecary's shop, wherein are all remedies for all infirmities of mind, purgatives, cordials, alternatives, lenatives. Every disease of the soul . . . hath a peculiar medicine in the Scripture."[11]

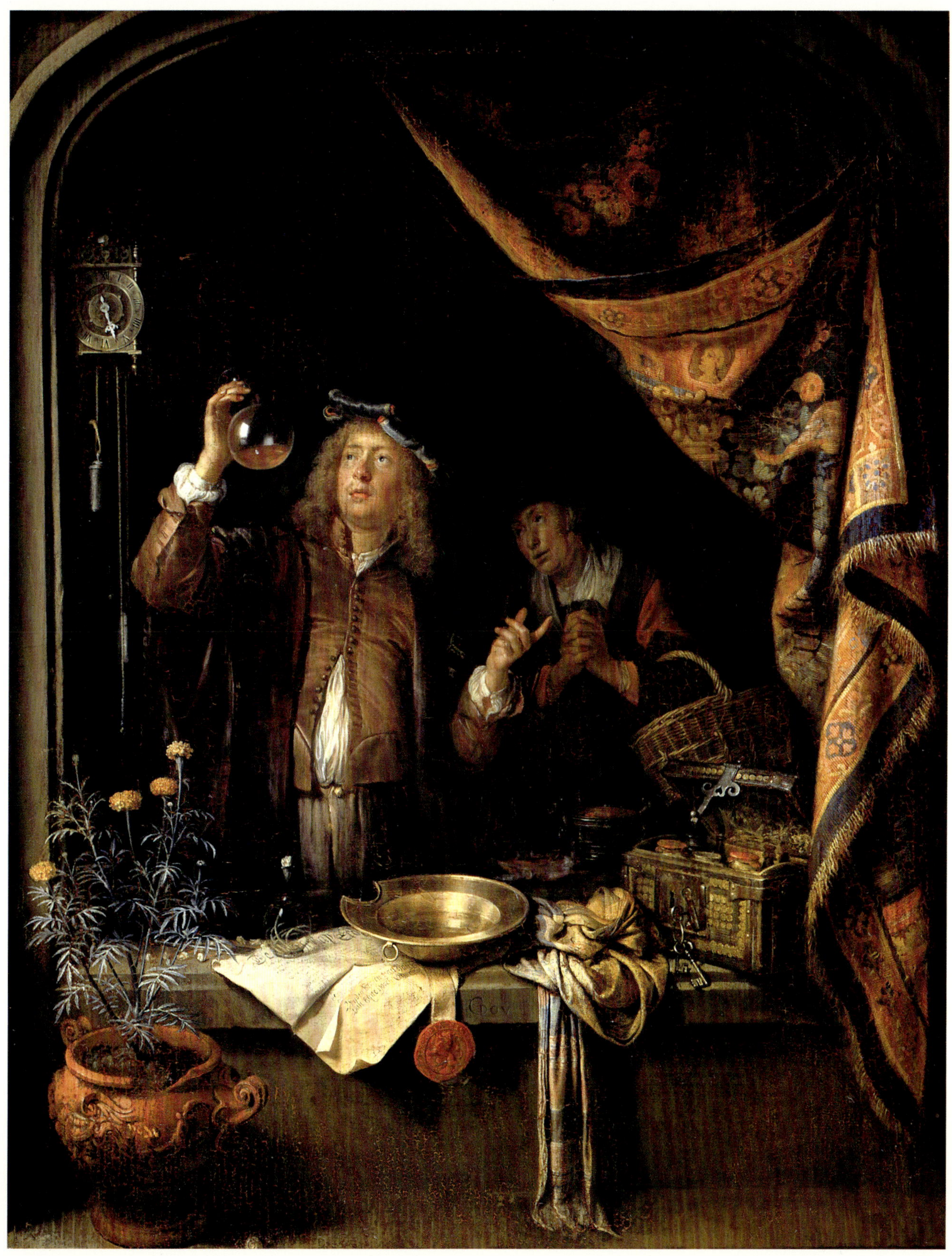

27.
Self-Portrait

1663; oil on panel; with added strips 54.7 x 39.4 (21 ½ x 15 ½); The Nelson-Atkins Museum of Art, Kansas City, Missouri (Purchase: Nelson Trust)

Signed and dated on base of column at right: GDov 1663 (*and turning the corner of the base*) Aet. 50; *signed again on the edge of the table at proper left:* GDov

· *Provenance* Possibly acquired with several other Netherlandish pictures by Kurfurst Max Emanuel (r. 1679–1726) for his residence and gallery at Schleissheim; in Schleissheim inventory of 1770; in Hofgarten Galerie, Munich, in 1799 (inv. no. 713); Bayerische Staatsgemäldesammlungen, Alte Pinakothek, Munich, by 1836; (D. Hoogendijk, Amsterdam, 1932); Gallery of Western Art, Kansas City, 1932; The Nelson-Atkins Museum, 1933.

· *Bibliography* J. Smith 1829, no. 109; J. Smith 1842, no. 65; Moes 1897, no. 2096.9; Martin 1901, no. 100; Hofstede de Groot 1907, no. 274; Martin 1911, no. 48; Martin 1913, 20; Plietzsch 1960, 37; Van Hall 1963, no. 5; Hunnewell 1983, 120–130; Sumowksi 1983, no. 304; Raupp 1984, 265; Baer 1990, no. 88; Sluijter 1993, 50; Lammertse 1997, 116–119.

· *Exhibitions* New York 1940, no. 4 (cat. untraced); The Hague and San Francisco, 1990–1991, no. 18.

· This self-portrait may well be the painting noted by the Danish scholar Ole Borch during his visit to Dou's studio on 9 November 1662: "We saw at his place his portrait of himself, finished in a delicate manner, with the aid of a mirror."[1] Indeed, this self-portrait is skillfully and delicately rendered, combining passages of painstaking brushwork (for example, the unblended, multicolored strokes that compose the artist's forehead) with freely painted details (such as the sumptuous, pigment-loaded white of his tie and sleeves).

Dou is clearly making a statement about himself in this grand and grandiose image. The setting of the elegant portico is patrician, and the artist's stance is proud. Instead of a bust- or half-length format, Dou presents himself in three-quarter length. His fur-trimmed coat and hat are luxurious, and the walking stick he carries has gentlemanly associations.

It is clear from the inscription that Dou's age held special significance for him. The half-century mark was then, as now, a milestone, perhaps a time to reflect on and assess one's achievements.[2] The clothes, comportment, and environment clearly signal the wealth and social position that the artist had attained through his labors. Both print and emblematic traditions, as well as Philips Angel's tract on the art of painting, extol the rewards of a lifetime of diligent activity. Dou here personifies the good to be gained through vigilance, diligence, and decorum.[3]

Dou's profession as painter is nowhere alluded to in this portrait. He poses before the Blauwpoort, the seigneur of his native city. Built between 1601 and 1610, this gate was one of the most important landmarks of Leiden. It was also the meeting place of the city's *rederijkers*—the Chamber of the White Columbine (*Witte Akelei*)—an amateur performance society that explicated moral issues for its audiences through instruction and entertainment.[4] Without associating Dou specifically with the *rederijkers*, the inclusion of the Blauwpoort imbues the portrait with a rhetorical air, referring in a general manner to the cultural and artistic associations that the chamber might have evoked. It may also be that Dou included the gate as an indication of his ongoing allegiance to Leiden. Indeed, only shortly before he executed this work, he had refused the invitation of Charles II to come to the English court, stating that he was not prepared to abandon his native city for "the favor of princes."[5]

The form of the Blauwpoort in the painting is decidedly anachronistic. The painting is signed and dated 1663, but the tower did not appear in this form until 1667—four years later.[6] X-radiography reveals that a balustrade extended from the table edge across the entire breadth of the painting.[7] The balustrade was painted out and a much shorter wall (on which Dou is leaning) inserted. Dou apparently had a mantle draped over his right arm in the painting's first state. The Blauwpoort, however, is not visible in the x-radiograph, and there is no lead white (which would indicate the presence of another, earlier form) in its place.

As Friso Lammertse has convincingly argued, Dou must have taken up the painting again after 1667 (at which date it appears in its first state as a painting-within-a-painting on the back wall of the *Lady at Her Toilet* [cat. 32]), transforming the wall into a table, including a carpet and book, altering the clothing, adding the Blauwpoort, and signing the panel (but not dating it) for a second time.[8]

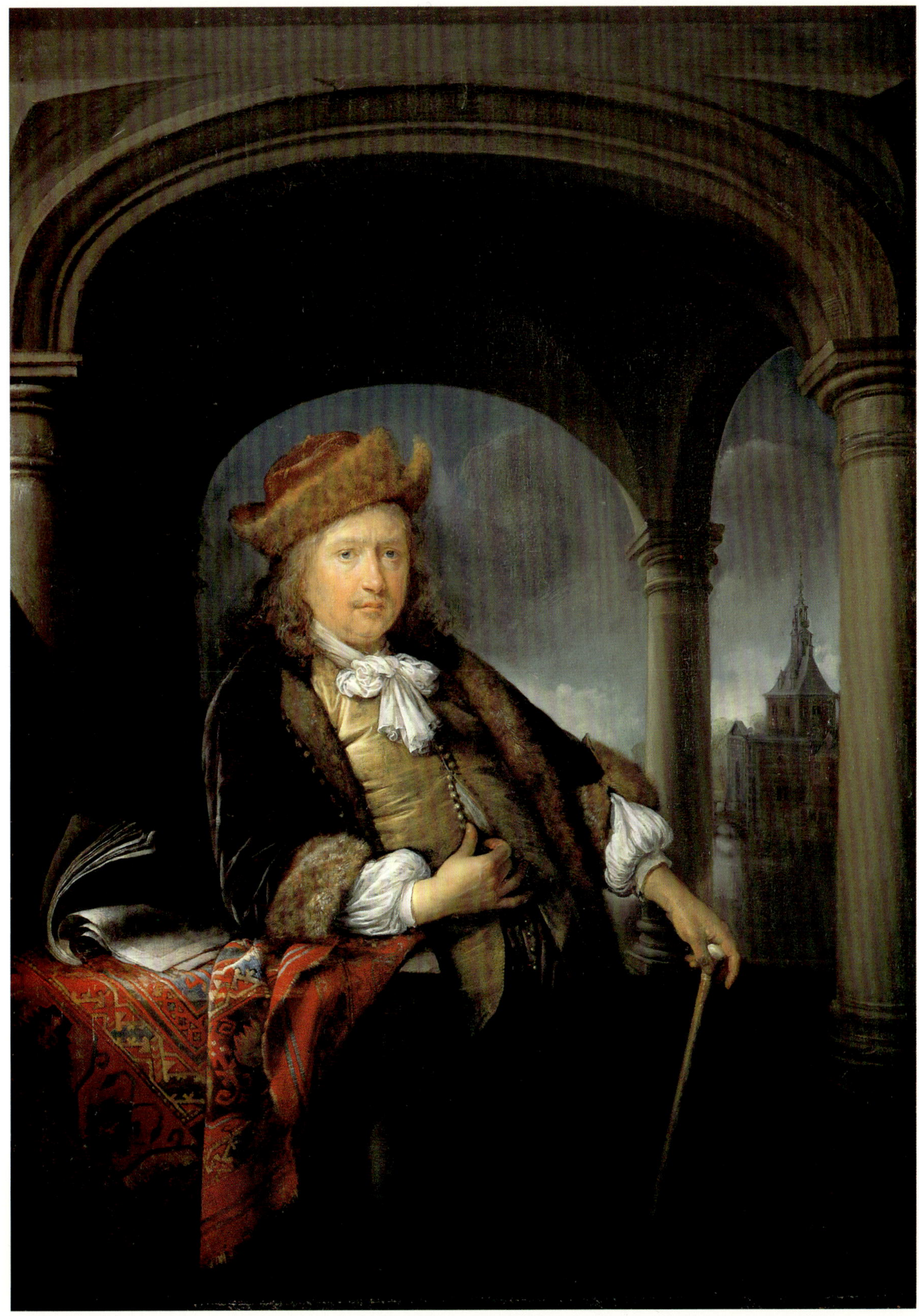

28.

The Night School

Before 1665; oil on panel; 53 x 40.3 (20 7/8 x 15 7/8); Rijksmuseum, Amsterdam

Signed at lower right corner of the platform: GDov

· *Provenance* Johan de Bye, Leiden, 1665 (no. 8); by bequest to Anna de Bye; by descent to Marya Knotter; by descent to Adriaen Wittert van der Aa, 1701. Pieter de la Court van der Voort through Karel de Moor, 1710; De la Court van der Voort sale, Leiden, 8 September 1766 (no. 19) (*f* 4000, to Mossel); to G. van der Pot van Groeneveld, 1783, from Mossel (*f* 4900); Van der Pot van Groeneveld sale, Rotterdam, 6 June 1808 (no. 28) (*f* 17,500, to J. Eck for the museum).

· *Bibliography* J. Smith 1829, no. 79; Martin 1901, no. 320; Hofstede de Groot 1907, no. 206; Moes and Van Biema 1909, 113, 158, 182, 186; Martin 1911, no. 176; Martin 1913, 170; Wiersum 1931, 211; Martin 1936, 2: 218–219; Gerson 1952, 34; Plietzsch 1960, 40; Rijksmuseum 1976, no. A87; Gaskell 1982, 21; Sumowski 1983, 1: no. 289; Brown 1984, 152; Haak 1984, 272; Baer 1990, no. 110.

· *Exhibitions* Laren 1969, no. 17.

· The last and most ambitious of Dou's series of school scenes, *The Night School* probably dates from shortly before 1665, the year in which it was exhibited by Johan de Bye in Leiden. It incorporates elements found in the left wing of the famous *Triptych* of c. 1660, which was lost at sea in 1771 but whose composition is preserved in a mid-eighteenth-century copy by Willem Joseph Laqui (page 17, fig. 4).[1]

The composition contains an uncharacteristically large number of figures and a much deeper background space than is usually found in Dou's paintings. *The Night School* differs most markedly from Dou's other schoolroom scenes, however, in its anecdotal character. The schoolmaster raises an admonitory finger at the boy in the shadowed middle ground. The girl at the center of the composition, strongly lit by a candle, strains forward with her lips parted as she recites her lesson. Only the dramatic sweep of the parted curtain removes the scene from the ordinary.

School sessions in seventeenth-century Holland might last from early in the morning until after nightfall, perhaps to keep children out of mischief.[2] Candlelight here does not merely indicate the hour, nor simply demonstrate Dou's ability to render the effects of artificial light (a skill noted by the artist's contemporaries).[3] The prominent candles also refer to the light of understanding,[4] a meaning underscored by the contrast between the unlit lantern at the left (a sign of ignorance that teaching is meant to combat), and the prominent glowing lantern in the middle of the floor. The girl at the far left bears a striking resemblance to the figure of *Cognitione* (*Kennisse*, or understanding) in Cesare Ripa's *Iconologia* (1644) (fig. 1). Dou's figure holds a candle and points to the slate on which the seated boy writes. The text that accompanies Ripa's image explains that, like our eyes, which need light to see, so our reason needs our senses, especially that of sight, to achieve true understanding.[5]

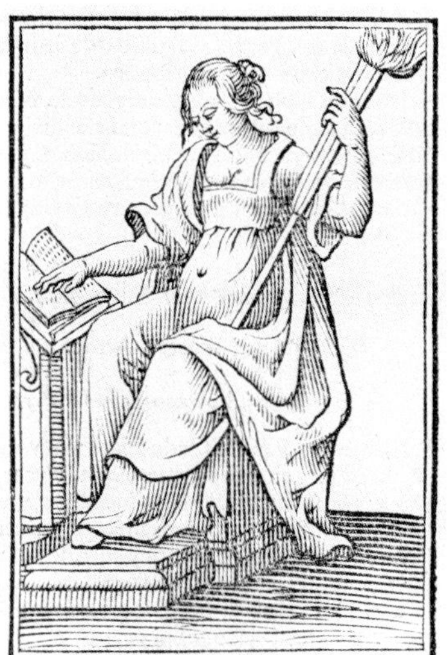

FIGURE 1
"Cognitione," woodcut, from Cesare Ripa, *Iconologia*, Amsterdam 1644, National Gallery of Art, Washington

During the nineteenth century, *The Night School* was among the most famous works of art in Holland. It was the signature piece of an important collection assembled by Gerrit van der Pot van Groeneveld, who had himself portrayed by Jan Baptist Scheffer in 1802 with *The Night School* in the background.[6] John Smith, writing in 1829, noted that "[n]othing in art can surpass the magical effect of light and shade in this painting; the master appears to have chosen difficulties, in order to show how well his superior talents could overcome them. Some connoisseurs consider this as the most capital of his works. . . ."[7] Johannes Immerzeel describes the painting as "the famous Night School with five lights that was bought in Rotterdam in 1808 at the sale of Gerrit van der Pot for *f* 7,500."[8] Théophile Thoré in 1858, while protesting that he was unmoved by the work, described *The Night School* as a painting of "first importance."[9]

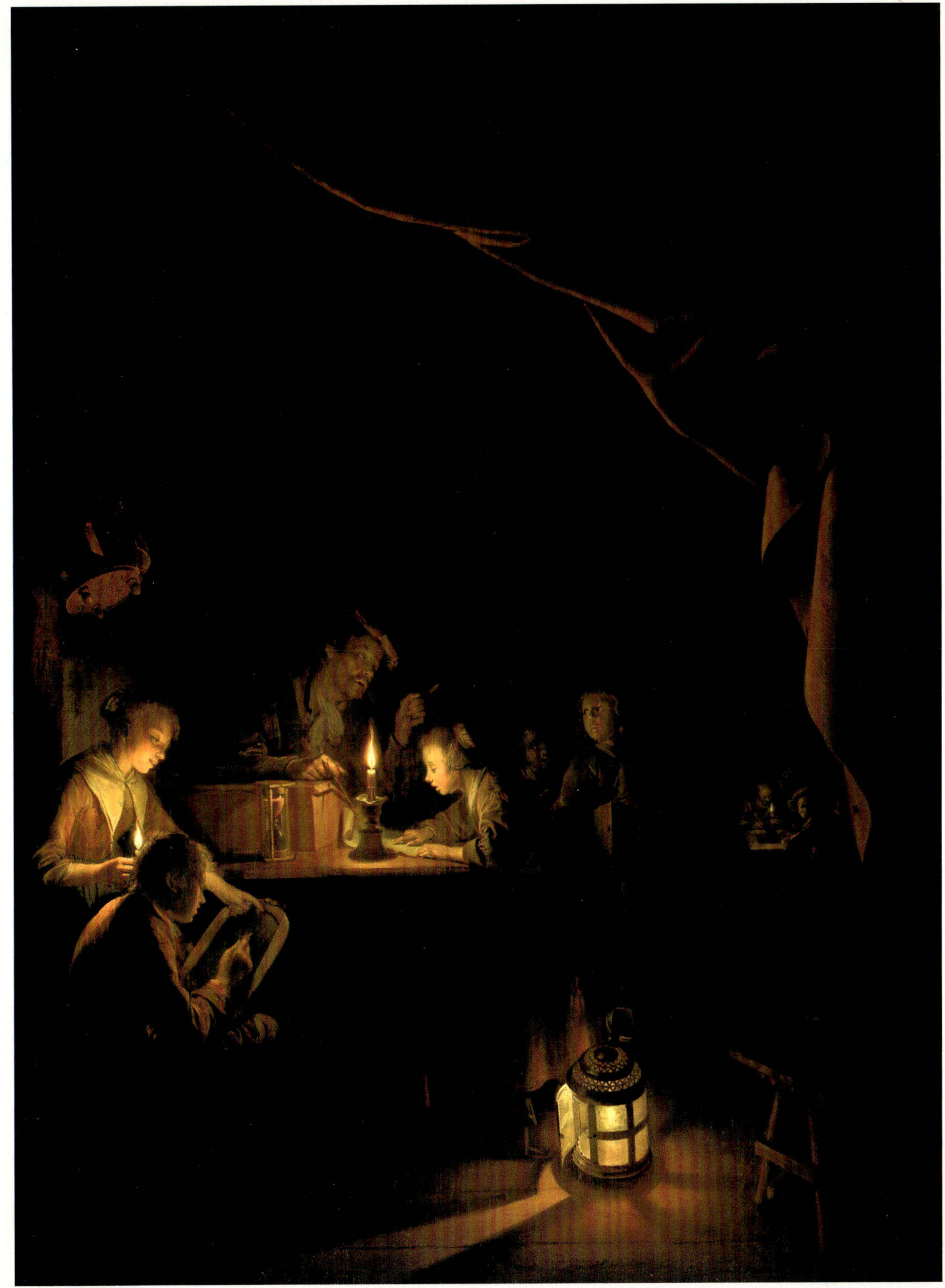

29.

Self-Portrait

c. 1665; oil on panel; arched top, 59 x 43.5 (23 1/4 x 17 1/8); private collection, Boston

Signed in cartouche: GDov

· *Provenance* Baroness Wilhelm von Rothschild, Frankfurt am Main, before 1906. (Johnny van Haeften, London, 1997); sold shortly thereafter to present owner.

· *Bibliography* Hofstede de Groot 1907, nos. 75 and 271; Martin 1911, no. 52; Martin 1913, 19.

· Dou appears slightly older in this painting than in the Kansas City *Self-Portrait* (cat. 27), which it otherwise resembles. Whereas the earlier work is a statement of Dou's social standing, this self-portrait emphasizes Dou's artistic aspirations.

A strong light from the left falls directly on the large open book, causing a dance of shadows along the right wall of the window opening. The beautifully rendered tapestry curtain, pulled to either side above Dou's head, underscores the revelatory and presentational aspects of the painting. The work's illusionism is enhanced by the window ledge, on which objects that seemingly invade the viewer's space—the cast, the book, the sash—are arranged. The emphasis on Dou's artistry is intended both to delight and to prompt speculation about the relationship between the real and the represented worlds.

In many ways, this painting is the culmination of Dou's self-portraits. Read as a group, the images that lead up to this work show Dou subtly varying the accoutrements that surround him, his choice of attire, and the structure of the mise-en-scène.[1] These self-portraits, in which Dou surrounds himself with objects that function on both a prosaic and a metaphorical level, have the character of a personal manifesto. The allegorical character of Dou's images, however, always takes precedence over the literal.

Here, Dou has clearly situated himself in an artist's studio, evident from the easel and *écorché* figure on the table in the background, the plaster cast on the front ledge, and the palette and brushes in his hand.[2] His dress, however, is by no means that of an ordinary painter. The fur-lined scholar's *tabbaard* that he wears, the sash of which lies on the window sill, alludes to his erudition, as well as to his advanced years.[3] Like his costume, many of the objects in the painting carry *studium* and *vanitas* connotations. In addition to their associations with learning, the violin, books, and globe were all common symbols of ephemerality.

In many respects, this approach to portraiture has its roots in the series of engraved prints of artists titled *Pictorum Aliquot Celebrium Germaniae Inferioris Effigies*, published by Domenicus Lampsonius and Hieronymus Cock in Antwerp in 1572.[4] Dou's self-portrait shares several elements with these images: the format (half-length with the hands displayed); the pyramidal composition; the steady, essentially expressionless regard; the dignified, costly dress; and the prominent display of the painter's implements. As in the prints, the formal elements combine in the painting to create a *memoria*, an image that will transcend death. The sitter himself is no longer a simple, plebian craftsman; rather, he represents *ars* in the service of *virtus*.[5] Dou's intellectually based art (as opposed to a manually based craft), illustrated in this programmatic image, is ultimately the means by which he will triumph over his own mortality: *ars longa vita brevis.* The message contained in this late self-portrait is much the same as it was in his earliest presentation of himself (compare cat. 14).

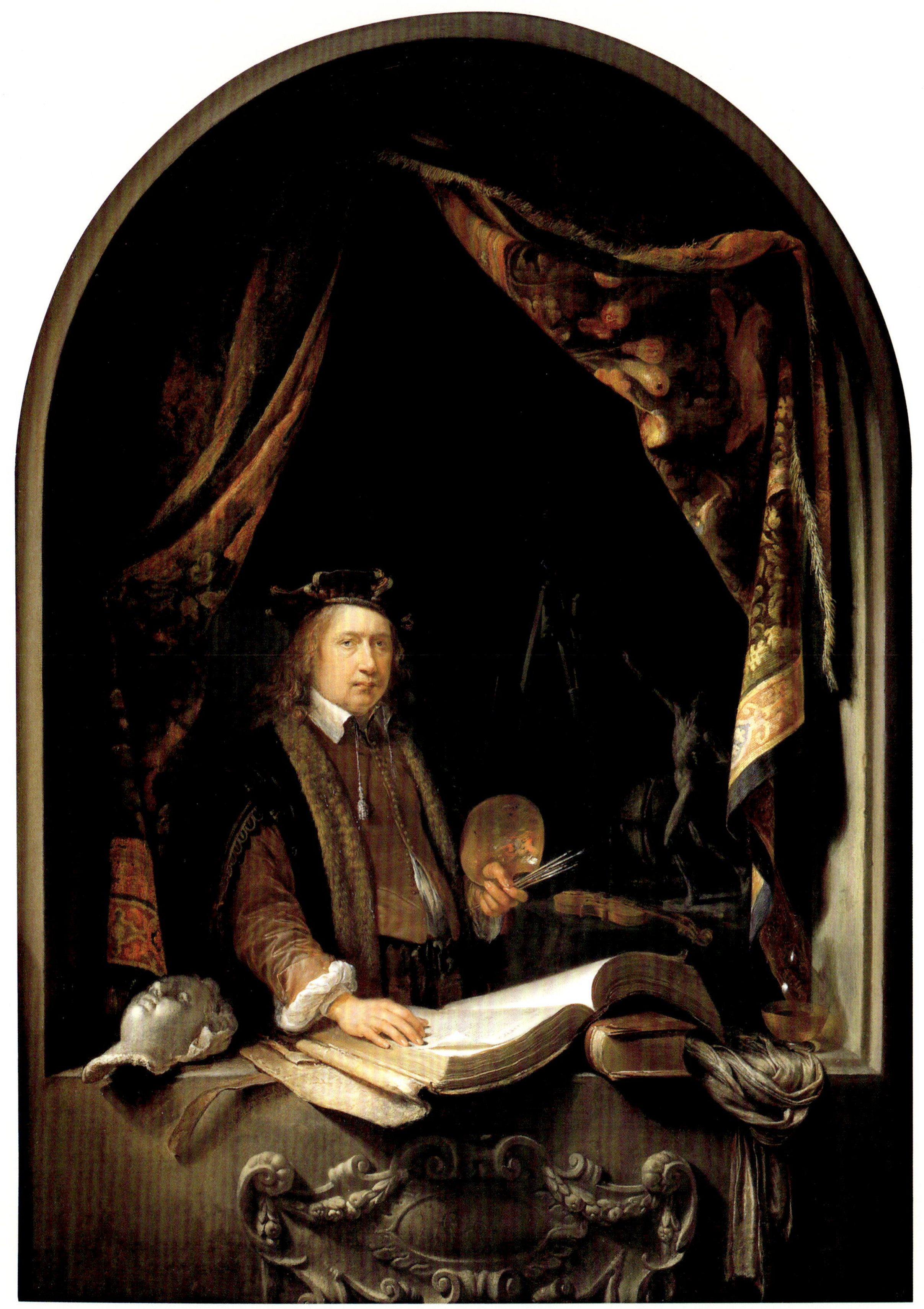

30.

Woman at the Clavichord

c. 1665; oil on panel; 37.7 x 29.8 (14 3/4 x 11 3/4); Trustees of Dulwich Picture Gallery, London

· *Provenance* Possibly Johan de Bye, Leiden, 1665 (no. 2). Possibly Issenghien, 1754.[1] Comte de Dubarry sale, Paris, 21 November 1774 (no. 30) (FF5100, to Lebrun). Prince de Conti sale, Paris, 8 April 1777 (no. 325) (FF5000, to Langlier).[2] Paul Benfield sale, London, 30 May 1799 (no. 64) (£242.11). (Noel Desenfans sale 18 March 1802, [bought in];) by bequest to Peter Francis Bourgeois, 1807; Bourgeois bequest, 1811.[3]

· *Bibliography* J. Smith 1842, no. 14; Hofstede de Groot 1907, no. 132; Martin 1901, no. 301; Martin 1911, no. 162; Martin 1913, 99; Dulwich Picture Gallery 1980, 12; Sumowski 1983, 1: no. 287; Brown 1984, 137; Baer 1990, no. 111; Sluijter 1991, 59; Sumowski 1994, 3597; The Hague 1994, 368; Washington and The Hague 1995, 202; Beresford 1998, no. 56.

· *Exhibitions* Royal Academy, London, 1854 (cat. untraced); London 1947, no. 11 (wrongly described as signed); London 1976, no. 32; London 1980, no. 8.

· Keyboard players, most commonly women, were a popular subject in seventeenth-century Dutch art.[4] Music-making was often associated with love, as for example, in verses by Jacob Westerbaen: "Learn to play the lute, the clavichord. The strings have the power to caress the heart."[5] A sense of expectation is communicated here in the woman's direct gaze (interruption is implicit in the placement of her fingers on the keyboard), the half-filled glass (the wine is cooling in a basin at the lower right), the viola da gamba and flute, and the empty stool.[6] With its allusions to harmony and fruitfulness (a grapevine figures prominently at the lower right), the work is a paean to female comeliness and an invitation to the viewer to fulfill the role of the absent lover, to be seduced both by the woman's beauty and by the beauty of the painting itself.

A reference to a "claversimbelspeelster" in the contract for Johan de Bye's exhibition of Dou's paintings suggests a date of no later than 1665 for this work. The painting's composition (including its spatial construction, the use of a diaphragm arch, the full-length figure set back in space, the seat and basin that bracket the figure), its specific details (the metal birdcage, tapestry, basin, leather wall-hanging on the back wall), and Dou's approach to the subject closely resemble those of *Lady at Her Toilet* of 1667 (cat. 32). However, the woman's direct confrontation of the viewer, her less sumptuous clothing, and the closed birdcage suggest a more guileless vision than that of the more knowing, assured, and flirtatious woman in *Lady at Her Toilet*. The closed birdcage in *Woman at the Clavichord* may allude to the notion that love is strengthened by having limits placed around it (and that with freedom comes danger).[7] The love that this woman seeks is thus faithful and true.

The refined setting and elegant subject reflect Dou's changing social affinities in the 1660s.[8] A warm chiaroscuro envelops the room, infusing it with atmosphere. Light streams in from the window at left, highlighting the woman and the viola da gamba, which is carefully modeled, with careful attention paid to the properties of the wood. The pillow on the stool at the left edge, thickly brushed crimson with pink areas of light, is inviting and beautifully painted. Saturated royal blue, orange, pink, green, gold, and yellow enliven the surface of the painting. The combination of thick and thin brushwork invite the viewer's close scrutiny. As in *Lady at Her Toilet*, both the sweeping arch at the top of the painting and the tapestry hitched up at the right reveal the elegant subject in an almost theatrical manner. Nothing bars the spectator's entrance into the pictorial space; to the contrary, everything—subject, composition, execution—is designed to invite him in.

Woman at the Clavichord features *leitmotifs* that run throughout Dou's mature work: woman as temptress and seductress and the transience of beauty and material pleasures. The painting invites the male viewer—perhaps voyeuristically—to watch, delight in, and contemplate the woman's charms and the beautifully painted surface of the picture. At a safe distance (the distance between the actual and fictive worlds), he runs no true risk of moral taint.[9]

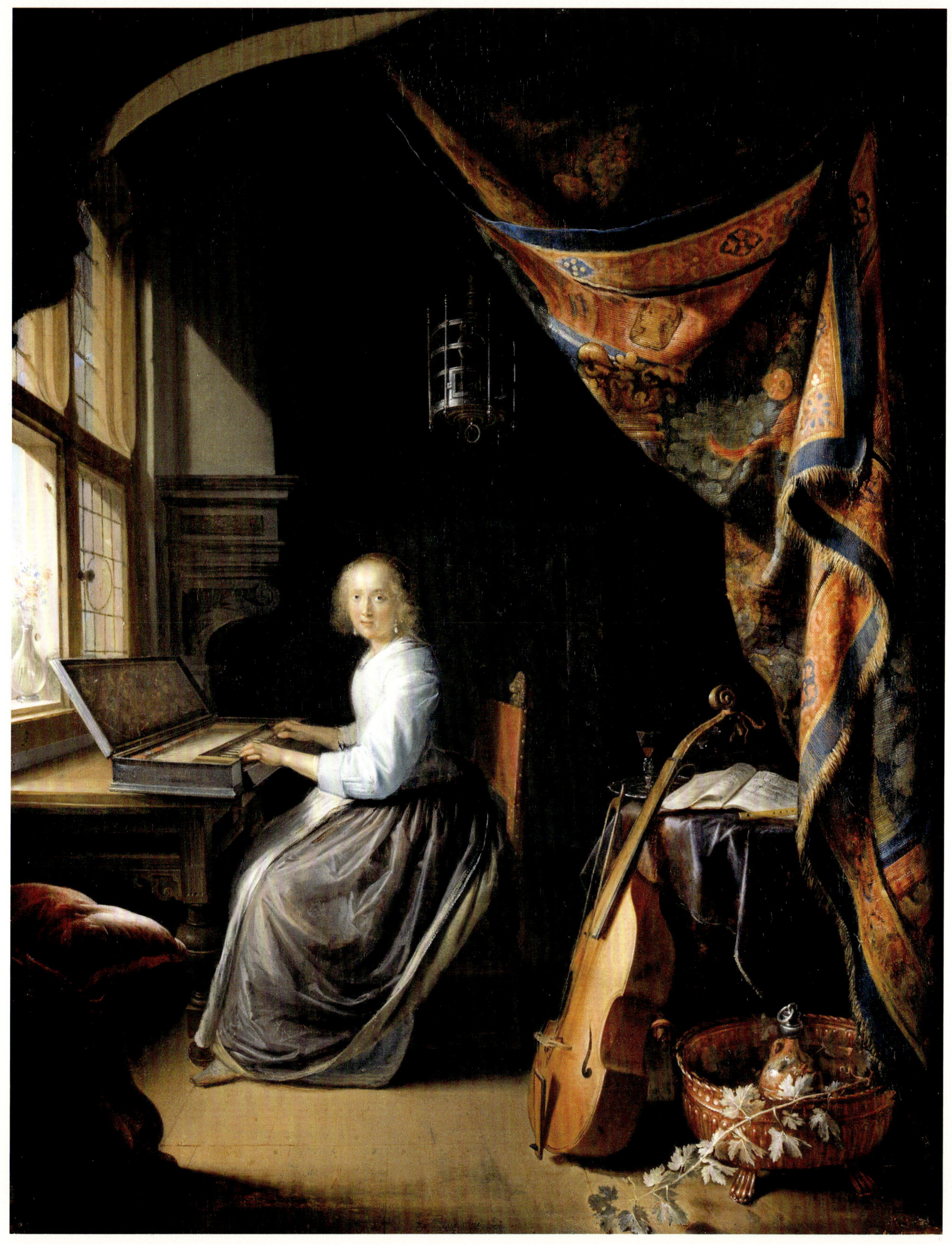

31.
Astronomer by Candlelight

c. 1665; oil on panel; arched top, 32 x 21.2 (12 5/8 x 8 3/8); The J. Paul Getty Museum, Los Angeles

Signed on pages of closed book at left: GDov

· *Provenance* Probably in Adriaen van Hoek sale, Amsterdam, 7 April 1706 (no. 2) (*f* 505). Willem Six sale, Amsterdam, 12 May 1734 (no. 18) (*f* 905). Wilhelm VII, Landgrave of Hesse-Cassel. Possibly Lapeyrière sale, Paris, 14 April 1817 (no. 19) (FF7100, to Paillet). (Joseph Barchard sale, Christie's, London, 6 May 1826 [no. 12] [300 gns, to John Smith]); (John Smith, London); William Beckford, London; by exchange to Hume, London. R.H. Fitzgibbon, second earl of Clare, London, by 1839; Earl of Clare sale, London, 17 June 1864 (no. 38) (670 gns). (William Delafield sale, Christie's, London, 30 April 1870 [no. 79] [798 gns to M. Colnaghi for Albert Levy]); (A. Levy sale, Christie's, London, 6 April 1876 [no. 329] [680 gns to Piercer]). Barkley Field, London, by 1888. The Lords Astor of Hever, after 1907; (sale, Sotheby's, London, 6 July 1983 [no. 80] [Johnny van Haeften]); Gerald Guterman, New York; purchased by the J. Paul Getty Museum, 1985.

· *Bibliography* J. Smith 1829, no. 96; J. Smith 1842, no. 15; Martin 1901, nos. 52 and 314; Hofstede de Groot 1907, nos. 63c and 210; Baer 1990, no. 109.

· *Exhibitions* British Gallery 1839, no. 30 (cat. untraced); Royal Academy, London, 1873, no. 76 (cat. untraced); Royal Academy, London, 1888, no. 84 (cat. untraced); Philadelphia, Berlin, and London 1984, no. 35.

· Like Jan Vermeer's *Astronomer* in the Musée du Louvre, Paris (fig. 1), Dou's figure has an open book before him, probably a practical treatise on astronomy similar to the book in Vermeer's painting. However, unlike Vermeer's scholar, Dou's figure is not specifically placed in a study. Armed with a compass, the traditional attribute of both astronomy and geography,[1] and guided by the instruction contained in the volume before him, Dou's astronomer, plotting the course of the stars on the celestial globe, is a personification of the pursuit of knowledge. The hourglass at the figure's left, like the compass, was a common attribute of geometry as well as of astronomy; it was also, of course, an instrument for measuring time. In Cesare Ripa's *Iconologia* (1644), the hourglass is an attribute of *studio*, and by extension a reminder to make good use of fleeting time.[2] Here the emphasis is on the assiduousness of the astronomer, hard at work late into the night (though the late hour is, of course, essential to his work).[3]

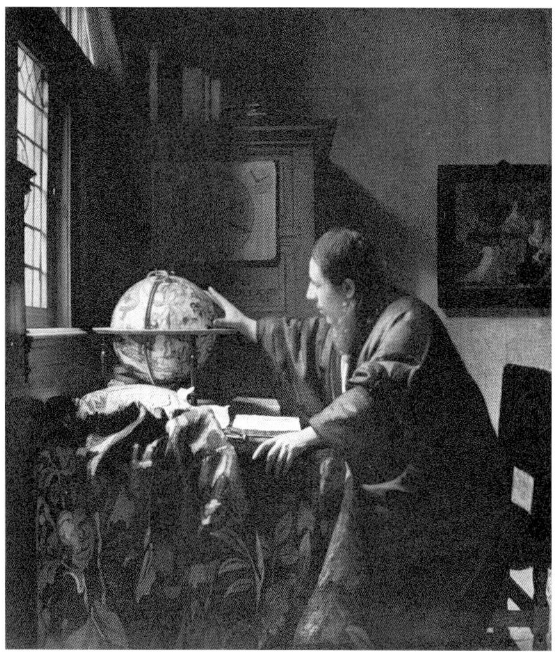

FIGURE 1
Johannes Vermeer, *The Astronomer*, 1668, oil on canvas, Musée du Louvre, Paris

The stone surround in this painting serves as a ledge and a pictorial framing device rather than as a window. The columns silhouetted against the dark background create the effect of a very deep space.

Tiny multicolored strokes describe the young man's face, features, and long, curly hair, whereas his hands are more smoothly brushed. The wrinkles in his costume are relatively broad and freely painted, especially considering the small scale of the panel. An undulating line describes the spine of the book. The globe, on which the signs of the zodiac are visible, was probably painted with the aid of a template; the incised line describing its perfect circle is still visible. A bright blue—the only cool color in the composition—delineates the edges of the candle flame. Shades of brown and red (notably for the sand in the hourglass and the liquid in the carafe) predominate. Dou has carefully traced the shadows cast by each object on its proximate surface.

The groin-vaulted setting, the handling, the light effects and motif of the figure holding a candle, and the proportion and placement of the figure in space point to a date of c. 1665. The Getty picture may well be the painting owned and exhibited by Johan de Bye in 1665, described in the inventory (no. 18) as "Een kaerslicht met een astrologue" (A candlelight [scene] with an astronomer).[4]

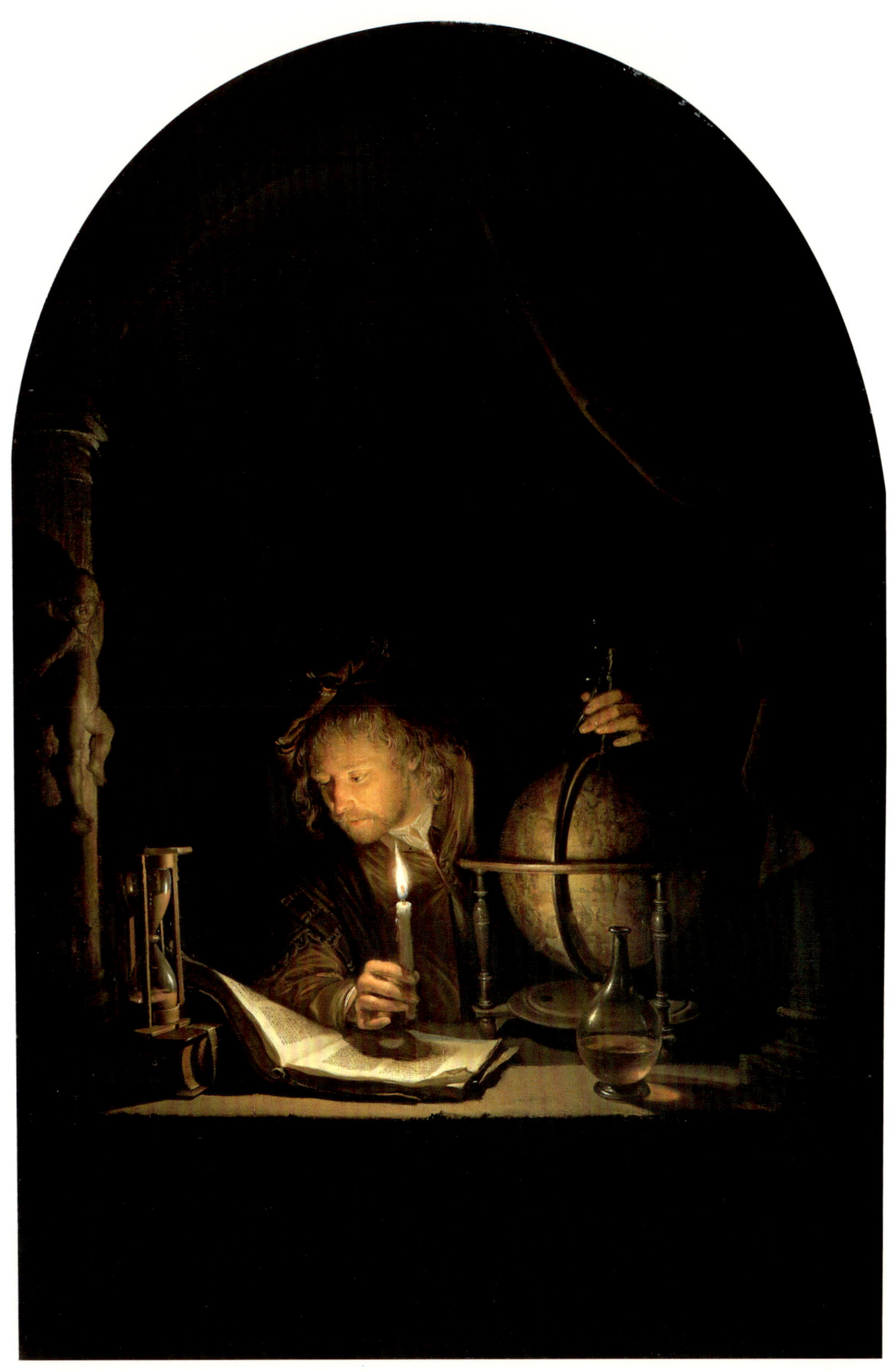

32.
Lady at Her Toilet

1667; oil on panel, 75.5 x 58 (29 3/4 x 22 3/4); Museum Boijmans van Beuningen, Rotterdam

Signed and dated on the crossbar of the chair at center: GDov 1667

· *Provenance* Probably François de le Boë Sylvius, Leiden 1673; by descent to Jean Rouyer, Amsterdam (described in 1678 valuation at *f*450: "sijnde een vrouwtje dat gekapt wordt, met openslaende deur en daerop een suygent vrouwtje bij de lamp").[1] Arend van der Werff van Zuidland sale, Dordrecht, 31 July 1811 (no. 24) (*f*75, to A. van der Werff); A. van der Werff sale, Rotterdam, 19 April 1816 (no. 8) (*f*430, to Durselen). Maximilian I Joseph of Bavaria, before 1823; Bayerische Staatsgemäldesammlungen, Alte Pinakothek, Munich. (D. Hoogendijk Amsterdam), 1930(?). Gift of Sir Henry Deterding to Boymans Museum, 1936.

· *Bibliography* J. Smith 1829, no. 123; Martin 1901, no. 303; Hofstede de Groot 1907, no. 129; Martin 1911, no. 164; Martin 1913, 95; Plietzsch 1960, 39; Snoep-Reitsma 1973, 288; Sluijter 1988c; Sluijter 1988d, 163 and fig. 14; Amsterdam 1989, 56; Baer 1990, no. 114; Lammertse 1997, 117–119.

· *Exhibitions* Leiden 1988, no. 16.

· The impression of a uniform surface in this major, dated painting is belied by close examination. The women's faces and hands are smoothly rendered. Wisps of hair, painted with the finest brush, frame the face of the maid, who wears the same earring and hairstyle as her mistress. Whites have been applied delicately—in thin, fuzzy stripes of varying pigment density—to indicate the texture of the mistress' red velvet jacket. The "pointillist" technique evident on the underside of the tapestry contrasts with the more descriptive rendering of the elaborate design in the heavy carpet covering the table. Dou varies his technique to capture the particular qualities of each element.

The perspective in this painting seems skewed; the wine cooler and chair tilt downward. Although Willem Martin's critique of Dou's flawed perspective in the late works may be justified, in this instance the effect may also have been deliberate: as Annetje Boersma argues, the painting may have been intended to be viewed from an elevated and close distance.[2]

The subject of a woman at her toilet was explored by Gerard ter Borch and subsequently taken up by Frans van Mieris, Gabriel Metsu, and Quirijn van Brekelenkam. Dou's treatment combines the typical "upper-class" subject with the more refined surroundings characteristic of his paintings after c. 1660, when his work began to reflect the influence of Ter Borch, Vermeer, and Van Mieris. The appointments of the room—the rich chair-covering on which the woman sits, the tooled leather wall hangings, the elaborate ewer and basin,[3] the marble wine jug and footed cooler—are particularly luxurious.

The action of *Lady at Her Toilet*—a woman primping as her maid dresses her hair—resembles that of a painting of 1654 by Rembrandt (now in the State Hermitage Museum, St. Petersburg) depicting a young woman examining her earring.[4] One commentator has identified the Hermitage painting with a description in Rembrandt's inventory of "a courtesan grooming herself."[5] In Dou's painting, the cooling wine and the chair positioned as if to receive a visitor suggest an analogous interpretation: that the subject of *Lady at Her Toilet* is seduction. The open birdcage—a conventional symbol of immorality—is positioned directly above the mistress' head and occupies the very center of the composition.[6] The figure of a woman before a mirror, moreover, was traditionally associated with pride and lust.[7]

Who, then, is the lady seducing? She glances directly at the spectator through her reflection in the mirror: it is the male viewer that she hopes to attract, seduced as well by the beautiful surface of the painting, a rendering so faithful that the lines between illusion and reality are blurred (*schijn zonder zijn*). The play of illusion—the woman herself and her reflected image—is echoed in the presentational devices of parted curtain and diaphragm arch. These pictorial devices also separate the depicted from the real, rendering the woman even more inaccessible and, hence, more desirable. The play of seduction in *Lady at Her Toilet* involves all these factors: painting as object of beauty and value, painting as illusion, and painting as intellectual puzzle.[8]

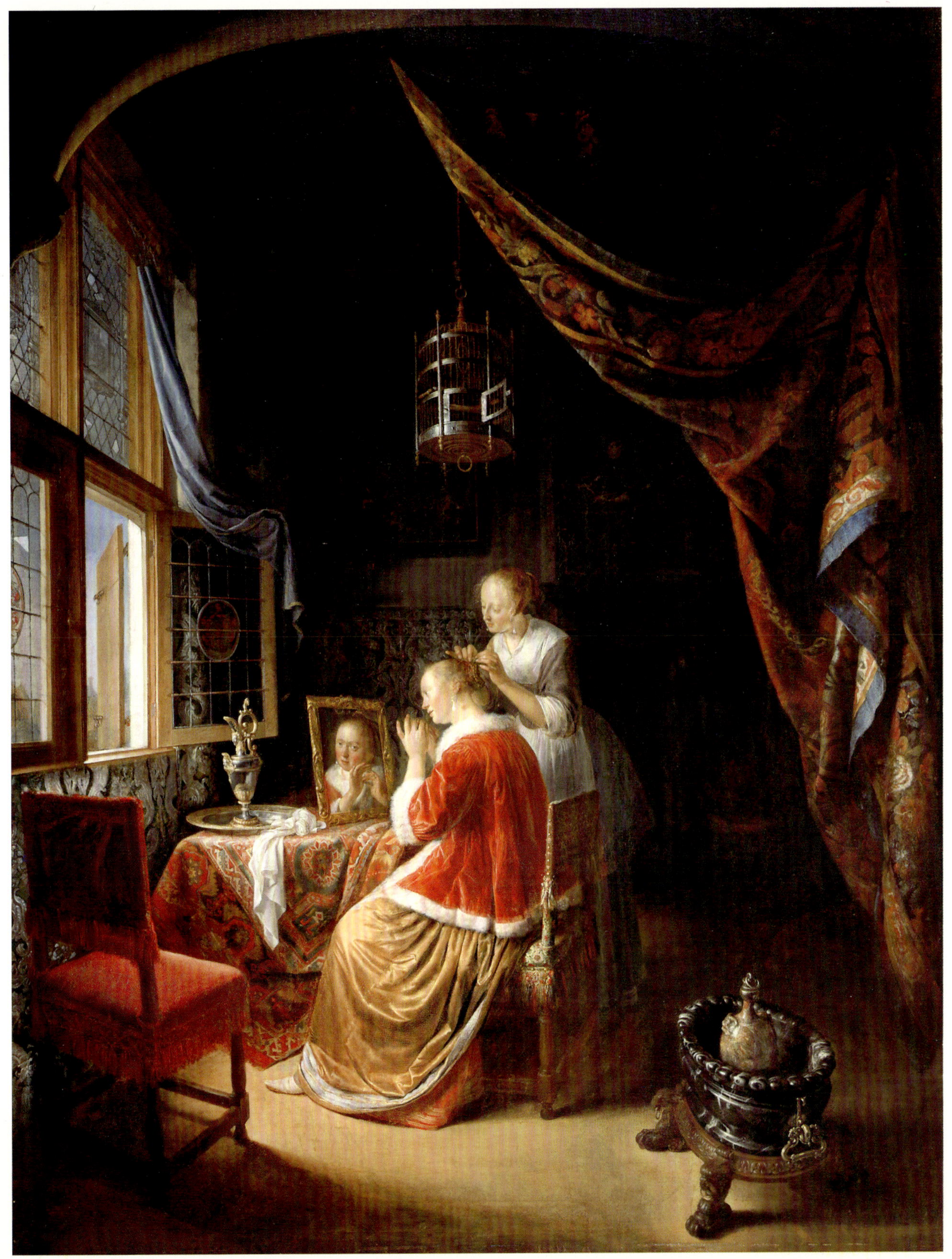

33.
Hermit Praying

1670; oil on panel; 33.6 x 27 (13 ¼ x 10 ⅝);
The Minneapolis Institute of Arts,
The William Hood Dunwoody Fund

Signed and dated on flap of book cover:
GDov 167[0]

· *Provenance* (Trafalgar Galleries, London); acquired by the museum in 1987.

· *Bibliography* Van de Watering 1985; Baer 1990, no. 120; Baer 1995; Sumowski 1994, no. 2246.

· This painting and *The Hermit* (cat. 34) are the only two works by Dou dated 1670. Here Dou uses subtle effects of dark and light and the expressive possibilities of the brush to describe the figure and his milieu. The hermit's hair and beard are a tangle of long, thin, individual strokes of powder-blue, yellow, black, and white. These colors recur in the succession of very small strokes that describe the flesh and veining of the figure's hand. The cloth of the hermit's habit is thinly and loosely painted. Dou has brushed a lighter tone over the predominant brown to give texture and weight to the garment. Irregular, broad strokes for the milky highlights, applied over more even, horizontal, parallel dashes capture the roughness of the burlap. In other passages, smoothly rendered surfaces skillfully obscure the hand of the artist. Highlights and color gradations on each rosary bead give the illusion of three-dimensionality. This picture testifies to the fact that Dou's painterly abilities did not necessarily diminish with age.

A strong beam of light, falling from the upper left, glances off the tree and strikes the monk's forehead. The still life at the right receives its own, more subdued light. A patch of white pigment in the blue sky above the monk's cowl implies that dawn is breaking. The glowing chiaroscuro gives the work its overall harmony.

The half-length format, with the figure shown in three-quarter view and pushed up close to the picture plane, was Dou's preferred compositional type for his many depictions of hermits. This arrangement invites scrutiny of the most expressive parts of the human body (the face, head, neck, and hands) and provides the artist with an opportunity to render physiognomic minutiae and psychological nuances.[1] In adopting this compositional type, Dou here emphasizes the figure's reverential attitude rather than creating an evocative atmospheric context for his act of prayer (as he does in his contemporaneous full-length depiction of the subject [cat. 34]).

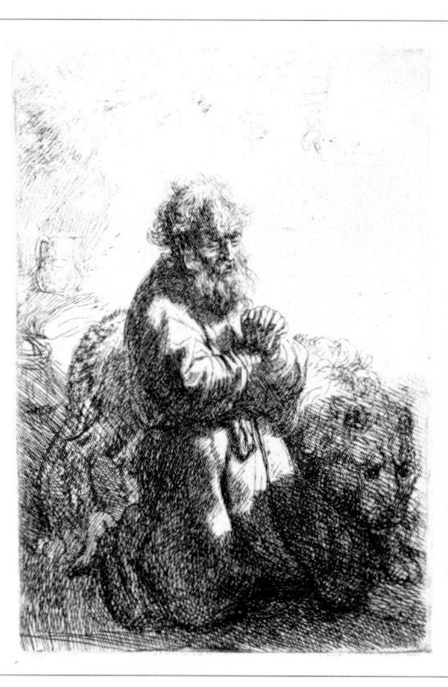

FIGURE 1
Rembrandt van Rijn, *St. Jerome*, c. 1635, etching, The Pierpont Morgan Library, New York

The figure may be loosely based on Rembrandt's etching of St. Jerome, c. 1635 (fig. 1). Dou, however, has not specifically identified the hermit with an attribute, such as the lion that appears in Rembrandt's etching. Dou's figure retains Rembrandt's grizzled, elderly type, but the hands that Rembrandt portrays clasped fervently in prayer here hold a rosary. The tightly shut eyes of the figure in the etching are here open in meditation and rumination.

The image, enhanced with accoutrements and placed close to the viewer, also follows other pictorial traditions.[2] The brick arches of the setting recall those in earlier depictions of hermits reading or praying in the ruins of ancient buildings.[3] The arches both frame the figure and suggest a grotto or cave.[4] Symbols of the hermit's faith—the rosary, crucifix, and Bible—are counterbalanced by the basket in the background, a reference both to his meager earthly sustenance and his status as a pilgrim. The standard *vanitas* accoutrements—extinguished candle, hourglass, and skull—are all reminders of the transitoriness of life on earth. Placed opposite the *vanitas* symbols and next to the hermit, the dessicated tree alludes to the hermit's triumph over death through Christian prayer and study of the Scriptures.[5]

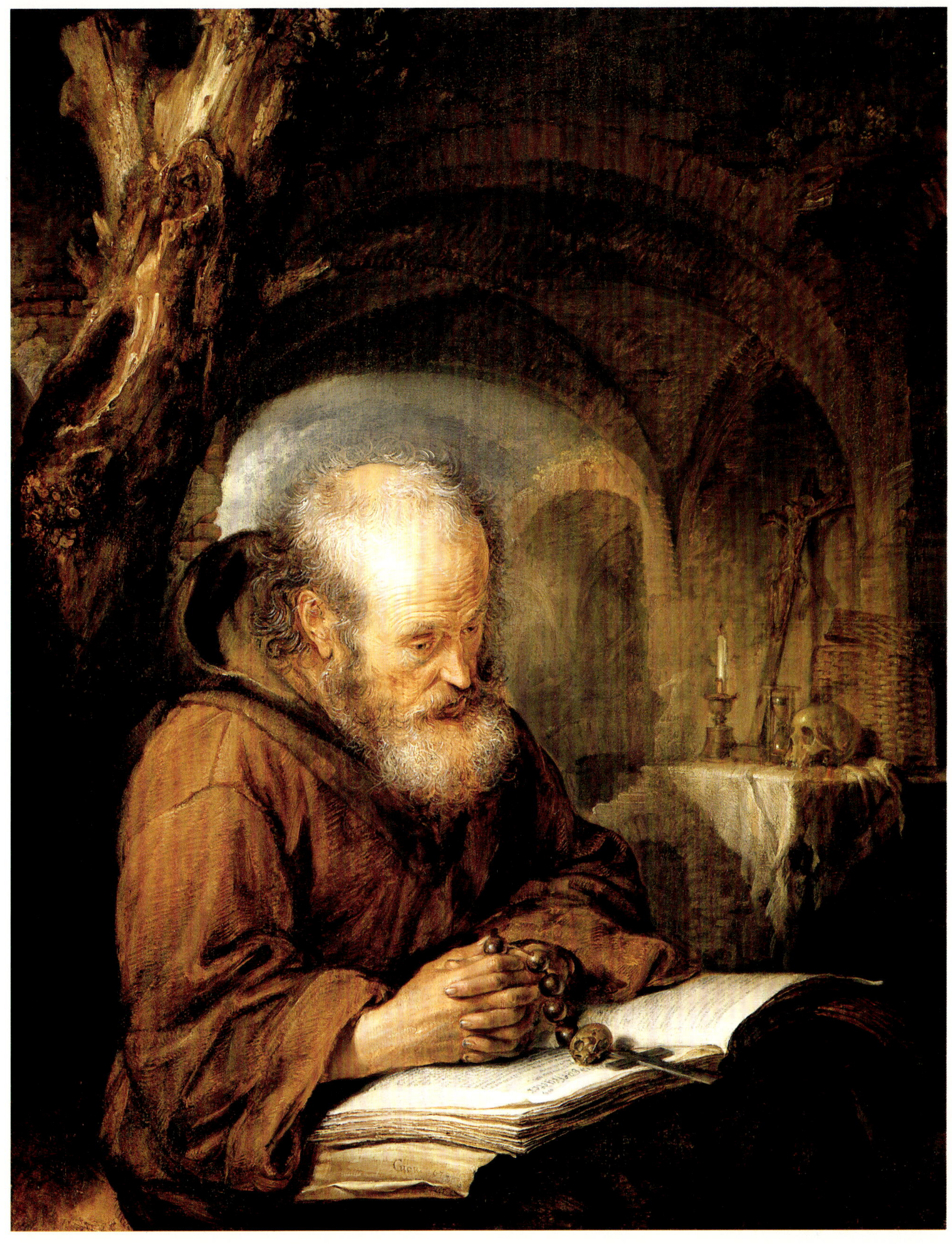

34. The Hermit

1670; oil on panel; 46 x 34.5 (18 1/8 x 13 5/8); National Gallery of Art, Washington, Timken Collection

Signed and dated on book strap at center: GDov 1670; *signed at top of right page in book:* GDov

· *Provenance* Probably Kurfürst Karl Albrecht (1697–1745), Munich, by 1742;[1] in the Electoral Gallery, Munich; Bayerisches Staatsgemäldesammlung, Alte Pinakothek, Munich, by 1829; deaccessioned in 1927; Galerie van Diemen, Berlin; William R. Timken (d. 1949), New York; by inheritance to Lillian S. Timken (d. 1959), New York; bequest to the National Gallery of Art, 1960.

· *Bibliography* J. Smith 1829, no. 111; Martin 1901, no. 20; Hofstede de Groot 1907, no. 19; Martin 1911, no. 11; Martin 1913, 6; Baer 1990, no. 121; Wheelock 1995, 57–60; Baer 1995, 25 and fig. 2.

· In 1911, Willem Martin singled out *The Hermit* as the clearest example of the weaknesses in Dou's late paintings, which he described as dry, lacking in tonal harmony, and plagued by faulty perspective and drawing errors.[2] In dismissing the painting, Martin overlooked a range of approaches to the depiction of materials and surfaces that the artist has ably captured. The wrinkles of the hermit's hand are painted in small, regular strokes of powder-blue, pink, and ochre. The grasses that grow from the water at the bottom of the panel are painted in single, tapering sweeps of the brush, as different one from the other as the grasses they describe. White highlights on the overturned earthenware jug suggest both the reflection of light and the working of the clay. Dou's characteristically fine brushwork is both spirited and free.

Subtle color harmonies and a gentle serpentine rhythm unify the composition. Red accents pepper the painting—in the lantern, the sand of the hourglass, the book strap, and the bricks. The leaves sprouting from the tree branches restate the color and brushwork of the grasses below. The great sweep of the central arch is answered by the bend in the old tree trunk, and carried through by the circular form of the surface on which the hermit leans.

The distance beyond the ruined architecture is marked by a glowing yellow light. The source of the light is obscure, lending the scene an atmosphere of mystery and deep religiosity. As tends to be characteristic of the late works, the lighting is uniform and does not display the dramatic contrasts found in Dou's early depictions of hermits.

The wide cracks in the dark portions of the paint surface point to the use of bitumen in the black underpaint laid down in many areas over the white ground. Dou's use of bitumen, probably intended to enhance the depth of color and tone, has been documented in the underpaint of *The Young Mother* (cat. 21);[3] it was likely used by Dou in other paintings as well.

Dou's signature appears twice on this work, as it does in *The Quack* (cat. 19) and his *Self-Portrait* of 1663 (cat. 27). Like both works, it has been substantially reworked. X-radiography and craquelure in the area indicate that Dou altered the position of the open book. Unlike most of Dou's other depictions of hermits, the figure must therefore originally have been positioned more frontally, in a pose that Dou favored for his paintings of the penitent Magdalen. The alteration suggests the importance that Dou attached to the book in this image; certainly, the emphasis on the written word was a significant component of Protestant belief.[4]

Dendrochronological analysis of the panel indicates a likely felling date of 1633 (plus or minus five years).[5] This finding suggests that Dou may have begun work on the panel in the mid-1630s and reworked it much later in his career, as he did with *The Quack* (cat. 19) and the 1663 *Self-Portrait* (cat. 27).[6]

The painting is replete with symbols alluding to the vanity of life, the constancy of the hermit in his devotions, and his eventual triumph over death through meditation and prayer. The latter is underscored by the flowering branches that sprout from the dead tree stump at the right.

A similar representation of a hermit at prayer hangs on the back wall of a double portrait that has traditionally been attributed to Dou.[7] A man and his wife are posed in an interior, surrounded by indications of their worldly interests and material possessions. The painting of the hermit praying in the wilderness here is clearly meant to be a paradigm of the contemplative life, in contrast to the couple's active life. The suspended glass sphere hanging from the rafters nearby symbolizes heaven, the reward of a life that combines spiritual and material pursuits.[8] The hermit, therefore, was probably regarded by the Dutch public as the personification of piety and devotion, virtues necessary to balance the demands of an active life.

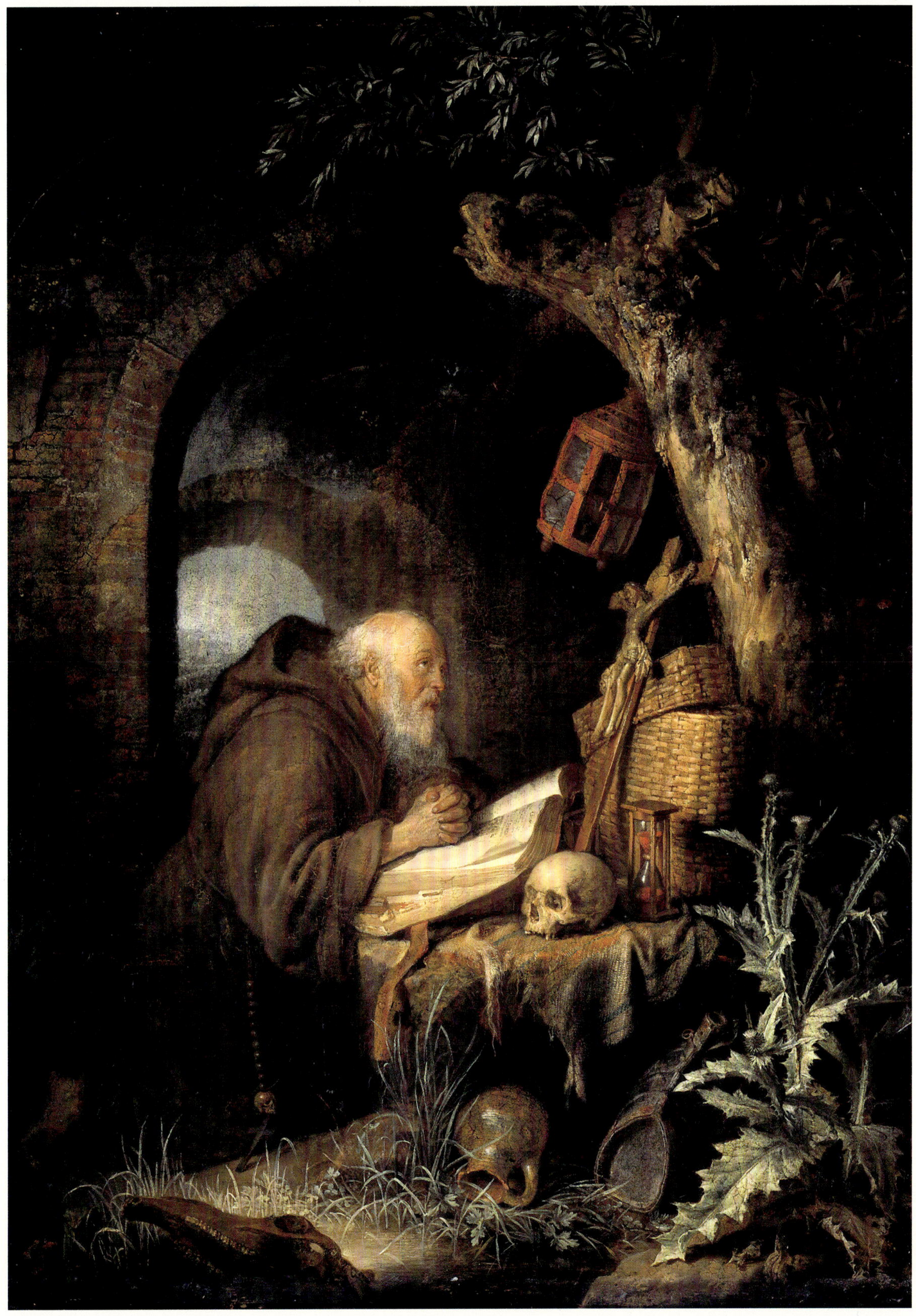

35.
The Grocery Shop

1672; oil on panel; arched top, 48.8 x 35 (19 ¼ x 13 ¾); Lent by Her Majesty Queen Elizabeth II

Signed and dated lower right: GDov 1672; *signed again on box in background*

· *Provenance* Duc de Choiseul, Paris, in 1756; Chosieul-Praslin sale, Paris, 18 February 1793 (no. 92) (FF 34,850, to Paillet). Purchased by William Buchanan in Paris, 1817. Purchased by George IV from Thomas Thompson Martin, 21 June 1817 (1,000 gns).

· *Bibliography* J. Smith 1829, no. 23; Martin 1901, no. 261; Hofstede de Groot 1907, no. 187; Martin 1911, no. 139; Martin 1913, 135; Royal Collection 1982, no. 46; Baer 1990, no. 125

· *Exhibitions* London 1946–1947, no. 342; London 1971, no. 57

· As in his other late dated works, Dou here returns to a theme he favored early in his career.[1] A shopkeeper, scales in hand, is about to weigh the grapes indicated by the girl standing next to her with a shopping pail. In the background, an elegant woman carrying a silver pot looks out at the viewer as she leaves the shop.

A new modish elegance is apparent in the dress of the shopper and the clothing of the woman in the doorway at right. The painting also includes exotic goods: lemons on a blue-and-white export platter, sweet confections in a sealed jar, and sponges. This fashionable taste reflects the appeal of things French and the opening of Dutch markets to imports, as well as social changes occuring in Holland during the third quarter of the seventeenth century.

The scene depicted takes place in a *comenij*, or general store, which sold eggs, dairy, and meat products. The poppies hanging from a nail in the center of the stone arch, used to make a syrup with narcotic properties, are commonly associated with apothecary shops.[2] Dou's shop scenes were avidly imitated by his followers. Willem van Mieris (1662–1747), the son of Dou's most successful student, Frans, specialized in the genre, as did his son, Frans the Younger (1689–1763). These two artists, however, depicted identifiable types of shops—dry-goods stores, poulterers, or apothecary shops—rather than the generalized locale depicted by Dou.

Dou's painting technique is less detailed here than in his earlier works. His brushwork, moreover, does not distinguish among various textures, whether the wood of the bucket, the straw of the basket, or the terracotta flowerpot. Although individual strokes are evident in the girl's hair, Dou has not meticulously described each strand as he did in earlier works. The blue, red, and gray in the rapidly brushed striped curtain at the upper right are the primary color notes of the painting.

The stone arch that frames the scene is placed at a greater distance from the viewer than is often the case in Dou's work and removes the spectator from the image. The organization of space, with a surface projecting perpendicular to the windowsill, is a device used by Dou in other late works. Here, Dou has concentrated more on the interaction between the figures, and the background vignette, less monochromatic than usual, is more fully integrated into the scene as a whole.

The background scene of a woman cutting bread for a young boy is a familiar one in Dou's oeuvre. His earlier representations of the subject allude to moral and spiritual education, as well as to domestic virtue and accomplishments.[3] It may be that the act of cutting bread is intended here to reinforce the implied virtues of the careful shopper in the foreground.

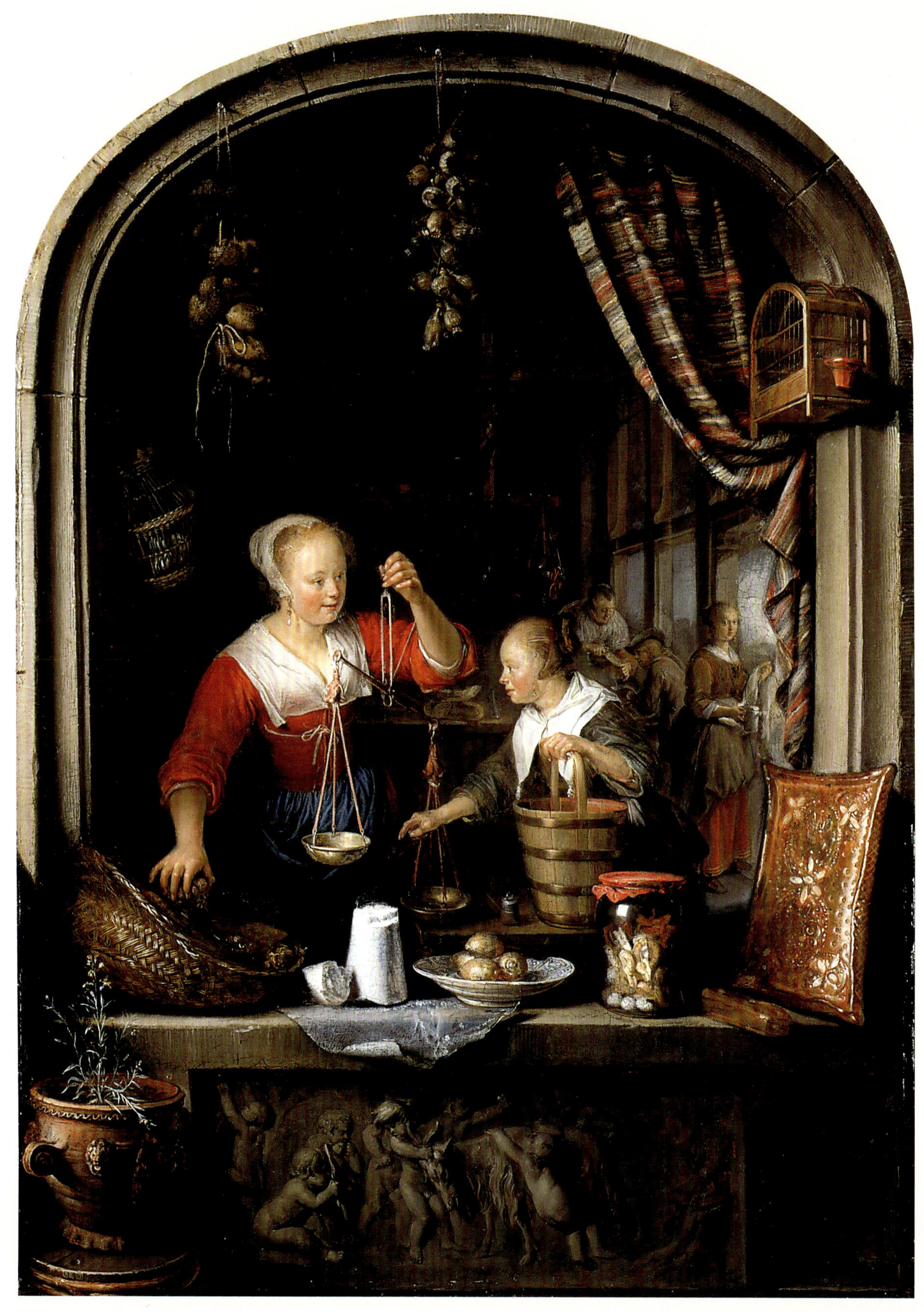

Notes for Catalogue

1.

Artist in His Studio

1 Adams 1985, 151 ff.

2 Raupp 1984, 276–277.

2.

Old Woman Reading

1 Bruyn, in *Corpus* 1982–, 1: 356. Jan Bialostocki (1984, 16) identifies images of old women reading religious texts as personifications of piety, an interpretation that is probably just as valid as the more specific one offered by Bruyn.

2 Rotermund 1957, 134–138. The lectionary, originally used by ecclesiastics and in public worship, came to be a domestic devotional book in the sixteenth century.

3 The model has traditionally been identified as Rembrandt's mother, but no documented likenesses of her exist. An etching of "Rembrandt's Moeder" is mentioned in Clement de Jonghe's inventory of 1679, but the print has not been identified. Nevertheless, because the woman's features appear in numerous early Rembrandt etchings and paintings (Bartsch 1802–1821, nos. 343, 348, 349, 351, 352, 354, and *Corpus* 1982–, 1: A27 and A32), the identification has found general acceptance.

4 Alpers 1983, 188.

3.

Man Writing by an Easel

1 Courtesy of Sotheby's.

2 On Dou's probable use of a magnifying device, see above, page 51, note 137.

3 Dou also adapted Rembrandt's motif of the easel turned away from the viewer that is found in *Artist in His Studio* of c. 1627 / 1628. See above, cat. 1.

4 See, for example, Hunnewell 1983, 172–173; Naumann in Philadelphia, Berlin, and London, 1984, 182; Brown in Berlin, Amsterdam, and London 1991, 304.

4.

Man Interrupted at His Writing

1 The *tabbaard*, a fur-trimmed mantle with ornamental loops and braid, was a house garment worn by scholars during the seventeenth century; see De Winkel 1995.

2 For example, *Corpus* 1982–, 2: A44 and A95.

3 For this tradition, see Van de Waal 1974, 143, and above, pages 27–28.

4 In several of his portraits from the 1630s, Rembrandt affixed his signature to a letter or document held by the sitter. See, for example, *Corpus* 1982–, 2: A43 and A52.

5 See Miedema 1975.

5.

Old Man Lighting a Pipe

1 Willem Martin notes that Theodor von Frimmel thought this painting a copy; Abraham Bredius attributed it to Jacob van Spreeuwen (1611–after 1650).

2 On the *tabbaard*, see De Winkel 1995.

3 Usually such images show the figure warming his (or occasionally her) hands over a similar coal pan; see *Allegory of Winter* by Hendrick Bloemaert (1601–1672) in the Rijksmuseum, Amsterdam, or the work of the same title by Cesar van Everdingen (1616/1617–1678) in the Southampton City Art Gallery (illustrated in Van Straaten 1997, 39, figs. 64 and 65). Curiously, the hearth behind the elderly man in Dou's painting is unlit.

4 For seventeenth-century Dutch attitudes toward smoking, see Schama 1987, 198; Gaskell 1987, 117–137; and Auckland 1982, 101–105.

5 The same sitter appears in Rembrandt's *Old Man Asleep by the Fire* (Galleria Sabauda, Turin) (*Corpus* 1982–, 1: A17) and *Bust of an Old Man in a Fur Cap* (Tiroler Landesmuseum Ferdinandeum, Innsbruck) (*Corpus* 1982–, 1: A29); in Lievens' *Oriental* (Gemäldegalerie, Potsdam) (Sumowski 1983, 3: 1236); and in Dou's *Man with a Globe* (State Hermitage Museum, St. Petersburg) (Martin 1913, 22 left) and *The Dentist* (Musée du Louvre, Paris) (Sumowski 1983, 1: 563 [no. 266]).

6.

Still Life with Globe, Lute, and Books

1 Sumowski 1983, 1: 538 (no. 307).

7.

Self-Portrait

1 Dou had recently begun to employ the arched-top panel in such works as *An Interior with Young Violinist* (cat. 8).

2 Hunnewell 1983, 30.

8.

An Interior with Young Violinist

1 My thanks to Hugh Macandrew at the National Galleries of Scotland for identifying the seal.

2 J. Smith 1829, 35.

3 Bailly's portrait (and, by extension, Dou's) also resembles De Keyser's influential *Portrait of Constantijn Huygens and His Clerk* (1627) (MacLaren and Brown 1991, 2: pl. 184). Huygens is depicted as a virtuoso, surrounded by objects that represent the range of his interests and accomplishments; see Adams 1985, 120. Adams (on 100–106), interprets the sword and book in Huygens' portrait as an allusion to the ideal of the humanist-courtier, skilled not only in arms but also in the arts. The spurs in the De Keyser painting allude to Huygens' service as a diplomat; they are identified as his "spurs of knighthood."

4 Castiglione 1528, 1: xlvii–xlviii: "niuno riposo de fatiche e medicina d'animi infermi ritrovar si po più onesta e laudevole nell'ocio, che questa." This book, a manual of etiquette for the successful courtier, was influential well into the seventeenth century and beyond.

5 Munich 1999, 96–97.

6 X-radiographs of *The Hermit* in the National Gallery of Art, Washington (cat. 34) reveal a similar compositional change. Hugh Macandrew was kind enough to arrange to have *An Interior with Young Violinist* x-rayed for me.

7 "[U]n petit tableau où un homme joue du violon selon la tabulature." Stockholm, Kungl. Biblioteket S4a, inventory number 3.

8 Von Sandrart, ed. Peltzer 1925, 195: "Ein Lautenschlager an einem Tisch sitzend / der vor ihme Bücher ligen hat / ungefähr einer Spannen groß."

9.

Portrait of a Young Woman

1 Kettering 1983, 65.

2 See Louttit 1973, 321–322, 325; Kettering 1983, chap. 4.

3 Kettering 1983, 70 ff.

4 For an idea of what the headdress would have looked like when in place, compare Rembrandt's so-called portraits of Saskia in the Rijksmuseum, Amsterdam (1633; *Corpus* 1982–, 2: A75) and in the National Gallery of Art, Washington (probably begun 1634/1635 and completed 1638/1640; see Wheelock 1995, 210–215).

5 The other profile portraits in Dou's oeuvre are the *Bust of a Youth* in the Fitzwilliam Museum, Cambridge (Sumowski 1983, 1: 556 [no. 259]), the *Portrait of a Woman* (cat. 10), and the *Bust of a Negro* in the Statens Museum for Kunst, Copenhagen (Martin 1913, 36). Rembrandt employed both the profile format and the arcadian type during his early years in Amsterdam. For the format, compare Rembrandt's 1632 *Young Woman in Profile* in the Nationalmuseum, Stockholm (*Corpus* 1982–, 2: A49), his *Portrait of Amalia of Solms* in the Musée Jacquemart-André, Paris (*Corpus* 1982–, 2: A61), and the *Profile Portrait of Saskia* in the Gemäldegalerie Alte Meister, Kassel (*Corpus* 1982–, 2: A85). For the arcadian type, see *Flora* in the State Hermitage Museum, St. Petersburg (*Corpus* 1982–, 2: A93), and *Flora* in the National Gallery, London (*Corpus* 1982–, 3: A112).

The profile view was especially favored by Jan Lievens in his Leiden work; see Sumowski 1983, 3: nos. 1249, 1251, 1252, 1255–1258, 1261, and 1280. Lievens' profiles are more *tronies* than portraits.

10.

Portrait of a Woman

1 Courtesy of the Noortman Gallery, Maastricht.

2 See, for example, the paintings in the Nivaagards Malerisammling (Martin 1913, 54, left); the Manchester City Art Galleries (cat. 9); and the Staatliche Museen, Berlin (Martin 1913, 38, left). The costume of the sitter in the present painting, with the addition of the fur jacket, resembles that in the *Portrait of a Girl* (c. 1638–1640) in the Gemäldegalerie Alte Meister, Dresden (Martin 1913, 54, right).

11.

Bust of a Man

1 The pose also appears in Dou's *Bust of a Negro* in the Statens Museum for Kunst, Copenhagen (Martin 1913, 36, left). Lievens used it in his *Man in a Ruff Collar* in the State Hermitage Museum, St. Petersburg (Sumowski 1983, 3: no. 1283) from the late 1630s, which Hans Schneider sees as dependent on the 1620 *Portrait of Abraham Graphaeus* by Cornelis de Vos (1584–1651) (Schneider and Ekkart 1973, 48). Hals and Rembrandt often employed the pose, imbuing otherwise static compositions with a sense of liveliness.

2 Although the early provenance of the Corcoran painting cannot be unconditionally established, if it does correspond to that suggested above, it would differ from the early provenance of the London *Man with a Pipe* (cat. 15). The paintings do not in any event read as pendants, compositionally or in subject.

3 Arthur Wheelock (1978, 61) has also questioned the identification of the sitter as Dou's father.

12.

Portrait of a Man

13.

Portrait of a Woman

1 The pendants in the Gemäldegalerie Alte Meister, Kassel (Martin 1913, 22, right, and 38, right), are imaginative figure studies, or *tronies*, not portraits.

2 Several of Rembrandt's female sitters from the 1640s are similarly dressed. Compare, for instance, the millstone ruff, the double form of cap enclosing hair and ears, the long sleeves and the black solemnity of the dress of Aeltje Gerritdr. Schouten in the *Double Portrait* with Cornelis Claesz. Anslo (1641) in the Staatliche Museen, Berlin (*Corpus* 1982–, 3: A143), or the *Portrait of Ariaentje Hollaer* (1647) in the Westminster Collection, London (Bredius 1969, 370).

3 D. Smith 1982, 78–79.

4 J. Smith 1829, 43 (no. 132).

14.

Self-Portrait

1 Similarly diminutive self-portraits were painted by Frans van Mieris (1635–1681) (see Naumann 1981, 1: pls. 29, 38, and 41) and Adriaen van der Werff (1659–1722) (see Gaehtgens 1987, pl. 105), among others.

2 Rembrandt's famous *Self-Portrait* of 1640 in the National Gallery, London (*Corpus* 1982–, 3: A139), derives directly from this composite image (which loses its stable, pyramidal form in the later states of the print). The resemblances between Rembrandt's 1640 painting and the present work were remarked upon in the Christie's sale catalogue, London, 8 December 1995 (33A), and by Peter Sutton in Melbourne and Sydney 1997, 232.

3 Von Sandrart, ed. Peltzer 1925, 196.

4 This dating was also suggested by Willem van de Watering, as quoted in the entry for the painting in the Christie's sale catalogue, London, 8 December 1995 (33A), and is not contradicted by Marieke de Winkel's assessment that the costume dates, at the earliest, from the second half of the 1640s; see London and The Hague 1999, 253 note 288.

15.

Man with a Pipe

1 Opinion as to whether this is a self-portrait remains evenly divided. As Eric Jan Sluijter has indicated (Leiden 1988, 100 note 2), a painting of the same sitter in the Rijksmuseum, Amsterdam (Sumowski 1983, 1: 271 [= cat. 16]) was identified as a self-portrait as early as the eighteenth century (Hoet 1752–1770, 2: 407: "Een Tabaks rooker zynde 't Pourtrait van G. Dou door hem zelfs geschildert" [A tobacco smoker, being the portrait of G. Dou painted by himself]). Although MacLaren, Sumowski, Hunnewell, and Sluijter do not consider it a self-portrait, Martin, Naumann, Raupp, Haak, and Brown's revision of MacLaren do. The composition of *Man with a Pipe* resembles that of a painting in the Fogg Museum, Cambridge, identified as a self-portrait by Michael Sweerts (1618–1664) (see Raleigh 1960, no. 11).

2 Compare, for instance, the smoking man on the far right of Buytewech's *Merry Company* in the Bredius Museum, The Hague (Haverkamp-Begemann 1959, no. 6) or the similar figure on the far left of Buytewech's painting of the same subject in the Szépmüvészeti Muzeum, Budapest (Haverkamp-Begemann 1959, no. 8). The figure of the smoker is commonly identified as emblematic of the sense of smell, but Werner Sumowski interprets it as a reference to the transitoriness of youth: see Sumowski 1994, 3596.

3 The scale of the figure, the hairstyle, and the turn of the woman's body resemble those in the *Portrait of a Girl* in the Nivaagards Malerisammling (Martin 1913, 54, left), but she appears to be older and she faces the viewer.

4 For example, see *Corpus* 1982–, 1: A8, A20, A32, and A33 (two self-portraits and two *tronies*); and Van de Wetering 1982, 32–33.

16.

Painter with Pipe and Book

1 See Dijon 1982–1983, 267–269.

2 Mastai 1975, 190.

3 The illusionistic curtain was a common device among Dou's contemporaries. Rembrandt used it in the *Holy Family* (1646, in the Gemäldegalerie Alte Meister, Kassel; Bredius 1969, 486), although, unlike Dou, he executed the curtain with broad, painterly strokes, drawing attention to the painting's surface. See Sluijter in Leiden 1988, 98. Eddy de Jongh (in Auckland 1982, 145) observed that trompe l'oeil "is the creation of the fullest possible illusion in paint, whereby the paint as a material is repudiated and the demands of style are subject to the reality of appearance," an apt description of Dou's painting technique here.

4 See Sluijter 1993, 20. Traudenius (1662, 17) praised Dou's "Boere-Keucken, Zeer aertig afgebeeldt" (Peasant kitchen, very artfully executed).

5 See Leiden 1988, 11, and Sluijter 1988b, 19–21.

6 Raupp 1984, 237–241; Leiden 1988, 98; Sluijter 1990b, 298. Sluijter makes the intriguing suggestion that because the painter must capture that which is fleeting, smoke is the perfect metaphor for *schijn zonder sijn*. For the negative connotations of smoking, see Amsterdam 1976, 55–57.

7 For this conceit in Rembrandt's prints, see Dickey 1986, 253–262.

17.

Still Life with Hourglass, Pencase, and Print

18.

Still Life with Book and Purse

1 Ingvar Bergström suggested that the Hartford panel was originally a cover for a picture box (see Bergström 1956, 182), but there is no physical evidence to support this conjecture. The argument against identifying the Hartford still life as a *kas* cover is made by Otto Naumann in Wadsworth Atheneum 1978, 131 note 3.

2 Miedema 1975, 15.

3 Wadsworth Atheneum 1978, 131 and note 5.

4 See Bergström 1956, 183. This idea is taken up in Amsterdam and Cleveland 1999, 183.

5 Sluijter 1993, 24–27.

19.

The Quack

1 Spanish cedar (*Cedrela odorata*) is a tropical wood grown in Central America, specifically in Brazil, with which Holland had much trade in the seventeenth century. It is noteworthy that had Dou used oak, he would have had to use several planks; here he has used a single board. See Lammertse 1997, 111.

2 The clothing and gesture of Dou's quack recall those of Rembrandt's charlatan in his etching dated 1635 (B. 129).

3 As Sluijter 1993, 72, noted, the placement of this woman directly under the quack underscores the nature of his discourse.

4 Sluijter 1993, 73. Sluijter identifies the bystanders as carefully chosen (stereo)types associated with gullibility and stupidity.

5 E. de Jongh 1967, 70.

6 Although the date is somewhat illegible, Jeroen Giltaij, the curator of Old Master paintings at the Boijmans, has assured me that the painting bears the date of 1652, the date given as well in the Munich catalogue of 1936. Nevertheless, Raupp gives the date as 1657; according to a fiche in the RKD, the Düsseldorf catalogue of 1778 states that the painting is dated 1632 (perhaps an error of transcription). P. J. M. de Baar, the Leiden archivist, has noted that the Blauwpoort tower as it is shown in the painting was not completed until 1 November 1667. See Lammertse 1997, 115. As Lammertse observed, it is not clear what Dou changed in the building, nor can the succession of changes be definitively worked out.

7 Compare, for example, *The Grocery Shop* of 1647 (p. 39, fig. 15), and *Woman with Poultry* of 1650 (Martin 1913, 120), both in the Musée du Louvre, Paris, and to a lesser extent *The Mousetrap* in the Musée Fabre, Montpellier (Martin 1913, 124).

8 E. de Jongh 1967, 70–74.

9 Lammertse 1997, 119, asserts that if this is indeed the central conceit of the painting, it could not originally have been so, since neither the self-portrait nor the window was originally included. Hunnewell 1983, 114–116, is the sole author rightly to consider Dou's self-portrait not only on a symbolic level but on a pictorial and artistic level as well. He notes that through his "niche of transition," Dou visually assumes the painter's role of intermediary between the viewer's world and the painted illusion of it. The figure of the artist in the painting both comments on the scene unfolding below, and acts as a foil, providing the viewer with a model worthy of emulation.

10 Eddy de Jongh and Jan Emmens extend the comparison between artist and quack both to their products—the quack's remedies as merely imitative, and the artist's paintings as requiring thought—and to their manner of operation—the quack's hasty chatter versus the artist's (and most emphatically, Dou's) smooth and painstaking technique. Curiously, the technique used to depict the two figures in the painting contradicts one's expectations; the artist has been quickly and hastily sketched in (his lopsided face is curiously unfinished) while the quack receives Dou's most assured handling.

11 Alpers 1983, 116–118.

12 Gaskell 1982, 18–20. Dixon 1995, 190, also attempts to reconcile the two, indicating the historical unity of painters and doctors in the Guild of St. Luke. These professions were traditionally linked because the physician St. Luke was honored with the privilege of painting the Virgin and Child. Dixon interprets *The Quack* (whose identity she disputes because of his dress in full academic regalia and the diplomas [sic] surrounding him) as Dou asking his viewers "to compare the arts of painting and medicine, both disciplines based on learning, and both utilizing deception as a desirable, even necessary strategy."

13 As quoted in Gaskell 1982, 19.

14 Sluijter 1993, 72.

15 Eric Jan Sluijter, "Humor en bedrog: Inleiding," an unpublished lecture delivered in Leiden in a colloquium on humor on 30 March 1999.

16 Jan Emmens' article, "De kwakzalver" of 1971, was originally delivered as a lecture to the annual meeting of the Vereniging van Nederlandse Kunsthistorici te Rotterdam on 21 December 1963. The ideas formulated by Emmens were elaborated and refined by Eddy de Jongh in De Jongh 1967, 70–74, and in Amsterdam 1976, 87–89. To summarize their findings: Dou has enlarged the seal hanging from the parchment on the table with the intention of alluding to Roemer Visscher's emblem with the motto "Dat cera fidem," (the seal inspires trust) (Roemer Visscher, *Sinnepoppen*, Amsterdam, 1614, no. 46). The implication of the seal is that the quack is as dependable as his fake diploma; he will earn money under false pretenses. The inscription associated with Jan van der Veen's emblematic image of a pancake baker (Jan van der Veen, *Zinnebeelden oft Adams appel*, Amsterdam, 1642, no. 104), reads: "Het ongerijmt geklap of reedenloose reeden, Verderven soet verhaal en alle goede zeeden" (Speech without rhyme or reason spoils all good tales and all good virtues), likening undercooked pancakes to the "half-baked" prattle of the quack. Johan de Brune's emblem with the motto "Dit lijf, wat ist, als stanck en mist?" (What is life but stench and excrement?) (Johan de Brune, *Emblemata of zinnewerck*, Amsterdam, 1624, no. 17) implies that the attraction of the sensual life is deceptive. Another emblem by Jan van der Veen of a boy trying to catch a bird is an obvious analogue to the quack luring the gullible public. The seduction is easy; one must guard against choosing the wrong path (the choice between good and evil as represented by the two trees, one living and one dead). This imagery is based on Roemer Visscher's emblem with the motto *Keur baert angst* (choice brings anxiety) (*Sinnepoppen*, no. 11). While in no other painting did Dou use emblems in a programmatic way, the sheer number

of correspondences in this work to emblematic images suggests that he may have intended these thematic associations.

17 See E. de Jongh 1967, 74. Gaskell 1982, 19, suggested that moral anxiety and the decline in his fortune following the death of Spiering motivated Dou to examine his role as deceiver. Lammertse 1997, 111, argues that Dou had the freedom to determine the size and subjects of his paintings because of his fame. Nevertheless, *The Quack* differs significantly enough from Dou's usual production—both in iconography and size—that a specific commission should not be ruled out.

20.

Violin Player

1 The painting reproduced by Martin is a copy after this work by Van der Mijn.

2 For an exhaustive study of this theme, see Raupp 1978, 106–129.

3 Painters are known to have played music in their studios for their own entertainment or inspiration. See Amsterdam 1983, 124, which cites Houbraken's account of Gerard de Lairesse's playing the violin before he set to work. Albrecht Dürer counseled a young painter exhausted by his work to distract himself by playing a stringed instrument to get his blood moving again. For this anecdote and the notion of music as a relaxing stimulant, see Dijon 1982–1983, 195.

4 Eric Jan Sluijter (in Leiden 1988, 101), sees this as the most likely intended meaning of the picture, contrasting the musician's art with the more craftsmanly aspect of painting embodied in the background. This interpretation, with the background echoing or adding to the central meaning of the picture, is consonant with that proposed for the *Painter with Pipe and Book* (cat. 16).

5 Dou's earliest depiction of a bas-relief below a windowsill appears in the *Kitchenmaid at a Window* (1652) in the Staatliche Kunsthalle, Karlsruhe (page 38, fig. 13), featuring rinceaux and grotesques in a decorative pattern. The first appearance of the bas-relief by Duquesnoy of putti playing with a goat (the original, also known as *Sacred and Profane Love*, is in the Galleria Doria Pamphilj, Rome) occurs in *The Doctor* of 1653 in the Kunsthistorisches Museum, Vienna (page 37, fig. 11). In that painting, contemporary with the present work, the tapestry thrown over the sill distances the climbing putto at the far left of the relief from the masked putto who appears next to him in the actual and the present relief; Dou manipulated the composition of the bas-relief to accommodate the tapestry. His pictorial solution in the *Violin Player* is to drape the rug over the right portion of the relief, thereby obscuring only a subsidiary putto and a tree.

The same relief, or portions thereof, appears in many of Dou's other genre paintings, among them, Dou's *Self-Portrait* in the Metropolitan Museum of Art, New York (Martin 1913, frontispiece); *The Violinist* in the Gemäldegalerie Alte Meister, Dresden (Sumowski 1983, 1: 589 [no. 292]); *The Trumpeter* in the Musée du Louvre, Paris (Martin 1913, 86); *The Poulterer's Shop* in the National Gallery, London (Sumowski 1983, 1: 593 [no. 296]); *The Grocery Shop* in Buckingham Palace (cat. 35); and *Girl with a Candle at the Window* in the Thyssen Collection, Madrid (Sumowski 1983, 1: 588 [no. 291]). Sluijter's conclusion—that this painting could be seen to express, both literally and figuratively, the power of painting to capture appearances and material riches that, according to Angel, delight the eye of the amateur (Leiden 1988, 101)—would then have to apply to all of the paintings in which this bas-relief is featured. The bas-relief more plausibly simply signals Dou's painterly abilities and *Pictura*'s deceptive qualities, but has little bearing on the particular interpretation of the scene depicted.

21.

The Young Mother

1 For a description of the painting as it figured in the royal inventories, see Brenninkmeyer-de Rooij et al. 1988.

2 For a discussion of contemporary associations evoked by needlework, see Franits 1987, 34–38; for the meaning of the discarded shoe, see Franits 1987, 64.

3 This idea was credited by Wayne Franits (1987, 176 note 87) to E. Haverkamp-Begemann.

4 Whether there was a tradition of commissioning paintings of an idyllic view of family life or of the exemplary role of the woman to commemorate a marriage remains uncertain.

5 Mauritshuis 1895, 95–96.

6 This interpretation was proposed by Ben Broos (1987, 117). It should be pointed out that visitors to Dou's studio did not remark on whether Dou maintained a stock of paintings; see, for example, the accounts of Ole Borch 1662 (quoted in Madsen 1907, 228) and De Monconys 1666, 152–153. As Broos observed, Dou managed to provide the paintings for the "Dutch gift" on very short notice. He was named as appraiser of De Graeff's painting on 23 September 1660 (Logan 1979, 78–79 note 88), and the paintings he furnished were shipped shortly after 18 October of that same year.

7 Mahon 1949, 350; Broos 1987, 112. For Dou's role in assembling the Dutch gift, see above, pages 31–32.

22.

Young Woman in a Black Veil

1 The form of this signature is unusual; the monogram is more commonly—indeed, almost always—intertwined.

2 Willem Martin suggested a date of c. 1640–1645; on the unspecified grounds of style and costume, Neil MacLaren opted for c. 1655–1660; Werner Sumowski connected it stylistically to *The Young Mother* in the Gemäldegalerie, Staatliche Museen zu Berlin (Sumowski 1983, 1: 583 [no. 286]) and *The Lacemaker* in the Staatliche Kunsthalle, Karlsruhe (Sumowski 1983, 1: 590 [no. 293]) and thus dated it c. 1660; and Christopher Brown, on the basis of the "relative freedom of handling on a small scale . . . more characteristic of the earlier years of [Dou's] career," dated it c. 1640. In type, certainly, this painting resembles the panels of c. 1635–1640 in the Nivaagards Malerisammling (Martin 1913, 54, left), and the Manchester City Art Galleries (cat. 9). In execution, however, it is more assured and sophisticated, resembling *Man with a Pipe* of c. 1645 (cat. 15) with respect both to handling and conception.

3 Compare *Woman with Grapes*, 1662, Galleria Sabauda, Turin (Martin 1913, 110); and *Lady on a Balcony*, c. 1660, Narodni Galerie, Prague (Martin 1913, 52).

23.

The Wine Cellar

1 Otto Naumann shares the belief that it was the present painting and not a version of the picture formerly in Dresden (see Martin 1913, 166) that was originally protected by the *Still Life with Candlestick, Pipe, and Pocket Watch* in the Gemäldegalerie Alte Meister, Dresden. In an unpublished catalogue entry on *The Wine Cellar* that he generously allowed me to read, Naumann argues that the version formerly in Dresden had an arched top instead of the rectangular format of the *Still Life*, and that it most likely entered the Dresden collections at an earlier date than did the latter (the Dresden *Wine Cellar* is first recorded in the Guarienti inventory, which dates from before 1753, while the *Still Life* is first mentioned only in the inventory of 1754). For the function of the *kas*, see Martin 1901, 76–78; Boström 1949; and above, page 49, note 111.

24.

Woman Asleep

1 Dou has shuffled the figures he introduced in the *Cardplayers by Candlelight*, in the Residenzgalerie, Salzburg (Martin 1913, 176): the cavalier has risen from his chair to light his pipe, his companion has put down the violin and taken a seat, and the woman has loosened her bodice and fallen asleep.

2 Salomon 1984, 51, points out that the depictions of mocked sleepers in Dutch art may stem from the theater. A clearly theatrical image, such as the Caravaggesque painting by Nicolas Regnier (c. 1590–1667) in the Musée des Beaux-Arts, Rouen (see *Gazette des Beaux Arts*, ser. 6, 85 [1975]: supp. 73), depicting a masked figure holding a smoking wick under the nose of a male sleeper, may lie behind them. The humor in these scenes depends on the next moment within the narrative, when the drunken sleeper begins to stir, wave away what he thinks is a fly or an insect, but is not yet fully awake. The action of the cavalier lighting his pipe may also derive from a Caravaggesque source.

3 Dou was greatly admired for his ability to paint artificial light; see *The Night School*, cat. 28.

4 It is uncertain whether this action is meant to revive the sleeper (for this, a foul-smelling substance would have been used) or arouse her. As Nanette Salomon suggested in conversation (9 June 1989), sweet-smelling incense could have been used to provoke erotic dreams, as blowing into a sleeper's ear was supposed to do.

5 Salomon 1984, 51 ff.

6 "Die slapen gaat, veet niet hoe hij ontwaken sal"; "De wyn is een Spotter," quoted in Salomon 1984, 45.

7 For more on the connection between smoke and drink, see Utrecht 1986–1987, 107–108.

8 Salomon 1984, 52.

9 These pearls are most likely the "satanic" pearls of prostitutes mentioned by E. de Jongh 1975–1976, 82.

25.

Old Woman with Jug at a Window

1 Schama 1980, 7.

2 De la Perrière 1553, no. 71.

26.

The Doctor

1 This distinction was made by B. Feer (1985, 17). It is implied as well by Einar Petterson (1987, 193–194), who distinguishes among scenes of consultation (as here), the doctor's visit, and images of "the faint."

2 Dixon 1995, 50–51.

3 Dixon 1995, 6, 114.

4 "Langt hier een veynigh een Choffoor, En warmt d'Uryne door en door." Quoted in Van Gils 1917, 75.

5 "Laet se mij noch eens sien/en wiltse wel heeten." Quoted in Van Gils 1917, 76.

6 See Dixon 1995, 79. For a discussion of uroscopy and its use in determining pregnancy, see Sutton 1982–1983, 24, and Amsterdam 1976, 135.

7 See Amsterdam 1976, 221.

8 The *vanitas* elements are most obvious in Dou's *Doctor* in the State Hermitage Museum, St. Petersburg (Martin 1913, 72). B. Feer (1985, 57), argues that the clock and snail set the moral tone of the painting but offers an altogether different interpretation of the iconography: the painting, she argues, stresses the importance of striving toward self-knowledge and a sober life. For the snail as a symbol of self-knowledge and independence, see Henkel and Schöne 1967, 619–620; for the clock as a symbol of moderation and temperance, see Amsterdam 1976, 184.

9 See E. de Jongh 1967, 85–86, and Amsterdam 1976, 117–119.

10 See Naumann 1981, 1: 100.

11 Quoted in Naumann 1981, 1: 100.

27.

Self-Portrait

1 Madsen 1907, 228: "Nous avons vu chez lui son portrait de lui-même, qu'il a fini d'un travail délicat en se servant d'un miroir." This description of finish certainly does not apply to the roughly contemporary self-portraits in the Musée du Louvre, Paris (Martin 1913, 21) or the Metropolitan Museum of Art, New York (Martin 1913, frontispiece), although it is more likely that a mirror would have been used for a bust- or half-length portrait.

2 Werner Sumowski (1983, 1: 537) called this a "jubilee" self-portrait; Richard Hunnewell (1983, 123–124), as well, suggested that the painting might commemorate Dou's prosperity and fame at half century.

3 Hunnewell 1983, 126–128. For Angel in this context, see *Still Life with Book and Purse*, cat. 18.

4 See Muller, ed. 1997, 329 (s.v. "Rhetoricians chambers").

5 Broos in The Hague and San Francisco 1990–1991, 220–223. On the king's invitation to Dou, see above, page 32.

6 P.J.M. de Baar, the Leiden archivist, was the first to notice this discrepancy, which also figures in *The Quack* (cat. 19). For the form of the gate's tower as it appears earlier in Dou's work, see *Lady on a Balcony* in the Narodni Galerie, Prague (Martin 1913, 52).

7 Lammertse 1997, 116, and Broos in The Hague and San Francisco 1990–1991, 220. The balustrade would have resembled the one that appears in Rembrandt's *Self-Portrait* of 1640 in the National Gallery, London (see *Corpus* 1982–, 3: A39). The mantle that was originally draped over Dou's right arm in the early state of the *Self-Portrait* of 1663 also echoes the full sleeve in Rembrandt's *Self-Portrait*.

8 Lammertse 1997, 116–119.

28.

The Night School

1 Compare also *The Night School* (c. 1660–1665) in the Uffizi, Florence (Martin 1913, 171). The motif of the youth writing on a slate, overseen by another, for example, was introduced in the *Triptych*. For an important discussion of this work, particularly illuminating in its discussion of Dou's school scenes, see Emmens 1963, 125–136.

2 Durantini 1983, 168; De Planque 1926, 9–10; Schotel 1903, 80–86; Peeters 1966, 171–172; Philadelphia, Berlin, and London 1984, 318.

3 See, for example, Van Hoogstraeten 1678 (reprint 1969), 268.

4 Emmens 1963, 133; Miedema 1975, 6.

5 Ripa 1644, 273, quoting Aristotle's dictum "Daer is niet in 't verstand, dat niet eerst geweest is in de sinnen" (There is nothing in understanding that was not first in the senses). As the authors of Amsterdam 1976 have shown, it is inconceivable that Dou did not make use of this source.

6 See Wiersum 1931, 214.

7 J. Smith 1829, 27.

8 Immerzeel 1842, 1: 191.

9 Thoré (Bürger) 1858, 81–82. See above, pages 15–16.

29.

Self-Portrait

1 This is most evident in the self-portraits in the Gemäldegalerie Alte Meister, Dresden (page 35, fig. 10), the Musée du Louvre, Paris (Martin 1913, 21), and the Metropolitan Museum of Art, New York (Martin 1913, frontispiece).

2 The *écorché* is based on what is probably a late sixteenth-century bronze by an unknown artist; almost identical versions of the bronze are housed in the Musée Bonnat, Bayonne, and the Statens Museum for Kunst, Copenhagen. See Amerson 1975, fig. 211 (no. 28) and fig. 212 (no. 29). The *écorché*, a model of the body with the skin removed and the superficial muscles displayed, was kept in artists' studios as an example of the structure of the body, obviating the need to study anatomy by dissection; see Kornell 1996 and Nottingham and Kenwood 1991. This is the sole appearance of an *écorché* in Dou's oeuvre.

3 On the associations of the *tabbaard* during the seventeenth century, see De Winkel 1995.

4 See Raupp 1984, 383–385, pls. 6, 7, and 9.

5 Raupp 1984, 19–23.

30.

Woman at the Clavichord

1 The provenance of the present work has long been confused with that of *Woman at the Spinet*, formerly in the Gould collection (Martin 1913, 98). Neither painting can securely be identified as the one described by Descamps in 1754 (Descamps 1753–1765, 2: 225): "Chez M. le Maréchal d'Issenghien, une jeune Femme qui touche du Clavecin."

2 A note in the catalogue reports that the painting had previously been sold at Langford's, London, as Schalken after Dou.

3 Giles Waterfield in Washington and Los Angeles 1985–1986, 9–37, esp. 15–17.

4 According to Van Dijck and Koopman 1987, about 90 percent of the keyboard players pictured by Dutch artists are women and girls. Although, as MacLaren 1960, 439, has observed, the design of Vermeer's painting *A Lady Seated at the Virginal* (c. 1675) in the National Gallery, London, differs in many respects from that of Dou's, the viola da gamba, with the bow placed between the strings, and the tapestry just visible in the upper left corner are reminiscent of the earlier work. The suggestion that *Woman at the Clavichord* might have influenced Vermeer was first proposed by Boström 1949, 24, and recently discussed by Wheelock in Washington and The Hague 1995, 202.

5 *Gedichten*, The Hague, 1672, 2: 721: "Leert op de Luyt, leert op de Clavecijmbel speelen/De snaeren hebben macht om yemands hert te steelen." The comparison between Westerbaen's poem and Dou's painting was first made by Christopher Brown in London 1976, no. 32.

6 An infrared photograph indicates that the tablecloth was painted over a metal ewer, suggesting that Dou radically altered the still life in the course of painting the panel. See Beresford 1998, no. 56. Compare cats. 8, 27, and 34 for other examples of significant compositional changes in Dou's work.

7 Arthur Wheelock has proposed that the closed birdcage in *Woman at the Clavichord* could refer to the emblem in P.C. Hooft's *Emblemata Amatoria* (Amsterdam, 1611), 66–67 (28) with the motto "Voor vryheyt vaylicheyt" (Instead of freedom, safety). See Washington and The Hague 1995, 203 note 12.

8 For the relationship of Dou's art to that of Gerard ter Borch, Johannes Vermeer, and Dou's student Frans van Mieris, see above, pages 37–38, 39, 40–41.

9 The themes of lust and vanity, among others, were presented for the spectator's moral edification in addition to his delectation. See Sluijter 1986, 268, and Enschede 1987–1988, 11.

31.

Astronomer by Candlelight

1 Welu 1986, 263: "In practice these two branches of cosmography were more closely related during the seventeenth century than they are today. A person active in one was usually active in the other. . . . Globes of this period were always produced and sold in pairs, a practice that demonstrates the close connection between astronomy and geography at the time."

2 Miedema 1975, 15.

3 For a similar example, see Müller Hofstede 1988, 19. The interpretation of the painting as a youth reading his amorous fortune in the stars (Sluijter in Leiden 1988, 107), seems strained, nor are allusions to *vanitas* particularly strong.

4 During the seventeenth century, astronomy was viewed as closely related to astrology: see Amsterdam 1976, 84; Braunschweig 1978, 65; Brown 1984, 101–102; and above, page 36.

32.

Lady at Her Toilet

1 "Being a little woman being coiffed, with a door opening outward on which is a sucking woman by candlelight." The subject on the *kas* cover was probably a woman nursing a baby. See Sluijter 1988c, 152.

2 See above, page 57, for a discussion of the vanishing point revealed by recent conservation of *Lady at Her Toilet*.

3 Eric Jan Sluijter (1988c, 160) thinks it probable that Dou owned this ewer and basin, which figure in others of his paintings. It was the type of gift that an affluent patron would have been likely to bestow upon the artist. Outside of their iconographic connotations, Dou may have included these objects to draw attention to his success and artistic standing.

4 Sluijter 1988c, 152.

5 Schwartz 1985, 244 (272).

6 The birdcage was originally placed higher and did not have an open door; the change is further support for the iconographic significance of this element. For the open birdcage as a symbol of immorality, see Amsterdam 1976, 226–227; Sluijter 1988c, 159.

7 For an exhaustive account of the symbolism of mirrors and the detailed iconographic interpretation on which the present discussion is based, see Sluijter 1988c.

8 Sluijter 1988c, 60, also sees the theme of vanity, the fleeting nature of appearances, and the short-lived beauty of youth as implicit in this painting, an argument that *Lady at Her Toilet* is both an object of enjoyment and a symbol of illusion and transitoriness. Sluijter views Dou's inclusion of the ewer and basin and his own self-portrait on the back wall (in its first state; see cat. 27) as allusions to *vanitas*. However, as in many of Dou's self-portraits, art is in this case an antidote to decay, a triumphant victor over time, rather than the idle striving of the painter to capture the temporal. The beauty of the painting, and hence the artist's endeavor, would outlast the seductive (and transitory) beauty of the woman.

33. Hermit Praying

1 Ringbom 1965, 50–52.

2 Jan Sanders van Hemessen's *St. Jerome* (Veca 1981, 47, fig. 48; on the art market in Vienna in 1981) shows a half-length bearded saint with clasped hands placed just beyond a ledge that is pushed against the picture plane. A skull, hourglass, snuffed-out candle, crucifix, and large open book—the same objects that figure in Dou's painting—appear on the ledge.

3 Examples of this type of painting include Jan Brueghel the Elder's *Landscape with Ruins and St. Anthony* of 1596 in the Ambrosiana, Milan (Ertz 1981, 12), Pieter Lastman's *Hermit* of 1611, last recorded in a private collection, Brussels (Freise 1911, fig. 7), and Bartholomeus Breenbergh's painting of *St. Anthony Among Ruins* of 1635 (sold by Philips, London, 8 December 1987 [no. 72]).

4 Williams 1962, 36 ff, argues that monks who retired to their wilderness caves were reliving the birth of Christ and, consequently, were reborn there; the cave also represented both the womb of Mary and Paradise itself. Falckenburg 1985, 135–136, discusses a desolate landscape setting for Joachim Patinir's *St. Jerome and the Lion* (in the Prado, Madrid) as an allusion to the hermit's difficult choice to follow the path of Virtue.

5 In the caption to the 1596 engraving of *St. Jerome* by Hendrick Goltzius (1558–1617) after Palma Giovane, the man of piety is described as one who shuns the deceitful allurements of the flesh for solitude and Christian meditation. For this and the dead tree in images of St. Jerome, see Kuretsky 1974, 573–574.

34. The Hermit

1 Wheelock 1995, 60 note 1, traces the painting's early provenance: "On the back of the painting are two wax seals that were detached from the original panel when it was cradled and then reapplied. One of these seals is that of Kurfürst Karl Albrecht . . . [which] was used until 1742. The other seal may also be that of Karl Albrecht, or alternatively of Kurfürst Maximillian II Emmanuel (1662–1726)."

2 Martin 1913, xix.

3 See Struick van der Loeff 1987, 48; White 1986, 62; and above, pages 40, 60, and 63 note 24.

4 While the image of a hermit in prayer before a crucifix would seem to be a Catholic image, it apparently had no such specific denominational appeal. See Wheelock 1995, 58, and Baer 1995, 33 note 46.

5 Letter from Peter Klein of the Ordinariat für Holzbiologie, Universität Hamburg, 28 January 1987 (NGA curatorial files). See also Bauch and Eckstein 1970, 45–50, esp. 49, with the caveat that "the dating of a solitary panel will be limited if no comparative panels by the same artist are available."

6 See Lammertse 1997.

7 Wheelock 1995, 60, fig. 2.

8 E. de Jongh 1975–1976, 74. For a more detailed discussion of the Brooklyn painting, see this author's entry in the forthcoming catalogue of Old Master paintings in the Brooklyn Museum.

35. The Grocery Shop

1 Dou's earliest treatment of this subject, in the Musée du Louvre, Paris (page 39, fig. 15), is dated 1647. *The Hermit* of 1670 (cat. 34), *The Pen Sharpener* of 1671 (Sumowski 1983, 1: 592 [no. 295]), and *The Dentist* of 1672 (Sumowski 1983, 1: 594 [no. 297]), the latter two in the Gemäldegalerie Alte Meister, Dresden, illustrate Dou's return to earlier themes in his late paintings.

2 Leiden 1988, 141.

3 Compare for example, the paintings (both c. 1660) in a private collection, Essen (Martin 1913, 173), and in the Museum Boijmans van Beuningen, Rotterdam (Martin 1913, 174, right).

DETAIL
The Young Mother, 1658, oil on panel, Royal Cabinet of Paintings Mauritshuis, The Hague (cat. 21)

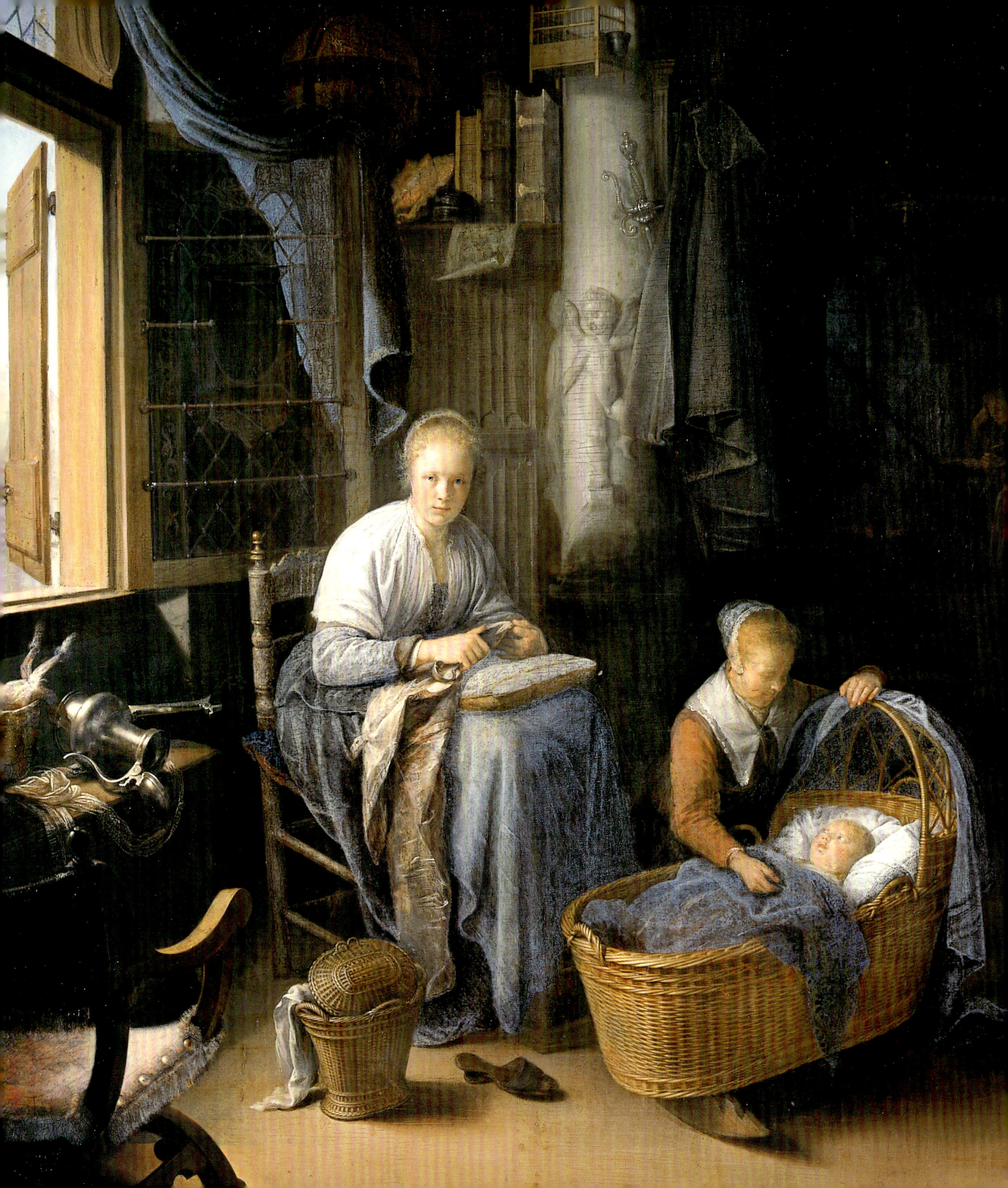

ADAMS 1985
Adams, Ann Jensen. "The Paintings of Thomas de Keyser (1596/7–1667): A Study of Portraiture in Seventeenth-Century Amsterdam." Ph.D. diss., Harvard University, 1985.

ALPERS 1976–1977
Alpers, Svetlana. "Describe or Narrate? A Problem in Realistic Representation." *New Literary History* 8 (1976–1977): 15–41.

ALPERS 1983
Alpers, Svetlana. *The Art of Describing.* Chicago, 1983.

AMERSON 1975
Amerson, Price. "The Problem of the Écorché: A Catalogue Raisonné of Models and Statuettes from the Sixteenth Century and Later Periods." Ph.D. diss., The Pennsylvania State University, 1975.

AMMAN AND SACHS 1568
Amman, Jost, and Hans Sachs. *The Book of Trades.* New York, 1973 (facsimile reprint of 1568 edition).

AMSTERDAM 1929
Hoogendijk, D.A., et al., eds. *Oude schilderijen.* Exh. cat., Rijksmuseum. Amsterdam, 1929.

AMSTERDAM 1952
Dantzig, M.M., et al. *Vals of echt?* Exh. cat., Stedelijk Museum. Amsterdam, 1952.

AMSTERDAM 1965
Het Nederlandse Geschenk. Exh. cat., Rijksmuseum. Amsterdam, 1965.

AMSTERDAM 1976
De Jongh, Eddy, ed. *Tot Lering en Vermaak: Betekenissen van Hollandse genrevoorstellingen uit de zeventiende eeuw.* Exh. cat., Rijksmuseum. Amsterdam, 1976.

AMSTERDAM 1983
Blankert, Albert, et al. *The Impact of a Genius: Rembrandt, His Pupils and Followers in the Seventeenth Century: Paintings from Museums and Private Collections.* Exh. cat., Waterman Gallery. Amsterdam, 1983.

AMSTERDAM 1984
Ornstein-van Slooten, Eva. *Bij Rembrandt in de leer.* Exh. cat., Museum Het Rembrandthuis. Amsterdam 1984.

AMSTERDAM 1989
Hecht, Pieter. *De Hollandse fijnschilders: Van Gerard Dou tot Adriaen van der Werff.* Exh. cat., Rijksmuseum. Amsterdam, 1989.

AMSTERDAM AND CLEVELAND 1999
Chong, Alan, and Wouter Kloek. *Still-Life Paintings from The Netherlands 1550–1720.* Exh. cat., Rijksmuseum; Cleveland Museum of Art. Amsterdam and Zwolle, 1999.

ANGEL 1642
Angel, Philips. *Lof der Schilder-konst.* Leiden, 1642 (facsimile ed., Utrecht, 1969).

ANGEL 1996
Angel, Philips. "Praise of Painting." Trans. Michael Hoyle with an introduction by Hessel Miedema. *Simiolus* 24 (1996): 227–258.

ARMSTRONG 1904
Armstrong, Sir Walter. *The Peel Collection and the Dutch School of Painting.* London, 1904.

ARNHEM 1953
Zeventiende eeuwse meesters uit Gelders. Exh. cat., Gemeentemuseum. Arnhem, 1953.

ASKEW 1969
Askew, Pamela. "The Angelic Consolation of St. Francis of Assisi in Post-Tridentine Italian Painting." *Journal of the Warburg and Courtauld Institutes* 32 (1969): 280–306.

AUCKLAND 1982
De Jongh, Eddy. *Still-Life in the Age of Rembrandt.* Exh. cat., Auckland City Art Gallery; Robert McDougall Art Gallery, Christchurch; National Art Gallery, Wellington. Auckland, 1982.

AVERY 1971
Avery, Charles. "François Dieussart in the United Provinces and the Ambassador of Queen Christina." *Bulletin van het Rijksmuseum* 19 (1971): 143–164.

DE BAAR AND MOERMAN 1991
De Baar, P.J.M., and Ingrid W.L. Moerman. "Rembrandt van Rijn en Jan Lievens, inwoners van Leiden." In Christiaan Vogelaar et al., eds., *Rembrandt and Lievens in Leiden*, exh. cat., Stedelijk Museum De Lakenhal. Zwolle and Leiden, 1991: 24–38.

BAER 1990
Baer, Ronni. "The Paintings of Gerrit Dou (1613–1675)." Ph.D. diss., New York University, 1990.

BAER 1995
Baer, Ronni. "Image of Devotion: Dou's 'Hermit Praying'." *Minneapolis Institute of Arts Bulletin* 67 (1995): 22–33.

BARTSCH 1797
Gersaint, Edme François. *Catalogue raisonné de toutes les estampes qui forment l'oeuvre de Rembrandt et ceux de ses principaux imitateurs. Composé par les sieurs Gersaint, Helle, Glomy et P. Yver.* Revised and enlarged edition by Adam Bartsch. 2 vols. Vienna, 1797.

BARTSCH 1802–1821
Bartsch, Adam. *Le peintre graveur.* 21 vols. Vienna, 1802–1821.

BAUCH AND ECKSTEIN 1970
Bauch, Josef, and Dieter Eckstein. "Dendrochronological Dating of Oak Panels of Dutch Seventeenth-Century Paintings." *Studies in Conservation* 15 (1970): 45–50.

BAUCH 1960
Bauch, Kurt. *Der frühe Rembrandt und seine Zeit.* Berlin, 1960.

BEDAUX 1975–1976
Bedaux, Jan Baptist. "Minnekoorts-, zwangerschaps- en doodverschijnselen op zeventiende-eeuwse schilderijen." *Antiek* 10 (1975–1976): 17–42.

BERESFORD 1998
Beresford, Richard. *Dulwich Picture Gallery: A Concise Illustrated Catalogue.* New Haven, 1998.

BERGER 1883
Berger, A. "Inventar der Kunstsammlung des Erzherzogs Leopold Wilhelm von Osterreich." *Jahrbuch der Kunsthistorischen Sammlungen des Allerhöchsten Kaiserhauses* 1 (1883): lxxix–clxxvii.

BERGSTRÖM 1956
Bergström, Ingvar. *Dutch Still-Life Painting in the Seventeenth Century.* London, 1956.

BERLIN, AMSTERDAM, AND LONDON 1991
Brown, Christopher, Jan Kelch, and Pieter van Thiel. *Rembrandt: The Master and His Workshop: Paintings.* Exh. cat., Altes Museum, Gemäldegalerie, Staatliche Museen zu Berlin; Rijksmuseum, Amsterdam; National Gallery, London. New Haven and London, 1991.

BERNHARD 1965
Bernhard, Marianne. *Verlorene Werke der Malerei in Deutschland in der Zeit von 1939 bis 1945 zerstörte und verschollene Gemälde aus Museen und Galerien.* Munich, 1965.

BIALOSTOCKI 1984
Bialostocki, Jan. "A New Look at Rembrandt Iconography." *Artibus et Historiae* 10 (1984): 9–19.

DE BIE 1661
De Bie, Cornelis. *Het Gulden Cabinet van de edele vry schilderconst.* Antwerp, 1661.

DE BIÈVRE 1995
De Bièvre, Elisabeth. "The Urban Subconscious: The Art of Delft and Leiden." *Art History* 18 (June 1995): 222–252.

BILLE 1961
Bille, Clara. *De Tempel der Kunst, of Het Kabinet van den Heer Braamcamp.* 2 vols. Amsterdam, 1961.

BIRMINGHAM 1934
Commemorative Exhibitions of the Art Treasures of the Midlands. Exh. cat., City of Birmingham Museum and Art Gallery. Birmingham, 1934.

BLANKERT 1980
Blankert, Albert. Introduction to *Gods, Saints, and Heroes: Dutch Painting in the Age of Rembrandt*, ed. Albert Blankert et al. Exh. cat., National Gallery of Art. Washington, 1980: 15–33.

BLANKERT 1982
Blankert, Albert. *Ferdinand Bol (1616–1680): Rembrandt's Pupil.* Doornspijk, 1982.

BLANKERT 1983
Blankert, Albert. "Rembrandt's Pupils and Followers in the Seventeenth Century." In Amsterdam 1983: 13–34.

BLOK 1916
Blok, Petrus Johannes. *Geschiedenis eener Hollandsche Stad.* 3 vols. Leiden, 1916.

VON BODE 1906
Von Bode, Wilhelm. *Rembrandt und seine Zeitgenossen.* Leipzig 1906.

BOGTMAN 1944
Bogtman, Willem. *Nederlandsche Glasschilders.* Amsterdam, 1944.

DU BOIS DE SAINT GELAIS 1727
Du Bois de Saint Gelais, Louis François. *Description des tableaux du Palais Royal: Avec la vie des peintres à la tête de leurs ouvrages.* Paris, 1727.

VAN DER BOOM 1940
Van der Boom, Anton. *Monumentale Glasschilderkunst in Nederland.* The Hague, 1940.

BOSTRÖM 1949
Boström, Karl. "Peep-show or Case?" *Kunsthistorische Mededeelingen van het Rijksbureau voor Kunsthistorische Documentatie* 4 (1949): 21–24.

BRAUN 1980
Braun, Karel. *Alle tot nu bekende schilderijen van Jan Steen.* Rotterdam, 1980.

BRAUNSCHWEIG 1978
Müller, Wolfgang J., Konrad Renger, and Rüdiger Klessmann, eds. *Die Sprache der Bilder: Realität und Bedeutung in der niederländischen Malerei des 17. Jahrhunderts.* Exh. cat., Herzog Anton Ulrich-Museum. Braunschweig, 1978.

BRAUNSCHWEIG 1979
Ekkart, Rudolf E.O., et al. *Jan Lievens, ein Maler im Schatten Rembrandts.* Exh. cat., Herzog Anton Ulrich-Museum. Braunschweig, 1979.

BRECKENRIDGE 1955
Breckenridge, James Douglas. *A Handbook of Dutch and Flemish Paintings in the William Andrew Clark Collection.* Washington, 1955.

BREDIUS 1886
Bredius, Abraham. "Een rederijkers-blazoen, door Bartholomeus Dolendo gesneden." *Oud Holland* 4 (1886): 130–131.

BREDIUS 1969
Bredius, Abraham. *Rembrandt: The Complete Edition of the Paintings.* Revised by Horst Gerson. London, 1969.

BRENNINKMEYER-DE ROOIJ ET AL. 1988
Brenninkmeyer-de Rooij, Beatrijs, et al. *Paintings from England: William III and the Royal Collections.* The Hague, 1988.

BRISTOL 1946
Souvenir Catalogue of the Exhibition of Dutch Old Masters. Exh. cat., Red Lodge, Park Row, Bristol. Bristol, 1946.

BROOS 1983
Broos, Ben. "Fame Shared Is Fame Doubled." In Amsterdam 1983: 35–58.

BROOS 1987
Broos, Ben. *Meesterwerken in het Mauritshuis.* The Hague, 1987.

BROWN 1984
Brown, Christopher. *Images of a Golden Past.* New York, 1984.

BRUSSELS 1946
Van Schendel, Arthur François Emile. *De hollandsche schilderkunst van Jeroen Bosch tot Rembrandt.* Exh. cat., Palais des Beaux-Arts. Brussels, 1946.

BRUYN 1951
Bruyn, Josua. "David Bailly 'fort bon peintre en pourtraicts et en vie coye'." *Oud Holland* 66 (1951): 148–164, 212–227.

BRUYN 1953
Bruyn, Josua. "Twee late portretten van David Bailly." *Oud Holland* 68 (1953): 113–114.

BRUYN 1982
Bruyn, Josua. "The Documentary Value of Early Graphic Reproductions." In *Corpus* 1982–, 1: 35–51.

BRUYN 1989
Bruyn, Josua. "Studio Practice and Studio Production." In *Corpus* 1982–, 3: 12–50.

BRUYN 1991
Bruyn, Josua. "Rembrandt's Workshop: Its Function and Production." In Berlin, Amsterdam, and London 1991: 68–89.

CASTIGLIONE 1528
Castiglione, Baldassare. *Il libro del Cortegiano.* Venice, 1528. (Ed. Giulio Carnazzi, Milan, 1987).

CHAPMAN 1990
Chapman, H. Perry. *Rembrandt's Self-Portraits.* Princeton, 1990.

CHIARINI 1989
Chiarini, Marco. *I Dipinti Olandesi del Seicento e del Settecento: Gallerie e Musei Statali di Firenze.* Rome, 1989.

CHICAGO 1969
Haverkamp Begemann, Egbert, et al. *Rembrandt after Three Hundred Years: An Exhibition of Rembrandt and His Followers.* Exh. cat., Art Institute of Chicago; Minneapolis Institute of Art; Detroit Institute of Art. Chicago, 1969.

CHONG 1987
Chong, Alan. "The Market for Landscape Painting in Seventeenth-Century Holland." In Peter C. Sutton, *Masters of Seventeenth-Century Dutch Landscape Painting,* exh. cat., Rijksmuseum, Amsterdam; Museum of Fine Arts, Boston; Philadelphia Museum of Art. Boston, 1987: 104–120.

COPENHAGEN 1951
Royal Museum of Fine Arts, *Catalogue of Old Foreign Paintings.* Copenhagen, 1951.

CORPUS 1982–
Bruyn, Josua, et al. (Rembrandt Research Project). *A Corpus of Rembrandt Paintings.* 3 vols. to date. The Hague, Boston, and London, 1982–.

COX 1909–1910
Cox, Kenyon. "Dutch Pictures in the Hudson-Fulton Exhibition—III." *Burlington Magazine* 16 (1909–1910): 305.

DESCAMPS 1753–1765
Descamps, Jean Baptiste. *La Vie des peintres flamands, allemands et hollandais.* 4 vols. Paris, 1753–1765.

VAN DEURSEN 1991A
Van Deursen, Arie Th. *Plain Lives in a Golden Age: Popular Culture, Religion and Society in Seventeenth-Century Holland.* Cambridge, 1991.

VAN DEURSEN 1991B
Van Deursen, Arie. Th. "Rembrandt and His Age: The Life of an Amsterdam Burgher." In Berlin, Amsterdam, and London 1991: 40–49.

DICKEY 1986
Dickey, Stephanie S. "'Judicious Negligence': Rembrandt Transforms an Emblematic Convention." *Art Bulletin* 68 (1986): 253–262.

VAN DIJCK AND KOOPMAN 1987
Van Dijck, Lucas, and Ton Koopman. *Het klavecimbel in de Nederlandse kunst tot 1800.* Zutphen, 1987.

DIJON 1982–1983
Georgel, Pierre. *La Peinture dans la peinture.* Exh. cat., Musée des Beaux-Arts, Dijon, 1982–1983.

DIXON 1995
Dixon, Laurinda S. *Perilous Chastity.* Ithaca and London, 1995.

DORDRECHT 1949–1950
17de eeuwse meesters uit de collectie Leendert Dupper. Exh. cat. Dordrechts Museum, Dordrecht, 1949–1950.

DUDOK VAN HEEL 1991
Dudok van Heel, Sebastien A.C. "Rembrandt van Rijn (1606–1669): A Changing Portrait of the Artist." In Berlin, Amsterdam, and London 1991: 50–67.

DULWICH PICTURE GALLERY 1980
Murray, Peter. *The Dulwich Picture Gallery: A Catalogue.* London and Tottowa, N.J., 1980

DURANTINI 1983
Durantini, Mary Frances. *The Child in Seventeenth-Century Dutch Painting.* Ann Arbor, 1983.

VAN DYKE 1895
Van Dyke, John C. *Old Dutch and Flemish Masters.* New York, 1895.

ECKARDT 1971
Eckardt, Götz. *Selbstbildnisse niederländischer Maler des 17. Jahrhunderts.* Berlin, 1971.

EDINBURGH 1992
Williams, Julia Lloyd. *Dutch Art and Scotland: A Reflection of Taste.* Exh. cat., National Gallery of Scotland. Edinburgh, 1992.

EKKART 1963
Ekkart, Rudolf E.O. *Isaac Claesz. van Swanenburg 1537–1614.* Zwolle, 1963.

EKKART 1974
Ekkart, Rudolf E.O. "Leidse schilders, tekenaars en graveurs uit de tweede helft van de 16de en het begin van de 17de eeuw." In *Leiden '74: Leven in oorlogstijd in de tweede helft van de zestiende eeuw*, exh. cat., Stedelijk Museum De Lakenhal. Leiden, 1974: 171–196.

EKKART 1998
Ekkart, Rudolf E.O. *Isaac Claesz. van Swanenburg, 1537–1614: Leids schilder en burgemeester.* Leiden, 1998.

EMMENS 1963
Emmens, Jan A. "Natuur, Onderwijzing en Oefening. Bij een drieluik van Gerrit Dou." In *Album Discipulorum J.G. van Gelder*, ed. Josua Bruyn et al. Utrecht, 1963: 125–136.

EMMENS 1964–1965
Emmens, Jan A. "Inleiding." In *De Schilder in zijn wereld.* Delft, 1964–1965: 9–13.

EMMENS 1969
Emmens, Jan A. "A Seventeenth-Century Theory of Art: Nature and Practice." *Delta: A Review of Arts Life and Thought in The Netherlands* (summer 1969): 30–40.

EMMENS 1971
Emmens, Jan A. "De kwakzalver van Gerard Dou." *Openbaar Kunstbezit* 15 (1971): 4.

EMMENS 1981
Emmens, Jan A. "De trompetter van Gerard Dou." *Kunsthistorische Opstellen*, vol. 2, Amsterdam, 1981: 181–187.

ENSCHEDE 1987–1988
Van Schaamte Ontbloot: He naakt in de Nederlandse kunst ca. 1500–heden. Exh. cat., Rijksmuseum Twenthe. Enschede, 1987.

ERTZ 1981
Ertz, Klaus. *Jan Brueghel der Ältere (1568–1625).* Cologne, 1981.

EVELYN 1818
Evelyn, John. *Memoirs of John Evelyn, Esq. F.R.S.* Vol. 1. London, 1818.

FALCKENBURG 1985
Falckenburg, Reindert L. *Joachim Patinir: Het landschap als beeld van de levenspelgrimage.* Nijmegen, 1985.

FEER 1985
Feer, B. "Dokterstaferelen in het oeuvre van Gerrit Dou." Doctoraalscriptie, Leiden University, 1985.

FITZHUGH 1997
Fitzhugh, Elisabeth West, ed. *Artists' Pigments: A Handbook of Their History and Characteristics.* Vol. 3. Washington, 1997.

FIX 1991
Fix, Andrew C. *Prophecy and Reason: The Dutch Collegiants in the Early Enlightenment.* Princeton, 1991.

FRANITS 1987
Franits, Wayne E. "'The Vertues which Ought to be in a Compleate Woman': Domesticity in Seventeenth-Century Dutch Art." Ph.D. diss., New York University, 1987.

FRANITS 1993
Franits, Wayne E. *Paragons of Virtue: Women and Domesticity in Seventeenth-Century Dutch Art.* Cambridge and New York, 1993.

FRANKFURT 1993
Schulze, Sabine, ed. *Leselust: Niederländische Malerei von Rembrandt bis Vermeer.* Exh. cat., Schirn Kunsthalle, Frankfurt. Stuttgart, 1993.

FREISE 1911
Freise, Kurt. *Pieter Lastman.* Leipzig, 1911.

FRIEDLÄNDER 1926
Friedländer, Max J. *Die Kunstsammlung von Pannwitz.* Munich, 1926.

GAEHTGENS 1987
Gaehtgens, Barbara. *Adriaen van der Werff.* Munich, 1987.

GASKELL 1982
Gaskell, Ivan. "Gerrit Dou, His Patrons and the Art of Painting." *Oxford Art Journal* 5 (1982): 15–23.

GASKELL 1987
Gaskell, Ivan. "Tobacco, Social Deviance and Dutch Art in the Seventeenth Century." In *Holländische Genremalerei des 17. Jahrhundert: Symposium Berlin 1984*, ed. Henning Bock and Thomas W. Gaehtgens. Berlin, 1987: 117–137.

GEISENHEIMER 1911
Geisenheimer, H. "Beiträge zur Geschichte des Niederländischen Kunsthandels in der zweiten Hälfte des 17. Jahrhunderts." *Jahrbuch der Königlich Preussischen Kunstsammlungen* 32 (1911): 34–61.

VAN GELDER AND JOST 1985
Van Gelder, Jan G., and Ingrid Jost. *Jan de Bisschop and His Icones and Paradigmata*. Doornspijk, 1985.

GERARDS-NELISSEN 1986
Gerards-Nelissen, Inemie. Review of Hans-Joachim Raupp. *Untersuchungen zu Künstlerbildnis und Künstlerdarstellung in den Niederlanden im 17. Jahrhundert*. (Hildesheim and New York, 1974). *Simiolus* 16 (1986): 263–266.

GERSON 1942
Gerson, Horst. *Ausbreitung und Nachwirkung der hollandischen Malerei des 17. Jahrhunderts.* Haarlem, 1942.

GERSON 1952
Gerson, Horst. *De Schoonheid van Ons Land*. 2 vols. Amsterdam, 1952.

VAN GILS 1917
Van Gils, Johan B. F. *De dokter in de oude nederlandsche tooneelliteratur.* Haarlem, 1917.

GOLDBERG 1983
Goldberg, Edward L. *Patterns in Late Medici Art Patronage.* Princeton, 1983.

VAN GOOL 1751
Van Gool, Jan. *De nieuwe schouburg der nederlantsche kunstschilders en schilderessen*. 2 vols. The Hague, 1751.

VAN DE GRAAF 1958
Van de Graaf, Johannes Alexander. *Het De Mayerne manuscript als bron voor de schildertechniek van de barok*. Mijdrecht, 1958.

GRAFTON 1988
Grafton, Anthony. "Civic Humanism and Scientific Scholarship at Leiden." In *The University and the City: From Medieval Origins to the Present*, ed. Thomas Bender. New York and Oxford, 1988: 59–78.

GREENVILLE, S. C. 1957
Valentiner, Wilhelm R. *The Hammer Collection: Dutch, Flemish, German, Italian XV–XVII Century Paintings.* Exh. cat., Bob Jones University, Greenville, South Carolina, 1957.

GROEN 1993
Groen, Karin. "Krokodillen Craquelé en Ultramarijnziekte." *Kunstenaars Materiaal* 5 (spring 1993): 8–10.

GUDLAUGSSON 1945
Gudlaugsson, Sturla J. *De Komedianten bij Jan Steen en zijn Tijdgenooten*. The Hague, 1945.

GUDLAUGSSON 1959–1960
Gudlaugsson, Sturla J. *Gerard Ter Borch*. 2 vols. The Hague, 1959–1960.

GUDLAUGSSON 1965
Gudlaugsson, Sturla J. "Gerrit Dou." In *Kindlers Malerei Lexikon*, vol. 2, Zurich, 1965: 131–135.

VAN GULIK 1975
Van Gulik, E. "Drukkers en geleerden. De Leidse Officina Plantiniana (1583–1619)." In *Leiden University in the Seventeenth Century: An Exchange of Learning*, ed. Theodoor H. Lunsingh Scheurleer and G. H. M. Posthumus Meyjes. Leiden, 1975: 367–393.

HAAK 1984
Haak, Bob. *The Golden Age: Dutch Painters of the Seventeenth Century.* New York, 1984.

THE HAGUE 1988–1989
Brenninkmeyer-de Rooij, Beatrijs, and Rieke van Leeuwen. *Paintings from England: William III and the Royal Collection (betwiste schilderijen van de koning-stadhouder)*. Exh. cat., Royal Cabinet of Paintings Mauritshuis, 1988–1989. The Hague, 1988.

THE HAGUE 1994
Buijsen, Edwin. *The Hoogsteder Exhibition of Music and Painting in the Golden Age.* Exh. cat., Hoogsteder & Hoogsteder, The Hague; Hessenhuis Museum, Antwerp. The Hague and Zwolle, 1994.

THE HAGUE 1997–1998
Princely Patrons: The Collection of Frederick Henry of Orange and Amalia of Solms in The Hague. Exh. cat., Royal Cabinet of Paintings Mauritshuis. The Hague, 1997–1998.

THE HAGUE AND SAN FRANCISCO 1990–1991
Broos, B. P. J. *Great Dutch Paintings from America*. Exh. cat., Royal Cabinet of Paintings Mauritshuis, The Hague; Fine Arts Museums of San Francisco. The Hague and Zwolle, 1990–1991.

VAN HALL 1963
Van Hall, H. *Portretten van Nederlandse beeldende Kunstenaars.* Amsterdam, 1963.

HARTFORD 1938
The Painters of Still Life. Exh. cat., Wadsworth Atheneum. Hartford, Conn., 1938.

HAVELAAR 1919
Havelaar, Just. *Oud-Hollandsche Figuurschilders.* 2nd ed. Haarlem, 1919.

HAVERKAMP-BEGEMANN 1959
Haverkamp-Begemann, Egbert. *Willem Buytewech*. Amsterdam, 1959.

HECHT 1998
Hecht, Peter. "Rembrandt and Raphael Back to Back: The Contribution of Thoré." *Simiolus* 26 (1998): 162–178.

HENKEL AND SCHÖNE 1967
Henkel, Arthur, and Albrecht Schöne. *Emblemata: Handbuch zur Sinnbildkunst des XVI. und XVII. Jahrhunderts.* Stuttgart, 1967.

HOBSON 1982
Hobson, Marian. *The Object of Art: The Theory of Illusion in Eighteenth-Century France.* Cambridge, 1982.

HOET 1752–1770
Hoet, Gerard. *Catalogus of naamlyst van schilderijen. . . .* 2 vols. Supplement by Pieter Terwesten. The Hague, 1752–1770.

HOFSTEDE DE GROOT 1907
Hofstede de Groot, Cornelis. *A Catalogue Raisonné of the Works of the Most Eminent Dutch Painters of the Seventeenth Century.* Vol. 1. London, 1907.

HOLLÄNDER 1923
Holländer, Eugen. *Die Medizin in der Klassischen Malerei.* Stuttgart, 1923.

HOOGEWERFF 1919
Hoogewerff, Godefridus J. *De twee reizen van Cosimo de Medici, Prins van Toscane door de Nederlanden (1667–1669).* Amsterdam, 1919.

VAN HOOGSTRATEN 1678
Van Hoogstraten, Samuel. *Inleyding tot de hooge schoole der schilderkonst.* Rotterdam, 1678 (Davaco reprint, Doornspijk, 1969).

HOUBRAKEN 1718–1721
Houbraken, Arnold. *De groote schouburgh der nederlantsche konstschilders en schilderessen.* 3 vols. Amsterdam, 1718–1721.

HOUBRAKEN 1753
Houbraken, Arnold. *De groote schouburgh der Nederlantsche konstschilders en schilderessen.* 2nd ed. The Hague, 1753.

HUNNEWELL 1983
Hunnewell, Richard. "Gerrit Dou's Self-Portraits and Depictions of the Artist." Ph. D. diss., Boston University, 1983.

IMMERZEEL 1842
Immerzeel, Johannes. *De levens en werken der Hollandsche en Vlaamsche kunstschilders,* 2 vols. Amsterdam, 1842.

E. DE JONGH 1967
De Jongh, Eddy. *Zinne- en minnebeelden in de schilderkunst van de zeventiende eeuw.* Amsterdam, 1967.

E. DE JONGH 1975–1976
De Jongh, Eddy. "Pearls of Virtue and Pearls of Vice." *Simiolus* 8 (1975–1976): 69–97.

W. M. DE JONGH 1878
De Jongh, W. M. "De Staatsarchieven te Florence." *De Nederlantsche Spectator* (6 July 1878): 212–214.

KEMP 1989
Kemp, Wolfgang. *Rembrandt: La Sainte Famille, ou l'Art de lever un rideau.* Paris, 1989.

KETTERING 1983
Kettering, Alison McNeil. *The Dutch Arcadia: Pastoral Art and Its Audience in the Golden Age.* Montclair, N. J., 1983.

KLIBANSKY ET AL. 1964
Klibansky, Raymond, et al. *Saturn and Melancholy.* Cambridge, 1964.

KNIPPING 1940
Knipping, John B. *De Iconografie van de Contra-Reformatie in de Nederlanden.* 2 vols. Hilversum, 1940.

KORNELL 1996
Kornell, Monique. "Écorché." In *The Dictionary of Art,* ed. Jane Turner, vol. 9. London and New York, 1996: 706.

KUNSTHISTORISCHES MUSEUM VIENNA 1972
Demus, Klaus, ed. *Holländische Meister des 15., 16. und 17. Jahrhunderts.* Vienna, 1972.

KURETSKY 1974
Kuretsky, Susan Donahue. "Rembrandt's Tree Stump: An Iconographic Attribute of St. Jerome." *Art Bulletin* 56 (1974): 571–580.

LAMMERTSE 1997
Lammertse, Friso. "Veranderen na verloop van jaren. Over Gerard Dou's *Kwakzalver* in Rotterdam en het *Zelfportret* in Kansas City." In *Album Discipulorum J. R. J. van Asperen de Boer,* ed. Peter van den Brink and Liesbeth M. Helmus. Zwolle, 1997.

LAMMERTSE 1998
Lammertse, Friso. *Nederlandse genreschilderkunst uit de 17de eeuw: Eigen collectie Museum Boijmans van Beuningen.* Rotterdam, 1998.

LAREN 1969
Het kind in de noord-nederlandse kunst. Exh. cat., Singer Museum. Laren, 1969.

LEICESTER 1988
Dutch and Belgian Paintings: The Baron de Ferrières Collection. Exh. cat., University of Warwick, Leicester; Dulwich Picture Gallery. London, 1988

LEIDEN 1956
Rembrandt als leermeester. Exh. cat., Stedelijk Museum De Lakenhal. Leiden, 1956.

LEIDEN 1976–1977
Geschildert tot Leyden anno 1626. Exh. cat., Stedelijk Museum De Lakenhal. Leiden, 1976–1977.

LEIDEN 1988
Sluijter, Eric Jan, et al., eds. *Leidse Fijnschilders: Van Gerrit Dou tot Frans van Mieris de Jonge 1630–1760*. Exh. cat., Stedelijk Museum De Lakenhal, Leiden. Leiden and Zwolle, 1988.

LEUPE 1878
Leupe. "Brief van de Gezanten in Engeland." *Nederlandsche Spectator* 16 (1878): 82–83.

VAN LEEUWEN 1672
Van Leeuwen, Simon. *Korte Besgryving van het Lugdunum Batavorum Nu Leyden*. Leiden, 1672.

LOGAN 1979
Logan, Anne-Marie S. *The "Cabinet" of the Brothers Gerard and Jan Reynst*. Amsterdam, 1979.

LONDON 1929
Exhibition of Dutch Art, 1450–1900. Exh. cat., Royal Academy of Arts. London, 1929.

LONDON 1946–1947
Catalogue of the Exhibition of the King's Pictures, 1946–1947. Exh. cat., Royal Academy of Arts. London, 1947.

LONDON 1947
Some Pictures from the Dulwich Gallery. Exh. cat., National Gallery. London, 1947.

LONDON 1964
The Orange and the Rose: Holland and Britain in the Age of Observation, 1600–1750. Exh. cat., Victoria and Albert Museum. London, 1964.

LONDON 1965
Assheton Bennett, Mrs. Edgar. *The Assheton Bennett Collection*. Exh. cat., Royal Academy. London, 1965.

LONDON 1971
Millar, Sir Oliver. *Dutch Pictures from the Royal Collection*. Exh. cat., Queen's Gallery, Buckingham Palace. University Park, Penn., 1971.

LONDON 1976
Brown, Christopher. *Art in Seventeenth-Century Holland*. Exh. cat., National Gallery. London, 1976.

LONDON 1980
David Carritt, Ltd. *Ten Paintings by Gerard Dou, 1613–1675*. Exh. cat., David Carritt, Ltd. London, 1980.

LONDON 1999
Wright, Christopher. *The Cabinet Picture: Dutch and Flemish Masters of the Seventeenth Century*. Exh. cat., Richard Green Gallery. London 1999.

LONDON AND THE HAGUE 1999
Van der Wetering, Ernst, et al. *Rembrandt by Himself*. Exh. cat., National Gallery, London; Mauritshuis, The Hague. London and The Hague, 1999.

LOS ANGELES 1987
Masterworks from the Sixteenth and Seventeenth Centuries. Exh. cat., Fisher Gallery, University of Southern California. Los Angeles, 1987.

LOUTTIT 1973
Louttit, M. "The Romantic Dress of Saskia van Ulenborch: Its Pastoral and Theatrical Associations." *Burlington Magazine* 115 (May 1973): 317–326.

LUNSINGH SCHEURLEER 1975
Lunsingh Scheurleer, Theodoor H. "Un Amphithéâtre d'anatomie moralisée." In *Leiden University in the Seventeenth Century: An Exchange of Learning*, ed. Theodoor H. Lunsingh Scheurleer and G.H.M. Posthumus Meyjes. Leiden, 1975: 217–277.

LUNSINGH SCHEURLEER ET AL. 1988
Lunsingh Scheurleer, Theodoor H., et al. *Het Rapenburg: Geschiedenis van een Leidse gracht*. 6 vols. Leiden, 1988.

MACLAREN 1960
MacLaren, Neil. *National Gallery Catalogues: The Dutch School*. London, 1960.

MACLAREN AND BROWN 1991
MacLaren, Neil and Christopher Brown. *National Gallery Catalogues: The Dutch School*. 2 vols. London, 1991.

MADSEN 1907
Madsen, Karl. "Une Visite chez Dou et une note sur Rembrandt." *Bulletin uitgegeven door den Nederlandschen Oudheidkundigen Bond* 8 (1907).

MADSEN 1911
Madsen, Karl. *Billeder af Rembrandt og hans Elever*. Copenhagen, 1911.

MAHON 1949
Mahon, Denis. "Notes on the 'Dutch Gift' to Charles II." *Burlington Magazine* 91 (1949): 303–305, 349–350.

MANCHESTER 1929
Dutch Old Masters. Exh. cat., City of Manchester Art Gallery. Manchester, 1929.

MANCHESTER 1965
Assheton Bennett, Mrs. Edgar. *Paintings from the Assheton Bennett Collection*. Exh. cat., Manchester City Art Gallery. Manchester, 1965.

MARTIN 1901
Martin, Willem. *Het leven en de werken van Gerrit Dou*. Leiden, 1901.

MARTIN 1902
Martin, Willem. "Bladvulling." *Oud Holland* 20 (1902): 64.

MARTIN 1911
Martin, Willem. *Gérard Dou, sa vie et son oeuvre*. Trans. L. Dimier. Paris, 1911.

MARTIN 1913
Martin, Willem. *Gerard Dou: Des Meisters Gemälde*. Stuttgart and Berlin, 1913.

MARTIN 1936
Martin, Willem. *De Hollandsche Schilderkunst in de Zeventiende Eeuw.* 2 vols. Amsterdam, 1936.

MASTAI 1975
Mastai, Marie Louise d'Orange. *Illusion in Art.* New York, 1975.

MAURITSHUIS 1895
Bredius, Abraham, and Cornelis Hofstede de Groot. *Musée Royal de la Haye [Mauritshuis]: Catalogue raisonné des tableaux et des sculptures.* The Hague, 1895.

MAURITSHUIS 1985
Hoetink, Hans R., ed. *The Royal Picture Gallery Mauritshuis.* Amsterdam and New York, 1985.

MELBOURNE AND SYDNEY 1997
Blankert, Albert, ed. *Rembrandt: A Genius and His Impact.* Exh. cat., National Gallery of Victoria, Melbourne; National Gallery of Australia, Canberra. Melbourne, Sydney, and Zwolle, 1997.

MERRIFIELD 1967
Merrifield, Mary P., ed. *Original Treatises on the Arts of Painting.* 2 vols. New York, 1967

MIEDEMA 1973–1975
Miedema, Hessel. "Schilderen is een ambacht als een ander." *Proef* 3 (1973–1975): 124–144.

MIEDEMA 1975
Miedema, Hessel. "Over het realisme in de Nederlandse schilderkunst van de zeventiende eeuw." *Oud Holland* 89 (1975): 2–18.

MIEDEMA 1981
Miedema, Hessel. *Kunst, kunstenaar en kunstwerk bij Karel van Mander.* Alphen aan den Rijn, 1981.

MOES 1897
Moes, Ernst Wilhelm. *Iconographia Batava.* Vol. 1. Amsterdam, 1897.

MOES AND VAN BIEMA 1909
Moes, Ernst Wilhelm, and Eduard van Biema. *De Nationale Konst-Gallery en het Koninklijk Museum.* Amsterdam, 1909.

DE MONCONYS 1666
De Monconys, Balthasar. *Journal des Voyages de Monsieur de Monconys... Seconde Partie: Voyage d'Angleterre, Païs-Bas, Allemagne et Italie.* Lyon, 1666.

MONTIAS 1982
Montias, John Michael. *Artists and Artisans in Delft: A Socio-Economic Study of the Seventeenth Century.* Princeton, 1982.

MONTIAS 1987
Montias, John Michael. "Cost and Value in Seventeenth-Century Dutch Art." *Art History* 10 (1987): 455–466.

MONTIAS 1990
Montias, John Michael. "Estimates of the Number of Dutch Master-Painters, Their Earnings and Their Output in 1650." *Leidschrift Historisch Tijdschrift* 3 (August 1990): 59–74.

MONTREAL 1969
Rembrandt and His Pupils / Rembrandt et ses élèves. Exh. cat., Montreal Museum of Fine Arts; Art Gallery of Ontario, Toronto. Montreal, 1969.

MÜLLER HOFSTEDE 1988
Müller Hofstede, Justus. "Artificial Light in Honthorst and Terbrugghen: Form and Iconography." In *Hendrick ter Brugghen und die Nachfolger Caravaggios in Holland: Beiträge eines Symposions aus Anlass der Ausstellung "Holländische Malerei in neuem Licht, Hendrick ter Brugghen und seine Zeitgenossen" im Herzog Anton Ulrich-Museum Braunschweig vom 23. bis 25. März 1987.* Braunschweig, 1988: 13–43.

MULLER, ED. 1997
Muller, Sheila, ed. *Dutch Art: An Encyclopedia.* New York, 1997.

MUNICH 1999
Vignau-Wilberg, T. *O Musica du Edle Kunst: Musik und Tanz im 16. Jahrhundert.* Exh. cat., Neue Pinakothek, Staatliche Graphische Sammlung, Munich, 1999.

NAUMANN 1978
Naumann, Otto. "Frans van Mieris as Draughtsman." *Master Drawings* 16 (1978): 3–34.

NAUMANN 1981
Naumann, Otto. *Frans van Mieris the Elder (1635–1681).* 2 vols., Doornspijk, 1981.

NEW YORK 1940
Self-Portraits, Baroque to Impressionism. Exh. cat., Shaeffer Galleries. New York, 1940.

NORDENFALK 1966
Nordenfalk, Carl. "Christina and Art." In Stockholm 1966: 416–421.

NOTTINGHAM AND KENWOOD 1991
Bignamini, Ilaria. *The Artist's Model: Its Role in British Art from Lely to Etty.* Exh. cat., University Art Gallery, Nottingham; The Iveagh Bequest, Kenwood. Nottingham, 1991.

OBREEN ET AL. 1877–1890
Obreen, Frederik D.O., et al. *Archief voor Nederlandsche Kunstgeschiedenis.* 7 vols. Rotterdam, 1877–1890.

OMAHA 1977
Cloudman, Ruth H. *The Chosen Object: European and American Still Life.* Exh. cat., Joslyn Art Museum. Omaha, Neb., 1977.

ORLERS 1641
Orlers, Jan J. *Beschrijvinge der Stadt Leyden.* 2nd ed. Leiden, 1641.

PARIS 1961–1962
Connaissance des arts: Le Tabac dans l'art, l'histoire et la vie. Exh. cat., Musée des arts décoratifs, Palais du Louvre, Pavillon de Marsan. Paris, 1961–1962.

PARIS 1970 – 1971
De Lavergnée, Arnauld Bréjon. *Le Siècle de Rembrandt: Tableaux hollandais des collections publiques françaises.* Exh. cat., Musée du Petit Palais. Paris, 1970–1971.

DE PAUW-DE VEEN 1969
De Pauw-de Veen, Lydia. *De begrippen 'schilder', 'schilderij' en 'schilderen' in de zeventiende eeuw.* Brussels, 1969.

PEETERS 1966
Peeters, H.F.M. *Kind en jeugdige in het begin van het moderne tijd (ca. 1500–ca. 1650).* Hilversum, 1966.

PELINCK 1957
Pelinck, E. "Een prent met het ontzet en het profiel van Leiden door Barthelomeus Dolendo." *Leids Jaarboekje* 49 (1957): 99–101.

DE LA PERRIÈRE 1553
De la Perrière, Guillaume. *La Morosophie.* Lyon, 1553 (reprint, Aldershot, 1993).

PETTERSON 1987
Petterson, Einar. "*Amans Amanti Medicus:* Die Ikonologie des Motivs Der ärztliche Besuch." In *Holländische Genremalerei des 17. Jahrhundert: Symposium Berlin 1984*, ed. Henning Bock and Thomas W. Gaehtgens. Berlin, 1987: 193–224.

PHILADELPHIA, BERLIN, AND LONDON 1984
Sutton, Peter C. *Masters of Seventeenth-Century Dutch Genre Painting.* Exh. cat., Philadelphia Museum of Art; Gemäldegalerie, Staatliche Museen Kulturbesitz, Berlin; Royal Academy of Arts, London. Philadelphia, 1984.

DE PILES 1715
De Piles, Roger. *Abrégé de la vie des peintres avec des reflexions sur leurs ouvrages, et un traité du peintre parfait; de la connoissance des desseins; de l'utilité des estampes.* 2nd ed. Paris, 1715.

DE PLANQUE 1926
De Planque, Pieter A. *Valcooch's 'Regel der Duytsche Schoolmeesters.'* Groningen, 1926.

PLIETZSCH 1960
Plietzsch, Eduard. *Holländische und flämische Maler des XVII Jahrhunderts.* Leipzig, 1960.

POPPER-VOSKUIL 1973
Popper-Voskuil, Naomi. "Self-Portraiture and Vanitas Still-Life Painting in Seventeenth- Century Holland." *Pantheon* 31 (1973): 58–74.

POSTHUMUS 1939
Posthumus, Nikolaas W. *De Geschiedenis van de Leidsche Lakenindustrie: De Nieuwe Tijd.* 3 vols. The Hague, 1939.

PRINZ 1971
Prinz, Wolfram. *Die Sammlung der Selbstbildnisse in den Uffizien.* Berlin, 1971.

RALEIGH 1956
Valentiner, Wilhelm R. *Rembrandt and His Pupils: A Loan Exhibition.* Exh. cat., The North Carolina Museum of Art. Raleigh, 1956.

RALEIGH 1960
Tobacco and Smoking in Art. Exh. cat., The North Carolina Museum of Art. Raleigh, 1960

RAUPP 1978
Raupp, Hans-Joachim. "Musik im Atelier." *Oud Holland* 92 (1978): 106–129.

RAUPP 1984
Raupp, Hans-Joachim. *Untersuchungen zu Künstlerbildnis und Künstlerdarstellung in den Niederlanden im 17. Jahrhundert.* Hildesheim, 1984.

REUTERSWÄRD 1956
Reuterswärd, Patrik. "Tavelförhanget." *Konsthistorisk Tidskrift* 25 (1956): 97–113.

REYNOLDS 1781
Reynolds, Sir Joshua. *A Journey to Flanders and Holland, 1781.* In *The Literary Works of Sir Joshua Reynolds*, ed. H.W. Beechy, vol. 2. London, 1890.

RIJKSMUSEUM 1976
Van Thiel, Pieter J.J. *All the Paintings of the Rijksmuseum: A Completely Illustrated Catalogue.* Amsterdam and Maarsen, 1976.

RINGBOM 1965
Ringbom, Sixten. *Icon to Narrative: The Rise of the Dramatic Close-Up in Fifteenth-Century Devotional Painting.* Abo, 1965.

RIPA 1644
Ripa, Cesare. *Iconologia of uytbeeldinghe des verstants . . . vertaalt door D. Pers.* Amsterdam, 1644.

ROBINSON 1974
Robinson, Franklin W. *Gabriel Metsu (1629–1667): A Study of His Place in Dutch Genre Painting of the Golden Age.* New York, 1974.

ROSENBERG AND SLIVE 1966
Rosenberg, Jakob, and Seymour Slive. *Dutch Art and Architecture.* Harmondsworth, 1966.

ROTERMUND 1957
Rotermund, Hans Martin. "Rembrandts Bibel." *Nederlands Kunsthistorisch Jaarboek* 8 (1957): 123–150.

ROTTERDAM 1939 – 1940
Catalogus tentoonstelling van schilderijen, beeldhouwwerken en teekeningen uit particuliere verzamelingen in Nederland. Exh. cat., Museum Boymans. Rotterdam, 1939–1940.

ROTTERDAM 1991
Giltaij, Jeroen, and Guido Jansen. *Perspectiven: Saenredam en de architectuurschilders van de 17e eeuw.* Exh. cat., Museum Boijmans van Beuningen. Rotterdam, 1991.

ROYAL COLLECTION 1982
White, Christopher. *The Dutch Pictures in the Collection of Her Majesty the Queen.* Cambridge, 1982.

SALOMON 1984
Salomon, Nanette. "Dreamers, Idlers, and Other Dozers: Aspects of Sleep in Dutch Art." Ph.D. diss., New York University, 1984.

SALZBURG LANDESSAMMLUNGEN 1980
Salzburger Landessammlungen: Residenzgalerie mit Sammlung Czernin und Sammlung Schönborn-Buchheim. Salzburg, 1980.

VON SANDRART 1675–1679
Von Sandrart, Joachim. *Teutsche Academie der edlen, Bau-, Bild-, und Mahlerey-Künste.* 2 vols. Nuremberg, 1675–1679.

VON SANDRART, ED. PELTZER 1925
Von Sandrart, Joachim, ed. A.R. Peltzer. *Teutsche Academie der edlen, Bau-, Bild-, und Mahlerey-Künste.* 4 vols. Munich, 1925.

SCALLEN 1999
Scallen, Catherine B. "Rembrandt's Reformation of a Catholic Subject: The Penitent and the Repentant St. Jerome." *The Sixteenth-Century Journal* 30 (1999): 71–88.

SCHAMA 1979
Schama, Simon. "The Unruly Realm: Appetite and Restraint in Seventeenth-Century Holland." *Daedalus* 108 (1979): 103–123.

SCHAMA 1980
Schama, Simon. "Wives and Wantons: Versions of Womanhood in Seventeenth-Century Dutch Art." *The Oxford Art Journal* 3 (1980): 5–13.

SCHAMA 1987
Schama, Simon. *The Embarrassment of Riches: An Interpretation of Dutch Culture in the Golden Age.* New York, 1987.

SCHMITT 1990
Schmitt, Sibylle. "Das Pettenkoferische Regenerationsverfahren." *Zeitschrift für Kunsttechnologie und Konservierung* 4 (1990): 30–76.

SCHNEIDER AND EKKART 1973
Schneider, Hans. *Jan Lievens: Sein Leben und seine Werke.* Supplement by Rudolf E.O. Ekkart. Amsterdam, 1973.

SCHOTEL 1903
Schotel, Johannes C. *Het Oud-Hollandsch huisgezin der zeventiende eeuw.* Arnhem, 1903.

SCHWARTZ 1985
Schwartz, Gary. *Rembrandt: His Life, His Paintings.* New York, 1985.

SLIVE 1995
Slive, Seymour. *Dutch Painting 1600–1800.* New Haven, 1995.

SLUIJTER 1986
Sluijter, Eric Jan. *De 'Heydensche Fabulen' in de noordnederlandse schilderkunst circa 1590–1670.* Leiden, 1986.

SLUIJTER 1988A
Sluijter, Eric Jan. "Belering en verhulling?" *De zeventiende eeuw* 4 (1988): 3–28. (Reprinted in English translation as "Didactic and Disguised Meanings?" in *Art in History / History in Art.* Santa Monica, 1991: 175–207.)

SLUIJTER 1988B
Sluijter, Eric Jan. "Schilders van 'cleyne, subtile ende curieuse dingen'." In Leiden 1988: 15–55.

SLUIJTER 1988C
Sluijter, Eric Jan. "'Een stuck waerin een jufr. voor de spiegel van Gerrit Douw'." *Antiek* 23 (1988): 150–161.

SLUIJTER 1988D
Sluijter, Eric Jan. "'Een volmaekte schilderij is als een spiegel van de natuer': spiegel en spiegelbeeld in de Nederlandse schilderkunst van de zeventiende eeuw." In Nico J. Brederoo et al., *Oog en oog met de Spiegel.* Amsterdam, 1988: 146–163.

SLUIJTER 1990A
Sluijter, Eric Jan. "Hoe realistisch is de Noordnederlandse schilderkunst van de zeventiende eeuw? De problemen van een vraagstelling." *Leidschrift Historisch Tijdschrift* 3 (1990): 5–39.

SLUIJTER 1990B
Sluijter, Eric Jan. "Een zelfportret en 'de schilder in zijn atelier': het aanzien van Jan van Mieris." In *Nederlandse Portretten. Bijdragen over de portretkunst in de Nederlanden uit zestiende, zeventiende en achttiende eeuw*, ed. H. Blaase-Hegeman, et al. (*Leids Kunsthistorisch Jaarboek* 8 [1990]): 287–307.

SLUIJTER 1991
Sluijter, Eric Jan. "Over fijnschilders en 'betekenis'." *Oud Holland* 105 (1991): 50–60.

SLUIJTER 1993
Sluijter, Eric Jan. *De lof der schilderkunst: Over schilderijen van Gerrit Dou en een traktaat van Philips Angel uit 1642.* Hilversum, 1993.

D. SMITH 1982
Smith, David R. *Masks of Wedlock: Seventeenth-Century Dutch Marriage Portraiture.* Ann Arbor, 1982.

D. SMITH 1987
Smith, David R. "Irony and Civility: Notes on the Convergence of Genre and Portraiture in Seventeenth-Century Dutch Painting." *Art Bulletin* 69 (1987): 407–430.

J. SMITH 1829
Smith, John. *A Catalogue Raisonné of the Works of the Most Eminent Dutch, Flemish, and French Painters.* Vol. 1. London, 1829.

J. SMITH 1842
Smith, John. *A Catalogue Raisonné of the Works of the Most Eminent Dutch, Flemish, and French Painters.* Vol. 4 (supplement). London, 1842.

SNOEP-REITSMA 1973
Snoep-Reitsma, A. Elisabeth. "De waterzuchtige vrouw van Gerard Dou en de betekenis van de lampetkan." In *Album Amicorum J. G. van Gelder*, ed. Josua Bruyn et al. The Hague, 1973: 285–292.

ST. AUBIN 1910
Catalogue des Ventes illustrés par Gabriel de St. Aubin. Vol. 3. Paris, 1910.

STAATLICHE MUSEEN BERLIN 1978
Picture Gallery Staatliche Museen Preußischer Kulturbesitz Berlin: Catalog of Paintings, Thirteenth–Eighteenth Century. Trans. Linda B. Parshall. 2nd rev. ed. Berlin-Dahlem, 1978.

STATENS MUSEUM FOR KUNST 1951
Royal Museum of Fine Arts: Catalogue of Old Foreign Paintings. Copenhagen, 1951.

STECHOW 1969
Stechow, Wolfgang. "Some Observations on Rembrandt and Lastman." *Oud Holland* 84 (1969): 148–162.

STOICHITA 1997
Stoichita, Victor I. *The Self-Aware Image: An Insight into Early Modern Meta-Painting.* Cambridge and New York, 1997.

STOCKHOLM 1966
Bjurstrom, Per. *Queen Christina of Sweden. A Personality in European Civilisation.* Exh. cat., Nationalmuseum. Stockholm, 1966.

STONE-FERRIER 1989
Stone-Ferrier, Linda A. "Gabriel Metsu's 'Vegetable Market at Amsterdam': Seventeenth-Century Dutch Market Paintings and Horticulture." *Art Bulletin* 71 (1989): 428–452.

VAN STRAATEN 1977
Van Straaten, Evert. *Kout tot op het bot: De verbeelding van de winter in de zestiende en zeventiende eeuw in den Nederlanden.* The Hague, 1977.

STRAUSS AND VAN DER MEULEN 1979
Strauss, Walter L., and Marjon van der Meulen. *The Rembrandt Documents.* New York, 1979.

STRUICK VAN DER LOEFF 1987
Struick van der Loeff, Luuk. "Problemen, Overwegingen en Beslissingen bij de Conservatie en Restauratie van het Schilderij door Gerard Dou 'Jonge Moeder', 1658, Mauitshuis Inv. Nr. 32." *Centraal Laboratorium Themadag* 12 (1987): 40–50.

STRUICK VAN DER LOEFF AND GROEN 1993
Struick van der Loeff, Luuk, and Karin Groen. "The Restoration and Technical Examination of Gerard Dou's *Young Mother* in the Mauritshuis." In ICOM, Committee for Conservation: Tenth Triennial Meeting, Washington, D.C., 22–27 August 1993 (preprints): 98–103.

SUMOWSKI 1980
Sumowski, Werner. *Drawings of the Rembrandt School.* Vol. 2. Ed. and trans. Walter Strauss. New York, 1980.

SUMOWSKI 1983
Sumowski, Werner. *Gemälde der Rembrandt-Schüler.* 5 vols. Landau and Pfalz, 1983.

SUMOWSKI 1994
Sumowski, Werner. *Gemälde der Rembrandt-Schüler.* Vol. 6 (Supplement). Landau and Pfalz, 1994.

SUTTON 1980
Sutton, Peter C. *Pieter de Hooch: Complete Edition.* Oxford, 1980.

SUTTON 1982–1983
Sutton, Peter C. "Jan Steen: Comedy and Admonition." *Bulletin of the Philadelphia Museum of Art* 78 (1982–1983): 3–63.

THORÉ (BÜRGER) 1858
Thoré, Théophile E.J. (William Bürger). *Les Musées de la Holland.* Paris, 1858.

THORÉ (BÜRGER) 1859
Thoré, Théophile E.J. (William Bürger). *Galerie d'Arenberg à Bruxelles avec le catalogue complet de la collection.* Paris, 1859.

TOKYO 1992
Brown, Christopher. *Rembrandt, His Teachers and His Pupils.* Exh. cat., Bunkamura Museum of Art, Tokyo; Kawamura Memorial Museum of Art, Chiba; Yamaguchi Prefectural Museum of Art. Tokyo, 1992.

TRAUDENIUS 1662
Traudenius, Dirck. *Tyd-Zifter, dat is, kort bericht of onderwijs van de onderscheidinge en afdeelinge des tydts. Met een rym-bundel.* Amsterdam, 1662.

UTRECHT 1986–1987
Blankert, Albert, and Leonard Slatkes. *Nieuw licht op de Gouden Eeuw. Hendrick ter Brugghen en tijdgenoten.* Exh. cat., Centraal Museum, Utrecht; Herzog Anton Ulrich-Museum, Braunschweig. Utrecht, 1986.

VALENTINER 1930
Valentiner, Wilhelm R. "Important Rembrandts in American Collections." *Art News* 28 (26 April 1930): 3.

VECA 1981
Veca, Alberto. *Vanitas.* Bergamo, 1981.

VOGELAAR 1991
Vogelaar, Christiaan. "Een jong en edel Leids schildersduo. Inleiding." In Christiaan Vogelaar et al., eds. *Rembrandt and Lievens in Leiden*, exh. cat., Stedelijk Museum De Lakenhal. Zwolle and Leiden, 1991: 12–23.

J. DE VRIES 1976
De Vries, Jan. *The Economy of Europe in an Age of Crisis, 1600–1750.* Cambridge, 1976.

L. DE VRIES 1977
De Vries, Lyckle. "Jan Steen 'de kluchtschilder'." Ph.D. diss., Rijksuniversiteit Groningen, 1977.

L. DE VRIES 1990
De Vries, Lyckle. "Tronies and Other Single-Figured Netherlandish Painting." In *Nederlandse portretten: Bijdragen over de portretkunst in de Nederlanden uit de zestiende, zeventiende en achttiende eeuw*, ed. H. Blaase-Hegeman, et al. (*Leids kunsthistorisch jaarboek* 8 [1990]): 185–202.

WAAGEN 1854–1857
Waagen, Gustav Friedrich. *Treasures of Art in Great Britain.* 3 vols. London, 1854–1857.

VAN DE WAAL 1974
Van de Waal, Henri. "Rembrandt's 'Faust' Etching: a Socinian Document, and the Iconography of the Inspired Scholar." In *Steps Towards Rembrandt.* Amsterdam, 1974: 133–181 (originally published in *Oud Holland* 79 [1964]: 6–48).

WADSWORTH ATHENEUM 1978
Haverkamp-Begemann, Egbert, ed. *Wadsworth Atheneum Paintings.* Vol. 1: *The Netherlands and the German-Speaking Countries.* Hartford, Conn., 1978.

WADUM 1994
Wadum, Jørgen. *Vermeer Illuminated: Conservation, Restoration and Research.* The Hague, 1994.

WADUM 1995
Wadum, Jørgen: "Vermeer in Perspective." In Washington and The Hague 1995: 67–79.

WASHINGTON 1979
Bohlin, Diane DeGrazia. *Prints and Related Drawings by the Carracci Family: A Catalogue Raisonné.* Exh. cat., National Gallery of Art. Washington, 1979.

WASHINGTON AND THE HAGUE 1995
Wheelock, Arthur K., Jr., ed. *Johannes Vermeer.* Exh. cat., National Gallery of Art, Washington; Royal Cabinet of Paintings Mauritshuis, The Hague. Washington and The Hague, 1995.

WASHINGTON AND LOS ANGELES 1985–1986
Collection for a King: Old Master Paintings from the Dulwich Picture Gallery. Exh. cat., National Gallery of Art, Washington; Los Angeles County Museum of Art. London, 1985.

VAN DE WATERING 1985
Van de Watering, Willem L. "Gerrit Dou: A Hermit Praying." In *Trafalgar Galleries at the Royal Academy IV.* London, 1985: 8–11.

WELU 1986
Welu, James A. "Vermeer's *Astronomer:* Observations on an Open Book." *Art Bulletin* 68 (1986): 263–267.

VAN DE WETERING 1982
Van de Wetering, Ernst. "Painting Materials and Working Methods." In *Corpus* 1982–, 1:11–33.

VAN DE WETERING 1983
Van de Wetering, Ernst. "Isaac Jouderville, a Pupil of Rembrandt." In Amsterdam 1983: 59–69.

VAN DE WETERING 1986
Van de Wetering, Ernst. "Problems of Apprenticeship and Studio Collaboration." In *Corpus* 1982–, 2: 45–90.

VAN DE WETERING 1988
Van de Wetering, Ernst. "Some Remarks on Light, Colour and Form with the Dutch Caravaggists." In *Hendrick ter Brugghen und die Nachfolger Caravaggios in Holland: Beiträge eines Symposions aus Anlass der Ausstellung "Holländische Malerei in neuem Licht, Hendrick ter Brugghen und seine Zeitgenossen" im Herzog Anton Ulrich-Museum Braunschweig vom 23. bis 25. März 1987.* Braunschweig 1988: 45–50.

VAN DE WETERING 1991
Van de Wetering, Ernst. "Rembrandt's Method—Technique in the Service of Illusion." In Berlin, Amsterdam, and London 1991: 12–39.

WHEELOCK 1976
Wheelock, Arthur K., Jr. Review of Franklin W. Robinson, *Gabriel Metsu (1629–1667); A Study of His Place in Dutch Genre Painting of the Golden Age* (New York 1974)." *Art Bulletin* 58 (1976): 456–459.

WHEELOCK 1978
Wheelock, Arthur K., Jr. "A Reappraisal of Gerard Dou's Reputation." In *The William A. Clark Collection.* Exh. cat., The Corcoran Gallery of Art. Washington, 1978: 60–67.

WHEELOCK 1995
Wheelock, Arthur K., Jr. *Dutch Paintings of the Seventeenth Century.* The Collections of the National Gallery of Art Systematic Catalogues. Washington, 1995.

WHITE 1986
White, Raymond. "Brown and Black Organic Glazes, Pigments and Paints." *National Gallery Technical Bulletin* 10 (1986): 58–71.

WHITE AND KIRBY 1994
White, Raymond, and Jo Kirby. "Rembrandt and His Circle: Seventeenth Century Dutch Paint Media Re-examined." *National Gallery Technical Bulletin* 15 (1994): 64–78.

WIERSUM 1931
Wiersum, Eppe. "Het ontstaan van de verzameling schilderijen van Gerrit van der Pot van Groeneveld te Rotterdam." *Oud Holland* 48 (1931): 201–214.

WILLIAMS 1962
Williams, George Huntston. *Wilderness and Paradise in Christian Thought: The Biblical Experience of the Desert in the History of Christianity and the Paradise Theme in the Theological Idea of the University.* New York, 1962.

WILSON 1968
Wilson, Charles H. *La République hollandaise des Provinces Unies.* Paris, 1968.

DE WINKEL 1995
De Winkel, Marieke. "Eene der deftigsten dragten: The Iconography of the Tabbaard and the Sense of Tradition in Dutch Seventeenth-Century Portraiture." In *Beeld en zelfbeeld in de Nederlandse kunst, 1550–1750/Image and Self-Image in Netherlandish Art, 1550–1750.* (*Nederlands Kunsthistorisch Jaarboek* 46 [1995]): 144–167.

WOODALL 1990
Woodall, Joanna. "Honour and Profit: Antonis Mor and the Status of Portraiture." In *Nederlandse portretten: bijdragen over de portretkunst in de Nederlanden uit de zestiende, zeventiende en achttiende eeuw*, ed. H. Blaase-Hegeman et al. (*Leids Kunsthistorisch Jaarboek* 8 [1990]): 69–89.

WOLTJER 1975
Woltjer, J.J. Introduction to *Leiden University in the Seventeenth Century: An Exchange of Learning*, ed. Theodoor H. Lunsingh Scheurleer and G.H.M. Posthumus Meyjes. Leiden, 1975: 1–19.

WRIGHT 1988
Wright, Christopher. *Catalogue of Foreign Paintings from the de Ferrières Collection.* Cheltenham, 1988.

VAN YSSELSTEYN 1936
Van Ysselsteyn, Gerardina T. *Geschiedenis der Tapijtweverijen in de Noordelijke Nederlanden.* 2 vols. Leiden, 1936.

ZURICH 1953
Falsch oder echt? Exh. cat., Kunstmuseum Basel; Kunsthaus Zurich. Basel, 1953.

Photo Credits

Except where otherwise noted, all photographs were provided by the owners.

Annetje Boersma, page 59, fig. 7; page 61, fig. 12

Bridgeman Art Library, cat. 7, plate

©*The British Museum*, cat. 14, fig. 1

©*DOWIC Fotografi*, cat. 26, plate

courtesy Instituut Collectie Nederland, Amsterdam, page 57, fig. 3 (Reni Gerritsen); page 58, fig. 4 (E. Klusman); page 59, fig. 8; page 60, figs. 9, 10, and 11 (a and b)

©*Manchester City Art Galleries*, cat. 9, plate

©*Mauritshuis, The Hague*, page 58, fig. 5; cat. 21, plate

courtesy of Museum of Fine Arts, Boston. Reproduced with permission. © 2000 *Museum of Fine Arts, Boston. All Rights Reserved*, cat. 1, fig. 1

courtesy of Museum Boijmans van Beuningen, Rotterdam, page 58, fig. 6

©*National Gallery, London*, cat. 15, fig. 1

courtesy of National Gallery of Scotland, cat. 8, fig. 1

courtesy of Noortman Gallery, Maastricht, cat. 10, plate

Photo Prauder, cat. 23, fig. 1

©*Réunion des Musées Nationaux, France*, page 16, fig. 2; cat. 31, fig. 1

RKD, The Hague, page 34, fig. 8

The Royal Collection ©*Her Majesty Queen Elizabeth II*, cat. 35, plate

courtesy of Sotheby's, cat. 3, plate

©*Sterling and Francine Clark Art Institute, Williamstown, Mass.*, page 38, fig. 14